W9-BAM-662

Praise for *Sams Teach Yourself Maya in 24 Hours*

"Autodesk Maya is no easy program to master, requiring the skills of an artist and programmer to effectively navigate. Kenny and Fiona's simple hour-by-hour breakdown, filled with common questions and answers, will give you the knowhow you need to traverse Maya's many channels. I would recommend this book to any newcomer seeking passage."

David Andrade, Co-founder, Theory Animation

"*Sams Teach Yourself Maya in 24 Hours* is a great book to get your feet wet in learning one of the most powerful 3D applications available. Kenny Roy and Fiona Rivera present the tools and techniques to understanding Maya in a very friendly and straight-to-the-point manner. By the end of the book, you will have learned all the basics needed to be familiar with Maya's interface. You will also have created a neat character that you'll animate and render to showcase your very own fully completed CG shot. I recommend this book to novices looking to get up to speed quickly in Maya. I also recommend it to pros looking for a refresher or interested in expanding their skillset in Maya."

George Castro, Senior Cinematic Artist, www.gcastro3d.com

"Autodesk Maya can cause struggling times, both for the experienced artist as well as for the newcomer. What Roy and Rivera do so well with *Sams Teach Yourself Maya in 24 Hours* is manage to highlight the essential steps in order to achieve their required result. This is further enhanced by the accompanying theory. As an animator I have already benefited greatly from Roy's *How to Cheat in Maya*, so on this alone I will be relying on *Sams Teach Yourself Maya in 24 Hours* the next time I need to further my knowledge in another discipline. The easy-to-follow tutorials really help to encourage a sense of adventure, and I for one will waste no time in putting my new found skills to use. As well as the strong lessons provided in this book, I feel its greatest strength is in its teachings of accessibility. The thousands of options provided in the software can soon be overlooked as we are taught to get the desired results at a much faster rate."

David Chambers, Character Animator, Studio Distract

"This is the perfect book for those wanting to learn Maya as quickly and efficiently as possible. The easy-to-understand approach will have you up and running in no time, and you won't be slowed down by the software as you begin your journey into the field of CG."

Chris Mayne, Freelance Character Animator

"Whether you are new to the program or looking to brush up on your Maya skills, this is the book for you. This book is the perfect way to learn Maya in a very short period of time! Loaded with insightful tips and meaningful tutorials that lead you seamlessly from one chapter to the next, I couldn't ask for anything more."

Steve Rector, Animation Professor, Prince George's Community College

"Yet another solid piece with purpose from the master of workflow, Kenny Roy. An outstanding training course guide for all newcomers to Maya interested in character animation and computer graphics. A simple, to-the-point reference tool for all experienced animators who wish to enhance their knowledge and skills."

David Yañez, Character Animator, Imagen Digital Creativa

Kenny Roy
Fiona Rivera

Sams **Teach Yourself**

Maya

in 24 Hours

SAMS 800 East 96th Street, Indianapolis, Indiana, 46240 USA

Sams Teach Yourself Maya® in 24 Hours

Copyright © 2014 by Pearson Education, Inc.

All rights reserved. No part of this book shall be reproduced, stored in a retrieval system, or transmitted by any means, electronic, mechanical, photocopying, recording, or otherwise, without written permission from the publisher. No patent liability is assumed with respect to the use of the information contained herein. Although every precaution has been taken in the preparation of this book, the publisher and author assume no responsibility for errors or omissions. Nor is any liability assumed for damages resulting from the use of the information contained herein.

Maya® is a registered trademark or trademark of Autodesk, Inc., in the USA and other countries. This book is independent of Autodesk, Inc., and is not authorized by, endorsed by, sponsored by, affiliated with, or otherwise approved by Autodesk, Inc.

ISBN-13: 978-0-672-33683-6

ISBN-10: 0-672-33683-9

Library of Congress Control Number: 2013940163

Printed in the United States of America

First Printing August 2013

Trademarks

All terms mentioned in this book that are known to be trademarks or service marks have been appropriately capitalized. Sams Publishing cannot attest to the accuracy of this information. Use of a term in this book should not be regarded as affecting the validity of any trademark or service mark.

Warning and Disclaimer

Every effort has been made to make this book as complete and as accurate as possible, but no warranty or fitness is implied. The information provided is on an "as is" basis. The authors and the publisher shall have neither liability nor responsibility to any person or entity with respect to any loss or damages arising from the information contained in this book or from the use of the DVD or programs accompanying it.

Bulk Sales

Sams Publishing offers excellent discounts on this book when ordered in quantity for bulk purchases or special sales. For more information, please contact

U.S. Corporate and Government Sales

1-800-382-3419

corpsales@pearsontechgroup.com

For sales outside of the U.S., please contact

International Sales

international@pearsoned.com

Editor-in-Chief
Mark Taub

Executive Editor
Laura Lewin

Development Editor
Songlin Qiu

Managing Editor
Kristy Hart

Project Editor
Elaine Wiley

Copy Editor
Bart Reed

Indexer
Tim Wright

Proofreader
Sarah Kearns

Technical Editor
Matthew Johnson

Publishing Coordinator
Olivia Basegio

Media Producer
Dan Scherf

Cover Designer
Mark Shirar

Compositor
Nonie Ratcliff

Contents at a Glance

Table of Contents

About the Authors

Kenny Roy started in the animation industry in 1997 as a dust buster on a children's animated feature. Since then, he has gone on to animate some of the most memorable characters on screen, from Scooby Doo to King Kong. In 2007, he founded Arconyx Animation Studios in Los Angeles, where he directs projects ranging from TV commercials to short films and visual FX. An animation teacher for almost 8 years, Kenny is also a multiple-published author in animation and a world-traveling lecturer. He also runs an animation training portal through www.kennyroy.com.

Fiona Rivera has animated and created 3D graphics for independent film, iPhone apps, marketing, university TV, and training courses. Fiona initially trained in 3D at Escape Studios, a premier visual effects academy in London, and went on to study character animation through Animation Mentor, where she met Kenny Roy. In addition to freelancing for companies such as Strange-Box.com, she has taught and developed undergraduate and postgraduate university courses in 3D animation, 3D modeling and rendering, and visual effects. Fiona has also created stereoscopic immersive virtual environments for European research projects and is currently researching related new technologies.

Dedication

For my ever-loving and supportive wife, Tamaryn.
Kenny Roy

For my most wonderful family—husband Mark, son Colin, and daughter Jessi—
for all the great love, support, and fabulous fun times together. And for Sue Stevens,
who would be slightly horrified to find her name in a book.
Fiona Rivera

Acknowledgments

Thanks Fiona for swooping in and being a savior on this book, and my wife Tamaryn for supporting me through even the toughest times. Thanks to the Pearson team for being always extremely organized and understanding.

—*Kenny Roy*

I owe considerable thanks to my fellow "Escapee" Phil Radford for his substantial contributions toward my input. Phil and I met when we attended Escape Studios for VFX training together, where his amazing abilities in all areas of 3D and VFX blew me away. After working at the BBC for 6 years, Phil established his own 3D and VFX company, Strangebox Ltd. His clients have included Virgin Atlantic, Google, Volvo, BBC, Virgin Media, Living, and Bravo, and many more. Phil's work can be seen at http://www.strange-box.com/.

I am also grateful to my friend, character animator Spencer Jones, for creating the arc tracker MEL script supplied as bonus content for Hour 17. Spencer's work can be seen at http://www.spence-animator.co.uk.

Thank you to the editorial team at Sams Publishing, including Laura Lewin, Olivia Basegio, and Songlin Qiu, plus Matthew Johnson for his hard work in checking the technical details. Special thanks also go to Kenny Roy and Laura Lewin for inviting me to be a part of this project, and even more thanks go to my family and friends for putting up with me while doing it.

—*Fiona Rivera*

We Want to Hear from You!

As the reader of this book, you are our most important critic and commentator. We value your opinion and want to know what we're doing right, what we could do better, what areas you'd like to see us publish in, and any other words of wisdom you're willing to pass our way.

We welcome your comments. You can email or write to let us know what you did or didn't like about this book—as well as what we can do to make our books better.

Please note that we cannot help you with technical problems related to the topic of this book.

When you write, please be sure to include this book's title and author as well as your name and email address. We will carefully review your comments and share them with the author and editors who worked on the book.

Email: consumer@samspublishing.com

Mail: Sams Publishing
         ATTN: Reader Feedback
         800 East 96th Street
         Indianapolis, IN 46240 USA

Reader Services

Visit our website and register this book at informit.com/register for convenient access to any updates, downloads, or errata that might be available for this book.

HOUR 1
Introduction to Autodesk Maya and This Book

What You'll Learn in This Hour:

▶ The aim of this book

▶ How to expand your knowledge after trying the examples in this book

▶ What to look for in screenshots

▶ Setting a pace for learning Maya

Welcome to the world of Autodesk Maya! In this hour, we will introduce you to the program itself and go over a few of the goals of this book. We will also describe how to get the most from this book and how to set yourself up for success in learning this amazing program. Wherever your interest in Maya comes from—be it a career change, a hobby, or just plain curiosity—you have embarked on a long and rewarding journey.

Our Goal

Our adventure begins at the very beginning: We assume you have little to no working knowledge of 3D graphics, much less any 3D software package. Each Hour will expose you to not just a menu item or a random button within Maya, but a little bit of the theory and concept behind the software. Because Maya is one of the most complex 3D animation packages available on the market, we won't inundate you with details, parameters you have to copy, or thousand-step-long tutorials that only serve to lead you too deep into the software with no way out.

Instead, the main tools and menus will be described and utilized to give you a deep enough understanding of Maya to feel like you can dive in further on your own. Our goal is to empower you to not be daunted by Maya's literal *thousands* of menus and options. We want you to not be afraid to try a new parameter or experiment with different attributes at will. An experimental attitude and a strong sense of adventure are both necessary to take on Autodesk Maya. Our goal is to take you through the steps to internalize this powerful software. Our goal is to give you the process to "teach yourself" Maya.

NOTE

Maya Version

Maya is updated every year with new features. This book is written using Maya 2014, the most recent version of the software available as of this writing. Throughout this book, numerous menus, tables, parameters, and functions will be presented. Nearly all of the features shown will be tools that are present in versions as old as 2010, but some tools new to 2014 offer paradigms that are too valuable to pass up. We will try to keep those sections to a minimum; just be aware that your version of Maya may not have a few functions here and there.

What Is Autodesk Maya?

If you feel like Maya is a behemoth of a program, it is. A piece of software does not become the industry standard for visual effects and feature animation without offering a complete toolset that caters to artists across industries.

Like all modern 3D programs, Maya is full featured, meaning it has all of the tools to create 3D imagery from start to finish. This includes tools for modeling, texturing, rigging, animating, lighting, rendering, and much more. Much of the task of learning this program is finding the right tool for the job; rarely is there actually no way to do something. This book will show you the layout of the program, and how to find the right tools.

At its heart, Maya is built on MEL script, a simple but powerful scripting language accessible to you within the program. This language is powerful enough that artists and technicians alike have created thousands of scripts that extend Maya's functionality even further than the amazing depth it already contains. Of course, you can actually get very far in Maya and a career in 3D without ever writing a single line of MEL script. Maya's user interface has seen incremental improvement ever since Autodesk took over its development. The UI is very streamlined and customizable. Labels are clear, the Help file is complete, to say the least, and most if not all of the features are accessible through more than one menu. The authors of the program have put an enormous emphasis on making Maya artist-friendly. I'm always happy to say that I believe they are succeeding.

Maya is limited only by your imagination. At the same time, certain skills take a lot of practice to become familiar with their nuances. Many of the concepts presented in this book will be completely new paradigms for you. For instance, you will be asked to imagine what a texture on a 3D object would look like if the object was pounded flat and laid out onto a grid (the basic approach to creating and editing UV sets covered in Hour 6, "Unfolding UVs and Applying Textures"). You may be asked to imagine a bumpy surface's height expressed as an image with values from black to white representing low to high areas. This will be a new way to think of the world around you, but it can be exciting as well. Many artists have confirmed that I'm not the only one that starts to stare off in the distance imagining how to model an object. You can also get too immersed; if you find yourself reaching for the Undo key when you drop a plate on the kitchen floor, it's probably time to take a break!

Maya has so much depth that it's easy to get lost. Most professionals in the CG field understand that to be competitive in today's market, specialization is key. This means that the different tasks, such as modeling, texturing, and lighting, are all given out to different artists in a production. Because it is impossible to be an expert in every single aspect of CG, we will not try to go so far into a concept that you miss some broader topics within Maya. Also, good generalist knowledge is a huge advantage when you decide on your specialty. Animators who understand lighting can be more effective on the job because they are thinking about issues that affect their work down the pipeline. Riggers who can model are able to fix small problems they encounter when they receive a mesh from the modeling department. You are beginning that generalist training right now. And although the program can swallow you up, this book will give you the tools you need to avoid getting lost. Your experience in learning it will be greatly improved if you commit first to learning *how* to teach yourself the program as opposed to thinking all the answers are right at your fingertips.

Our Approach

We will use a few different tools to get you comfortable experimenting and teaching yourself this amazing program. Each Hour will be packed with a wealth of information, including background on the concept in the broader CG world, as well as focused description of how Maya specifically handles tasks. In addition, there will be a few callouts designed to grab your attention when needed. These will come in the form of:

NOTE

When a concept needs to be annotated, a Note will provide this extra information. Notes offer good information and provide an extra tidbit or a jumping-off point for your further experimenting with a concept. We will also use the Notes to steer you clear of common pitfalls of Maya, and to explain processes that will reduce the learning curve.

TIP

Tips are provided when you are learning a process and a valuable piece of information is available. These are "good-to-know" bits of info, and can come in the form of presets that help you achieve quicker results, known parameters and attributes that produce great images, and more.

▼ TRY IT YOURSELF

At certain points throughout the Hours, you will be asked to try applying a concept that has just been explained in a guided mini tutorial called Try It Yourself. Follow the instructions in these sections to get a quick hands-on experience with some of Maya's tools. To learn the most from this book, however, you should always be following along and identifying the steps that are being taken as we discuss Maya's features. To get a deeper understanding of the material, it will prove worthwhile to repeat each exercise a few times after finishing the Hour. In doing so, you will challenge your memory recall, which will give you an even firmer grasp of the concepts. Because Maya has literally thousands of options, we will show you everything you need to get started teaching yourself, but there's plenty more to see after the Hour is done. The last best piece of advice is to continue exploring the menus and settings when you are done "trying it yourself." Take a cue from the examples given in the book, and see if you can apply your knowledge to features that lay just beyond the purview of an introductory book like this one.

How We Use Screenshots

Because much of what goes on in Maya is visual, we will be using screenshots extensively in this book. Here's some guidance as to how to get the most out of a screenshot like Figure 1.1.

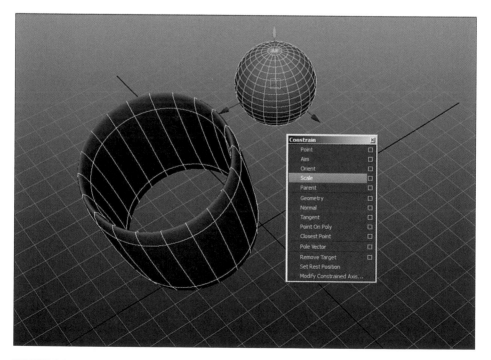

FIGURE 1.1
A typical screenshot in this book. Objects will be centered, menus will be shown, and when possible, the menu selection will be highlighted.

As you can see in Figure 1.1, the screenshots will be presented with as much information as possible without crowding the frame. Menus are typically all arranged at the top of the Maya window; however, Maya allows you to "tear off" menus (remove them from their dock and have a floating menu window wherever you choose). In order to present the important details to you, often the menu being discussed will be torn off and the menu option we have chosen for the task at hand will be highlighted, as it is in Figure 1.1. Try to not let the floating menu confuse you; your Maya screen will look different because your menu will be located in its original position at the top of the screen. Although having the menus expand from the top is good for saving on screen real estate, it makes for a little bit of trouble when showing you a nicely composed screenshot, as illustrated in Figure 1.2.

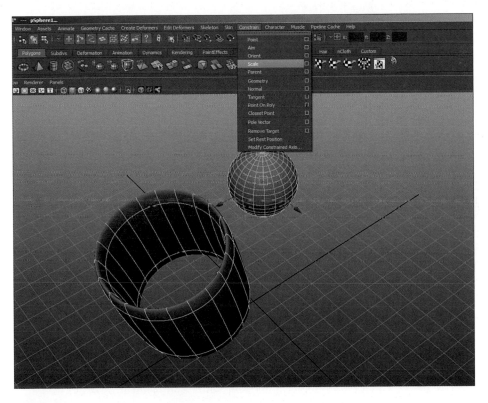

FIGURE 1.2
The exact same menu and option is shown as in Figure 1.1, but in the default position. Selecting the dotted line at the top of a menu allows you to "tear off" the menu into a floating window. Don't let the position of a menu in a screenshot fool you.

Occasionally we'll be highlighting a button and not a menu item. In these instances, sometimes Maya does not highlight the button in a very visible way. In order to make sure you do not get lost, we will emphasize the button by applying a mask on the figure, as you can see in Figure 1.3.

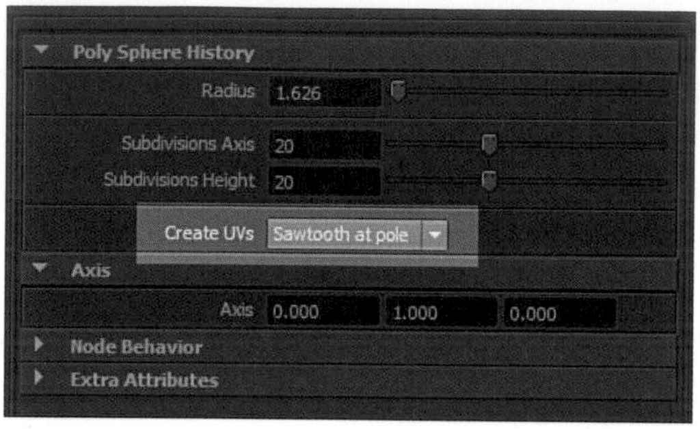

FIGURE 1.3
When a button or a field is the focus of the lesson, the area in question will be masked to draw your attention.

NOTE

Keyboard and Mouse Clicks

In this book, whenever there is a keystroke you need to press, it will be explained clearly. Maya, however, distinguishes between capital letters and lowercase letters when using keystrokes. Maya's documentation is a little bit confusing because you are meant to know that because they show "Ctrl+A" that means that you are supposed to press Shift as well, due to the A being capitalized. Unlike Maya's documentation, whenever the capital letter is required, we will write "Shift," so you know that you are supposed to press it (for example, Ctrl+Shift+A). Also, we will refer to the left mouse button as LMB, the middle mouse button as MMB, and the right mouse button as RMB whenever we refer to mouse clicks.

Supplementing Your 3D Training

3D graphics is a very technical industry. At the same time, a traditional art foundation really brings a depth of understand of the "why" of 3D. Maya has a wealth of options to create colored lights and shadows. Why? Great painters know that using subtle complementary colors in lighting brings richness to the frame. Maya's skinning tools are top notch, allowing for rigged characters to be posed in almost any way imaginable. Why would we go for that much flexibility? Because great traditional animators were constantly pushing the limits of their character's bodies to get their poses to be dynamic and appealing. With one foot firmly planted in 3D, supplementing your 3D training with other artist pursuits can be a boon to your growth. Here are some other disciplines that will help you further build your skills:

▶ **Drawing**—Perhaps the most beneficial skill to have as you dive into the world of animation is the ability to draw. For most, drawing is a painful task that usually ends in frustration. Have a sketchbook with you at all times, and try to force yourself to draw at least once a day. First of all, the best CG artists are masters of observation. Lighters get inspired by the way that light and shadow react in the real world and get lost staring at seemingly mundane things. Animators try to find the nuance in motion, and spend a lot of their time observing. Modelers also need to have an attention to detail so they do not have to spend too much time gathering a mass of reference material for every little thing they are assigned to create. Drawing teaches us to observe details. Moreover, drawing is visual communication. Sketching ideas to show your supervisor, thumbnailing a scene, and even creating a few drawings to pitch an idea to a client are all scenarios that are frequent in this business. You don't want to be left out of the communication loop because of a barrier like not being able to draw.

▶ **Painting**—Like drawing, painting is a form of visual art that contributes to your overall appreciation of beauty. Plus, it's hard as heck. Animation, modeling, and nearly all of the tasks involved in CG can be characterized as moments of sheer excitement with hours and hours of painstaking work in between. I don't mean to suggest that all painting has to offer is to buff up your saint-like patience to cope with the monotony of CG; on the contrary, working on a painting in your free time is a fantastic wind-down from the high stakes world of production. Not to mention, the techniques of classic painters such as color mixing, contrast, and understanding the fine properties of light can make you a powerful asset to a team.

▶ **Photography**—Another fine pursuit for individuals wanting to round out their artistic knowledge. Photography teaches us to compose a shot, thinking about issues such as framing, composition, positive and negative space, and focus. So much of the way that we see the world changes when we look through a camera; it is a huge advantage in your career and your training to understand how to re-create what the lens sees. Particularly if you are planning to enter the visual effects industry, photography is a worthwhile hobby.

▶ **Acting**—Animators are known as the "shyest performers in the world." We create tear-jerking subtle performances, nail-biting action scenes, all the while sitting in dark rooms hiding behind a big computer monitor. It's true—many fantastic animators are very shy people. To break out of that shell can mean a huge boost in your work. As scary as it is, enroll in an acting class, or better yet (to me anyway), an improv class could be just the thing you need to take your animation to the next level. You learn subtext, character development, physicality, and the truth to be found in every scene. Best of all, it's a blast (once you get over the crippling fear part, of course).

▶ **Music**—Believe it or not, music is extremely beneficial to learning CG. The benefits of playing an instrument cannot be overstated at combating the effects of Repetitive Stress Injury. Music is social, good for getting away from the desk every once in a while. For animators, understanding concepts such as rhythm and texture in music translates nearly 1:1 in physical work.

▶ **Sculpture**—We can't leave out sculpting, especially since a huge push of the last 5 or 6 years has been to make modeling organic shapes as near to the experience of working with clay as possible. Autodesk's flagship product in this arena is called Mudbox, and it tries to re-create the act of sculpting with great success. Force, form, structure, and silhouette are for some reason so much more apparent with real clay. It doesn't even have to be clay you use—wood, marble, wax, metal, any of the mediums can keep you grounded in the real world, the visceral. Perhaps all I have to mention is that the most amazing modelers I know, who work on *blockbuster* films, all sculpt in their free time.

Setting a Pace for Learning Maya

Although this book's title implies that you can learn Maya in 24 hours, the obvious reality is that mastery of such a robust program will take far longer than that. It is a good idea to set a pace for yourself even working through this book's lessons. The concepts are presented in a way that will open your mind to start "thinking in 3D." It is up to you to then take these new paradigms and apply them before moving on too quickly. Too often novice 3D artists try to rush to get to "the good stuff"—cartoony character animation or super-realistic visual effects. The truth is that all of the best Maya technicians have put years into training. Use this book as your launch point and guide to stepping into the world of 3D. Take the examples further and experiment with the program even after the hour is over. I promise that Maya will have new options to try and new features to explore to occupy you as long as you feel like sticking with it. Your energy will run out long before Maya's options do! That's okay. Take a break, relax, and come back to a new Hour with fresh eyes and an adventurous attitude.

VIDEO

Introduction and Demonstration
Watch Video 1.1 found in this Hour's folder to hear an introduction and watch me walk through a few of the menu conventions used in this book.

Summary

We're about to take our first look at the Maya interface and begin on our journey through the program's many features. Look out for the notes, tips, cautions, and warnings as we make our way through Maya. Know that we're going to cover a lot of information, but we'll also make building on the information easy. You'll have ample opportunities to "try it yourself," and should continue long after the Hour is done experimenting with different settings, tools, and commands. Take into consideration that a well-rounded *artist* is worth far more than just a technician. And, finally, work at a steady pace to not burn out before you have the skills to achieve your dreams.

Q&A

Q. I want to be able to do "X" in Maya. Will this book teach me how?

A. It is far more valuable to your growth as a 3D artist and to your career to know the concepts behind the tools of Maya. This book will show you the concepts and give you a starting point for learning as opposed to holding your hand through some specific tutorials.

Q. I've used another 3D program before. Should I start completely over with Maya?

A. Having some 3D experience is invaluable to the process of learning Maya. It can only help. At the same time, Maya has some very specific ways of doing things, specific terminology, and some tools that don't show up in competitor's software. Best to start at the beginning.

Q. Are there other learning tools you recommend?

A. Of course! I would turn to the Internet to give you extra information and support. For me, there is nothing like the support of fellow artists, so online forums such as www.cgtalk.com are amazing resources for connecting with like-minded individuals.

Q. I don't have Maya. How can I get it?

A. Autodesk offers a free evaluation of all of their software. The Maya evaluation period is 30 days—plenty of time to try it out and follow along with this book. Educational pricing is also available, as well as a free student license for those in an accredited school. Check www.autodesk.com for details.

Workshop

The workshop contains quiz questions and exercises to help you solidify your understanding of the material covered. Try to answer all questions before looking at the "Answers" section that follows.

Quiz

1. Name a few of the other artistic pursuits that will help you in your training.
2. How much time does it take to learn Maya completely?
3. When this book gives you an extra piece of information that steers you away from a potential roadblock or file crash, it will come in the form of a what?

4. The screenshots in this book are composed to maximize information, but that might mean a menu that normally appears at the top is depicted as floating in the middle of a panel. What is it called when you make a floating menu?

5. Name some of the tasks of CG artists.

Exercise

Learning Maya itself is an amazingly challenging but rewarding goal. Pursuing a career in visual effects or animation is even more so. Take a moment to reflect on your decision to dive into this amazing program, and/or to try to break into the fast-paced, competitive, and wondrous world of CG, and write down a few goals for yourself. Try to think of small goals you can accomplish in the next few weeks (such as finishing this book). Then move on to goals that will take a few months to achieve (such as doing a little bit of practice every day with the concepts you learned here). Finally, end this exercise with your pie-in-the-sky dream for yourself. Don't put a time limit on this one. Tack this up, or print it out and have it next to your computer workspace, and look at it as you read this book. Let it serve as a reminder to you when you get stuck, frustrated, and want to turn back. On the other side of the obstacles you will face is a world of imagination.

Answers

1. Drawing, painting, photography, acting, music, sculpture, and more.

2. It takes dedicated individuals years to fully understand even a facet of this program.

3. A "By The Way" keeps you from doing things that might truncate your file, or impede your learning.

4. A floating menu has been "torn off." Don't let this confuse you—look at the top of the screen for the equivalent menu.

5. Modeling, texturing, UV'ing, rigging, animating, lighting, rendering, and more!

HOUR 2
Menus and Navigating the Maya UI

What You'll Learn in This Hour:

▶ What menus are available to you
▶ How to navigate Maya's interface
▶ How to change menu sets
▶ How to navigate a scene file in 3D panels

Being familiar with Maya's interface and menus is the first essential step in learning to use this powerful program. There are hundreds of menus in Maya, but they are organized in a way that ensures they are not cumbersome as you try to get work done. The key skill is learning how to quickly access menus you need for your current task and how to let the rest of Maya's functionality wait in the background, ready to be used.

In this hour, you will open Maya and explore the different menu and dialog box types. You will load the different menu sets and see their functionality, and also learn the basic camera movements within panels for navigating in 3D.

The Maya Interface

Opening Maya, we are presented with the main application window. This layout presents the user with the most commonly used tools and menus. Many 3D programs first present the user with an array of very tightly packed menus and buttons, whereas Maya's interface contains primarily evenly spaced icons that have a helpful image to indicate what each option does. For this reason, Maya's interface stands out as one of the more user-friendly experiences available in CG. As you can see in Figure 2.1, the main Maya UI is clean and easy to browse.

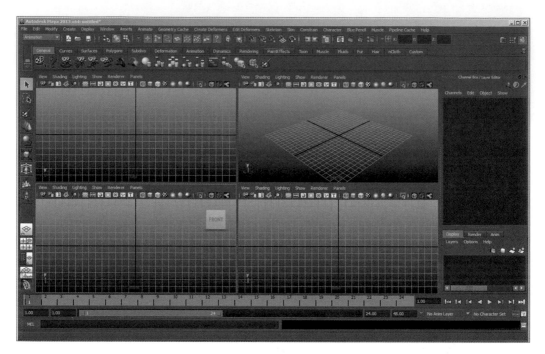

FIGURE 2.1
The main Maya window. These default loaded menus and buttons offer the user almost all of Maya's commonly used functionality at startup.

Starting from the Default Maya Interface

Make sure you are starting from the default Maya interface. If you are working from a fresh install, move ahead with this lesson. If not, you can get a default layout by either:

▶ In Maya, go to Window, Settings/Preferences, Preferences and then choose Edit, Restore Default Settings. Then go to Display, UI Elements, Restore UI Elements.

▶ Delete the "prefs" folder in My Documents\Maya\2013 (or whatever version you have).

Maya's interface has five main areas that contain the eight main UI elements. They are as marked in Figure 2.2:

▶ The top area, which contains the main menu, Status Bar, and Shelf

▶ The center area, which contains panels

▶ The left area, which contains the Tool Box and Tool Settings

▶ The right area, which contains the Attribute Editor and the Channel Box/Layer Editor

▶ The bottom area, which contains the Time Slider, Range Slider, Command Line, Help Line, and Status Line

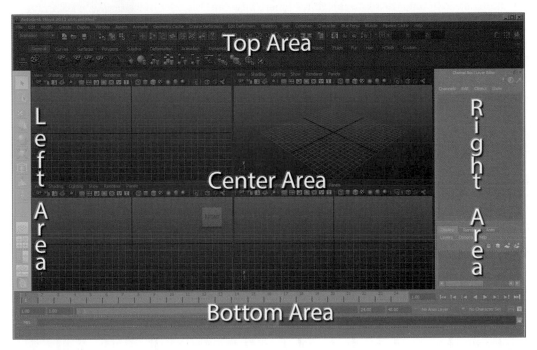

FIGURE 2.2
The interface can be simplified into five main areas. These areas will not change, though you can hide some or all of them to remove clutter from your workspace.

NOTE

Naming the Areas

The areas named in Figure 2.2 are not named as such in any official help file or resource; these are the naming conventions created for this book. I've found that designating general areas helps when trying to describe the location of menus, because as you can see, different areas have their own top menus.

The Top Area

We will start by looking at the top of the Maya interface. Almost all of the available commands are accessible through the menus and icons shown here. As you become more familiar with the software, you will return less frequently to the top area by the use of hotkeys and shortcuts, but it's good to know that Maya's core functionality is concentrated in one area.

The Main Menu

Maya's main menu area provides text-based menus at the top of the Maya window, and graphical buttons directly underneath in the Status Line. These buttons offer quick access to common tasks and options. Maya provides a variety of groups of menus (menu sets) to choose from, according to the task being carried out (see how to change your menus in the section "Switching Menu Sets"). This means that some of the listed text menus will change according to the menu set selected, but the good news is that a default set of menus remains constantly displayed: File, Edit, Modify, Create, Display, Window, and Assets (at the left of the listed menus) are shown in Figure 2.3. These menus contain tools, options, and commands common to every menu set. It is also good to note that "Help" is always displayed to the right of all the main menu items, and is also accessible by pressing **F1** at any time.

File   Edit   Modify   Create   Display   Window   Assets

FIGURE 2.3
The main menu. These first seven menus stay the same no matter what menu set you have loaded.

▶ The **File** menu contains options and commands for loading and saving files, setting and configuring your Maya project, using references, and interacting with other Autodesk software.

▶ The **Edit** menu contains commands for copying and pasting nodes; selecting, duplicating, and deleting nodes; and, finally, grouping and parenting.

▶ The **Modify** menu contains options, tools, and commands for manipulating object attributes, snapping and aligning objects, converting geometry, and access to the common tools in the Tool Box.

▶ The **Create** menu contains tools for creating all of the common object types in Maya.

▶ The **Display** menu contains options for controlling types of objects to display, changing display options for different object types, showing and hiding nodes, and controlling user interface display.

▶ The **Window** menu contains all of Maya's main windows and saved UI arrangements.

▶ The **Assets** menu contains options and tools for using Maya's Asset system to lock, unlock, and publish attributes on objects to reduce the possibility of errors introduced in production later.

These seven menus will never change no matter what menu set is currently loaded. They contain other menus, tools, options, and commands that are necessary to perform all of Maya's functionality.

NOTE

Accessing Menus

Maya has more than one way to access almost every menu. From the main menu, to hotkeys, to the hotbox, the menu you need is never more than a click away.

Switching Menu Sets

Maya allows you to load the different menu sets, arranged for convenient access to menus commonly used in conjunction. To switch between menu sets, you can hit the **F2** through **F6** keys, or use the drop-down box in the top-left corner of the screen. Changing menu sets replaces the menus to the right of the first seven menus (to the right of the "Assets" menu). Figure 2.4 shows the Menu Set drop-down list.

FIGURE 2.4
This drop-down box shows you the currently loaded menu set. Loading new menu sets is as easy as choosing a new one from this list.

Animation Menu Set

By pressing **F2** or choosing Animation on the Menu Set drop-down box, you can access the Animation menu set (see Figure 2.5). This menu set contains tools and commands to create deformers, create keyframe and path animation, set up skeleton and skinning, to cache your scene, and more.

FIGURE 2.5
The animation menu set contains all the menus you need for creating object movement.

Polygons Menu Set

Pressing the **F3** key or choosing Polygons in the Menu Set drop-down box will give you access to polygonal modeling tools and UV tools, as shown in Figure 2.6. Polygonal modeling is the standard surfacing type for modern animation and visual effects. Creating and editing UVs (or "UV'ing") is the method by which we define how textures stretch over a 3D object.

Select   Mesh   Edit Mesh   Proxy   Normals   Color   Create UVs   Edit UVs   Muscle   Pipeline Cache   Help

FIGURE 2.6
The Polygons menu set contains the menus you will need for modeling and texturing polygonal objects.

Surfaces Menu Set

Pressing the **F4** key or choosing Surfaces in the Menu Set drop-down box reveals all of the NURBS modeling tools as well as the Subdivision Surfaces tools. NURBS and "Sub-D's" (as they're called) are becoming antiquated technology, but support for these geometry types will persist for a few years yet. Figure 2.7 shows the Surfaces menu set.

Edit Curves   Surfaces   Edit NURBS   Subdiv Surfaces   Muscle   Pipeline Cache   Help

FIGURE 2.7
The Surfaces menu set contains tools and commands for creating and editing NURBS geometry.

Dynamics Menu Set

Pressing **F5** brings up the Dynamics menu set, which is also available by choosing it in the Menu Set drop-down box. This menu set loads Maya's legacy particles and dynamics systems, as shown in Figure 2.8. With the addition of nDynamics, Maya has been moving away from these tools, but support for them may persist for some time.

Particles   Fluid Effects   Fluid nCache   Fields   Soft/Rigid Bodies   Effects   Solvers   Muscle   Pipeline Cache   Help

FIGURE 2.8
The Dynamics menu set holds menus used to create dynamic animation and particles.

Rendering Menu Set

F6 is the last hotkey programmed to change the menu set, by default, and it is reserved for the Rendering menu set. You can also access the Rendering menu set by selecting it from the Menu Set drop-down box. This menu set offers access to Maya's lighting, texturing, rendering, toon shading, Paint Effects tools, and more, as seen in Figure 2.9.

Lighting/Shading   Texturing   Render   Toon   Stereo   Paint Effects   Muscle   Pipeline Cache   Help

FIGURE 2.9
This menu set is the hub of your lighting, surfacing, and rendering tasks. Also, toon rendering, muscle options, and paint effects reside here.

nDynamics Menu Set

Although no hotkey is defined for nDynamics, you can still access this menu set by selecting it in the top Menu Set drop-down box. nDynamics have replaced normal dynamics for most uses in

Maya. You can set up particles and fields as well as nCloth objects for cloth and soft body simu-lation. Figure 2.10 shows the nDynamics menu set loaded.

nParticles   nMesh   nHair   nConstraint   nCache   nSolver   Fields   Effects Assets   Muscle   Pipeline Cache   Help

FIGURE 2.10
The nDynamics menu set has no hotkey assigned, by default. This is only because the legacy Maya dynamics have not yet been written out of the program.

The Status Line

Below the main menu text buttons sits a bar containing graphical buttons. This menu is rarely changed because it contains some very important tools and menus. Starting from the left, as shown in Figure 2.11, we have the following items:

1. The Menu Set drop-down box

2. New File, Open File, Save File

3. Select by type: Hierarchy, Object, Component

4. Selection masks, for choosing what objects can and cannot be selected

5. Lock selection and highlight selected toggle

6. Snap to grid, curve, point, view plane, or make object live

7. Toggle construction history

8. Open render view, render the current frame, IPR render current frame, Render Globals

9. The input line box

FIGURE 2.11
Below the main menu is a menu bar called the Status Line. These buttons provide added control and options for manipulating objects and scene files.

The Shelf

The Shelf contains common commands and tools used frequently in Maya. The default shelves align basically with the default menu sets, but offer quick access to tools and commands that are a few extra clicks away if you were to navigate to them using the main menu. By far the most powerful aspect of the Shelf is that you can create your own shelves and organize your tools and commands in an infinite number of ways.

NOTE

Get Comfortable and Then Customize

It cannot be overstated how many different ways you can access the same menu, tool, or command in Maya. The main menu is a good go-to place and is simple to navigate, albeit rudimentary. Once you begin to use custom shelves, marking menus, and the like, you'll find your own comfortable workflow and can start removing clutter from your UI by hiding menus.

The Center Area

Although the top area contains the menus you will access most often, you will be working within the panels that occupy the center area 90% of the time. You can load almost any of Maya's many panels into the center area, as well as any camera or perspective view. If Maya was a tool shed, the top area would be where your tools hang and the center area would be your work bench.

Panels

The center area is where your main panels display (sometimes referred to as "viewports" or "workspace"). Which panels display here is entirely up to you, and you will find that part of a great workflow is finding convenient panel layouts and saving them for later use by going to the Panels, Saved Layouts menu. Any panel can display any camera or main application panel, such as the graph editor, outliner, or hypershade. You can maximize any panel to the entire panel area by tapping the spacebar when your mouse is hovering over it. Panels can also be resized by clicking on the panel borders.

Loading a new camera is simple: In the panel you want to change, select Panels and then choose either a Perspective, Stereo, or Orthographic view to change the camera. Alternatively, you can select the camera in the scene and go to Panels, Look Through Selected. A third way (there are many) to change cameras is to hold down the spacebar and then LMB click in the center of the hotbox that appears. The default camera choices will appear, and you can drag your mouse in the direction of the camera you would like to use. There are still more ways to change cameras, but let's get a little familiar with using panels so you can navigate your 3D scene.

TIP

Find the Menus Before the Hotbox

We are not going to go too deep into the hotbox in this book because although it is a timesaving tool for some tasks, it is fundamentally just a different presentation of the same menus you have available to you in the rest of Maya, albeit appearing in a panel whenever you hold down the space-bar. Learn to find your tools and commands in the normal Maya menus before you customize or even start to depend on the hotbox so when a command is not available to you there, you don't get lost searching for a menu you've misplaced. Again, it is a good timesaving tool for intermediate to advanced Maya users, but will be cumbersome to you as a beginner.

Using a Camera Panel

To rotate a camera in a panel, hold the **Alt** button while LMB dragging within the panel. The camera orbits around a center point. To move a camera along its Z axis (in other words, move the camera forward and backward), hold **Alt** and drag the right mouse button. This is mistakenly referred to as "zooming" in many tutorials and books. We'll cover true zooming in Hour 14, "Creating and Adjusting Cameras." Finally, to move your camera up and down, and side to side, hold **Alt** while dragging with your MMB.

The Left Area

The Toolbox and Tool Settings reside in the left area. By default, the Toolbox is displayed, but somewhat confusingly, the button to display the Tool Settings is in the top-right corner of the main Maya window. I've copied the button here because it can be quite hard to find without seeing it first. Take a look:

The Toolbox

This area holds commonly used tools, such as the move, rotate, and scale tools, but also the universal manipulator and soft selection. Most very experienced Maya users hide the Toolbox eventually, because of the easily learned hotkeys to access the tools. However, one very convenient feature of the Toolbox is that it shows the last-used tool below the Show Manipulator Tool. This can give you at-a-glance information that is useful for speeding up your workflow. To access the last-used tool, click on that button or press the **Y** key.

Tool Settings

To load the Tool Settings window, click the tool settings button in the top-right corner of the screen. Any tool that you load will display its options in this box. Alternatively, you can double-click on any tool loaded in the Toolbox, and the Tool Settings window will load with that tool selected. When you have loaded a tool and are ready to use it, the Tool Settings window gives you the options associated with your tool. These options range from the radius of your brush, with the Paint Skin Weights Tool, to the number of edge loops to insert with the Insert Edge Loop Tool. Remember that in Maya, any action that requires your input to determine the results is considered a tool. Although many commands have options boxes next to their name in the menu (which look like this □), you can bet that all tools have that box; you can set your tool's starting options by clicking that box before entering a tool. The settings will carry over when you open the Tool Settings window.

Common Tools

Maya delineates between a tool and a command. A command is executed and then the command is done. A tool is something that is able to be "in use." You manipulate a tool and your input changes the results you get onscreen. Some examples of commands are deleting geometry, removing history, and creating a sphere. Some examples of tools are the Insert Edge Loop Tool, the PaintFX Tool, and the Move Tool.

Select Tool

To select any 3D object that is displaying in a camera panel, press **Q** and use your LMB to click directly on the object or drag a selection box around the objects.

To toggle select objects (select if unselected, or deselect if selected), hold down the Shift key when selecting or dragging a selection box.

To add to selection, hold down **Ctrl+Shift** when selecting. To deselect, hold down just **Ctrl** when selecting.

Move, Rotate, and Scale Tools

All three of these tools will select an object if unselected: You simply LMB click on it. You can also use the selection box by clicking and dragging with your LMB to select, deselect, or toggle select, just like with the selection tool. These tools have manipulators, however, which look like axes that float in the panel. These are the literal handles you use to manipulate these tools. The advantage of using the selection tool over always making your selections with the Move, Rotate, and Scale Tools is that sometimes you will not be able to select an object that is blocked by a tool's manipulator (especially the Rotate Tool's manipulator, being the largest).

The **W** key activates the Move Tool. A three-axis move manipulator will appear at the pivot point of the selected object, or the last selected object if you have selected multiple objects. To move the object, select any one of the axis handles on the manipulator to move along that axis, or to move the object freely, relative to the camera, MMB drag anywhere in the panel and the object will follow.

The **E** key actives the Rotate Tool. A spherical rotation manipulator will appear at the selected object's pivot. LMB clicking on any of the three rotation axes will allow you to rotate along that axis, or LMB dragging anywhere within the radius of the rotation manipulator will activate a "virtual trackball" in which you can freely rotate the object. MMB dragging anywhere in the panel rotates the object on the currently selected axis.

Finally, the **R** key activates the Scale Tool. This tool resembles the Move Tool with its three-axis manipulator. Using the LMB to click-drag on any of the three axes scales along that axis. LMB clicking on the center of the manipulator and dragging scales the object uniformly. MMB dragging anywhere in the panel scales the object along the currently selected axis.

The Right Area

The right area of the Maya interface holds some of the most commonly accessed menus. The Channel Box, the Attribute Editor, and Layer Editor all reside here. Nearly all editable and animatable attributes can be accessed through the menus visible in the right area.

The Channel Box

By default, the Channel Box is the displayed menu in the right area. This menu shows you the channels (editable attributes) of the selected object in a list format. The channel name is on the left, and the current value is listed on the right, as you can see in Figure 2.12. You can select the value box and type in a new value, or you can MMB click-drag on the channel name to slide the value up and down. You'll learn how to add attributes later on.

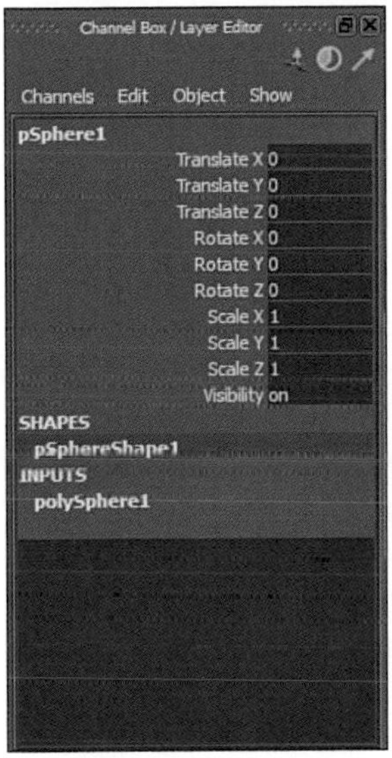

FIGURE 2.12
The Channel Box displaying the attributes of a selected object. The channel shows in the left column, the current value of a channel in the right.

The Attribute Editor

Clicking the Attribute Editor button or pressing **Ctrl+A** opens the Attribute Editor. By default, it will load and replace the Channel Box in the right area. When finer control is necessary, the Attribute Editor is the menu to use. This is where all of your "options" truly exist. Most of the editable top-level nodes are arranged across the top of the Attribute Editor in tabs. Clicking on a tab will load the attributes for that node, allowing you to change attributes as you see fit. Some nodes will always be shown, specifically an object's transform node and shape node, as you can see in Figure 2.13.

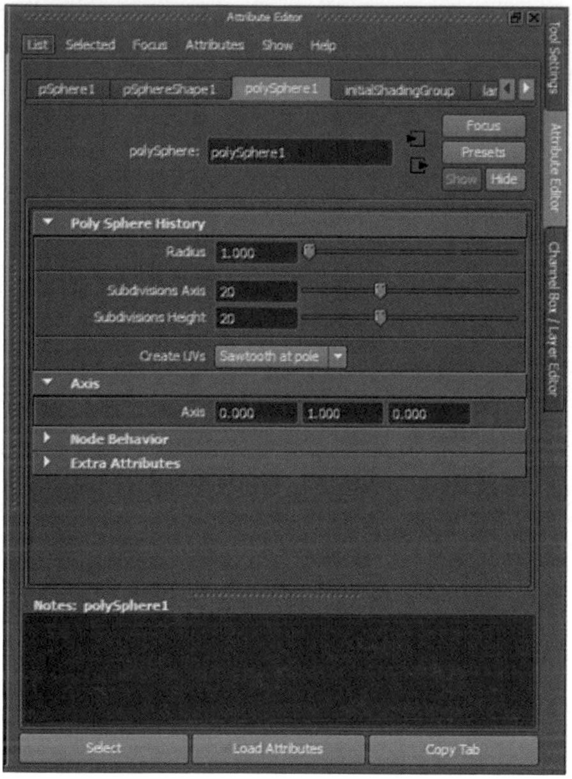

FIGURE 2.13
The Attribute Editor offers the most robust control over the attributes of nodes in Maya. All of the inputs and outputs associated with a selected node will normally display as tabs across the top of the Attribute Editor.

The Layer Editor

Beneath the Channel Box and Attribute Editor resides the Layer Editor. The three tabs here represent the three different types of layers Maya allows you to add to your scene (as shown in Figure 2.14):

▶ **Display layers** are like groups that control the visibility and selectability of objects in your scene. An object can belong to multiple display layers, but it should be known that an object will be hidden if the highest layer it belongs to is hidden, regardless if layers below are showing.

▶ **Render layers** allow you to separate objects into layers at render time. This is useful for rendering objects separately for compositing together into a single image later.

▶ **Animation layers** allow you to add multiple layers of movement onto objects. This is useful for applying movement that would be destructive to your overall animation if you had to change it later, such as adding a little bit of shivering on a character that is cold. Once you add the kind of small details it would take to make the shivering believable, the rest of the body animation would be very hard to change due to the amount of details piled onto the controls.

FIGURE 2.14
The Layer Editor contains the three layer types. Most of their functionality as far as adding and removing objects from a layer is the same among the layer types. We will make extensive use of these in later lessons.

The Bottom Area

This area may only hold a few menus, but it provides a lot of the power behind Maya's animation toolset. In addition, the feedback you get from the bottom area will be invaluable as you encounter errors or need tooltips as you work.

The Time Slider

The single most useful part of the bottom area is the Time Slider. As you start creating animation, you will see how easy it is to use; simply LMB click anywhere on the Time Slider to set the current frame. On the right of the Time Slider are normal VCR controls, with an additional frame forward, frame backward, keyframe forward, and keyframe backward. The keyboard shortcut to start playback is **Alt+V**, and **Esc** stops. To frame forward is **Alt+.** and frame backward is **Alt+,**.

The Range Slider

Here is where you determine how long, in frames, your scene file will be. You can type in values on the left and right side of this slider. When you have a scene length (the outermost numbers), you zoom in on a certain section of your scene by either typing in values in the innermost boxes, or even by LMB clicking and dragging the two handles on the ends of the Range Slider. This is useful when you have a long scene and you need to focus on a small section of keys. To the right of the Range Slider are options for choosing animation layers and character sets, to toggle AutoKey, and to change your animation preferences. We will go in depth on these options later.

The Command Line

The Command Line is a useful bar that gives you feedback about the commands you execute, as well as a small script box in which you can type in MEL or Python commands. Whenever you execute any command or finish using any tool, Maya will output some feedback on the Command Line. In essence, you are seeing simply the last line of the Script Editor (the button on the far right of the Command Line). It is still very useful, though, because sometimes feedback about errors that shows up here will cue you to open the Script Editor and take a closer look.

The Help Line

Hovering over any tool or command will make a helpful tooltip appear in the Help Line in most cases. From giving you the order in which you need to select objects to make a certain command work, to giving you a description of a tool and how to use it, the Help Line is your best friend when first starting in Maya. In fact, now would be a good time to hover with your mouse over some buttons and see what Maya has to say about them. With the feedback from the Help Line, it is quite possible to learn the basics about nearly all the tools once you have learned the basics of Maya.

Axes, Planes, Coordinates

As in all 3D programs, Maya has our standard Cartesian axes. The three axes are X, Y, and Z. All transforms (moving, rotating, and scaling) are done using these three axes. Because Z is normally considered "depth," you can consider this as the "forward and backward" axis. That leaves X to be "side to side" and Y to be "up and down." When Maya first loads, you are staring at the construction plane, or the world origin. This origin is at XYZ values of 0,0,0. This means that negative values on transforms, rotations, and scales are common. "Backward" in Z space is negative, "down" in Y space is negative, and "left" in X space is negative. You can see the current orientation of the XYZ plane by looking in the bottom-left corner of any panel (the lines point toward positive X, Y, and Z). Alt+LMB click and rotate the Persp panel around to see the effect on the coordinate axes.

The Outliner

The last important panel to become familiar with is the Outliner. You will, of course, encounter many menus as you go through this book and discover more about Maya, but the Outliner is used ubiquitously throughout all the steps of 3D production. Going to Window, Outliner loads the Outliner. As you can see, it is basically a hierarchical view of the entire Maya scene (see Figure 2.15). By default, the Outliner displays only nodes that have transform or shape nodes associated with them. Meaning textures, images, and other utility nodes are not displayed in the Outliner. This is a good thing because you need a way to see only the important nodes in your scene—nodes such as geometry, controllers, effects, and the like.

FIGURE 2.15
The Outliner will become your best friend. This simple hierarchical view of your scene file allows you to see how objects relate to one another. It also allows you to do simple tasks such as group and parent objects and, of course, make selections.

Typing in text in the top bar narrows the display to matching terms, and an asterisk (*) is a wildcard. For instance, if you want to find all of the spheres in your scene, you can type **pSphere*** in the box. Bear in mind this box is case sensitive, like all areas of Maya. Selecting an object by LMB and MMB dragging it will either move its position in the Outliner (only for organizational purposes; it is not like the Layer Editors). Or, if you MMB drag an object and let go while it is hovering directly on another object, the dragged object will "parent" underneath that object. This means the parent object controls the position, orientation, and scale of the child object. Don't worry too much about this now, because we will discuss hierarchies in depth in Hour 9, "Relationships and Making Nodes Work Together," and Hour 10, "Basic Rigging: Preparing Objects for Animation."

The one slightly odd thing about the Outliner is that while Ctrl+LMB is the action to *deselect* objects in the panel, it is how you *toggle* a selection in the Outliner. Shift+LMB selects all the objects between the two objects you clicked in the Outliner.

Summary

Maya's interface can be daunting, but it can also be very empowering and easy to use when you are used to it. The switching of menu sets allows you to focus on the task at hand, be it modeling, or animating. The rearrangement of panels makes it so that you can work in a way that suits your workflow. Tearing off menus means the tools you need are always at your fingertips. For ease of use, the same camera manipulation tools work in almost every single Maya panel—be it a perspective camera or the Graph Editor—so learning to move, dolly, and rotate the camera in panel will serve you in navigating all of Maya's many editors.

VIDEO

Menu Setups

Watch the bonus video included in this Hour's files for a quick run-through of common menu setups in Maya. You will see how fast it is to save menu layouts, and how to restore a layout saved previously.

Q&A

Q. I've been playing around in Maya and it doesn't look "default" anymore. How can I reset it?

A. Although it is possible to reset individual settings and preferences, a sure-fire way to revert your Maya installation back to default is to simply close Maya, delete the "prefs" directory on your computer found in the Documents/Maya/2013/ directory, and then reopen Maya.

Q. Can I access tools in one menu set when another is loaded?

A. Yes, however, it is almost always easiest to switch menu sets quickly. You can set hotkeys (discussed in Hour 24, "Ideal Settings, Preferences, and Hotkeys") for all of the Maya commands, but there are so many that you will quickly run out of keys if you are not careful. You can load any menu or command as a torn-off window too, which is a good alternative to having to switch menu sets constantly if you are doing a repetitive task.

Q. Is there a way to display both the Attribute Editor and the Channel Box at the same time?

A. You can move the Attribute Editor to either side of the Maya interface and tear it off. More powerfully, any menu that loads into the Attribute Editor can be torn off by clicking the Copy Tab button at the very bottom. The nice thing about this is that this copy of the Attribute Editor will always show the attributes for the object you had selected when you copied it.

Q. Can I change the coordinate system to have Z "up" like in other programs?

A. I highly recommend keeping your axes in their default configuration to avoid major problems down the road. However, if you are working closely with another program and need the interoperability, you can change it in Windows, Settings/Preferences, Preferences and then loading the Settings menu.

Workshop

The workshop contains quiz questions and exercises to help you solidify your understanding of the material covered. Try to answer all questions before looking at the "Answers" section that follows.

Quiz

1. How many areas are there in the default Maya interface?

2. What interface item holds sets of commonly used commands and tools, organized by menu set?

3. What area of the Maya interface is the Channel Box found in?

4. What is the 3D coordinate (X, Y, Z) of the world origin?

5. If an object is 4 units to the "left," 3 units "up," and 6 units "back," what is its 3D coordinate?

Exercise

Open Maya and make sure you are in your default interface. Load different menu sets, and tear off menus and arrange them how you like. Open the Attribute Editor, the Tool Settings window, and the Channel Box and get familiar with their layout. Choose a few layouts that are located below the Toolbox on the left and see how these arrangements make use of the five areas available. You can even create your own layout and save it by clicking the following in any panel: Panel, Saved Layouts, Edit Layouts.

Answers

1. Five areas. These can be hidden and re-arranged, but there are only ever five areas to dock menus and load items.

2. The Shelf holds these items. You can edit the shelves by right clicking on the Shelf (in Maya 2013).

3. The right area. It shows and hides depending on if the Attribute Editor is showing at the same time (Ctrl+A).

4. (0,0,0)

5. (-4, 3, -6). Remember to face the Cartesian plane with Z being your "depth" and you will not get confused.

File Types and Managing Assets

What You'll Learn in This Hour:

- ▶ The different file types Maya uses
- ▶ The Maya Project folder and file structure
- ▶ Converting files for use in Maya
- ▶ Common issues with files

Maya is a complex program. A major contributing factor to the complexity of Maya is the fact that it reads and writes so many different types of files. Even Adobe Photoshop, with all of its versatility, doesn't read anywhere near the number of files or generate the amount of different file types that Maya does. To understand workflow in Maya, you will learn what the different file types mean.

NOTE

Project Management

We will be covering the different Maya file types that are commonly used in this hour, but not how to organize them on your computer yet. To understand how to properly organize your files to be the most productive, you need to understand project management, which is covered in Hour 23, "Correct Project Management and Scene Workflow."

In this hour, you find out what file types are generally better than others to read and write with Maya. You will also gain a little bit more of an understanding of how the different assets work together as we look at file types and how they relate to one another in the pipeline. We won't get too ahead of ourselves here; it's important to get the basics of file types and asset types before we go too deep into a production workflow.

3D File Types

We'll first take a look at the many 3D file types. These are files that hold object information, animation information, particle information, cloth information, and so on. All of the following types have different uses and/or they are specifically designed to store a specific type of information.

Maya Scene Files

A Maya "scene" is all of the interconnected nodes and attributes in a single file. Everything from geometry to lights, cameras, and animation has information contained in the connected nodes that needs to be saved when you create a scene. Maya can save scene files in two different formats: binary and ASCII. The binary format file extension is .mb (Maya Binary) and the ASCII format file extension is .ma (Maya ASCII).

There are numerous reasons to choose either of the Maya scene files formats, so let's go over each one.

Maya Binary

Maya binary files are greatly smaller in size than ASCII format due to the fact that the nodes and associated edits are saved into this format in a computer-readable-only format. The amount of size reduction between a binary and ASCII file depends greatly on the type of information within the file, but it is safe to say that if file transfer or storage space is an issue for you, or if you are just starting out with Maya, a binary file should be chosen.

Binary files are also known for saving the information in a little more "clean" manner, meaning that sometimes when a file is in .ma format and causes errors, one of the first things to try is to save it as an .mb file instead. This has not been detailed specifically in developer documentation, and it is extremely case specific, so you will have to leave it up to fate to be able to test this. Suffice it to say that for some reason, *some* scene files seem to work better in .mb format. My personal testing indicates slightly that the more advanced Maya features save better in .mb than .ma, such as complex rig systems, nCloth, and so on.

These are the two main advantages. The disadvantages of the .mb format are that it is not human readable and not generally backward compatible (although improved recently, but still not bulletproof).

Maya ASCII

As a tradeoff for file size, ASCII files are "human readable." You can open an .ma in any text editor and see every single command that built your scene. In fact, Maya executes your .ma file almost exactly like you are typing in MEL script when you open it. The major advantage of this is that you can make edits to an .ma file without even having to open it. For instance, if a particular node is causing your scene to crash, you can comment out that node in the ASCII file using a text editor and then open the cleaned file in Maya. You can also change the file path for a referenced node, change the plugins required to open a scene, and even change the version number of Maya that is saved into the file. This makes .ma files generally much more backward compatible with previous versions of Maya than their binary counterparts. All nodes may not load correctly when you do this, but it is still generally a better bet to use .ma files when multiple versions of Maya are involved in your pipeline. Again, the tradeoff is file size. It is common for an .ma that contains a very high polygon environment, with textures, lighting information, and maybe some dynamics and effects to be in the hundreds of megabytes. With Incremental Save (described next) turned on, a folder with a few versions of a work-in-progress high-poly model might balloon to the gigabytes.

Nearly all visual effects studios save their files in ASCII format so that Technical Directors can make fixes to crashed or corrupted files. They are normally on the cutting edge of network speed and storage capacity as well, so the issue of file size does not come into play.

TRY IT YOURSELF ▼

Setting the Default Maya Scene File Type

We're going to set the file type for saving our files in Maya to ASCII format. We're doing this so that we have the option of making some simple changes to the files in a text editor, and because we are not going to be creating massive scene files. Therefore, disk space is not an issue.

1. Open Maya, and in the main menu, click File, Save Scene As □. (The □ denotes you need to click on this icon to open the options dialog for a given menu.)

2. Change the file type from Maya Binary to Maya ASCII and then choose Save and Close.

3. Check that your file type has been changed to ASCII by clicking on File, Save. The save options dialog should open, and Maya ASCII is loaded as default.

We'll keep the default Maya file type as ASCII for the time being. Only switch to binary if you are positive you will not have to read the file in a text editor to make changes or fixes, or if the .ma file is continuously crashing or freezing.

Other 3D File Types

You'll find that in the course of creating a fully fleshed-out 3D scene, Maya may read and write a dozen different file types. The formats Maya displays by default only represent a portion of the files it can potentially read, and yet still there is quite a long list of them, as shown in Figure 3.1. There are a few you should know, and many others you will learn as you work in Maya and the program generates them automatically.

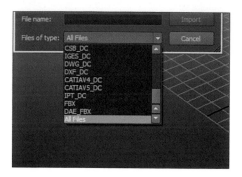

FIGURE 3.1
The File, Import dialog box shows just a portion of the types of files Maya can read.

OBJ

A simple 3D geometry format, OBJ stores polygonal models without textures. This format is both readable and writeable by Maya and most other 3D software. This format stores UV information as well (the information as to how 2D images are stretched onto the 3D geometry).

You will be exporting and importing .obj files when you use other software to create textures or high-detail geometry from a base mesh from Maya. You may even elect to save your models as .obj so that you always have a very simple copy of them if you want to import them at a later time. Most online 3D model repositories offer their models in OBJ format to accommodate Maya users.

FBX

The FBX file format is a robust format that contains much more information than OBJ, but still less than the full .ma or .mb Maya scene file. This format offers the ability to export and import a variety of materials, animation data, as well as lights and camera data. This format was designed to provide a high degree of interoperability between Autodesk products. You work with FBX files when you are working with other Autodesk programs extensively, such as 3ds Max and MotionBuilder. Because it can export most basic material types, FBX is good for saving models and is preferred over OBJ for downloading models from an online repository.

ANIM

The ANIM file format is not loaded by default, but it is very useful. Therefore, you should load the import/export plugin. This format saves the animation data on selected nodes for later use. You might do this if you want to reuse a piece of animation in another scene, if your current file is getting cumbersome and you'd like to apply the same animation to a fresh scene, or if you want to save your animation to a library for future projects.

TRY IT YOURSELF ▼

Load Plugins to Gain More Functionality

To access a few more of the file types Maya can read and write, you need to load the plugins. This is very simple:

1. In Maya's main menu, click on Windows, Settings/Preferences, Plug In Manager.

2. A window appears showing the plugins that are loaded and available to you.

3. Find the plugin called animImportExport.mll and check the Loaded and Auto Load boxes.

4. Now let's load a few more. Check both the Loaded and Auto Load boxes for the plugins atomImportExport.mll and objExport.mll (OBJ files can import by default, but you must enable the exporter plugin to create them).

ATOM

The new ATOM file format is an update to the ANIM file format, and is very powerful. This format allows you to not only apply the animation to the same hierarchy, but to use search strings to apply the animation to differing hierarchies. On top of that, this format exports and imports animation data on constraints and driven keys.

2D File Types

For the most part, you will be working within Maya scene files and loading and creating 2D images from the program. These 2D file types include texture files (images that are used to give color or shading properties to objects, as discussed in Hour 6, "Unfolding UVs and Applying Textures"), images that control attributes such as skin weight maps, and renders that you save from the program.

Texture File Types

You may already be familiar with some of the different file types that Maya reads based on your use of them in other programs or in general everyday use. Now that you are applying them in a high-end 3D animation software package, you have a few things to consider when working with the following file types.

JPG

Maya can read and write JPG files (pronounced *jay-peg*). They can be saved as your render output or loaded as a texture. The upside to a JPG file is that it is a fairly compressed, 8-bit-per-channel image, meaning the file size is normally pretty small. Because Maya loads your textures into RAM as it renders an image, managing the amount of data going into the scene is very important. The huge downside of JPG files is that they are unsuitable for high-end production because of the amount of compression they contain. They also contain no transparency information (or "alpha channel"), so a separate transparency image must be loaded if you are using JPG files for textures. We compare them to TGA files next. However, if you are doing a lot of post-processing to your renders, are using a non-photorealistic renderer, or if you want to preview effects and lighting, JPG files are fine to use.

TGA

The standard image file format for high-end usage is TGA (Targa). These images can be saved with 8 bits per channel and an extra 8 bit alpha per pixel, so they have a transparency channel. This format is relatively ubiquitous (can be read and written by all other high-end graphics software) and, as such, is a good format to use for textures. The format can be saved lossless, which is another good reason to use this format for textures. If the situation calls for high-quality 8-bit-per-channel images, TGA is the right choice. See how TGA files compare to JPG files for use as textures in Figure 3.2 (top) and Figure 3.3 (bottom).

EXR

For some instances, an image with more color depth is necessary. OpenEXR is a format designed for just that. Each channel has 32 bits, meaning that the number of colors possible in the format is in the trillions. When would you need this much color information? Imagine you are using an image to displace geometry (in other words, to make a relief-map). If you are only using an 8-bit-per-channel image format, you have only 256 (2^8) possible levels of detail. Imagine if you are trying to displace or extrude a mountain range out of a highly detailed plane. With only 256 possible levels of detail, that mountain is going to look pretty jagged. With an EXR image instead, the mountain will have as much detail as you can imagine in its topology (you'll actually run out of RAM calculating the geometry long before you run out of detail in the EXR displacement map to drive the geometry in the first place).

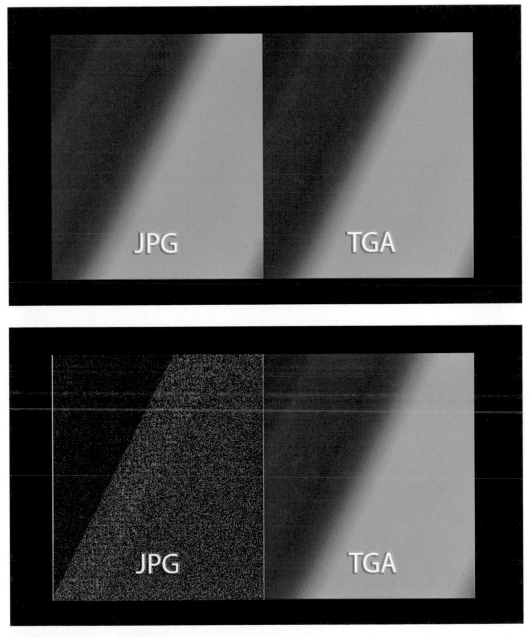

FIGURE 3.2 (top) and **FIGURE 3.3** (bottom)
The same rainbow-colored image was saved as a JPG and a TGA file. I then rendered these two images as textures from Maya (top). They look very similar, right? Well, when I overlay the original image onto the rendered image, the JPG reveals a lot of compression (bottom). The end quality of your renders depends on the quality of your source images.

Maya can write EXR images as well, which is useful for compositing for television VFX and film, where color needs to be matched to a raw image with high color depth. For most intents and purposes, however, animation destined for the Web and TV that has no color matching does need to take advantage of this format.

▼ TRY IT YOURSELF

Load the OpenEXR Plugin

We won't need to worry about rendering anything for a while, but because we're talking about the different image file formats, let's make sure Maya has loaded the plugin that reads and writes this incredible format:

1. In the main menu, go to Window, Settings/Preferences, Plug-in Manager.

2. Find the entry for OpenEXRLoader.mll and check the Loaded and Auto Load boxes.

PNG

Comparable to the size of JPG files, but with the added benefit of carrying a transparency channel, PNGs are a good middle ground for most users. For most of your work, a PNG offers the best of both worlds, with lossless compression and transparency. You should be careful using PNGs, because Maya will automatically load a transparency even if you are not using one. Some attributes do not like PNGs for the way they handle transparency.

IFF

The Maya Image File Format (IFF) is the default format written from Maya. This format does not have much compression, but it reads fast. It also supports alpha channel, and goes up to 16 bits per channel, giving you film-quality color in your renders. Maya, for lack of a better word, "loves" IFF files. It reads them and writes them quickly, and can use IFFs in any texture slot without problems.

NOTE

Choosing the Right Image Format

Choosing the correct image format can be a very important decision. Although Maya reads over two dozen formats and can read even more with plugins, there *is* such thing as the wrong format for the job. You don't need a 32-bit image as your transparency channel, the same way an 8-bit-per-channel image will not work for a displacement map. In general, TGAs are safe to use for textures, rendering as IFFs is fine for Web and TV, and if there's film or color matching involved, a 16-bit IFF or EXR is perfect.

Miscellaneous Formats

Maya writes dozens and dozens of files when creating scenes—from particle cache and geometry cache files, swatch files, render settings presets, render logs, and more. You will learn about these files types in their respective Hours. All the same, whenever you are working with Maya, it is important to set your project. When you do so, Maya will create the respective folders you need to store these files. Let's learn how to set a project and save your files in the correct folders.

VIDEO

File Types
In this video, I demonstrate some of the pros and cons of the many file types that Maya can read and write. You will see me save and open a few formats, as well as edit a Maya ASCII file using a text editor.

Maya Projects

The Maya Project folder structure is set up so you have all the directories you need to organize your files. Maya also looks for your files in their respective folders automatically, so keeping them organized is pivotal to your success. We will go over higher-level project management in Hour 23.

Set Project

In Maya, in the File menu, you have the option to set your project. This chooses a folder on your hard drive or a network location as a type of home directory. By default, Maya chooses the "default Project" folder in your My Documents folder if you are using Windows, or your Users folder if you are using a Mac. If the appropriately named and organized folders are present, Maya will save automatically generated files into their respective directories. If there are files present in the directories, Maya knows where to look for them by looking at the workspace.mel file created in every Project directory.

TIP

Default Workspace
Setting a project in a directory that is not in the normal Project directory structure will prompt Maya to ask you to either use a default workspace (a workspace.mel file that will assume your asset files are in the normal directories) or create a new one. It's a good idea to work with Maya's Project structure, so creating a default is a good bet.

Creating a Project

To create a project, you simply choose the directory you want to create the project within and then choose a project name. In its simplest form, Maya is creating a few default folders and a workspace.mel file to tell the program (whenever you set this project) where to look for certain files. To create a project, go to File, Project Window and then choose New. You will have the chance to choose a directory and a name for your project (see Figure 3.4).

As you can see, the default directories are created for you. These directories hold almost all of the files you will ever create in conjunction with a 3D project in Maya. When creating a project, you have the option to remove the directories you do not think you will need by clearing the fields before clicking Accept. Most Maya users learn how to look past the infrequently used directories and focus on the important ones; deleting unused directories doesn't really clear up clutter, and can be a pain when it's time to generate an asset and the folder needs to be created by hand. In Figure 3.5, we see the folder structure of a Maya project as viewed in Windows Explorer.

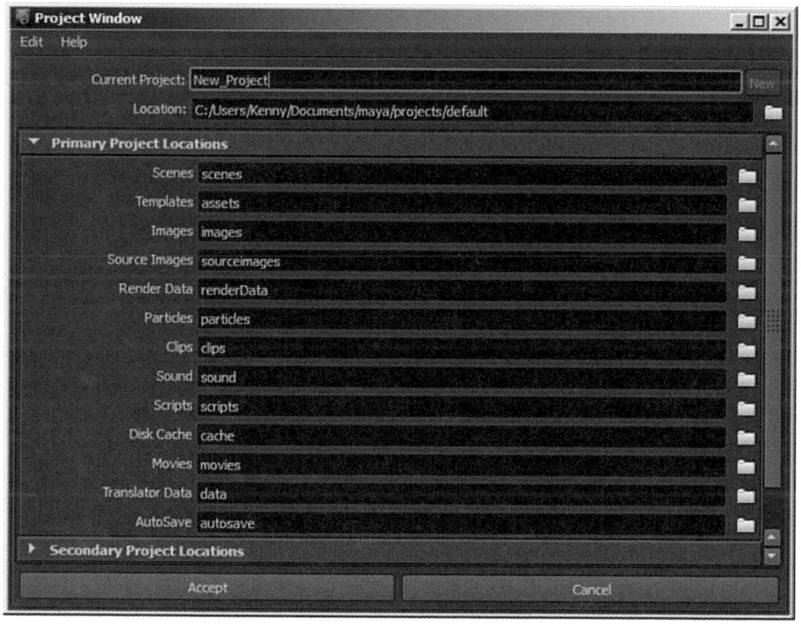

FIGURE 3.4
The Project window, where you can make a new project.

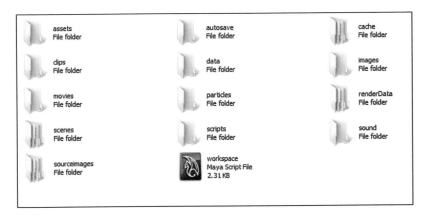

FIGURE 3.5
The Maya Project folder structure, as seen from Windows Explorer.

You will rarely need to change this structure, and we will discuss when and why to do so in Hour 23.

Summary

We've taken a look at what a Maya file contains and a few of the issues of saving using the different file types. We've also looked at the other types of 3D assets that Maya can read and write. Because you will be using many different image file formats in Maya, we also discussed the advantages and disadvantages of popular formats, and decided on some good ones to use for most tasks. We talked about the miscellaneous formats Maya will create when working in a scene, and finally where they will all be saved to, by creating your first Maya project.

Q&A

Q. It sounds like I should always be saving as .ma for all the benefits it has, right?

A. The file size issue can actually become pretty prohibitive. I have seen Maya files in the hundreds of megabytes. If you are transferring files frequently, .mb makes sense. Major visual effects studios that have blazing-fast networks and petabytes of storage space don't worry about these issues though.

Q. Shouldn't I use the highest bit depth images I possibly can for all my 2D needs?

A. No, it depends on the final destination of your 3D project. If you are rendering for display on the Web, for instance, you should keep in mind that monitors only display 8 bits per channel. Although it's true you will get slightly different values in your final renders if you use a very "deep" format, the amount of scene overhead and RAM required to render your scene will quickly become overwhelming.

Q. Do I have to set my project to work?

A. No, you can work in Maya without setting your project to the correct one. Maya creates a default project in your Documents directory that it will use until you make your first project. After that, it will always load the last-used project when it opens. Beware: Even though it's not necessary to set your project to work on a file, you could overwrite important files if you don't set it correctly.

Q. Can I delete the unused folders in my project directory?

A. Yes, but it's probably a better idea to get used to them. Different scenes will require different assets. If you are constantly trying to trim down your directory structure, you will by definition be spending less time creating.

Workshop

The workshop contains quiz questions and exercises to help you solidify your understanding of the material covered. Try to answer all questions before looking at the "Answers" section that follows.

Quiz

1. What does .ma stand for? What does .mb stand for?

2. Which exportable/importable format saves the most information within it?

3. Which image format has the least amount of information within it and is the most compressed? Which has the most amount of information in it?

4. What is the window called that is used to set the directories Maya will use to locate files associated with your scene?

5. The MEL script that is created within all projects and lists the project's directory settings is called what?

Exercise

We will be using a lot of different types of files in this book. It is a good idea to set up a project for the files you will be loading and editing. Create a folder on your computer called STYMAYA (for *Sams Teach Yourself Maya*). Within this folder, create a new project called 3D. Accept the defaults for the project that Maya gives you. Close Maya and navigate in Windows to the 3D directory and make sure it created a workspace.mel file. Reopen Maya and double-check that the project is set correctly. Try saving the empty file as an .mb and .ma file in the scenes directory as well.

Answers

1. .ma stands for Maya ASCII, and .mb stands for Maya Binary. Only ASCII files are editable and human readable, and they are generally backward compatible.

2. FBX files have the most robust information saved within, saving everything from geometry and texture information, to lights and camera data. Some formats that only save one type of data are OBJ (geometry) and ANIM (animation).

3. JPG has the least amount of information in it, at 8 bits per channel and no alpha. JPGs are also highly compressed. EXR files can have up to 32 bits per channel (trillions of colors) and no compression.

4. This is called the Project window, and it is found under the File menu in the main menu.

5. Every project directory contains a workspace.mel file that contains the information as to where Maya should look for the files connected to your scene.

HOUR 4

Modeling with Polygonal Geometry

What You'll Learn in This Hour:

▶ How to create primitive polygon shapes

▶ The properties of a polygonal object

▶ Traditional polygonal modeling techniques

▶ Preparing a model for texturing and rigging

Like all 3D programs, Maya has incorporated the latest technology as it was discovered, researched, and developed. Interestingly, surface types have gone through many revolutions in the recent past. Starting with polygons, and moving onto splines, then NURBS, subdivision surfaces, and now finally back to polygons, we've done a large loop only to end up where we started. Polygons are simple to understand, yet in the beginning of computer graphics, it took far too much computing power to manipulate enough of them to create curved surfaces. Maya's polygonal modeling tools are top notch, and even more intuitive control is available through MEL scripts and plugins.

NOTE

Unlocking the Potential of Polygons

Indeed, the number of polygonal modeling tools freely available on the Web is nothing short of amazing. Visit www.creativecrash.com to see an enormous online repository of MEL scripts for modeling and all of the 3D disciplines. You can even download free 3D models for the purpose of looking at the topology and learning how other modelers work.

In this hour, we'll walk through the process of creating polygonal primitives, and also look at how Maya treats objects' nodes to get a closer look at geometry creation. We'll try out many of the modeling tools Maya has, as well as also go over the criteria for a "finished" 3D model.

Objects in Maya

Maya handles objects in a unique way that allows you to separate the information associated with a model. The simplest way to put it is that every object has a *transform node*, which holds the same information for all objects (3D position, orientation, scale, visibility, and so on) and a *shape node*, which holds all of the attributes of the object. This can be very confusing to first-time users of Maya, but it doesn't have to be. Think of it this way: Shape nodes do not have any 3D position and orientation information, until Maya places the shapes into an invisible container and then transforms the container into position in space. When you start working with groups later on, the idea of transform nodes will make more sense. One of the more confusing parts of this concept is that selecting the object in the panel actually selects the transform node and not the shape node. Therefore, it is almost as if when selecting an object, you are not selecting the object itself but rather the invisible group that acts as a container of the object, as you can see in Figure 4.1.

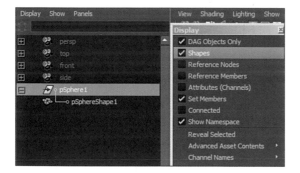

FIGURE 4.1
Displaying shape nodes in the Outliner shows you the relationship between a transform node (pSphere1) and a shape node (pSphereShape1). The transform node actually has the same icon as a group node, so you can think about it like your shapes are in their own personal group by default.

This relationship applies to all objects in Maya, but remember that not all objects are models. A hair system is an object, a dynamic field is an object, even a light is an object (although it has no mesh). Remember, also, that a shape node is not just model data but all of the attributes of an object (for instance, in the case of a light, you have intensity, shadow attributes, and light color).

Creating Polygons

Most 3D programs come with a set of prebuilt shapes, called *primitives*. Maya is no exception. A common modeling workflow is to begin by creating such a shape and then reshaping and building upon it to make the final model. To access the polygon modeling tools, first switch to the Modeling menu set by selecting it from the drop-down menu list, or by pressing **F3**.

Remember that the first seven menu items in the main menu are not going to change. Also, let's switch our Shelf to the Polygons shelf by clicking on the Polygon tab on the Shelf. The most common commands and tools are loaded into this shelf for you, as you can see in Figure 4.2.

FIGURE 4.2
The Polygons menu set and the Polygons shelf loaded.

You will see that the most popular polygon primitives are available in the Shelf for you to create. Clicking on any one of these buttons will bring up the interactive creation tool for the object. Maya will display onscreen instructions on how to create the object depending on the object you are trying to create. Therefore, as Figure 4.3 shows, if you choose to make a cube, you will be prompted to first drag to create the base and then pull up to make the height.

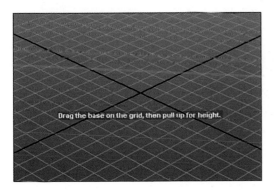

Drag the base on the grid, then pull up for height.

FIGURE 4.3
When you click any of the Shelf buttons to create a primitive, Maya gives you instructions on how to proceed. When I clicked on the "cube" primitive, my instructions displayed in the panel.

The list of objects that can be constructed solely out of primitives is very short. Maybe a hula hoop, a pipe, or a beach ball are simple enough that you can use the built-in shapes, but not much else. We need to start using Maya's polygonal modeling tools to model objects that have more than rudimentary forms. After you have familiarized yourself with the primitive shapes Maya offers, let's take a look at the skill of box modeling (a.k.a. polygonal modeling).

Polygons

A polygon is any straight-edged shape with three or more sides, and a polygonal mesh is an object made of multiple connected polygons. A triangle is the simplest polygonal shape, but Maya actually prefers working with four-sided polygons. You will find that the polygon primitives are largely formed of four-sided polygons by default. Although Maya supports polygons with any amount of sides, you will be introducing headaches down the road if you do not stick to clean, three- and four-sided polygons when you are modeling. Figure 4.4 illustrates the different types of polygons you can create in Maya.

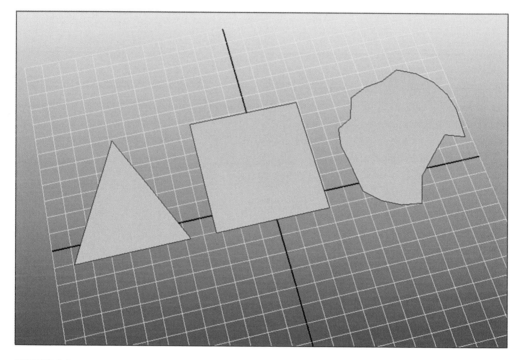

FIGURE 4.4
A three-sided, four-sided, and twenty-sided polygon. Generally, we want to stick to three- and four-sided polygons when modeling in Maya.

Let's begin to dive into the modeling tools Maya has to offer. We will use the most common tools to create a polygonal mesh of a hammer, starting from a single polygon and working all the way up to a finished model.

NOTE

Starting Your Mesh

Sometimes the easiest way to begin a mesh is with a single polygon. You may notice we could get to a further-along starting point by using one of the polygon primitives, but we'll save that knowledge for later. You will definitely want to start from a primitive that is close to your end goal when you are working in the future.

Polygon Plane

Using the Polygon shelf tools, we can create a polygon primitive by selecting the Polygon Plane button 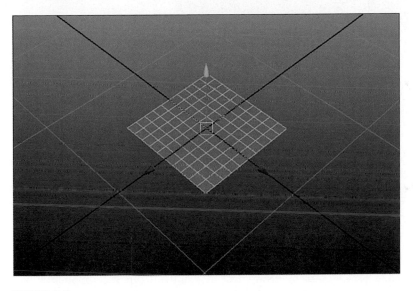 we can drag on the grid to get, as shown in Figure 4.5.

FIGURE 4.5
The result of creating the polygonal plane, pPlane1.

You will notice that the plane is made up from a large number of four-sided polygons, but we do not actually need that many. When modeling, it is usually best to keep the number of polygons to the minimum required for the task to avoid overcomplicating things. More polygons can be added later on, if needed. To remove the extra polygons, make sure the plane is still selected and expand the INPUTS section in the Channel Box (right area) by clicking on the label polyPlane1. This reveals the attributes of the pPlane1 shape node to specify the width, height, and how many subdivisions are required. The number of polygons our mesh is made from is dependent on how many subdivisions are specified. Because we want to keep the mesh complexity to a minimum at this point, set the subdivision height and width to 1, as shown in Figure 4.6.

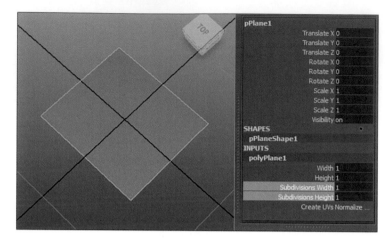

FIGURE 4.6
The plane with one subdivision, reduced from four polygons down to what we need to begin our mesh.

TIP

Wireframe and Shaded Mode

To view your models as just a wire mesh made up of your mesh's edges, press the **4** key on your keyboard. To see the geometry shaded smoothly in the panel, press the **5** key. (The **6** key and **7** key display your objects as textured and with lights, respectively, but it is normal to stay simply in smooth-shaded mode when modeling by pressing **5**.)

Components

In order to create models, you will be manipulating several different types of components that make up polygonal meshes. Before we start modeling, let's look at the different component types of a polygon mesh, displayed in Figure 4.7. The component parts of a mesh that are able to be manipulated in panel are as follows:

- ▶ **Vertices**—These are 3D points that define a mesh.

- ▶ **Edges**—These are the lines that connect the vertices.

- ▶ **Faces**—When at least three edges connect together at their endpoints, Maya creates a surface between them. This is called a face, or sometimes a polygon.

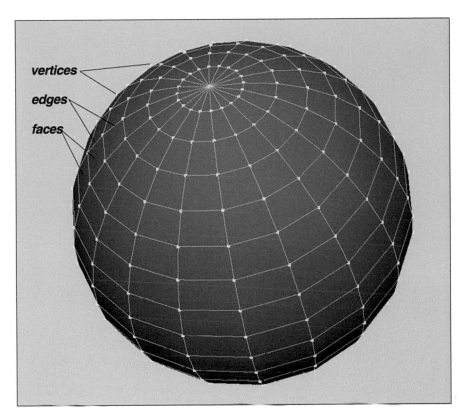

FIGURE 4.7
The three main component types that make up a polygon mesh.

Maya makes it simple and easy to access a mesh's components. The first way is to press **F8**, which takes you into component mode. If you don't have a type of component already selected, you will be brought into vertex mode. The second way to access the vertices is to RMB click and hold on the object you want to manipulate, and then drag the cursor to the component you need, as shown in Figure 4.8. The last way to access the components is to use the menu bar, select component mode, and then choose the component type or types you would like to access, as shown in Figure 4.9. All these methods give you the same access, although probably the RMB method is the most widely used (and easiest). No matter what method you use, pressing **F8** again is always the fastest way to return to object mode so you can select and manipulate your meshes rather than components.

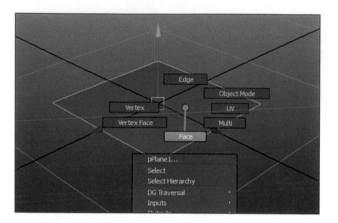

FIGURE 4.8
The RMB click method of accessing components.

FIGURE 4.9
The component mode toggled and faces selected.

▼ TRY IT YOURSELF

Explore the Polygon Primitives

Now that you've seen how to create a polygon primitive, you can create your own:

1. Create each one of Maya's many polygon primitive objects by clicking their respective button in the Shelf.

2. Use the Move (**W** key), Rotate (**E** key), and Scale (**R** key) tools to manipulate the objects in the panel.

3. Press **F8** or RMB drag on all of the objects to access their components—and while you are there, use the Move, Rotate, and Scale tools on the meshes' components as well.

Extrude

Extruding faces and edges is one of the most fundamental ways to create polygonal geometry. The Extrude tool creates new faces and edges from the selected components. Access Extrude and the other main modeling tools by making sure the Polygon menu set is active (**F3**) and going to the Edit Mesh menu. To actually extrude the face or edge, you need to select it first. Using our plane as an example, go into component mode (**F8**) to select faces. Select the plane's face and use the blue manipulator arrow to pull the face upward, like I did in Figure 4.10.

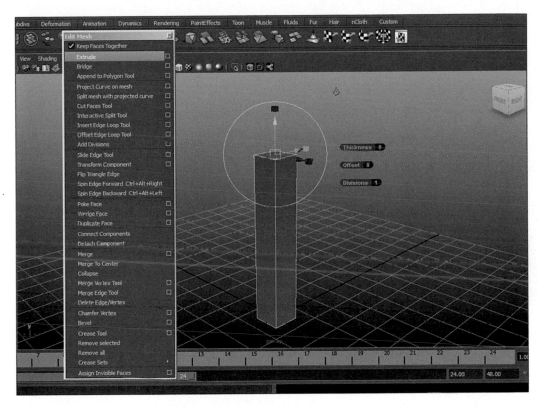

FIGURE 4.10
The polygon extruded upward in space. We are beginning to create the handle of our hammer.

The Extrude tool allows you to drag the extruded face by using the normal transform manipulator you are used to seeing with the Move and Scale tools, or you can use the sliders for Thickness, Offset, and Divisions to get different results. (Note that the Edit Mesh menu has been torn off.)

Bevel

Bevel is another of the most basic tools when working with polygons. It divides the selected geometry and creates an angle between the faces. If we select all the top edges and bevel them using the Bevel tool from the Edit Mesh menu, we can create the grip of the hammer. Figure 4.11 shows the top face of the hammer beveled inward, which starts to give us the shape that will turn into the grip.

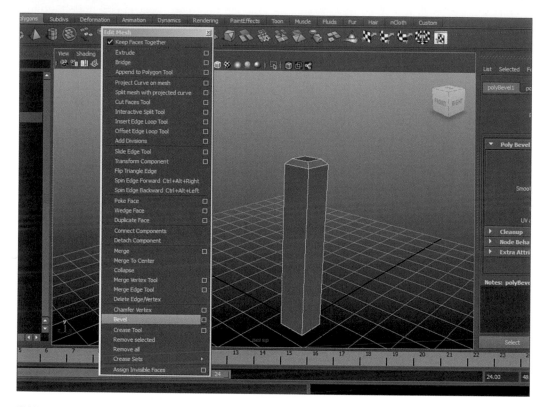

FIGURE 4.11
The top edge loop has been beveled to give us the hammer grip.

Insert Edge Loop

The Insert Edge Loop tool is very powerful. It creates a loop of edges to your model, adding a level of detail wherever you need it. To use it, select Insert Edge Loop from the Edit Mesh menu and then click-drag on an edge to place the new edge loop where you want it. With good modeling technique, you'll find this tool to be one of the most useful in your arsenal. To add detail to the hammer, insert an edge loop to the top section of the hammer, as I have done in Figure 4.12.

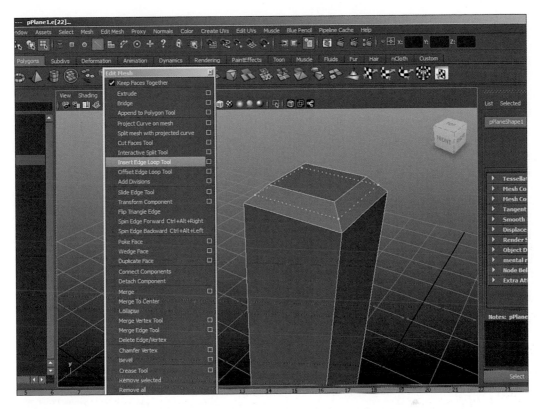

FIGURE 4.12
An edge loop has been added to this top part of the hammer. We will scale and translate this edge loop to make it cleaner.

As we continue to extrude faces, we get more polygons and therefore more detail in the mesh. We can then select the new faces and translate, rotate, and scale them to make our hammer take shape. Wherever we need extra detail, the Insert Edge Loop tool can normally provide the needed resolution on the mesh. As you can see, the most common workflow for polygonal modeling includes a lot of switching tools. We commonly go back and forth between creating new geometry and detail with tools such as Extrude and then adjusting the new polygons by using the Move, Rotate, and Scale tools on the mesh's components. See how the hammer form is starting to emerge in Figure 4.13.

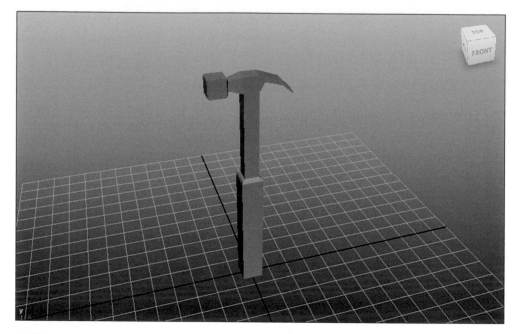

FIGURE 4.13
With just a little more extruding, the hammer model starts to take shape.

Subdividing

When you render a polygonal object, it is common that you will want to have a much more detailed model than you could ever create by hand. To give some perspective, the hammer in Figure 4.13 is made out of a paltry 50 polygons. Many feature-film-quality models are tessellated at render time to produce a scene with upwards of *5 million* polygons. Because it would be impossible to hand-extrude, bevel, move vertices, and add edge loops to get that level of detail, Maya has built-in polygonal smoothing tools. The main consideration is whether you want the tessellation to occur at render time after the scene is complete or you need to apply more edits, deformers, and manipulations to an already smoothed model. For the former, we will use the Mental Ray smooth mesh preview. For the latter, we will use Mesh, Smooth.

NOTE

Timing Matters

Maya keeps what's called "history" on the models. This is a record of the edits made to an object. If you apply a Smooth to a mesh and then make edits such as moving vertices or faces, these edits are dependent on the results of that Smooth—meaning you cannot change the parameters of the Smooth without unpredictable results to your mesh. This is because the Smooth is before the mesh edits in the history of the mesh. We'll talk more about this in future Hours.

Smooth

To smooth a mesh, we simply go to the Mesh, Smooth command. This command has many
options that alter the outcome of the model, but for now we'll simply adjust the number of
divisions to get a feel for changing parameters. We'll also use the Attribute Editor for the first
time. With the Smooth applied, we'll load the attributes. Pressing **Ctrl+A** with an object selected
brings up the Attribute Editor, as well as loads tabs across the top that correspond to that object's
inputs. Many of the commands and tools you use to create a model will load into tabs here as
well. Some of the inputs may even offer settings that you can change to get different results
(see Figure 4.14).

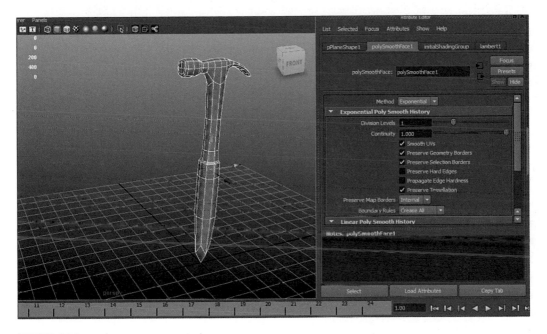

FIGURE 4.14
The Smooth is applied, and we are viewing the nodes connected to the hammer. The attributes of the Smooth
are accessed by clicking on the appropriate tab at the top. Sliding the Division Levels slider will give us more
or less detail, as we see fit.

Remember that because an object has history, you cannot make changes to a node that other
nodes depend on without potentially disastrous results. However, if you are happy with the
amount of smoothing you've achieved, you can remove all of the history of a model by choosing
Edit, Delete by Type, History (or by pressing **Alt+Shift+D**).

NOTE

There's No Going Back

Once you have hit the limit of your Undo queue, or close and open a scene again, deleting history cannot be undone. You should be sure that you will not have to make any edits to the construction history before doing so. As unpredictable as editing nodes deeper in history can be, there are actually instances in which making such edits is necessary and in fact part of the process, such as with rigging characters, texturing objects, and manipulating dynamics.

Smooth Mesh Preview

Instead of using the Mesh, Smooth tool, we can preview our smoothing in the panel. Pressing 3 with a piece of geometry selected activates the Smooth Mesh Preview. Maya will show you, in the panel, the amount of tessellation that will occur at render time. The advantage of this method is you can continue working on your low-poly mesh and then check the final result by pressing a single key. Pressing 1 takes you back to the base mesh, whereas 2 shows you both. You can change the amount of tessellation that you see in the Attribute Editor by navigating to the object's Shape Node tab and finding the Smooth Mesh expanding menu.

Crease

The last top-level tool we'll look at with polygonal modeling is the Crease tool. This powerful tool allows us to define hard edges on our model, making it so that when we use Smooth Mesh Preview, areas of detail are not lost. Go to Edit Mesh, Crease Tool to load the tool. The tool only works on edges, and to increase the hardness, simply select an edge and MMB drag, as I am doing on the hammer in Figure 4.15.

▼ TRY IT YOURSELF

Exploring the Modeling Tools

Take a few ideas for simple objects and try to model them from primitives:

1. Use the Extrude and Bevel tools to create new faces and edges.

2. Experiment with the other polygon modeling tools such as Merge (to connect edges and vertices) and Interactive Split (to make manual cuts in the geometry to add detail where desired).

3. When you are done with your model, go to Edit, Delete by Type, History to reduce scene overhead and reduce the complexity of calculating the mesh in panel.

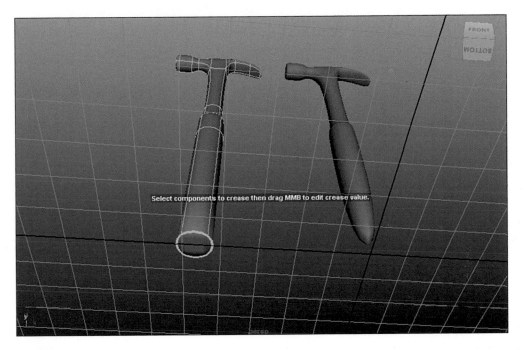

Select components to crease then drag MMB to edit crease value.

FIGURE 4.15
The difference between a creased edge loop and a non-creased edge loop on the bottom of our hammer mesh. Using creases to create hard edges as opposed to having edges really close to each other saves on modeling time.

BONUS

Extra Models

Take a look in this Hour's source files and you will notice a few extra completed models you can look at. These can be used in your animations if you wish, or you can continue to refine and edit these models to make them your own.

Summary

In this Hour, you learned how Maya handles objects in scene files, and we created a few standard primitive shapes. We then started with polygonal (box) modeling and explored the use of tools Maya has to offer. Once a mesh is complete, you can smooth it now with the Mesh, Smooth command, or you can smooth it later by pressing **3** with the object selected and using Maya's Smooth Mesh Preview function.

Q&A

Q. Do I have to start from a primitive?

A. No, but it is easiest to start from a primitive. Most people start from a box if they are doing polygonal modeling. If you want to create a single polygon, you can use the Create Polygon tool in the Mesh menu, but it takes more clicks than it would to start from a plane anyway.

Q. I have many different objects. Can I combine them into one?

A. Yes, with all of the objects selected, go to Mesh, Combine. You should note, however, that unless the vertices have been merged together on the seams of the objects after everything has been combined, the surface will not be smooth after you combine the objects. Combining should be viewed almost the same as grouping objects.

Q. I want to extrude faces that are next to each other, but they are connected by their shared edge. How do I fix this?

A. At the top of the Edit Mesh menu is a check box called Keep Faces Together. Unchecking this means that every single face that is extruded will not share any edges with any other polygon, even if they are adjacent.

Q. I created a mesh, but all of the edges appear hard and angled even though they flow into one another very smoothly. What's wrong?

A. Faces have something called "normals," which are basically the angle that Maya considers to be the "front" of the face. When two normals are far apart enough in angle, Maya draws the edges they share as a sharp edge. When you are box modeling, though, Maya doesn't calculate this value and therefore considers all new edges as "hard." To make your mesh smooth again, go to Normals, Soften Edge (or Harden Edge), with the edges you want softened (or hardened) selected.

Workshop

The workshop contains quiz questions and exercises to help you solidify your understanding of the material covered. Try to answer all questions before looking at the "Answers" section that follows.

Quiz

1. How many sides must a polygon have?

2. Name two ways to access an object's components.

3. The Extrude tool is found under which menu?

4. What is a series of unbroken edges called?

5. Why is using the Mesh, Smooth command an issue if you want to make further changes to an object?

Exercise

Choose a few simple models to create. Start from primitives with objects that might lend themselves to simple shapes, such as a cup or a wheel. Then move on to more complex shapes and extrude and manipulate the polygons by hand. Try modeling a simple spaceship, a chess piece, or another interesting prop. Don't move on to characters until you've read through Hour 8, "Character Modeling."

Answers

1. At least three. Polygons can have ostensibly an infinite number of sides, but Maya likes rendering objects that have three- or four-sided faces.

2. You can press **F8** and then choose the component type you want to manipulate in the top menu bar, or you can RMB click and drag to get a marking menu that will let you decide.

3. Like all of the component-level and box-modeling tools, Extrude is found under the Edit Mesh menu.

4. A series of unbroken edges is called an "edge loop." When an edge loop hits a vertex that has more than four edges going into it, the edge loop might be broken though. You will learn more about why edge loops are important in Hour 8.

5. Using a Smooth adds the command into the object's history, which means if you want to do further edits but do not want to work on the tessellated model, you have to first remove the Smooth node by deleting it and then add it later. An easier way to get a good preview of the smoothing is to press **3** and see the Smooth Mesh Preview.

HOUR 5
Modeling NURBS Curves and Surfaces

What You'll Learn in This Hour:

▶ What NURBS curves and surfaces are

▶ How to create simple NURBS geometry

▶ How to utilize NURBS' properties for good results

▶ What other uses NURBS curves have in Maya

3D graphics went through some very rapid change in the beginning. One of the most tumultuous areas of development was that of surfacing and geometry. The very earliest representation of a surface was a polygon. Other surface types and ways of rendering objects came and went quickly. Splines, voxels, point clouds, and subdivision surfaces all have their pros and cons. When NURBS first came about, apart from having a funny-sounding name, they were all the rage. Although they do not offer much benefit as a primary surfacing technology with today's technology of extremely high polygon tools, they are still very useful for specific purposes.

NOTE

Getting Terminology Straight

Maya calls any NURBS curve simply a "curve." In some menus, Maya will refer to a surface created from curves as a "surface" and sometimes as "NURBS," such as in the Edit, Convert menu. Although other 3D programs might have more than one type of spline technology, you should know that even though Maya sometimes drops the word "NURBS," we are still dealing with this technology whenever we use "curves" and "surfaces" within Maya.

In this Hour, you will get an overview of splines and how to create simple geometry using them. In addition, we'll look at what inherent properties of NURBS can be utilized to our benefit. We'll also walk through some of the most common uses for NURBS and how to manipulate them correctly for these purposes.

What Are NURBS?

The acronym stands for Non-Uniform Rational Basis Spline. Knowing the mathematics behind the equations that represent B-splines is not required to understand how they function in Maya (although you will be happy to know that mathematically, these curves are pretty versatile, stable, and fast to compute). It is interesting to point out that NURBS are not actually renderable surfaces; instead, they are tessellated at render time and made into polygons. The real power of NURBS and the reason they were en vogue in the late 1990s and early 2000s was because of the ease of creating and manipulating perfectly smooth surfaces. You see, up until that point, the other paradigms offered only cumbersome control over smooth surfaces, or traded intuitive control for the resolution of the geometry. NURBS seemed to offer the best of both worlds.

Curve Components

A NURBS curve is made up of edit points and control vertices (see Figure 5.1). Edit points are points on the curve that the curve passes through. Control vertices (CVs) are like handles that influence a NURBS curve, and they provide a more reliable way to adjust the shape of a curve. CVs are automatically created in between edit points when you make a curve.

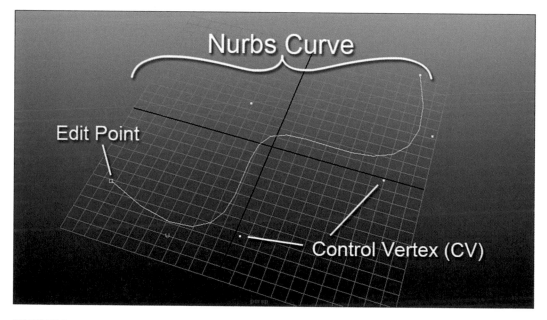

FIGURE 5.1
The components of a NURBS curve. Edit points lay directly on the curve, whereas CVs act like handles that "pull" the curve in different directions.

To create a NURBS curve, use the EP Curve tool. This is available by clicking on Create, EP Curve Tool when you have the Surfaces menu set loaded (**F4**). In the Curves shelf, the EP Curve tool is also prominently featured (see Figure 5.2).

FIGURE 5.2
The EP Curve Tool button, as it is shown in the Curves shelf.

Curves are parametric, meaning that they have a direction and along their path we can assign a value from 0 to 1. To put it another way, a curve's start point is always a value of 0 and the end point is always a value of 1, no matter the size or shape of a curve. Their direction is important when you're creating surfaces from two or more NURBS curves, because the surface will "stretch" between the same parametric values on each curve as it is drawn: 0 will connect to 0, 1 will connect to 1, and so on. Let's take a look at this, and at the same time, learn the components of a NURBS surface.

Surface Components

When a surface is created using curves (shown later in this Hour), the surface takes on some of the properties of the curves. The surface direction, the number of surface control points, and of course the shape are derived from the splines. You can see the components that make up a surface in Figure 5.3. In a similar fashion to polygonal modeling, NURBS modeling involves planning the flow of edges (in this case, splines). Some people call a surface a "patch," due to the fact that creating a character or complex object will require many surfaces to be "stitched" together, almost like a patchwork quilt. A very complex model might be made up of dozens of patches, created so that the geometry blends nicely from one patch to another. A surface will have control vertices (CVs) on its surface that behaves the same way they do on a curve. The placement of surface CVs is determined at creation time; therefore, in order to adjust the level of control, a surface needs to be rebuilt. We'll take a look at this procedure too.

FIGURE 5.3
A NURBS surface. The curves used to create this surface are selected. Notice the CVs on the surface that are generated automatically.

TIP

Keeping an Eye on CVs

Because control vertices determine pretty much the entirety of a surface's shape, I like to keep an eye on them without having to switch to component mode. With a surface selected, go to Display, NURBS, CVs and they will always be visible. Now as you work with the surface, you can troubleshoot at a glance.

A surface is made up two types of splines. The splines that run parallel to the direction of the creation curves are called "spans." The splines that cross the spans are called "isoparms." Isoparms are created where, due to the math that creates a NURBS curve, a new interior section needs to be created to continue the surface. You do not need to worry about the math or know how and why isoparms are created, only that adding resolution within a surface is a matter of adding and subtracting isoparms to and from your surface. Also know that the CVs you will use to manipulate the interior of a surface are created along isoparms, as you can see in Figure 5.4.

Creating complex geometry can be very cumbersome, so it's best to think of the simplest method to achieve the shape you want rather than create all of the small details with curves themselves. In other words, you should rely a little bit on your ability to adjust surfaces after you create them.

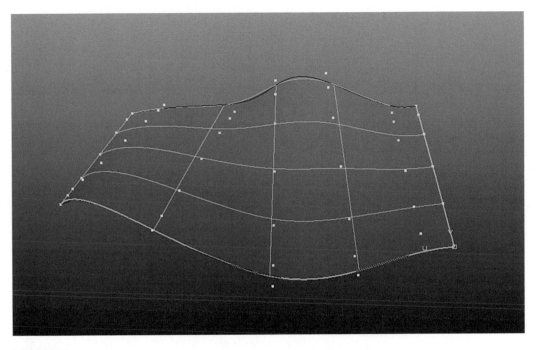

FIGURE 5.4
The NURBS surface has multiple isoparms that give us the resolution we need to adjust the surface however we'd like.

Modeling with NURBS

Some pretty complicated structures can be created using the surface tools Maya has to offer. In general, you will be concerning yourself with finding logical seams in the model, almost like UV'ing polygons. Think of NURBS as patches on a quilt that is stretched *over* your model. In stark contrast to polygons, NURBS have UVs built in already, so you do not have to worry about applying UVs to your NURBS model when you are done creating it.

NOTE

History in the Making

NURBS keep construction history like every surface type in Maya. The interesting thing about NURBS history is that it preserves very nicely throughout the creation process. The danger in this, however, is that you can make changes to a surface by manipulating the CVs of the curve that generated the surface, the position and orientation of the curve itself, or the surface CVs on the generated surface. In fact, there are still more ways to change the resulting model. You have to be very careful when modeling with NURBS to try to make changes on the *lowest level* you can to preserve the predictability of your results.

Creating a Simple Surface

We're going to create a surrealist checkerboard. Our model will be complete with a wavy checkerboard and a pawn floating above it.

First, we'll create two sides of the checkerboard. Remember, Maya automatically creates the detail within the surface (and it can also be rebuilt automatically with greater or lesser detail anyway), so our workflow will be to just create the simple shape. Using the EP Curve tool, draw two squiggly curves on the grid. Clicking on the grid will add an edit point, and pressing **Enter** will finish the curve (see Figure 5.5).

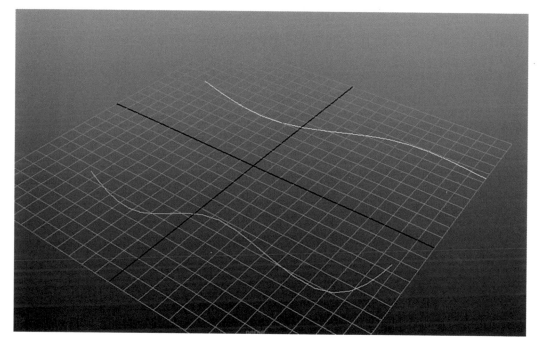

FIGURE 5.5
Our two curves. We don't care what their shape is, but you should create the curves in the same direction.

With our two curves created and selected, we will have Maya create a NURBS surface between them. A few tools can be used to achieve this, the simplest being the Loft tool. This is found under Surfaces, Loft. This tool basically grafts a surface from one curve to another. The nice thing about this tool is that it creates a surface that is parametric regardless of the shape of your curves, or if your curves have a different number of edit points. You can adjust the accuracy of the created surface later as well. See Figure 5.6 for an example of a lofted surface.

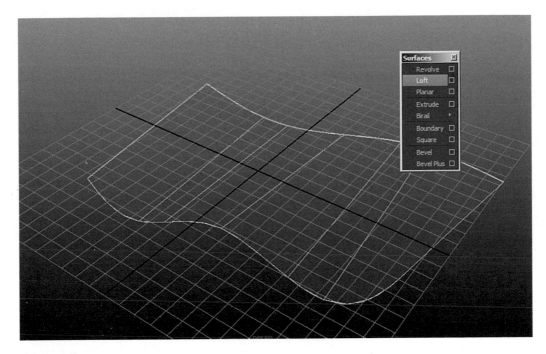

FIGURE 5.6
The Loft tool applied to the two NURBS curves. A surface is drawn between the curves. Note the spans are on the outside, and cross-section isoparms are generated across the surface.

Our surface needs to be rebuilt so that it has an even amount of detail spread across it. Maya knows how to create a new surface from this one that has evenly distributed isoparms—and therefore CVs for us to manipulate. By clicking on Edit NURBS, Rebuild Surfaces, we will get the result shown in Figure 5.7.

NOTE

Continuity

Keep in mind that if you are going to be creating a model made from multiple surfaces, the resolution needs to be uniform so that the surface appears to be smooth, continuous, and seamless. The Rebuild Surfaces tool has many options and parameters that allow the artist to control the end result. Although we're using the default parameters right now, this tool is worth exploring further when you move on to complex models.

Now by RMB dragging on the surface and choosing the CVs component mode, we can manipulate the surface. Drag the CVs up and down to make an interesting wavy surface (see Figure 5.8).

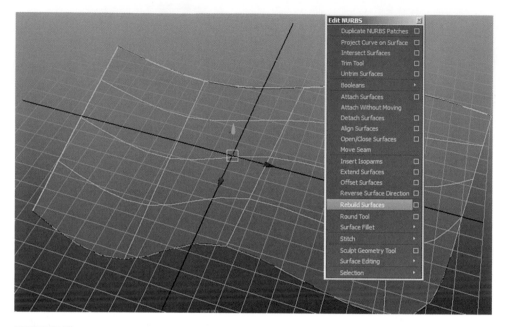

FIGURE 5.7
The Rebuild Surfaces tool applied to our NURBS surface. Notice how we have uniform distribution of our isoparms and therefore will get easy adjustment of the surface now.

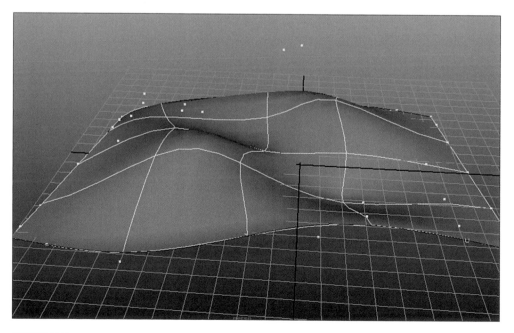

FIGURE 5.8
After pushing and pulling the CVs up and down a little, we have our wavy surface.

Now we can create our pawn. A great tool for creating shapes that are symmetrical about a point is the Revolve tool. It creates a surface by rotating the curve and extruding the surface along the resulting path—perfect for glasses, vases, table legs, or, in this case, a chess piece. Create the outline of our pawn in the side panel with the EP Curve tool. The center of the grid will be the point of rotation, so keep it centered like I have in Figure 5.9.

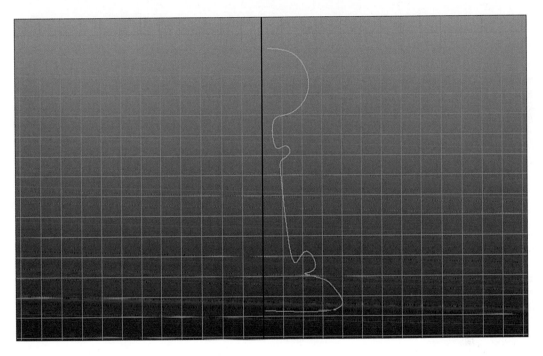

FIGURE 5.9
The profile of our pawn created in the side panel. Remember that because NURBS keep their construction history nicely intact, we can always adjust this original curve to get a nicer result if the revolved surface doesn't turn out exactly how we expect it to.

There are a few corners that I would like to make creased. The curved ridges in the side of the pawn should be hard edged, for example. You could always create more CVs by using the Insert Knot tool and then position them very closely, but in general it's a better idea to work with as few controls as possible to get the result you are looking for. Therefore, we'll instead use the CV Hardness tool. Go into CV component mode by RMB dragging on the curve. Select the CVs you want to be hard and then go to Edit Curves, CV Hardness. If it doesn't work, redraw your curve with more edit points to begin with (the tool requires that you have at least one CV on either side of the CV you are hardening that is not next to an edit point). Figure 5.10 shows the before and after of using the CV Hardness tool to get a crease in my curve.

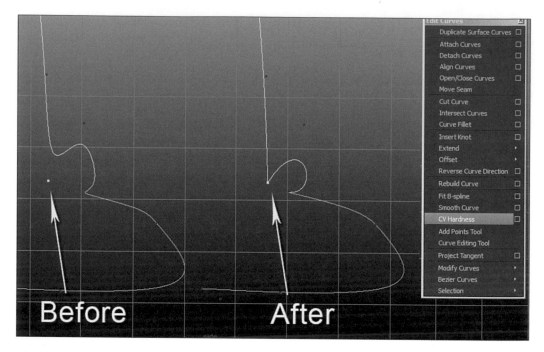

FIGURE 5.10
The CV in the corner before and after using the CV Hardness tool on it. Remember, you need to have enough edit points in your curve to use this tool. If hardening a CV does not work, redraw your curve with more edit points.

Now that the curve is cleaned up and ready to revolve, we're going to do just that. Select the curve and click Surfaces, Revolve, as shown in Figure 5.11.

Maya made quick work of that model! We are not done yet, though. If you look at the top of the model, you will see it has a hole in it. Switch to isoparm component mode by RMB clicking and dragging upward and then select the hole like I did in Figure 5.12.

Now click on Surfaces, Planer. A flat surface fills the hole (see Figure 5.13).

Adjusting the Model's History

We already have a good-looking pawn, so let's make a few adjustments and see the results in real time. Remember that construction history with NURBS is very powerful and intuitive. If we move the curve that we revolved, it will actually update the resulting surface. In fact, the planar cap that we just created will grow to cover the new sized hole as well. It's very easy to make adjustments to your NURBS model after you have created the basic structure. That is why it is good workflow to get your simple structure in place and make adjustments later to refine your model. I'm going to make the pawn a little fatter by transforming the curve away from the center gridline, and I'll shorten it by bringing down the top CVs, as shown in Figure 5.14.

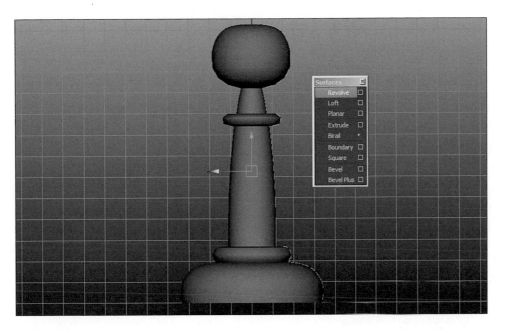

FIGURE 5.11
The newly created revolved surface. The default options work fine for us here because the surface is revolved around the Y axis 360 degrees.

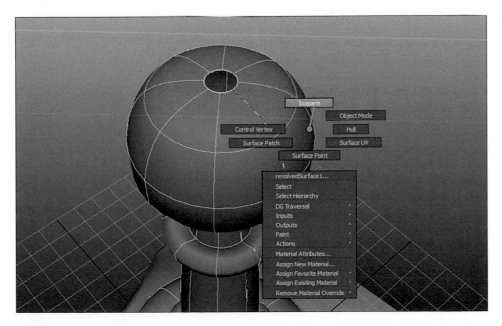

FIGURE 5.12
The hole in our revolved surface has an isoparm as its boundary. Choosing Isoparm and selecting it allows us to create a new surface to fill this hole.

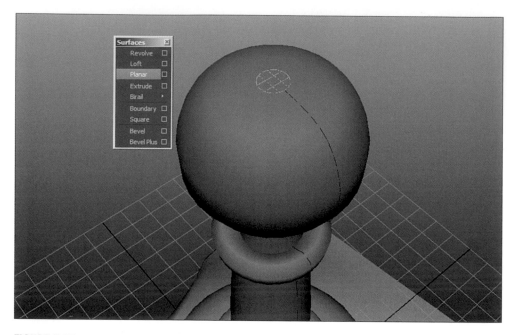

FIGURE 5.13
The top of the pawn is now filled in.

FIGURE 5.14
The pawn has been adjusted to be slightly fatter and shorter than before.

TIP

Many Ways to Get the Same Result

Once again, I chose to make my adjustments on the *lowest level* I could when modifying this model. Rather than scale the resulting surface or adjusting its CVs, I modified the source curve for the revolve. I will continue to make adjustments at this level for as long as I can.

Now that we have our chess piece and chessboard, let's throw some simple textures on them and put everything together.

Because NURBS have UVs built into their structure, all we need to do is apply the texture maps we want and we'll be done. We will create a Blinn by RMB clicking on the surfaces, choosing Assign New Material, and then clicking on Blinn. In the Attribute Editor that opens, apply a Checker texture to the Color attribute. Apply a Blinn to the pawn as well, this time using just black for the color attribute. Once all that is done, position and scale the pawn to look like it's floating above the surreal chessboard, and the image is complete (see Figure 5.15).

FIGURE 5.15
The final composed scene. The pawn surface has been moved and scaled to be in the position that I want.

TIP
_____

Putting It Together

Now that I am sure my image is ready to compose, I can select the end resulting surface of the pawn and move it where I want it. If you are following along in your own scene or have opened the file "05 - Curves and Surfaces.mb" included in this Hour, then see what happens when you edit the curve. It still affects the final pawn surface. This will affect it until you delete the history on the model, so it's a good idea to stay organized in your scene file in regard to where you are creating your NURBS geometry. Things can quickly get very messy and you may lose the ability to nicely edit your NURBS surface history.

More Uses for Curves

Curves are not just useful for modeling. They have a variety of other uses. Some of the most common uses for curves are for animation controllers, path animation, particle paths, and more. Let's take a look at a few of these uses.

Animation Controllers

Included in this Hour's files is Josh Burton's awesome character rig "Morpheus." If you open that file, you will see a professionally created character rig, complete with NURBS curves that act as controllers for the body parts. NURBS are chosen because they are clearly visible yet do not get in the way of seeing the body because they are basically wires. They also do not render. See Figure 5.16 for an example of control curves on an animation rig.

Path Animation

We can also use curves to create paths for our objects to follow. Because NURBS curves are parametric, Maya allows us to animate an object that travels from the start (U value of 0) to the end (U value of 1) of a curve. This is very powerful and used widely in production. Let's set one up so you can quickly get a feeling for this powerful animation tool.

Create a new scene, create a polygonal sphere, and then create a NURBS curve of any shape, as shown in Figure 5.17.

Now select pSphere1 and Shift-select curve1. Switch to the Animation menu set by pressing **F2** and then click on Animate, Motion Paths, Attach to Motion Path, as shown in Figure 5.18.

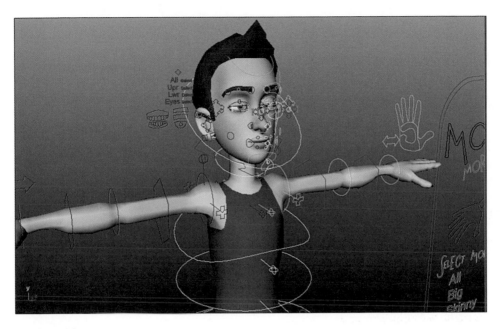

FIGURE 5.16
This character rig uses NURBS curves for the controllers. They are easy to see but don't get in the way.

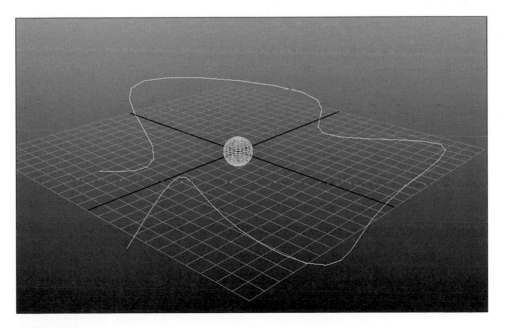

FIGURE 5.17
Our pSphere1 and curve1 are going to work together to make a path animation in a few easy steps. Don't forget you can either use the Create menu or the Shelf to create these shapes.

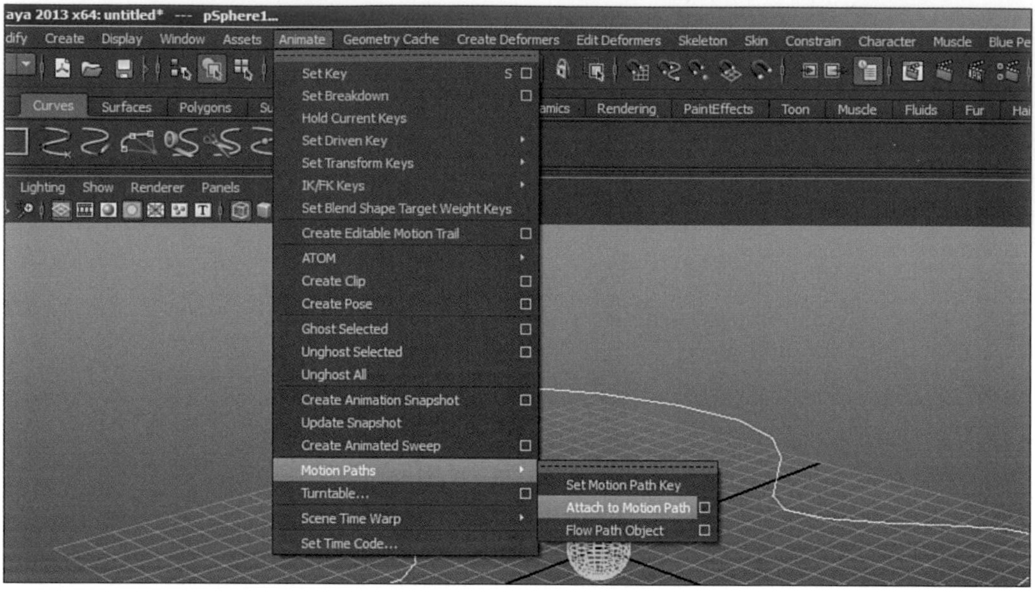

FIGURE 5.18
The sphere is now attached to the motion path. Maya creates an animation curve on the sphere by default that you can adjust easily in the graph editor. We will go over that in Hour 13, "Animation: Adding Movement to Your Scene."

If you press **Alt+V**, the animation will play back and you can watch the sphere move along the path of the curve, as shown in Figure 5.19. Just like all other functions in Maya, this operation saves history. If you manipulate the path, the sphere will continue to move along the new path.

▼ TRY IT YOURSELF

Create Some More Simple Objects Using NURBS

Create a small list of some simple objects that would lend themselves to being modeled with NURBS. Hard-surfaced objects and smooth shapes are best.

1. Find the most logical seams in the model and create NURBS curves that match those contours.

2. Experiment with the NURBS surfacing tools such as Loft, Revolve, Planar, Extrude, and Bevel.

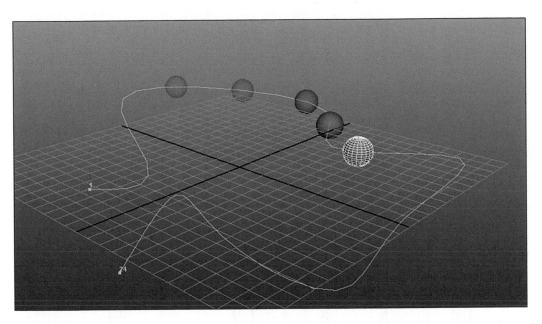

FIGURE 5.19
The sphere moving along its path. The four past frames are ghosted to show the direction of the moving sphere. Remember, you can change this path at any time and the animation will update in real time.

BONUS

Chess Pieces

You'll find some more NURBS models waiting for you in the Bonus folder for this Hour. Included are a nice chess board and some more chess pieces for you to work with. When you get to the Exercise, use these models as a reference to start from.

Summary

We took a look at the very powerful NURBS geometry type in Maya. First, we discovered the components that make up a NURBS curve. We then found the same components in a NURBS surface. We created a simple NURBS surface using the EP Curve tool and the Loft tool. Then we created a NURBS pawn by making a curve to represent the object's profile and using the Revolve tool. NURBS have more than just modeling applications, though. Because of their high visibility, low scene overhead, and how they don't block geometry substantially, we saw a finished character rig that makes ample use of NURBS objects as controllers. One last example of a good application of NURBS curves is as a path for an object to follow in an animation.

Q&A

Q. **What are the downsides to NURBS?**

A. NURBS are not widely used for characters in feature film and visual effects because of the advent of polygonal modeling tools that can handle immense amounts of detail. They do not deform as nicely as polygons do, and can be tricky to make appear seamless.

Q. **Why can't I use a certain NURBS tool on my curves?**

A. Some of the tools have specific requirements for them to work. Bevel needs a closed curve or two curves; it won't work on a straight, open NURBS curve. Look at the Command Line for feedback as to what the requirements are for the tool you are trying to use.

Q. **Even when I create the curves in a clean way, the surfaces don't seem to be seamless. Why?**

A. This is one of the more difficult aspects of NURBS. In order for there to not be a visible seam, the edges your surfaces need to have tangents that are parallel. Maya does not have automatic tools that will adjust the continuity for you, but modeling tools do exist that help with maintaining a perfectly smooth appearance across multiple NURBS curves. For further information on how NURBS surfaces fit together, do a search on the Web for "G1 continuity."

Workshop

The workshop contains quiz questions and exercises to help you solidify your understanding of the material covered. Try to answer all questions before looking at the "Answers" section that follows.

Quiz

1. What does NURBS stand for?

2. True or false? NURBS need to be UV'd after creation.

3. Cross-sections of a NURBS surface are called what?

4. Which curve creation tool is in the Curves shelf—the CV Curve tool or the EP Curve tool?

5. The Revolve tool revolves the curve around which axis by default?

Exercise

Model an entire chess set using the tools we discussed in this Hour. The Revolve tool is perfect for nearly all of the pieces. You may have to get a little tricky with the Bevel, Trim, and Loft tools when it comes time to make the Bishop and Knight.

Answers

1. Non-Uniform Rational Basis Spline. A basis spline is a form of Bezier spline, and you may hear people refer to NURBS as such.

2. False. They have UV information built into them inherently.

3. Isoparms. Adding Isoparms adds CVs to a surface as well.

4. The EP Curve tool. This tool allows you to place edit points exactly where you want them in the grid.

5. The Y axis. Our pawn was revolved like a spinning top. You can change this by going into the tool's option box □.

HOUR 6
Unfolding UVs and Applying Textures

What You'll Learn in This Hour:

▶ How to edit and align UVs on a polygonal mesh

▶ How to decide on a good UV layout

▶ How to create materials

▶ How to apply materials to your objects

Without materials, your models are going to be gray and lifeless. Maya has state-of-the-art shading tools, and you'll enjoy the flexibility the program offers. Your objects will get their color, shininess, even reflection from *texture maps*—image files that are projected or painted onto the surface of your geometry. But before you can apply a texture map to your objects, you have to edit the UVs of your object. What are UVs? Imagine you have a map of the earth and you want to paste it on a globe. If you just try to wrap up the globe inside the map, there's going to be excess paper hanging off the globe, and it won't fit correctly. This is where UVs come in. UVs represent the "flattened-out" version of your model, so that textures can be applied correctly. You decide where the seams should be and then essentially unfold the shell to be flat. Take that globe and hammer it flat, and you can simply lay the map on top of it.

NOTE

Shaders, Textures, and Materials

There is a difference between these three terms. A *shader* is the code that determines the render properties of a surface. A *texture* is any image that is applied to a node in a material. And, finally, a *material* is all of the connected nodes that make up the final rendered look. You may hear "materials" referred to as "textures" by some artists, but we will not confuse terms here.

In this Hour, you will see a proper UV layout for our hammer model, and how to get there. You will learn how we decide on material properties, and how to load textures into the appropriate slots. After all, the final quality of a 3D object is dependent at least 50% on the quality of the texture in conjunction with the geometric detail.

What Are UVs?

Let's take a look at a primitive object's UVs. A primitive sphere will illustrate our point nicely. To see an object's UVs, we open the UV Texture Editor with an object selected by going to Window, UV Texture Editor (see Figure 6.1).

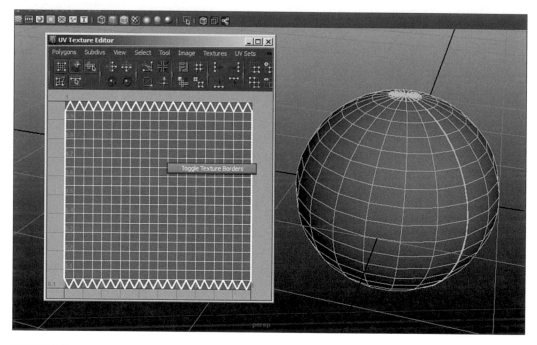

FIGURE 6.1
This sphere comes with UVs laid out nice and flat. As you can see, there is a seam where the flattened-out UVs wrap around the sphere and connect. To see the UV borders, Shift+RMB click in the UV Texture Editor.

Now let's look at how UVs actually work. Figure 6.2 shows a sphere with something called a "ramp" texture already applied. Ramp textures let you apply a gradient shading look to your objects. In this figure, you can see the association between the gradient colors on the object and the gradient colors in the UV Texture Editor. You can see the seam that is created by the UV border, and hopefully the concept of the "flattened-out" object will become very clear (see Figure 6.2).

With a texture applied, UVs become a lot more easy to understand. You can see the colors wrapped around this mesh as well as how the UVs line up in the UV Texture Editor.

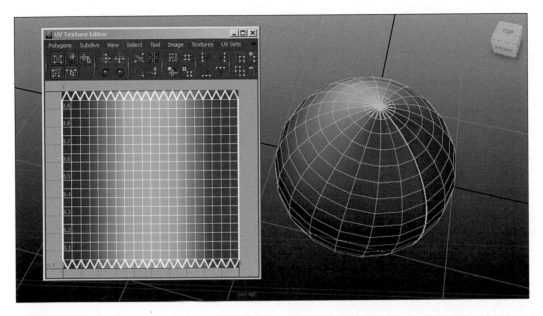

FIGURE 6.2
A basic ramp shader applied to the color channel of this sphere's material. As you can see, the color wraps around the sphere. Look closely where the seam is on the sphere, and you will see that the far-left color (red) and far-right color (blue) correspond to the borders of the UV space.

NOTE

Moving UVs

UVs can only be moved in the UV Texture Editor, not in a 3D workspace panel. In the UV Texture Editor, RMB clicking and dragging brings up the familiar marking menu that allows you to choose UVs, and the Move tool works as expected.

More Complicated Models

Now that you've seen how UVs work on a basic primitive, let's look at how they work on our hammer model from Hour 3, "File Types and Managing Assets." In this Hour's scene files, open the file hammer_Texture.ma. Once this file loads, selecting the hammer loads its UV sets into the UV Texture Editor as expected.

However, the UVs do not look nicely laid out as they do with the primitive sphere. It is up to you to create UVs and make them look nice on your custom models. Figure 6.3 shows the poorly laid-out UVs on the hammer model.

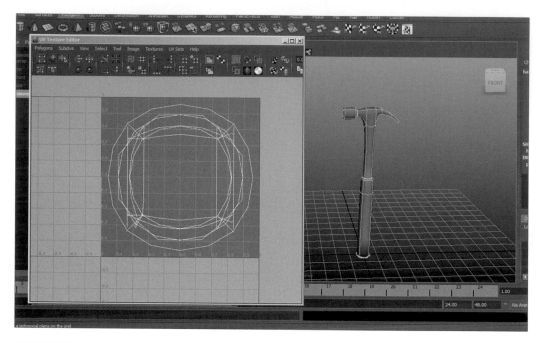

FIGURE 6.3
The UV Texture Editor shows polygonal objects' UVs. An object might not have UVs, or it might have a poor UV layout (like shown) for one reason or another, but we can create UVs easily.

TIP

Finding the UV Texture Editor Window

Even though we associate UVs with texturing, they are actually a *property of* a polygonal object. So, the UV Texture Editor window is found under the Polygons menu set (**F3**) under Edit UVs, UV Texture Editor. However, because this editor is so commonly accessed (like the Outliner), Maya also makes it available permanently under Windows, UV Texture Editor in the menu as well.

A common workflow to create nicely laid-out UVs is to begin with an automatically created UV set and then manually adjust the UVs in the UV Texture Editor to fit your model. To begin working with an object's UVs, press **F3** to get to the Polygons menu set and then go to the Create UVs menu. You will see a host of choices. In general, choose a mapping shape that matches your object roughly. A sphere will use spherical; a lamppost should be cylindrical. Automatic Mapping creates a series of cuts (seams) to make it so that the least amount of distortion occurs when applying your texture. You can't depend on Maya's automatic UV mapping to give you perfect results, but it will add UVs to the model that can be changed later. The exception to the rule of using a UV projection shape that is close to your model shape is if you have an object that is symmetrical, like ours:

▶ In the case of symmetry, you want to use Planar, so click Create UVs, Planar ☐ (remember, the ☐ symbol means you will be opening a tool's options before applying).

▶ Set the projection axis to Project From the Z Axis. Leave the rest of the options at their defaults for now and click Apply.

NOTE

Messy UVs Are Par for the Course

Whenever you use the box-modeling technique, the UVs are not going to be laid out correctly to apply textures immediately. The polygon primitives that you can create already have UVs, but because it's almost always necessary to edit primitives before they are ready to use in your scene, correct UV editing is an essential skill.

After you have applied automatic mapping to your object, you next must decide where the texture seams are going to be on your model. With a model that is symmetrical like this hammer, it makes sense that both sides should have the same texture. That means the UV seam can be right down the middle along the center edge loop that exists.

The two commands you absolutely need to know about (in the UV Texture Editor) are the Polygons, Cut UV Edges command and the Polygons, Sew UV Edges command, shown in Figure 6.4.

Using these two commands in conjunction with the Move and UV Smooth tools in the UV Texture Editor will get you 90% of the way there. Now follow these steps:

▶ Switch to Edge component mode by RMB clicking on your object in the panel and dragging upward. Select the new edge loop that runs up the center of the hammer in your perspective panel. You can do this by Shift+LMB clicking on each edge, double-clicking on a single edge in the edge loop (preferred method), or selecting a single edge loop and pressing the left arrow key on your keyboard.

▶ In the UV Texture Editor, go to Polygons, Cut UV Edges. Then select all the other edges *besides* the center edge loop. (You can quickly do this by holding down **Shift** and dragging a selection box around the entire hammer in the Persp panel. This toggles the selection and therefore will invert the selected edges.)

▶ Back in the UV Texture Editor, click Polygons, Sew UV Edges.

▶ Select the center edge loop one more time. Pressing Ctrl+RMB in the UV Texture Editor brings up a marking menu to convert your selection from one component type to another (from faces to vertices, or in this case, edges to UVs). This marking menu is available at all times and not just when you're working with UVs. Convert your selection to UVs, as shown in Figure 6.5.

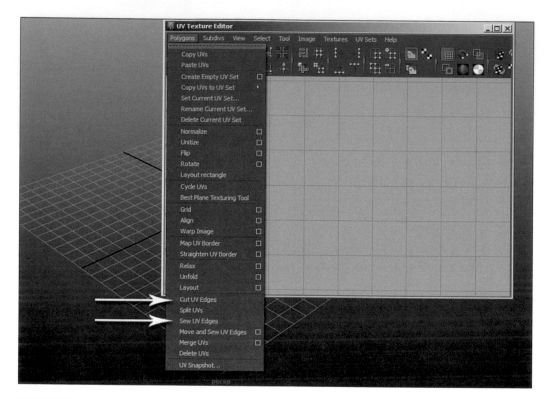

FIGURE 6.4
These two commands—Cut UV Edges and Sew UV Edges—are essential to your UV workflow. The two tools create and remove seams, respectively, in your UVs.

Now if we use the Smooth UV tool, the UVs in this middle seam will move out from behind the other UVs and get some UV space for themselves, as in Figure 6.6.

TIP

Symmetry Is Our Friend

Taking advantage of the symmetry of a model can be a great timesaver. This is especially true if the axis of symmetry runs through the axis of your object that isn't seen as much, like our hammer. The best way to take advantage of symmetry is to place your UV seam (cut UV edges) along the axis of symmetry.

Now that you understand how to arrange our UVs nicely, let's apply a custom texture and use some of Maya's great texturing tools.

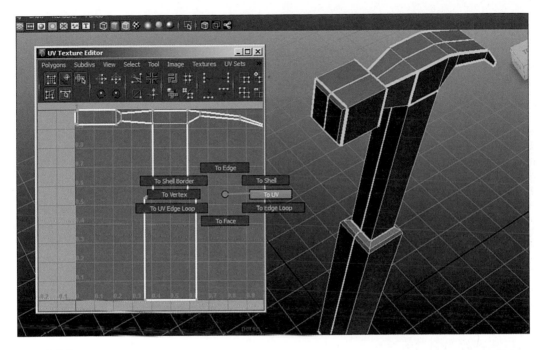

FIGURE 6.5
The hammer has planar mapping, but we want to make sure the UVs along this center seam are laid out; otherwise, they will not pick up any texture information when we apply a map.

NOTE

UV Space Is Limited

As you can see in all of the figures of the UV Texture Editor, only the space between 0,0, and 1,1 is shaded on the graph. UV space is parametric, meaning that you are manipulating points on a graph that will later tell Maya what value (between 0 and 1) to assign to each part of the model. When the image is rendering, Maya looks at the surface and then finds the corresponding UV coordinate to decide what part of the texture should be applied to the pixel. For correct texturing and rendering, all of your UVs must fall within the 0-to-1 range in UV space. Scaling, rotating, and assembling UV shells is a talent in and of itself. Look ahead to Hour 7, "Creating Node Networks in the Hypershade," if you want to see some complex character UV layouts.

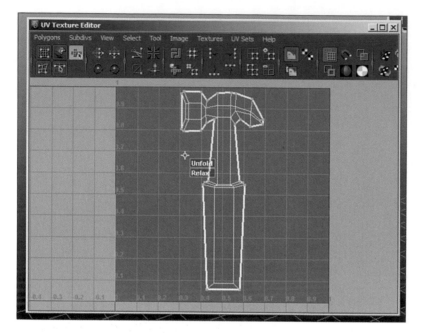

FIGURE 6.6
The Smooth UV tool (top left, highlighted) gives you interactive control over the Relax and Unfold commands. Selecting either Unfold or Relax and dragging the mouse will add or remove iterations in real time. I unfolded the UVs that made up the seam, and now they have some UV area dedicated to them.

Texturing in Maya

Maya has industry-standard (and some industry-leading) texturing tools available. These are the tools you will use to make your models go from gray and lifeless to colorful and beautiful. There are two basic types of textures in Maya: 2D textures and 3D textures. 2D textures such as ramps and image files require UVs to display correctly, as you just learned. 3D textures do not require UVs because Maya makes a projection in 3D space onto the model. Think of it like certain areas of the scene have paint floating in them; when you render, Maya finds the 3D position of the object it is drawing and takes the corresponding color from the paint floating in the same place, without regard for where the UVs sit on the surface.

The Hypershade is the main menu that deals with texturing. To access the Hypershade, go to Windows, Rendering Editors, Hypershade (see Figure 6.7).

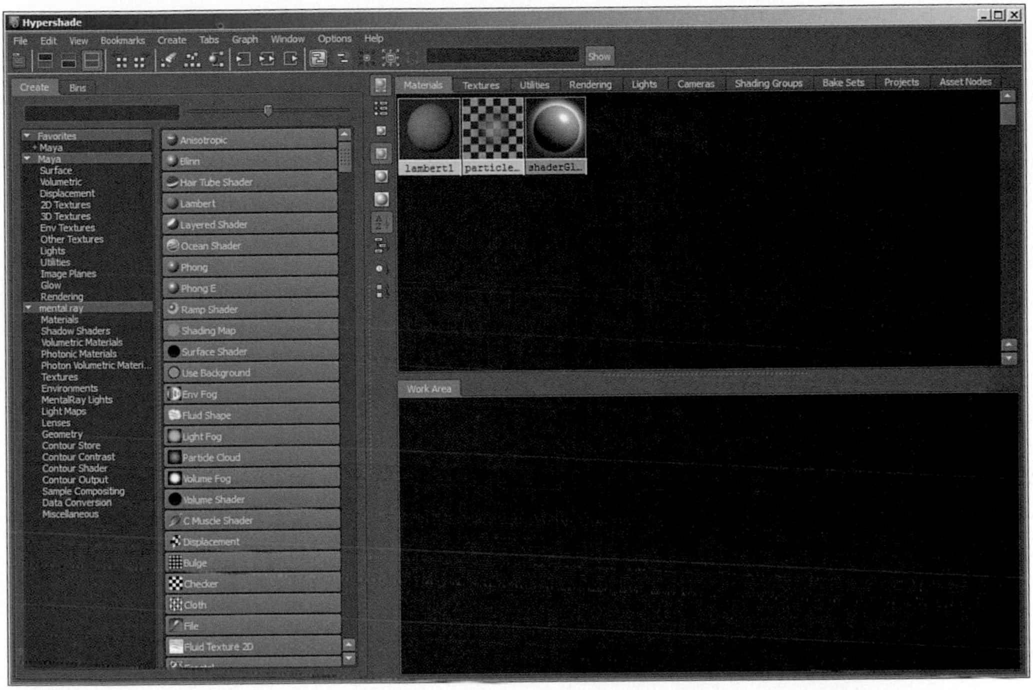

FIGURE 6.7
The Hypershade is broken into three main areas with the menus and buttons at the top. On the left is the Create panel; clicking on any of these buttons will created the associated node. The top-right box holds your nodes, and the bottom-right area is called the Work Area.

When you are connecting nodes together and building what are called "shading networks," you will primarily be using the Work Area. By default, every object is assigned the gray lambert shader called lambert1 when it is created. All of the objects we create in Maya will need custom materials, so let's start by creating a new material for our hammer.

NOTE

The Ubiquitous Lambert1

Maya requires unique node names to avoid conflicts when importing objects and references. If you edit lambert1 in one scene, it might either get lost when you import it into another scene or over-write the lambert1 already in that scene. Just don't touch lambert1—think of it as a necessary node Maya needs to display objects. It should never be used as a material for a production model.

With the Hypershade open, we can start creating some materials. You can follow this procedure to create nearly infinite combinations of materials in the Hypershade, but I'll show you how to put nodes together to make the hammer have some nicer material properties to it. First thing we'll do is create a Blinn material. Blinn is a material that has reflectivity and a specular highlight to it. It comes standard with most 3D programs. When you click on Blinn, the newly created node appears in the Work Area. Double-clicking any node in the Hypershade opens that node in the Attribute Editor, as shown in Figure 6.8.

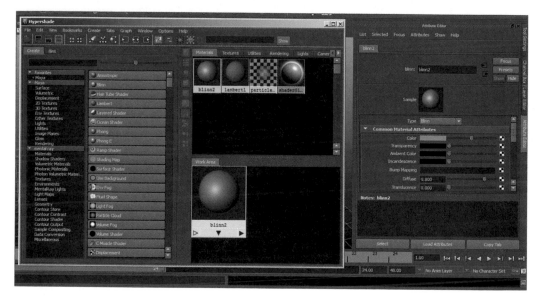

FIGURE 6.8
The Hypershade open and the Attribute Editor displaying the Blinn's properties.

Scrolling down the menus in the Attribute Editor reveals the great control Maya gives you over the look of your materials. Let's take a brief look at some of the material options, and go over what each one does. Most of the options are the same or similar for your standard materials.

Applying Our Texture

It's common to apply a material before you customize it to see your updates happening in panel and to make sure you are changing the attributes to the correct values. To apply the material, MMB drag this Blinn from the Hypershade onto the hammer in the Persp panel. Alternatively, you can select an object in any panel or the Outliner, and then in the Hypershade RMB, click and drag upward on the Blinn node. Then, in the marking menu that appears, choose Assign Blinn1SG to Selection, as I am doing in Figure 6.9.

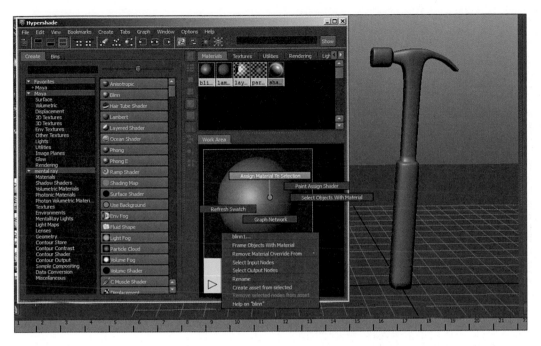

FIGURE 6.9
The process of applying a material to an object using the marking menu in the Hypershade. Alternatively, you can MMB drag the material directly from the Hypershade onto the surface of the object in the panel to apply it.

Standard Material Options

Listed here are the common options found in most materials in Maya. Understanding the function of these options will help you quickly learn which materials will give you the results you desire:

▶ **Color**—This channel is normally your main concern. It is what it sounds like—the color of the texture. Whether it is a Maya checker texture or a File node (the way to load your own images as textures), you can load almost any node into this channel.

▶ **Transparency**—This channel controls how see-through your material is. It determines the amount of transparency by black (value of 0) being completely opaque and white (value of 1) being totally clear. If you are using raytraced shadows, the shadow will be affected by this channel as well (more on shadows in Hour 19, "Lighting Your Scene Correctly"). You can use this channel to make "holes" in your material also, like a tattered pirate's flag for example.

▶ **Ambient Color**—This channel lightens and blends the color attribute with the color chosen here. If there are ambient lights in your scene, they will determine how this channel contributes to the final color of your texture.

▶ **Incandescence**—This channel makes the object appear to have a light source emitting from within it. Although it won't actually emit light from its surface when this attribute is used, it will appear to. The difference between Ambient Color and Incandescence is this: An Ambient Color of white will make an object in total darkness render its pure color channel, whereas an Incandescence of white will make the same object pure white (totally unaffected by shadow).

▶ **Bump Mapping**—This channel adds surface relief at render time. You can create the effect of subtle grain to your surfaces, or maybe small details such as rivets in metal, stitching in clothing, and so on. The surface is not actually displaced; bump mapping only gives the illusion that it is.

▶ **Diffuse**—Diffuse is the power of the reflection of light, put simply. Because we only see an object by the light that reflects off of that object back into our eye, changing the diffuse value is like raising and lowering the amount of light an object reflects. In turn, the Color value is affected by brightening and darkening. In a way, it's the opposite of Ambient— at 1.0, Diffuse will make the object render at brightest its pure Color value when *not* in shadow, and at 0.0, it will render black regardless of the lights in the scene.

▶ **Translucence**—The amount of light that passes through an object. This can be used to simulate surfaces that have light diffusing through them, such as wax, paper, leaves, and so on. The simplest way to describe the effect of adding translucency is to think of a thin object such as a leaf that has a shadow being cast on the bright side, and being able to see that shadow on the other side of the leaf (see Figure 6.10).

▶ **Translucence Depth**—Controls the way the light travels through the object by using a distance value.

▶ **Translucence Focus**—This controls how much the light is scattered in all directions or focused as it is transmitted through the surface. A low value is recommended for very thin objects such as paper where the shadows are going to be fairly sharp on the other side of the object. A high value is good for objects such as wax because the light truly spreads out very widely as it enters this material.

Notice how the shadow that the sphere is casting on the right plane can be seen from the back of the plane as if it is a piece of thin paper or a leaf. Also notice how the shadow on the ground is not affected (only transparency affects shadow color).

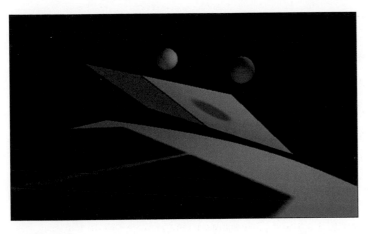

FIGURE 6.10
The effect of translucence on a material. The left plane has no translucence; the right plane has .5 translucence.

Standard Materials

Before we customize our Blinn to make it look like a shiny metal hammer, let's first take a quick look at a few of Maya's built-in materials. They are described here in laymen's terms:

- **Anisotropic**—This material has specular and reflection, but uses an algorithm than warps the specular highlight the way a brushed steel kettle would.

- **Blinn**—This material is a good standard material for shiny and reflective objects. You can get a good range of plastic to metal materials using Blinns.

- **Hair Tube Shader**—This material is useful for application on hair, due to its extremely warped specular highlight that simulates the way hair reflects light.

- **Lambert**—This material is good for objects that do not reflect or have any shininess to them and therefore don't need a specular highlight. Good examples would be clay and dirt.

- **Layered Shader**—To combine multiple shaders into one, you can use the layered shader. For instance, you can apply a Blinn's specular highlight to a Lambert's color to create the texture of dirt in a glass jar.

- **Ocean Shader**—This is a dynamic material that creates an animate ocean. The default settings create a simple, attractive water that is a good launch point for more advanced FX.

▶ **Phong**—Very much like the Blinn, the Phong shader is good for objects with shininess. The Phong specular highlight algorithm is geared a little bit more toward plastics.

▶ **Phong E**—The same as Phong, but with added control over the specular highlights.

▶ **Ramp Shader**—This powerful shader is useful for creating gradient effects based on properties of the scene. You can make the edges of objects a different color based on the angle the surface is relative to the camera, or you can make a stark two-tone color gradient for areas of shadow and light to simulate a cartoon render.

▶ **Shading Map**—This is a shader that mixes different shaders together, sort of like a Layered Shader, but uses properties such as the color and brightness of shaders to determine how they are mixed together rather than their transparency. It is not very commonly used.

▶ **Surface Shader**—This is a very commonly used material; it's a simple way to load color, alpha, and transparency to other channels in Maya. The color will always display pure no matter what the lighting condition.

▶ **Use Background**—This is an extremely useful shader; it displays whatever background is in your scene—be it a color or an image plane. This material is commonly employed when rendering effects for film and television, or for creating shadow renders for compositing.

Customizing Our Blinn

We will now customize our Blinn with the images that were created for it. We will apply a color map and a specular. First, we open the Hypershade and double-click on our Blinn. In the Attribute Editor, which should have just appeared, we will click on the little icon next to the "color" attribute that looks like a checkerboard, as shown in Figure 6.11. This icon means you can apply a map to a value.

FIGURE 6.11
The checkerboard icon means you can apply a texture or an image to an attribute.

Selecting File creates a file node, which is how we load our images as textures. Click the folder icon in the file1 attribute panel to open an explorer window to browse for the textures we've created for this hammer (see Figure 6.12).

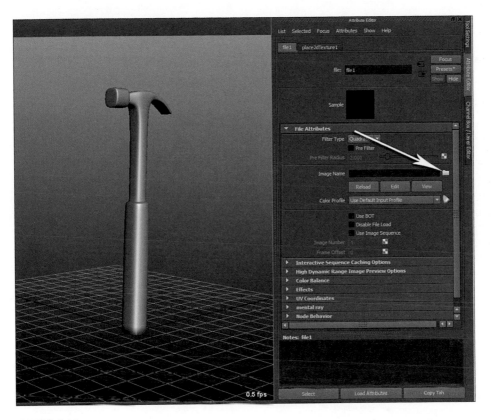

FIGURE 6.12
After you load a file node as a texture attribute, you must then load the image you created for this attribute. The file node has many options, but by default you will get results that are good for most common texture uses.

Navigate to the Hour 6 directory where the hammer's image maps are found and choose hammer_Color.tga for the color. Select the Blinn in the Hypershade one more time so we can load another map into its attributes. Click on the "specular color" map button and choose "file" one more time. In the new file node, click the browse button and choose hammer_spccColor.tga. This file has a white value on the metal parts and a black value on the handle area—to make it so there is no specular highlight on what is supposed to be the soft rubber grip. Figure 6.13 shows the hammer with the material edited to be more like rubber.

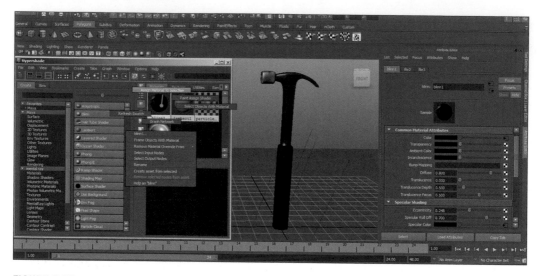

FIGURE 6.13
The Blinn material with color and specular color maps applied. Apply the texture to the selected hammer by RMB clicking on the marking menu in the Hypershade.

▼ TRY IT YOURSELF

Load Textures into the Many Material Attributes

The only way to learn how the many attributes of a material affect it is to experiment with the values:

1. Download or create some different images to apply as the color of the blinn1 material and see if you can change the color of the hammer to something more colorful.

2. Use the different textures such as "checker" and "noise" and see the effect they have on attributes such as transparency and ambient color.

3. Try adjusting all of the material attributes, and for help, don't forget that pressing **F1** brings up detailed explanations of the window you are using.

VIDEO

UV Layout Workflow

In this bonus video, I show you a common workflow for creating and laying out UVs for our finished character model, Sam. I walk through the first stages of creating automatic UVs and then move on to show you how to cut, sew, and lay out the UVs smoothly.

Summary

To apply texture in Maya, it is first necessary to lay out your UVs. We created UVs for our hammer model by using a planar projection, because it is common to create some form of automatic UV set and then adjust them. We next adjusted them by first making sure our seam was on the center edge loop using the Cut UV Edge and Sew UV Edge tools. We then moved the UVs into place by hand in the UV Texture Editor and then unfolded the UVs that were hidden using the UV Smooth tool. We then looked at the common material types and their common attributes, and applied a Blinn material to our hammer model. A common workflow is to apply the material first and then adjust the material's attribute to give yourself the effect you desire. We also loaded the custom images as textures in the color and specular color attributes, to give our hammer the color and shininess we expect. Open hammer_Textured_Finish.ma in this Hour's folder to see the final result.

Q&A

Q. When should I create/edit the UVs of a polygonal object?

A. You can wait until a model is finished to create its UVs, or if you don't want to have to remember to use a certain mapping type and so on, you can create and edit UVs as you go along. Manipulating geometry will not mess up already created and edited UVs, but it might create new UVs that get in the way of your customized ones.

Q. Can an object have more than one UV set?

A. Yes, you can add as many UV sets as you want to an object by going to the Create UVs menu and selecting Create Empty UV set. An instance when this might be useful is if you want a character's face to have a different material than his clothes, and you create a UV set for just his head.

Q. The UV Texture Editor is square. What do I do if my texture is not square?

A. You should be using square textures as a rule because of this reason, but if you absolutely can't, you can always resize the UVs to match the texture as it shows up in the UV Texture Editor.

Q. Can I apply more than one material to an object?

A. Certainly, and there are a few ways to do this. Let's say you want to use two different materials for the hammer (the metal part and grip). The easiest way is to RMB click and drag your mouse, choose "face" and select the faces you want to apply the new material to, and then MMB drag the material from the Hypershade onto these faces. You can also use a Layered shader and use an image as a mask to determine where the two materials are going to show up on the object.

Workshop

The workshop contains quiz questions and exercises to help you solidify your understanding of the material covered. Try to answer all questions before looking at the "Answers" section that follows.

Quiz

1. Where is the UV Texture Editor found?

2. What two tools do you use to create the seams in your UVs?

3. What material type would be the best for a nonreflective surface such as a tablecloth?

4. What material attribute controls how "see-through" an object is?

5. How do you create a new material in the Hypershade?

Exercise

Create a simple polygonal object, such as a can of soup, a box of cereal, or any other very simple 3D object. Look at the object's UVs in the UV Texture Editor and decide if you want to start over by creating UVs or if you can use the Cut and Sew tools to make your own seams. Unfold and Relax the UVs using the Smooth UV tool, and get your UVs to a place where they are laid out in a way they look nice and straight, and no unreasonable amount of stretching is occurring.

Open the Hypershade and create an appropriate material. Depending on the object you've made, load your texture file into the color attribute of your material. Finally, drag the material onto the object to apply it.

Answers

1. In the Polygon menu set (**F3**), Edit UVs menu, or in the main menu under the Windows menu.

2. The Cut UV Edges tool and the Sew UV Edges tool allow you to create the seams in your UVs so that the object can be flattened out nicely in the UV Texture Editor.

3. Lambert materials are good for objects with no shininess.

4. Transparency is the attribute that makes an object see-through. Do not confuse this with translucency, which creates the effect of light passing through an object.

5. The Create pane on the left side of the Hypershade houses all the buttons of material nodes you can use to build shading networks. Clicking on any one of these will create that node and place it in the Work Area.

Creating Node Networks in the Hypershade

What You'll Learn in This Hour:

▶ Navigating the Hypershade

▶ How to create nodes in the Hypershade

▶ Graphing networks in the Hypershade

▶ How to apply a material to an object

When we first encountered the Hypershade, it was in enough depth to create rudimentary materials. The Hypershade is extremely powerful and can be used to create some pretty complex relationships between nodes. Of course, the most common use of the Hypershade is for creating shading networks, but we'll explore some of its other functionality.

TIP

Dual Monitors

The Hypershade takes up a lot of screen space and can be cumbersome to have open in Maya, blocking other windows, particularly if you do not work with dual monitors on your workstation. Even with a large single screen, the Hypershade's necessary panels take up far too much real estate. I highly recommend dual monitors for texture work, but make sure they are the same brand or you may get inconsistent color results.

In this Hour, you find out just how essential the Hypershade is to creating complex hierarchies and networks. You will see that above being just a materials window, the Hypershade allows you access to some very high-level and very low-level functionality within Maya, all of which can be combined to produce some very interesting results.

Navigating the Hypershade

You've had a little bit of exposure to the Hypershade in the last Hour; now it's time to unlock its potential. Let's take a closer look at navigating this window.

The Panels

The Hypershade has its own three panels—the Create panel, the Bin, and the Work Area—along with a top main menu and menu bar with commonly used icons for your convenience. Look at Figure 7.1 to see the Hypershade in a default configuration.

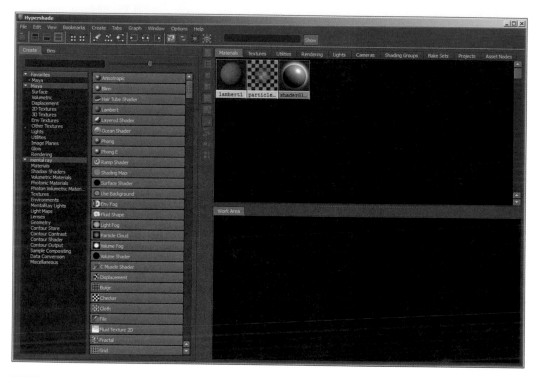

FIGURE 7.1
The Hypershade window in all its glory. The Create panel is on the left, displaying material nodes and many other nodes. The Bin is on the top right, and shows you the nodes you have created in your scene, arranged alphabetically by default. The Work Area is where you will connect nodes and build your shading networks.

NOTE

The Dependable Defaults

Notice that lambert1, particleCloud1, and shaderGlow1 are created by default in your scene. Lambert1 is applied to all geometry by default, just so that Maya can display the geometry in panel. ParticleCloud1 is a default particle shader, created for the same reason, and shaderGlow1 controls the glow on shaders. You can only have one shaderGlow node in your scene, so if you need more than one object to glow, you will have to use render layers.

The Main Menu

At the top of the Hypershade sits the main menu. This menu, shown in Figure 7.2, is not utilized too often because the most frequently used functions of the Hypershade are arranged in the form of buttons just below the main menu.

FIGURE 7.2
The main menu of the Hypershade is a necessary part of the UI, but you won't be using it very much when creating networks.

The two items here you will use most frequently are the File and Edit menus. You can import and export shaders and shading networks from the File menu, and you can perform some useful tasks such as deleting unused nodes and duplicating shading networks from the Edit menu. Bookmarks are useful as well; you can create a bookmark that will save any view you are looking at in the Work Area. This is helpful if you are working on a complex network and need to work on something else for a while. The Create, Tabs, Graph, Window, and Options menus contain options and commands that are more easily accessed through other panels and buttons or are very infrequently needed. Therefore, we don't even need to go through them to fully understand the Hypershade.

The Menu Bar

This collection of frequently used tools and commands will serve you very well when using the Hypershade, as seen in Figure 7.3.

FIGURE 7.3
Autodesk did a good job giving you the tools you need in this menu.

You will find that most of the tools you need from the Hypershade menu are found in the menu bar. Let's take a look across, from left to right, and see what each one does. Here are the icons and a brief explanation of their uses:

The first four buttons control how the Hypershade looks. You can hide the Create Panel, the Bins, or the Work Area.

These buttons show the previous graph and the next graph. Think of these almost as an undo and redo queue for views of your graphs—useful for when you have loaded many materials and are making changes to a few attributes on different materials in succession.

The next three buttons—Clear, Rearrange Graph, and Graph Selected—give you the main tools for sorting your Hypershade's Work Area. Clear does just that. Rearrange will arrange the nodes nicely in your Work Area to give you a clean layout. Graph Selected graphs all shaders in the Work Area that are connected to the selected object or objects. A very common workflow is to select the object whose shader you want to examine and just click this last button rather than finding a shader in the Bin and graphing it.

These buttons—Input, Input and Output, and Output—determine whether the Work Area displays the nodes that affect the selected node, are affected *by* the selected node, or both.

These buttons are the controls for working with assets. We'll come back to these tools in Hour 23, "Correct Project Management and Scene Workflow."

Finally, this area is used to search the Hypershade. It is very powerful and can use wildcards (*). Remember, though, that Maya is *always* case sensitive. For example, searching for Blinn will not show the node blinn1. The left icon with the arrows will highlight if a filter is in place; clicking it clears the filter.

The Create Panel

On the left you will see the Create panel. We briefly discussed this panel last Hour, but now we'll take an even closer look. At the top of this panel are two tabs: Create and Bins. The Bins panel is the area to the top right of the Hypershade, where your shading networks are displayed. The Create panel is used to create the nodes you will assemble together into complex shading hierarchies. To create any node listed in this menu, simply LMB click on it. The node will be created in the Work Area, and if it is a top-level material node such as Blinn or Lambert, it will appear in the Materials bin. Figure 7.4 shows blinn1 that just appeared after clicking the Blinn button in the Create panel.

The left side of the Create panel shows you the different categories of nodes you can create. Clicking any one or multiple filters will load them into the right side of the Create panel.

NOTE

All Displayed

Because Maya is so powerful, there's an almost overwhelming number of different nodes you can create, all of which are displayed by default. Get used to the filters by clicking on them and trying them out a bit.

The Work Area

The Work Area is where we will create all of the shading networks, as well as some interesting other relationships. The window responds to all of the normal orthographic view camera controls

(Alt+MMB for moving, Alt+RMB for zooming). Click on Blinn to create a new material node called blinn1. Double-clicking on any node will load that node in the Attribute Editor. Once the Attribute Editor is open, clicking on any node will load it into the Attribute Editor as well.

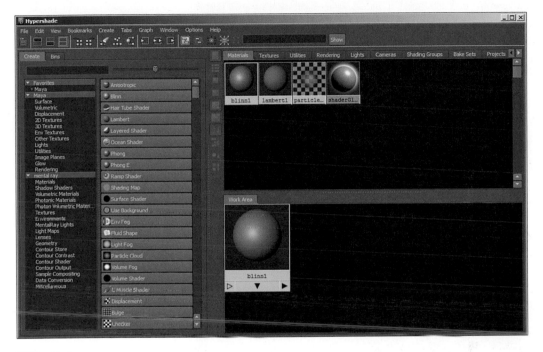

FIGURE 7.4
Clicking on the Blinn button in the Create panel creates the node and loads it into the Materials bin and the Work Area.

Right-Clicking

Most of the frequently used functionality of the Work Area is accessed by right-clicking on a node. Figure 7.5 shows the marking menu that appears.

The common workflow is to create a node and then start right-clicking and applying attributes and connections to it. You then create more nodes, and connect more attributes. In this way, you create a web of interconnected nodes, otherwise known as a *shading network*. Let's take a look at what that might look like.

Connecting Nodes

In the Create panel, click on the Checker button. It is in the list of nodes; you may have to scroll down to find it. Once you do, you will see the node has been created and loads into the Work Area. Remember, it won't show in the Bin because this is not a top-level material like blinn1 is.

Select the checker1 node and MMB drag it onto blinn1. In Figure 7.6, you see the marking menu that appears.

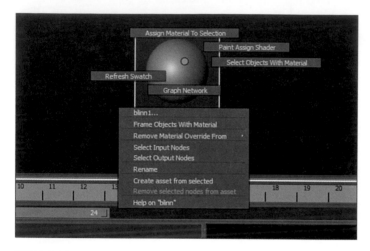

FIGURE 7.5
The right-click menu for the Work Area. Right-clicking on any node brings up this menu.

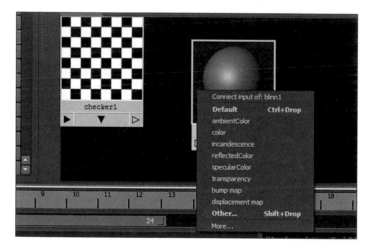

FIGURE 7.6
This marking menu gives you a lot of the common attributes; you can connect checker1 to blinn1.

The action of MMB dragging one node to another selects the default output of a node (in this case, the color) and gives you a selection of inputs to connect it to. The default input on blinn1 is also "color." So if you choose default, the checker texture will be assigned as the color channel of the blinn1 material. Alternatively, you can choose any of the attributes shown to connect the checker to, or you can choose Other to bring up the Connection Editor.

TIP
_____

Connecting Nodes Anywhere You Can

Maya does not care where you connect nodes, be it using the Hypershade, the Connection Editor, a script, or expressions. When you don't choose a default connection, Maya brings up the Connection Editor and gives you the option of connecting any output and input available on the selected objects. You should just note that the actual connecting of attributes is the same no matter what method you use, and that the Hypershade is just another way of connecting nodes that is material centric and very visual.
_____

Also, you can choose which output you want to connect on the checker node by right-clicking on the node's output (arrow icon on the bottom right) and then choosing whichever output you want. A menu with a list of choices will appear like in Figure 7.7.

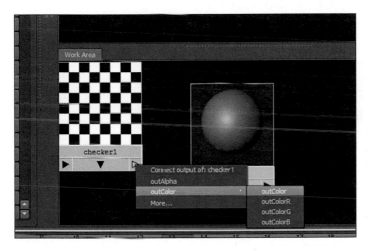

FIGURE 7.7
The other way to connect attributes; choose any output you like to connect to the input of blinn1.

Now that you know how to connect attributes, we will create a shading network in the next section. We are going to do some more complex arrangement of nodes that produces a simple result. We can attach almost any attribute to another attribute, provided that it produces the right type of data. For instance, we can connect the outColor attribute of checker1 to the Color attribute of blinn1, because it is looking for an RGB input. However, because the Reflectivity attribute is a single attribute that goes from 0 to 1, you could not connect the outColor to the reflectivity. You could, however, connect the outColorR (red) because this is a single channel.

You could also connect the outAlpha; again, one channel. This will make more sense as we start creating multiple connections.

Creating a Simple Network

Let's create a simple network for a cartoon eye material. It will need the iris and pupil color, it will need reflectivity and specular, and we'll even create a faux highlight so that the eye always looks like it's catching some of the light in the scene:

▶ We'll start with a Blinn. Create a Blinn material and move it (LMB click and drag) to the side of the Work Area to make room for the next couple of nodes we will create.

▶ Create a ramp texture (scroll down the Create menu; it's there).

▶ MMB drag the ramp texture onto the blinn1 material and then choose color, as shown in Figure 7.8.

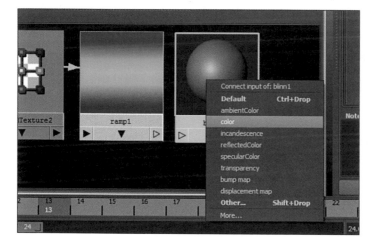

FIGURE 7.8
The ramp1 node's default output being connected to the "color" attribute of blinn1.

Now we have a connection. In the Attribute Editor, with the ramp1 node selected, you can see the many options for this texture:

▶ First, make sure the ramp's Type is set to "V Ramp" so that the color will be aligned correctly on the eyeball.

▶ Then click anywhere in the ramp's color area to add a color handle. You can move the created handles around by adjusting the round handle on the left, and remove a color handle by clicking on the box on the right. Add five or six color handles and make yours look like mine in Figure 7.9.

▶ To change the color, select a handle by clicking on the round icon and then click on the swatch that sits below the ramp's color. In Figure 7.9, the dots are arranged to have a nice gradient in the iris color.

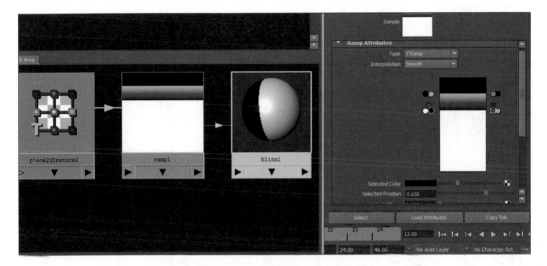

FIGURE 7.9
The ramp shader with the ramp1 colors set to create an iris color.

Now we'll add a little brightness to the edges of the material. Create another ramp shader and a samplerInfo node, as shown in Figure 7.10.

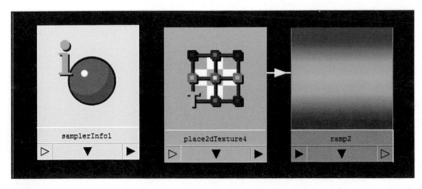

FIGURE 7.10
The new samplerInfo node and the new ramp node.

Now we will connect these two nodes in a unique way:

▸ MMB drag the samplerInfo node onto the ramp node.

▸ Choose Other.... The Connection Editor will open.

▸ Click on the samplerInfo node's facingRatio attribute in the left column of the Connection Editor. Then expand the uvCoord attribute and click on the vCoord attribute on the ramp node (right side of the panel).

You have just made it so that the amount a polygon faces the camera determines what position in the ramp Maya is going to use to display on that face. Figure 7.11 is a shot of the Connection Editor, and as you can see, connecting nodes is as simple as selecting them.

FIGURE 7.11
The samplerInfo node correctly connected to the ramp node. This creates an interesting effect we will tweak in a minute.

NOTE

Compatible Data

Keep in mind that Maya can connect attributes that read and write the same type of data. A samplerInfo returns a value between 0 and 1, depending on how much a face is turned toward the camera. It just so happens that the position of a color handle on a ramp can be any value between 0 and 1.

Now we will adjust the ramp's colors to make it so that the more "away facing" a polygon is, the brighter it is rendered. This gives a faux light-absorption effect:

▶ Adjust your ramp to look like mine in Figure 7.12 and then MMB drag the ramp onto the Blinn.

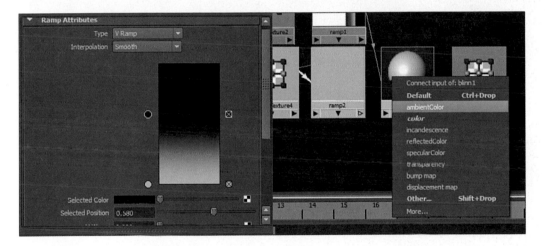

FIGURE 7.12
The shading network is starting to form. It is not uncommon to have a material with dozens of nodes interconnecting to create complex effects.

▶ Choose the ambientColor attribute when the marking menu pops up.

▶ RMB click and drag on the blinn1 node in the Work Area and choose Graph Network so that we can make sure your node network looks like mine in Figure 7.13.

NOTE

Graphing Networks and Clearing the Work Area

Be careful when using the Graph Selected button or the Rearrange Selected button in the Hypershade. The danger is that you will clear the Work Area unintentionally because either all your nodes are not selected or a new node you have created is not connected to a shading network yet.

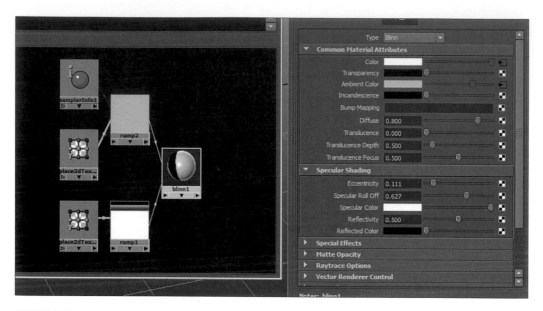

FIGURE 7.13
The blinn1 node as it exists so far.

There is just one more step to do: Add the faux highlight that we see in so many cartoon characters' eyes. This is a faked effect; the real highlight we see on a character's eye is the reflection of a light source. So although this method is not recommended for realistic materials, it gives us a good chance to look at the nodes a little closer and to give our eye a nice added effect:

▶ Create a new ramp by clicking the Ramp button in the Create panel of the Hypershade. It will load into the Work Area automatically.

▶ RMB drag the ramp onto blinn1 and choose "incandescence," as shown in Figure 7.14.

We will now adjust the placement of the ramp and turn it into the correct shape so that it appears to be a highlight:

▶ Create a polygonal sphere by clicking Create, Polygon Primitives, Sphere or by clicking the sphere icon in the Polygons shelf. Any size will do.

▶ In the Hypershade, and with the sphere still selected, RMB click and drag upward to choose Assign Material to Selection.

▶ Press the **6** key to make sure your panel is displaying textures.

▶ Lastly, open up the UV Texture Editor by clicking on Window, UV Texture Editor. Your workspace should look something similar to mine, as shown in Figure 7.15.

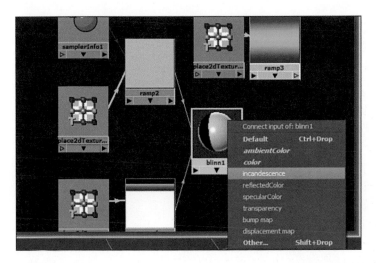

FIGURE 7.14
The incandescence attribute controls how much light appears to be coming out of a material.

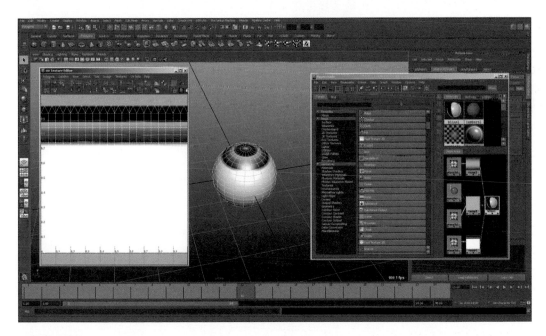

FIGURE 7.15
We will use this workspace layout to accomplish the final task of adding the highlight to the eye.

▶ Click on the newly created ramp3 and go into the Attribute Editor.

▶ Change the ramp type to Circular, change the interpolation to None in the drop-down box, and change the colors in the ramp to look like mine in Figure 7.16.

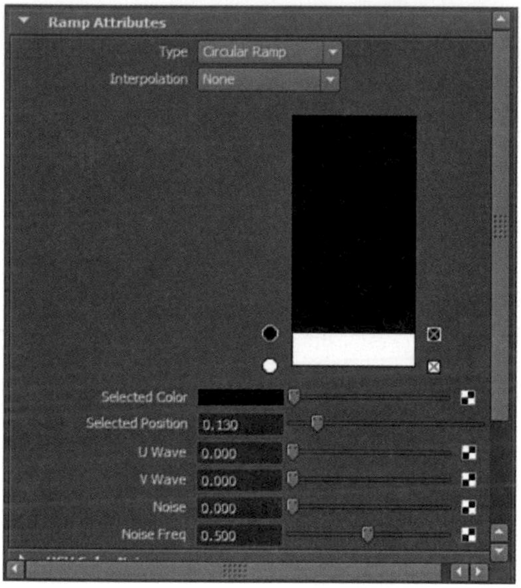

FIGURE 7.16
The correct settings to create the faux highlight on the eyeball.

▶ In the UV Texture Editor, go to Image and choose ramp3. It will load the ramp as the display image in the UV Texture Editor but also in the panel.

▶ Now in the Hypershade, choose the place2DTexture node that is connected to ramp3 and go into the Attribute Editor. Change the Y offset (second box next to the Offset attribute) to –0.3. You can also adjust the size of your highlight by moving the black color in the ramp3 node up or down in the ramp. If all goes well, your panel should look like mine in Figure 7.17.

Let's take a look at how this looks in render:

▶ Click in your panel and press **F** to frame the sphere.

▶ Then press **F6** to bring up the rendering menu set and click Render, Render Current Frame.

As you see in Figure 7.18, the sphere renders with our eye texture nicely, complete with the rim light that comes from the samplerInfo node and the faux highlight we just made with the circular ramp.

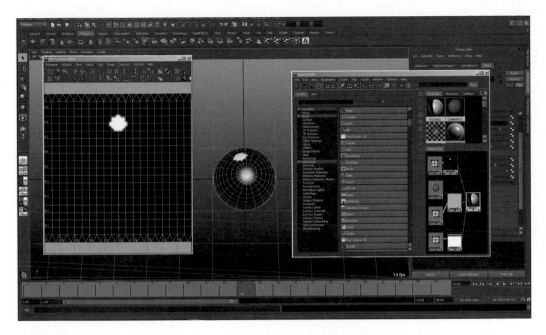

FIGURE 7.17
The ramp3 node displayed on the sphere and the offset correctly applied to the ramp.

FIGURE 7.18
The render of the eye texture on the sphere.

BONUS

Extra Materials

Included in this Hour's Bonus folder are a few Maya materials for you to import and apply to your objects. Graph the materials in your Hypershade and observe the connections that are being made to give you ideas on creating your own complex networks. You can open the .ma files to view the materials, or you can load them into your scenes by clicking in the Hypershade on File, Import and then choosing the material you would like to use.

Summary

The Hypershade offers Maya's most visual way to connect nodes together. Because creating materials involves creating multiple connections, naturally the Hypershade is organized into multiple panes to help you keep the nodes organized. You saw how creating nodes moves them automatically into the Work Area so you can begin connecting them together. Graphing a network organizes the Work Area neatly. You saw how a ramp texture is versatile and can be used to create a variety of effects. We used the UV Texture Editor, Hypershade, and Attribute Editor in unison to get the results we desired out of the highlight effect added to the eye material.

Q&A

Q. I created a node and then graphed the network, which cleared the Work Area, but now I can't see my node anymore. What happened?

A. The Graph Network command only arranges nodes that are connected in a network. The node you created still exists, but it might be in one of the other bins in the Hypershade. Look through the bins by clicking on the top tabs and see if you can find the node you are looking for. MMB drag it back into the Work Area to start connecting it to other nodes again.

Q. Why is my texture black in the panel?

A. To view textures in a panel, you press the **6** key. However, if the **7** key is pressed (lighting preview) and there are no lights, everything will be black. Press **5** to return the panel to smooth shading with no lights, then press **6** again and it should be fine.

Q. What are all these place2DTexture nodes that are generating automatically when I create any texture?

A. These nodes control the placement, orientation, scale, offset, and so on, of a 2D texture. As you can see in the UV Texture Editor in Figure 7.17, the offset value we put on the ramp3 node moved the circle from the center of the texture up toward the top. These are essential nodes that help you further define the placement of your textures on your objects.

Q. **How do I save a material so I can put it in another scene? Shouldn't I be saving all of my materials in some sort of "library"?**

A. That's a great idea. You can select a material in the Hypershade and click on File, Export Selected Network. Save them either to the Shaders folder in your project or to a new folder you create for the purpose of being your library. Note that there is no Material folder created in the default Maya project folder; this is one of the instances where terms are slightly confused.

Workshop

The workshop contains quiz questions and exercises to help you solidify your understanding of the material covered. Try to answer all questions before looking at the "Answers" section that follows.

Quiz

1. What is the difference between a material and a texture?

2. When you create a new node in the Hypershade, what panel does it show in immediately?

3. What are some of the different methods you can use to connect nodes?

4. When you want to see all of the connected nodes in a network, what do you do?

5. How do you only display a certain type of node in the Create panel?

Exercise

Create a small shader library using the skills you learned for connecting nodes in the Hypershade. You could make a themed library. For example, a city-themed library should contain some bricks, metals, old woods, and so on. We only have a few pages to explore the use of the Hypershade in this book, which is not enough to cover every single material and texture node. Therefore, you should create each material node one at a time and look at its attributes in the Attribute Editor. I also highly recommend you take a look at the Help for a node by clicking the Help menu at the top of the Attribute Editor. Choose the Help specifically for the node you are looking at. In other words, if you are looking at a lambert, choose "Help on Lambert." After you create a few simple networks, be a little more adventurous and start creating some more complex effects. Start applying image textures as values in a ramp, for example, or use a checker texture as both a color and a reflected color attribute to get an interesting mirror effect.

Answers

1. A *material* is a top-level node that connects a shader with associated textures and other render nodes. A *texture* is any image or node that is used in a material's attributes, such as color, transparency, and so on.

2. All newly created nodes appear in the Work Area immediately.

3. Middle mouse dragging one node on top of another in the Work Area allows you to connect the default output to a list of inputs. RMB clicking and dragging on the output (black arrow on the bottom right) of a node allows you to choose the output you would like to connect, and then LMB clicking on another node allows you to choose the input. You can also MMB drag a node right out of the Hypershade and drop it on any attribute in the Attribute Editor.

4. RMB click and drag down to choose Graph Network.

5. You can filter what types of nodes display in the Create panel by selecting the node type in the left of the panel. This filters the display in the right of the Create panel. You can also Shift-select multiple types or use the group filters (Favorites, Maya, and so on). To add a material to your favorites, just RMB click on the node in the Create panel and choose Add to Favorites.

HOUR 8
Character Modeling

What You'll Learn in This Hour:

▶ How to prepare for creating a character in Maya

▶ How to create a low polygon character

▶ What to consider when creating characters

▶ How to identify problem areas

Nearly all modern visual-effects-laden films and shows contain at least *some* character animation. From talking fuzzy animals to drooling insects, the television and film VFX markets rely heavily on modelers who can bring designs to life in 3D. This means that for your purposes as a CG artist, familiarity with the character-creation process is crucial. If you are planning on moving further down the character-modeling path, this Hour will be helpful for you to start getting accustomed to common considerations with CG character models.

NOTE

Working A-Head

We will go over common issues in character modeling that cover both the head and the body, although there are enough issues to discuss about head and face modeling to fill an entire book. Remember to use the concepts and exercises in this book as a jumping-off point for further study in CG and in Maya.

In this Hour, you will encounter the most common issues surrounding character modeling and learn how to overcome them. You will set up a scene in a way that allows for easy character creation and accurate modeling from a design. You will also learn about modeling considerations as they pertain to a production. Like most of the CG disciplines, character modeling is subject to personal workflows. Therefore, as you read this Hour, take note of the concepts that seem to come naturally to you, and those that are a little more difficult, so that in your personal exercises later on you can focus on finding your *own* way to achieve the goals explained here.

Character Model Basics

With a little bit of polygon modeling experience, you can pretty much intuit the process of creating a character model. The literal acts of extruding, adding edge loops, and merging vertices are all the same when you are modeling a character as when you are modeling a cell phone or a car. However, because characters are almost always meant to deform and move onscreen, certain important considerations must be made to ensure successful character modeling.

Working From Designs

One of the first considerations you have to make is whether you are going to be working from drawn character designs. If so, it is imperative that you have those drawings imported and arranged in your scene in a way that helps you get the 3D model as accurate as possible. Because it is common to work from designs, Maya makes it easy to get your images into the scene. Figure 8.1 shows how close to a design it is possible to create a character.

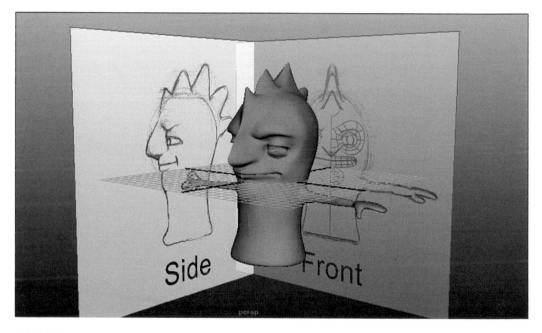

FIGURE 8.1
This finished character model looks very close to the design because we were careful to use all of Maya's available tools.

To begin, we must first create planes that will serve as guides in 3D space as to where our geometry is supposed to be placed. This is commonly achieved in one of two ways: using camera image planes or using polygonal planes with the designs as a texture. The first way involves importing the image as a background in your panel—otherwise known as an "image plane" (more in Hour 22, "Working with Film"). The advantages to this method are that Maya automatically retains the aspect ratio of your drawing, so an extra step is removed. The downside is that to move, rotate, or scale these planes, you must do so through the image plane's attributes in the Attribute Editor, which can be cumbersome when you are in the middle of modeling the character. Even with this drawback, the camera image planes are quicker and easier to create than polygonal planes, so we will use them.

First, we must locate our designs and make sure they have been created correctly. We just need to make sure that the front and side views' images line up perfectly. Navigate to this Hour's source files directory and open up design_Ortho.jpg (see Figure 8.2).

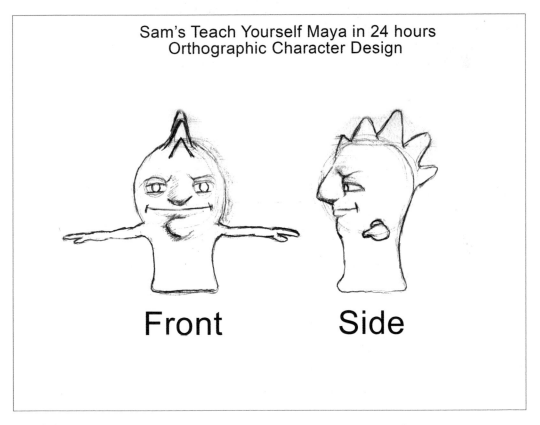

FIGURE 8.2
Notice how this design was created with the character perfectly lined up in both the front and side views. This makes it so that we have the most accurate guide and the easiest time matching the design.

You can clearly see that the front and side views line up correctly. So in order to use these designs, we must load them as image planes on their respective cameras. Open Maya, and in any panel, go to Layouts, Saved Layouts, Four Panes. This will reset your panel layout to the well-known standard layout shown in Figure 8.3.

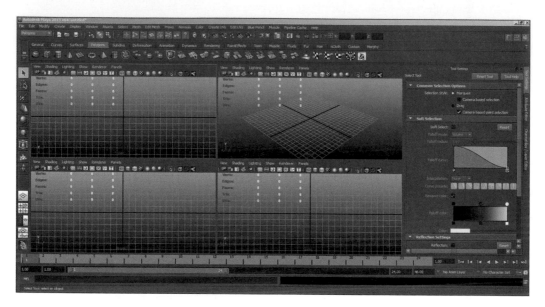

FIGURE 8.3
The layout in the well-known "four-pane" arrangement.

Next, we load the images as the image planes for the front and side cameras. In the front panel, go to View, Image Plane, Import Image.... Navigate to this Hour's source files and choose image_Front.jpg. The image has been cropped for the front view. In the Attribute Editor (which should open automatically when you create the image plane), one of the very first sliders is the Alpha Gain. This controls how "see-through" your image planes are. Set the Alpha Gain to .5 for the front image plane as well as the side image plane when you are done importing it. The properly loaded image is shown in Figure 8.4.

NOTE

Viewport 2.0

We are going to set our Persp panel to render with Viewport 2.0. This panel render engine has some quality features that give us great options for viewing models really beautifully in panel (even before rendering). In this case, however, we need Viewport 2.0 simply for the fact that it renders transparent image planes in the Perspective cameras correctly. In the Persp panel, go to Renderer, Viewport 2.0.

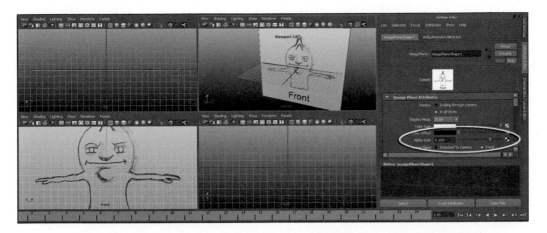

FIGURE 8.4
The front view of the design loaded as an image plane into the front panel. The alpha gain (circled) is set to
.5. Notice also that transparency is working correctly in the Persp panel with Viewport 2.0 set as our renderer.

Now do the same for the side panel. Go to View, Image Plane, Import Image... one more time
and find the image_Side.jpg file. Once it is loaded, you can see in the Persp panel that both
images are placed at the world origin, ready for your use, as shown in Figure 8.5.

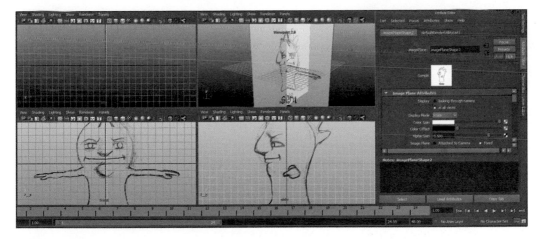

FIGURE 8.5
The two image planes loaded into Maya. Notice how they maintain their aspect ratio by default, which is an
extra step you have to take care of if you were to create polygon planes and arrange them yourself in this
manner.

We will want to move the image planes so they are not in the way of the character when we
start to model him. Select the front image plane and press **Ctrl+A** to bring up the Attribute
Editor. If you scroll down the attributes, you will see a section called Placement Extras. You can

resize your image plane and move it around the scene using these attributes. The Image Center attribute controls where the plane is placed. We want to move the image plane backward so it will be behind the model, so change the value in the far-right box next to Image Center (this is the Z value, even though it is not labeled) to –8. Select the side image plane and make the X value (first box) in its Image Center attribute –12. Figure 8.6 shows the planes with their correct positions.

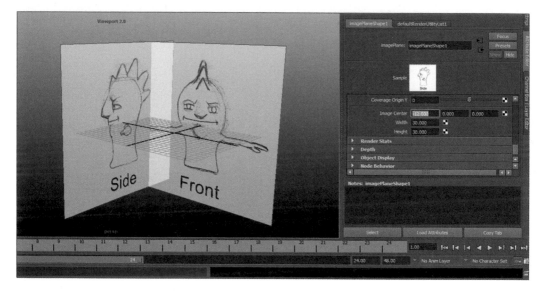

FIGURE 8.6
The image planes as they should be, lined up and ready to guide us as we create our geometry.

TIP

Seeing Three Boxes? It's XYZ!

Any time Maya has three inputs or attributes next to each other with no labeling, it is assumed that the three attributes control the X, Y, and Z values of whatever node you are editing. Be warned, though: Sometimes direction is relative, like in the sense of the Front and Side cameras, where Z is always away from camera, and might not line up with the Z axis in world space.

Once that is completed, we are almost ready to start creating geometry the same way we did with the hammer in Hour 4, "Modeling with Polygonal Geometry." There are just a few more steps to take to make sure we are going to have the most efficient workflow when modeling. Create a polygon sphere by going to Create, Polygons, Sphere. Click anywhere in the front panel and press the 5 key to shade the objects. As you can see, the sphere is opaque and we cannot see our image planes through it. To see through objects in a panel, click on (in your panel) Shading,

X-ray. RMB drag on the sphere and choose vertex. With the vertices highlighted, it's easy to see how intuitive and simple it will be to line up the polygons with details in the designs.

NOTE

Image Specifics

The importance of having accurate, well-drawn orthographic images cannot be overstated. If you try to use this method of creating image planes with designs that were not drawn from straight-on and side angles, your results will be highly skewed. It is also imperative that the images share at least one of the same dimensions—be it width or height—so that scaling the images (using the Width and Height attributes) can be done uniformly. The best practice is to combine the two images into one image to line them up, and then crop and save the two views out separately, retaining the image size.

Using Symmetry in Modeling

We're nearly ready to start modeling. Before we begin, we need to set up our model so that when we work on one side of the character, the other side will update as well. There are a wide variety of ways to do this, so I will show you the way that works the simplest—a "mirrored instance."

NOTE

Duplicates and Instances

The main difference between duplicating an object and instancing an object is that the instance will continue to update with modifications until it is converted into a separate object. Think about an instance as a duplicate with a continuous link to the other object, always updating and adjusting as you work. This link even persists if you delete history on both objects.

To create a mirrored instance, we are going to start with a single polygon. Create a polygon plane by clicking Create, Polygon Primitives, Plane and then the options box □. In the options box that appears, make sure the width divisions and height divisions are both set to 1 and then click Create. Now in the Persp panel, RMB drag and select the two vertices on the left side of the side image plane (the two vertices in negative X space) so that you can move them to the axis, as in Figure 8.7.

We are going to move these two vertices to the center of the world axis. Press **W** to switch to the Move tool. Now, holding down the **X** key makes it so that Maya will snap a vertex to the grid-lines (the **V** key snaps to vertices, and the **C** key snaps to curves). With the **X** key pressed, move these two vertices along the X axis until they snap to the center (they will be aligned with the side panel's image plane). Figure 8.8 shows the vertices in the correct position.

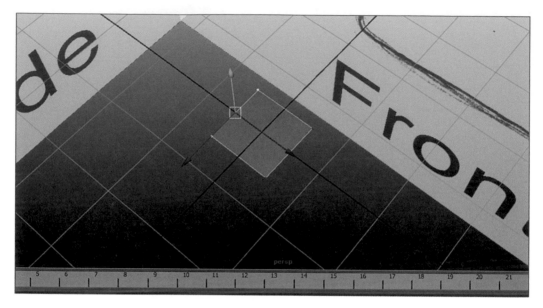

FIGURE 8.7
The newly created polygon plane, with the two vertices selected.

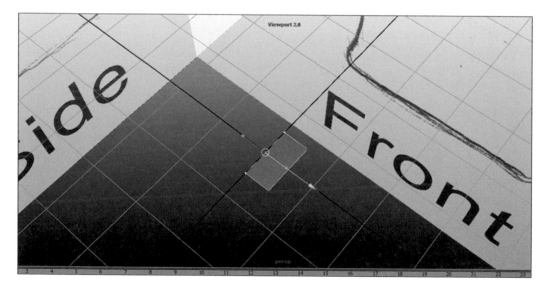

FIGURE 8.8
The vertices moved to the center of the grid.

Now we will instance this geometry. Press **F8** to return to object mode or RMB drag on the plane and choose "object." Go to Edit, Duplicate Special and then the options box □. In the options box, change "Geometry type" to "Instance," and in the first value box (the X value) for "Scale," enter –1 (remember that when you see three boxes, they are X, Y, and Z). Leave the rest of the settings at default and hit "Duplicate Special". A new plane will mirror across the X axis (the result of scaling it by –1), and it is an instance of our first plane. The two planes are now linked together, as shown in Figure 8.9, and all of the edits and modifications you do to the geometry of one will be applied to both simultaneously.

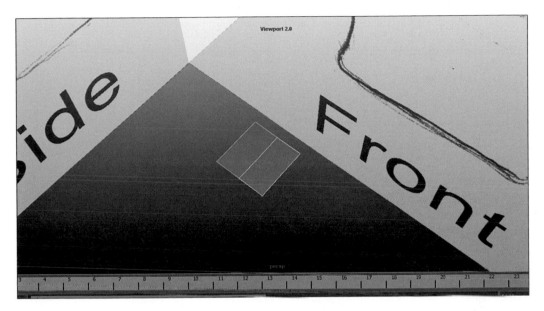

FIGURE 8.9
The final result of mirrored instancing. The two planes are instanced objects; therefore, when we make adjustments, and even add geometry onto these objects, they will give us a symmetrical model.

NOTE

Negative Transforms and Normals

Remember normals? They were mentioned in the Hour 4 quiz, and are basically the "direction" that Maya considers a polygon to be "facing." If you perform a Modify, Freeze Transformations on a piece of geometry with negative scale, it will flip the normal so that the surface is facing inward. This is a problem for UV'ing and rendering, and even some other effects that rely on face normals. Do not Freeze Transformations on a piece of mirrored geometry; we will perform the necessary steps to make sure we can combine the instanced objects correctly.

Starting a Model

We will begin by making some extrusions of this plane, working in the side and front panels to take advantage of the design we have.

Start by selecting the vertices and lining them up with the forehead in the side panel (see Figure 8.10).

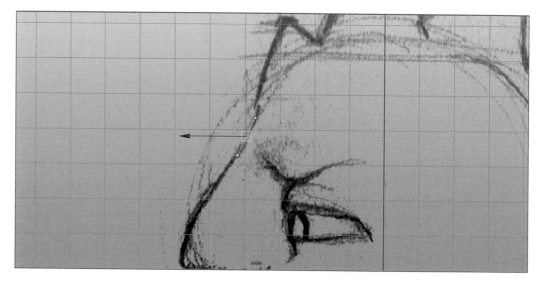

FIGURE 8.10
The first polygon is now lined up with the forehead area of our design. Get it close; there's no such thing as perfect at this stage. Remember to select both vertices when lining this up in the side panel.

Next, select the top edge and extrude it once (in the Polygons menu set, click Edit Mesh, Extrude), working in the side panel to line up the geometry with the design (see Figure 8.11).

Continue extruding the geometry until you have gone around the entire circumference of the character in the side panel. To connect the last two faces, line up the vertices as best you can in the side panel and then switch to the Persp panel. Select two vertices that are supposed to be connected and then select Edit Mesh, Merge. They should "weld" together.

TIP

Selecting Both Vertices

When you are selecting the vertices in the side panel, be very careful to not select single vertices. Some vertices are lined up with each other, so in the side panel it will look like there is only one. The easiest way to make sure you select both while you are doing this step is to drag small selection boxes around both vertices instead of LMB clicking.

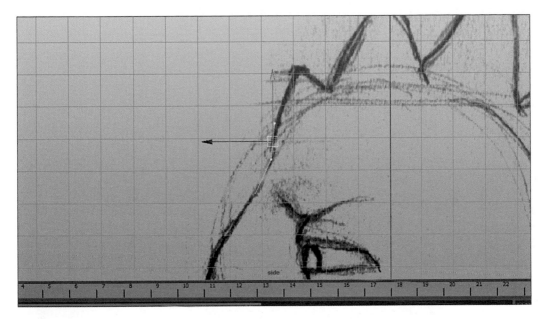

FIGURE 8.11
The top loop extruded and lined up with a higher point on the forehead.

NOTE

Extruding in the Right Direction

The Extrude tool will show you a manipulator when you engage the tool that corresponds to the direction of the face. If you are working only in the side panel, you don't have to worry about the polygons moving off of the center of the grid, but if you are working in the Persp panel, be careful: It is easy to accidentally move a face when extruding in the wrong direction.

Edge Loops

From Hour 4 you learned that edge loops are a series of continuous edges in a polygonal model. Edge loops are much more important in character modeling, because most of the time we are going to subdivide our mesh at render time and the results need to be predictable. Having good control over your edge loops means being able to have the "flow" of the model follow natural lines instead of fighting against them. A good example is the muscles of the arms; you would have a hard time really defining a nice bicep shape without edge loops that follow the curve of that muscle. Another instance when edge loop control is very necessary is when we have circular shapes in our mesh, such as mouths, eye sockets, and nostrils. It is common to draw a few edge loops on your design to give you a guide as to where the detail needs to go. Select the front panel's image plane, go into the Attribute Editor, and then replace the image with image_Front_ Loops.jpg, as seen in Figure 8.12.

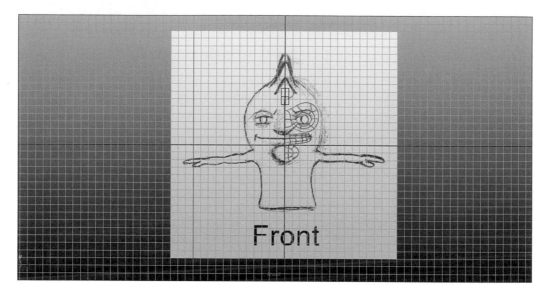

FIGURE 8.12
The updated front view image with a few important edge loops drawn over. We will integrate these edge loops as we work.

Let's create the edge loop that encircles the eye. One way is to create some polygons in the area of the eye and then use the Interactive Split tool and extrude to edit the polygons into shape. Instead, we will purposefully create the edge loops explicitly so that we know where they will be. Extrude the edges down the nose until your polygon is lined up with the edge loops drawn on the front image plane. Select the edge that is closest to the inside of the eye, as shown in Figure 8.13.

NOTE

Setting Up Polygon Display

We want to be able to see through the polygons we are manipulating so that we can see the design while we work. Turn on X-ray shading by clicking on the Shading menu in your front and side panels and clicking on X-Ray. Make sure you are in shaded mode as well by pressing **5** while your mouse is within the panel. You should now be able to see through the polygons.

Extrude the edge in the front panel two times toward the eye socket (see Figure 8.14).

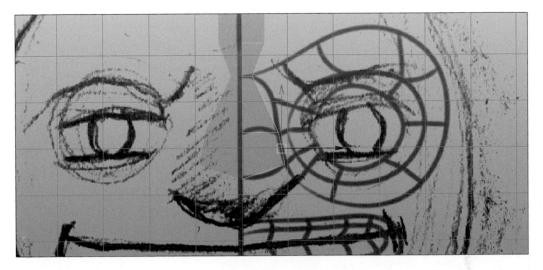

FIGURE 8.13
The edge that we are going to start with to create the edge loop that will encircle the eye socket.

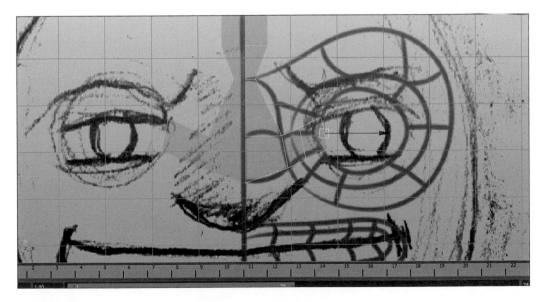

FIGURE 8.14
The edge extruded twice toward the eye socket.

Move the vertices of the extruded edges to be in line with the eye socket, like I did in Figure 8.15.

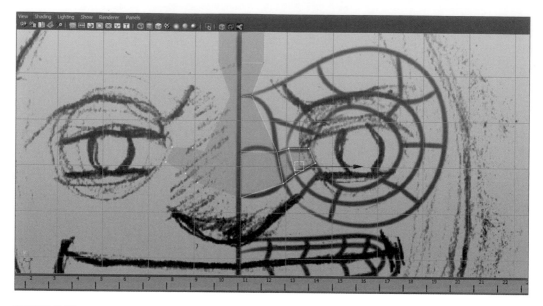

FIGURE 8.15
The polygons are lined up nicely with where the eye socket is.

Now extrude the edge all the way around the eye socket and then weld the vertices at the end when you are done (see Figure 8.16). Eight to ten extrusions is enough.

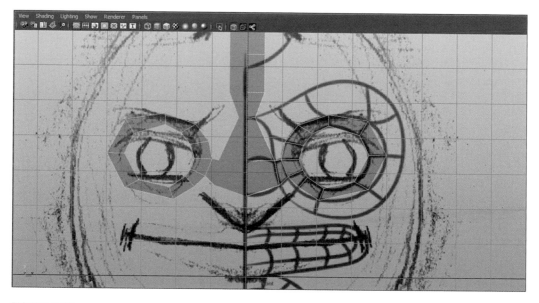

FIGURE 8.16
The edge loop we need to really define that eye socket shape is where we need it to be.

Now we must work simultaneously in the front and the side panels to move the vertices in the Z direction and line them up with the design in the side panel. Move them into place, as shown in Figure 8.17.

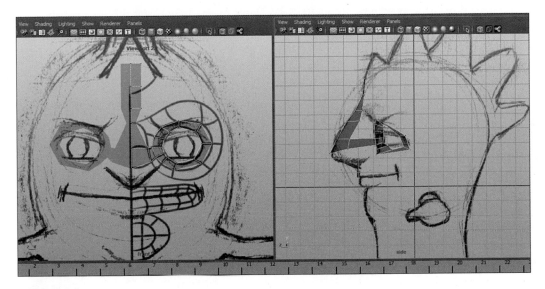

FIGURE 8.17
The edge loops look correct in both views now.

Continue Refining Your Model

Continue extruding and positioning faces to create the rest of the character's body geometry. Leave the arms out for now. You may want to make use of the Append to Polygon tool instead of merging vertices. To use this tool, select it by going to Edit Mesh, Append to Polygon Tool. Once it is active, select the open edge you would like to close. Triangular manipulators will appear on the edges in the mesh that you can select to create the new polygon. Click on any of them to create the new polygon; then press **Enter** to finish the tool. Once you have created the rough geometry for the entire character, you can go back and use the Interactive Split tool to redefine the edge loops. Look for areas where the edges are getting crossed and disorganized. You can use the Interactive Split tool to make some splits, and then delete the old edges to make things look like they are working better. In general, try to get the geometry evenly spaced and the edge loops looking smooth in all directions. As you get more practice, it becomes easier to predict how your geometry will turn out.

Multi-Edged Intersections: Poles

You may notice that you are getting many "poles" in your geometry. A *pole* is any vertex that is at the intersection of more than four edges. A certain number of poles is unavoidable because of the different elements you need to fit together in a single mesh. A character that has many circular edge loops close together is especially prone to having poles. Even our character has poles in his face near the eye socket. We do want to try to reduce the number of poles as much as possible because they are another problem for smoothing at render time. And we definitely want to try to get rid of poles in any place that is going to have a lot of deformation happening; they will introduce smoothing errors. Figure 8.18 shows some poles in our model.

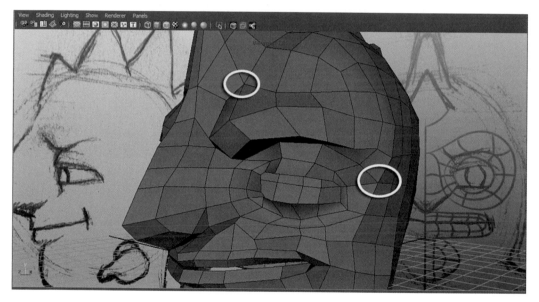

FIGURE 8.18
Poles are anywhere that more than four edges meet. Maya doesn't know how to subdivide these areas nicely.

Remember from Hour 4 we talked about how it is ideal to have three- and four-sided faces in our models? One way to reduce the number of poles you have from the outset is to try as hard as possible to make sure you only have four-sided faces, and that your edge loops are *as long as possible*. This will help ensure you are not creating tangled nests of polygons. Chances are your edge loops are terminating at poles; therefore, if you double-click on an edge, follow the selected edge loop to its ends to discover poles.

A place where poles are guaranteed to appear is anywhere a face is extruded from a plane. The vertices already have four edges intersecting at them, and you are essentially adding one more. If you think of the most low-poly bipedal shape possible, you will see that poles are unavoidable wherever appendages are extruded (see Figure 8.19).

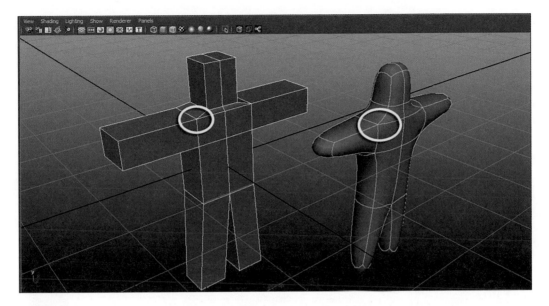

FIGURE 8.19
This very simple representation of a bipedal character illustrates how some poles are unavoidable. Even when smoothed (right), the poles remain. Keeping poles to a minimum is the mark of a good character modeler.

Adding the Arms

Seeing as having a few poles is unavoidable, we're going to extrude the polygons that make up the arms from the open edges on his side. If you want to start from the same point as I have, open character_Mid.ma in this Hour's source files. Go into the Edges component mode and double-click on the open edge loop on his sides. Use the Edit Mesh, Extrude tool to extrude his arms all the way to the wrists. This time, we're going to add detail using the Insert Edge Loop tool to give ourselves detail where we need it. Select Edit Mesh, Insert Edge Loop and click a few times along the arm, putting at least three loops near the elbow. When that is done, you can go into the vertex component mode and make the adjustments you need to get the vertices to line up with the design.

This character was designed with "mitten hands" so that it would not be too challenging to try to get the hands in place. Keep extruding, appending, and adjusting vertices to get the hands in place, as shown in Figure 8.20.

NOTE

Legs Cover the Real Center

Notice how our character's arms are basically not visible in the side panel's image plane. Because they don't block any geometry they are visible in the side drawing. Legs, however, *do* block crucial information—where the center edge loop goes from front to back through the groin area. On most side-view designs, the center edge loop is drawn even though it should be blocked by the leg (see Figure 8.21).

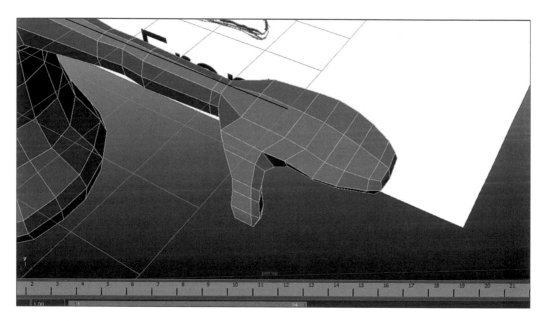

FIGURE 8.20
The completed hand has a thumb and a tapered "mitten" for fingers.

Low-Poly Workflow

As we move ahead, we should start thinking about the workflow that this character is going to go through. One of the more popular workflows is to export your geometry in a low-polygon state to a piece of 3D sculpting software to add details and then apply those details to the low poly at render time with something called a "displacement map." This workflow saves a lot of scene overhead because Maya does not handle millions of polygons in panel very well, nor could you possibly animate a character that had that much detail.

Working "low poly" means that you aren't necessarily trying to model detailed parts of the character into the geometry. This is particularly true for details such as buttons on a shirt, belts, arm bands, and so on. These small details would be better suited to be separate objects that you either constrain or rig to move along with the character geometry rather than being built into the single character mesh. A good rule of thumb is that anything that is "skin tight" can be a part of the character model, and anything that is not should be a separate object. Just imagine how hard it would be to have good edge loops if you had to add really tiny details to a low-poly object.

FIGURE 8.21
A common practice is to show the center edge loop even though it is blocked by the leg.

The last advantage to a low-poly workflow is the fact that you are simply dealing with fewer polygons. When we get to rigging and skinning this character, you will see that having fewer polygons to deal with is extremely advantageous. Particularly when we are creating shapes for the eyelids and mouth for animation, our low-poly character will be very simple to set up to take on some very dynamic shapes.

Problem Areas

Characters have some areas that traditionally can give us a lot of trouble. Therefore, you need to know what these areas are and some good methods for keeping out of trouble.

Inside the Mouth

Inside the mouth can be tricky to model because it is hidden by other geometry, and you have to decide what kind of mouth interior you want before you go about creating it. It can be a good idea to create a hollow mouth interior and have separate geometry for the teeth and tongue to avoid the problems mentioned before concerning detail and edge loop efficiency. The mouth interior does not have to be very big; a common beginner mistake is to make the mouth large, but we won't fall into that trap. Figure 8.22 shows a good-sized mouth interior.

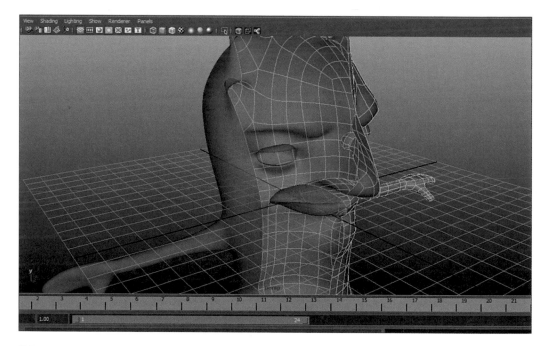

FIGURE 8.22
Our character with a hollow mouth added. We can add the teeth and tongue later if we wish.

Armpits and Shoulders

We created the arms by extruding an open edge loop on the side of the body, which created four poles. For our purposes, this shouldn't work out to be too disruptive in either the animation or the smoothing processes, but you should know anyway that armpits and shoulders are challenging. The reason they present such a challenge is that they have a very wide range of motion, and they take on very different shapes depending on if the arm is up, down, forward, or back. We create our character in T-pose (with arms perfectly out to the sides) because with most cartoon characters, this pose represents the middle of the range of motion. On some feature film rigs, the arms are modeled to be more relaxed, slightly lowered, and a little bit bent forward at the elbow. This is done because, in reality, our range of motion for most common tasks is very narrow. Because our character has very little armpit or shoulder definition, just a tiny bit of bulge on top and a little bit of indentation on the bottom of the arm will suffice. In Figure 8.23, the poles that were created on his arm area are shown, but there shouldn't be problems with smoothing or deformation here.

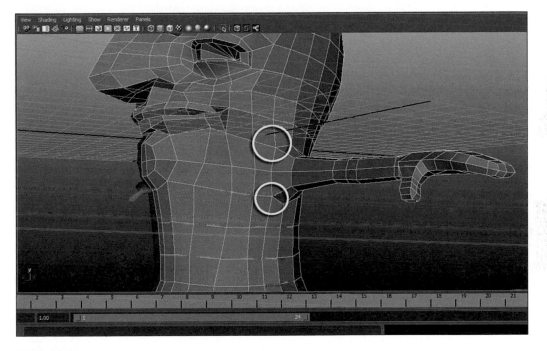

FIGURE 8.23
The arms of our character are not so bulky or defined that we'll run into deformation or smoothing problems with the poles that were created, but you should keep it in mind for future characters.

Hands

Our character's hands do not have much detail, but with realistic characters with multiple fingers, the hands are a challenge. The issue is getting enough edges into the fingers to nicely define the shape, without having to terminate too many of those edges at the wrist and create nasty poles. Most hand models use the same extrusion we did for this character's arms on each of the fingers, making it so the poles that would be created for the finger detail end up between the fingers and not all bunched up in the wrist.

Eyelids

Our character has very simple eyes with nice bulky eyelids. For characters with more realistic, thin eyelids, they are normally modeled *closed* so that by using rigging tools and deformers, they can be opened nicely. It is done this way because it is easier to rig an eye to open than it is to untangle the scrunched-up geometry of a closed eyelid and make it close nicely. Ours is modeled open solely because of the fact our character is cartoony, unrealistic, and, most importantly, low poly.

Elbows and Knees

These two areas are just like the armpits and shoulders in that they will either flatten out or get bunched up when deforming. Also, elbows and knees actually take on very different shapes (due to the bones changing position and pushing the skin out) when they are bent than when they are relaxed. We can use something called BlendShapes (described in Hour 15, "Making Diverse Shapes with BlendShapes") to change the shape of the elbows and knees depending on whether they are bent or not. Therefore, to avoid problems, model the knees and elbows in their clearly relaxed poses, not something halfway, which might be intuitive to avoid problems.

Density

When you're modeling characters, it's common to be focused on the section you are working on, and only worry about the overall model density later on. However, it is a good practice to have an idea of how dense the geometry is going to be on your character before you begin. Certain areas need more density, or they will not behave correctly when they deform. This is why we added extra edge loops near the elbow of our character. To make very sure we get the exact shape we want out of him, go back in and add some more detail on his elbow, as seen in Figure 8.24. When it comes time to rig these elbows, I know we'll have enough detail to get the results we want.

Besides areas that are going to deform, you also want more density in areas that are going to get the most screen time. For this reason, the face and head are typically the densest regions on your character model. Taking a step back and looking at our character model proves this is true, even with cartoony characters, as you can see in Figure 8.25.

The one other consideration for density is for any effect that relies on polygonal detail. Some particle systems generate particles per face, and if your mesh is too lopsided in detail, it can create some odd effects. Some third-party fur plugins generate hairs based on polygons as well; again, having far too much detail in one section and far too little in another can mean unpredictable results.

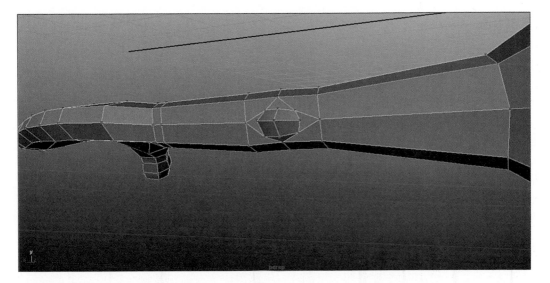

FIGURE 8.24
The elbows can be problem areas if you don't have enough geometric detail, or density, in the areas where they deform.

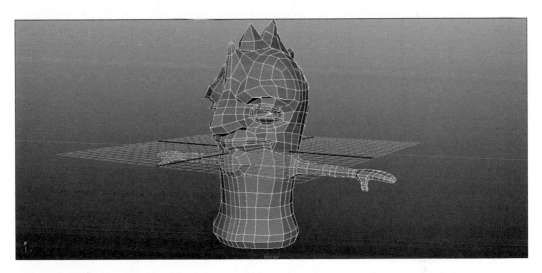

FIGURE 8.25
The detail is higher in the face than anywhere else because it will deform, but mostly because an audience spends the majority of their time watching the face!

Smoothing

We discussed smoothing in Hour 4, and the same considerations apply with characters. In some ways, it's more important to think about smoothing as you are working with characters, because as a character deforms in animation, the smoothing you apply will greatly affect how it looks in your final images.

Smoothing Reduces Detail

Remember that smoothing the geometry by tessellation does just that: It *smooths!* Wherever there are details that are not represented by enough polygons to really "define" it, you are going to lose that detail a bit when you smooth the mesh. Take a look at how the profile of the nose changes slightly when we press the **3** key and preview the smoothing, as shown in Figure 8.26.

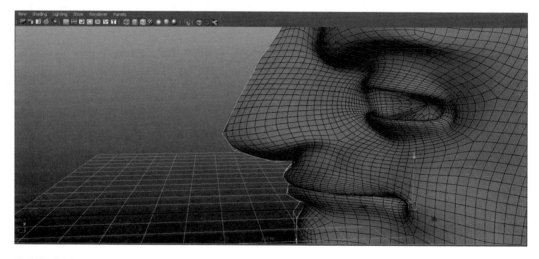

FIGURE 8.26
The nose before and after smoothing. Notice how the profile changes when smoothing is applied.

When you are getting close to making your final adjustments to a model, previewing the smoothing is important. Keep a close eye on areas where the geometry is protruding or receding, because smoothing will reduce the contrast in these areas the most.

Deciding on Smoothing

The issues regarding what type of smoothing to use are the same with characters as they are with non-organic geometry.

Under most circumstances, if you are using Mental Ray to render (and not the Maya software renderer or a third-party choice), smooth your geometry with Mental Ray's smooth mesh preview (by pressing **3** with geometry selected). This is when smoothing can happen as a last step before rendering.

In some rare cases, certain deformers, constraints, or miscellaneous nodes depend highly on the geometry and you will need to smooth your mode using the Mesh, Smooth command. Things such as toon lines depend on topology, and in order for them to follow the contour of the model, you will have to smooth the mesh using the Smooth command and not Mental Ray smooth mesh preview.

TIP

Adjusting the Smooth Mesh Preview

Unlike other inputs, the Smooth Mesh Preview settings are found in an object's shape node. Open the Attribute Editor with an object selected (**Ctrl+A**) and select the shape node (normally the second tab from the left at the top of the Attribute Editor). Scroll down to the section labeled "Smooth Mesh," and all of the attributes are available for you to change the preview to match your render settings or to be optimized for fast interaction.

Crease Edges

In Hour 4, we talked about using crease edges with polygonal geometry as a way to preserve sharp edges in your model when you smooth it. Find this tool under Edit Mesh, Crease Edges Tool. Crease edges only update interactively with Mental Ray's smooth mesh preview. If you want to take advantage of crease edges, know that they will not update interactively when you use the Mesh, Smooth command. If you make adjustments to the creases, you must delete the polySmooth node or delete history on the model and apply the Smooth again.

Combining Geometry

Once you are ready to combine both sides of the geometry into one mesh, follow these steps. First, delete history on both models by pressing **Alt+Shift+D** with the objects selected. Then, with the objects still selected, go to Mesh, Combine. It will create a new object and a blank group node that represents the transforms of the old geometry. These will not be used for anything, so delete history again, and the extra nodes will be removed. Now, there's a tricky thing happening right now: The center vertices are not welded together yet. It is quick to merge the vertices, but we'll need to make sure they are all lying on the world center axis first. Switch to Vertex components mode and, in the top panel, select all of the vertices that run through the center of the model by dragging a selection box around them. Figure 8.27 shows the center vertices selected correctly.

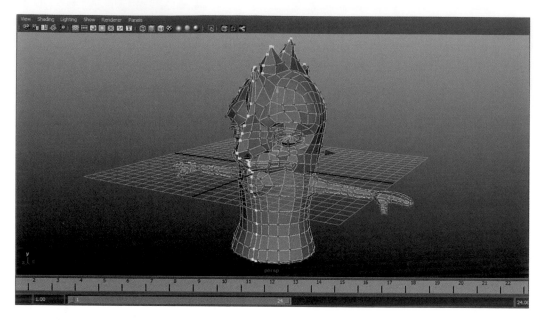

FIGURE 8.27
The model now combined, and with the center vertices selected.

With the **W** key pressed and held, LMB click in the panel and make sure your Move tool is set to "World" space (see Figure 8.28).

Go into the Move tool's settings (Windows, Settings/Preferences, Tool Settings—or double-click the Move tool in the toolbox). Scroll down to the section called "Move Snap Settings" and uncheck "Retain component spacing." This setting controls whether components you move are going to stay locked in their relative positions when you move them, or whether they will move absolutely. Now, with the center vertices still selected, hold the **X** key down and move the vertices on the X axis until they snap to the next gridline, and then move them back so they snap back to the center gridline. What you just did is moved all of the vertices to an adjacent gridline and snapped them to the grid and then moved them back into place. Now we know all of the center vertices are in the right position. Go to Edit Mesh, Merge, and the vertices will merge and close the center seam.

TIP

Double-Checking the Merge Worked

To make sure the merge vertices worked, you can always check to see if the number of vertices was reduced by half. To see the number of vertices you have selected, go to Display, Heads Up Display, Poly Count. Note the number of vertices it says you have selected (the far-right column) before you merge and after you merge. If you have followed the steps correctly, the number should be half of what you started with after you merge.

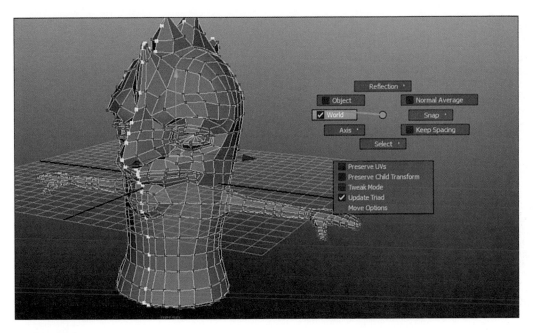

FIGURE 8.28
The Move tool is set to World space so that our next step is sure to work.

UVs Review

We are going to UV this character, which should be pretty straightforward. Also, he is symmetrical, and with characters it is better to *not* take advantage of symmetry. Characters seem a little bit more real with some asymmetry in their texture. To start from the finished model I am using, open character_Model_Finished.ma. Select the character, and in the Polygons menu set (**F3**), go to Create UVs, Cylindrical Mapping. Select all of the edges of the character, and in the UV Texture Editor (Windows, UV Texture Editor), go to Polygons, Sew UV Edges. Figure 8.29 shows the UV edges sewn correctly.

We will make a seam on each of his arms in the socket where it connects to the body, and a seam along the back of the arm so it can unfold flat. In the Persp panel, select the edges around the connecting point of *both arms*, select the edge loop at the wrist, and select the edge loop that runs through the center of the back of his arm, as you can see in Figure 8.30. In the UV Texture Editor, go to Polygons, Cut UV Edges.

Create another seam through the center of the back of his head, and seams around the top horns that protrude outward, using the Cut UV Edges tool. Also, create a seam around the edge loop just inside his lips.

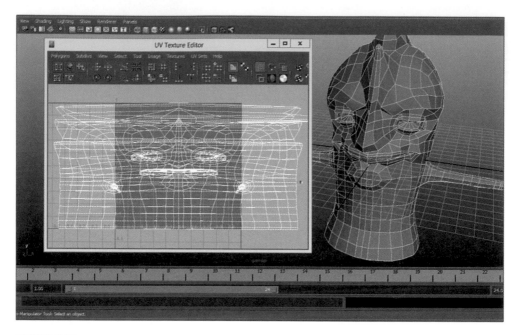

FIGURE 8.29
Don't worry about what the UVs look like in the beginning. Remember, the workflow is to start with an automatic mapping method and then refine by cutting seams and adjusting UVs.

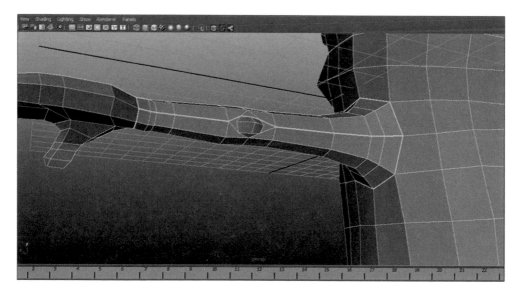

FIGURE 8.30
The seam we want to create on the arms is selected. This will allow us to unfold these UVs nicely.

With a little more cutting and sewing, you are ready to Unfold. Select each UV shell by clicking (in the UV Texture Editor) on a vertex and then Ctrl+RMB clicking until you see the option to convert "To Shell." To unfold the UVs all at once, in the UV Texture Editor, go to Polygons, Unfold. With a little moving, rotating, and scaling, the UVs are complete (see Figure 8.31). Open character_Model_Final.ma to see what the finished product looks like.

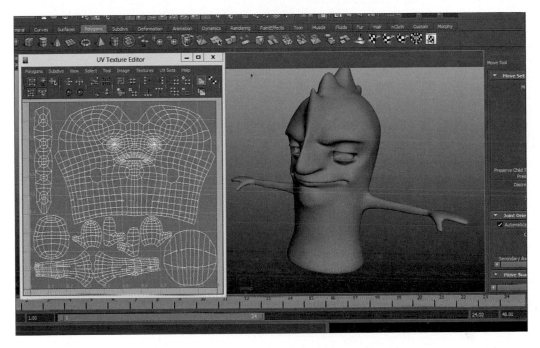

FIGURE 8.31
The finished model and UVs.

BONUS

Character Models

The Bonus folder for this Hour contains a handful of finished character models for you to open and dissect. Take a look at how each model has edge loops designed to work with the movement of the character. Also, look closely at how many three-, four-, and five-sided faces the characters contain.

Summary

Seeing as a wide majority of visual effects and films contain one if not hundreds of characters, character modeling is a valuable skill in any CG artist's arsenal. We discussed how to set up a modeling session. We went over bringing in designs as image planes as well as creating symmetrical low-polygon geometry that will be smoothed later. The model started coming to life as we extruded and moved edges. Finally, we combined the two halves and UV'd the character to get him totally ready for skinning.

Q&A

Q. How radically different are modeling workflows for different types of characters?

A. The workflow does not change drastically between highly realistic characters and cartoony characters. The only thing that changes is that most realistic characters are exported to a high-polygon sculpting software after they are finished in low-poly form.

Q. My image planes are not lining up with each other. What is wrong?

A. When this happens, it is because your image planes are not the same size. It is always easiest to take advantage of letting Maya size and position your image planes automatically by making the side and front images have the same dimensions.

Q. When I combine the two halves, and I select all of the center vertices to merge them, they do not all merge. Why?

A. You might have accidentally moved the models, or the center vertices are not exactly lining up with each other. To increase the distance that two vertices will travel to merge together, increase the Threshold value in the Merge command's option box.

Q. I noticed your character's eye socket is empty. Shouldn't we model an eyeball?

A. Remember any object that is not skin tight should be a separate object and not modeled into the character's model. That goes for eyes and teeth as well. Best bet is to have a sphere in place as you are creating the eye socket to give you a sense of what the eye shape is going to be, and remove it before you are done. Alternatively, you can use that sphere as a good starting point for your eye once the body mesh is complete.

Workshop

The workshop contains quiz questions and exercises to help you solidify your understanding of the material covered. Try to answer all questions before looking at the "Answers" section that follows.

Quiz

1. Why is it important to have orthographic designs when modeling a character?

2. What is the attribute called that adjusts the transparency of an image plane?

3. A copy of a polygon that is mirrored but takes on all of the changes to the original is called what?

4. Name a few areas where good edge loops are important.

5. What is a pole?

Exercise

After this Hour, you probably have many ideas for characters you'd like to create. Try to start with a very simple character and model him or her (or it) from scratch. Avoid starting with a polygon primitive. If you get stuck, open up any of the intermediate files in this Hour's source files to see how I've created my model and then try to follow some of the choices. Do not be too ambitious; if you bite off more than you can chew, you can get stuck—and discouraged.

Answers

1. Drawings with perspective will give a distorted view of a character and make it impossible to follow the designs working in a front or side panel in Maya.

2. The attribute is called Alpha Gain, and it can be adjusted in the Attribute Editor for an image plane. Remember that to see the transparency in the Persp panel, the "renderer" must be set to Viewport 2.0.

3. A "mirrored instance." This "link" between the polygons is preserved even if you delete history, but not if you combine the two halves.

4. Eye sockets, cheeks, mouths, muscles, and any area that has well-defined, curved detail.

5. A pole is any vertex that is at the intersection of *more* than four edges. This happens most often when you extrude faces, or have non-four-sided faces in your mesh.

HOUR 9
Relationships and Making Nodes Work Together

What You'll Learn in This Hour:

▶ How to see a relationship between objects
▶ How to create a relationship between nodes
▶ The different types of relationships you can create
▶ How to choose the right relationship to create

Maya's versatility stems mainly from the fact that Autodesk does not try to predict or control the way their users will take advantage of Maya's tools. Instead, they create a wide array of tools that can be connected in a near infinite number of ways. Ingenious Maya users around the world discover new ways to utilize Maya's features in new ways every day. We're going to take a look at how some relationships and connections are created for you, and how to create them yourself.

NOTE

Under the Hood

In actuality, every single node is connected in some way as you create it. A shape node is connected to a transform node to make up an object. Its surface is connected to a shading group so that it renders correctly. And all the lights in the scene are connected to the objects as well. Under the hood, Maya is connecting every node you create. You do not have to worry about connecting 99% of the nodes that make Maya work, only coming up with ingenious solutions to problems as they present themselves.

In this Hour, you will see the many subtle ways Maya connects nodes, and you'll connect some yourself. You will also see how the different nodes can work together to produce some pretty impressive results, and you will hopefully get ideas for new ways to elevate Maya's functionality further.

Viewing Relationships

Let's quickly take a look at the different connections that Maya generates for you automatically. Start a new Maya scene (press **Ctrl+N** or run the Maya program). Create a polygonal sphere by clicking Create, Polygons, Sphere. If you have not turned Interactive Creation off, you will need to click on the grid and drag the sphere's radius to create it. With the new sphere still selected, go to Windows, Hypergraph: Connections. It will look like Figure 9.1.

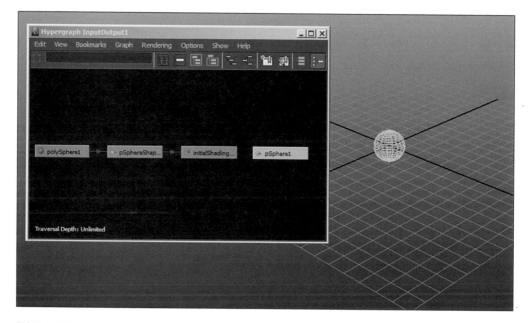

FIGURE 9.1
Even a simple sphere has a host of connections already created around it.

As you can see, even creating something as simple as a polygonal sphere creates multiple nodes that are connected. The creation node (with the sphere's creation attributes) outputs to the shape node, the shape node is a child of the transform node, and so on. Clicking on the initialShadingGroup node and then clicking on Windows, Hypergraph: Connections again will open a second Hypergraph, showing all of the connections that this shading group has created. Figure 9.2 shows just how many connections are present for default nodes! The number of connections that are created by default even for the most rudimentary objects and effects is quite staggering. Again, though, you need not concern yourself with 90% of the connections that are made; only how to make custom connections to achieve specific results.

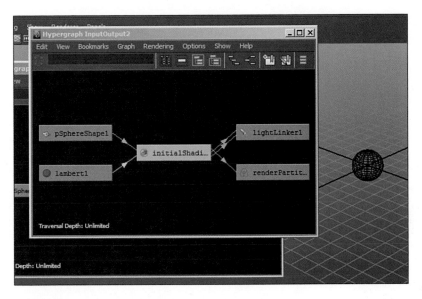

FIGURE 9.2
Even the default material generated by Maya when you create a new scene is "wired up" with plenty of connections. These relationships are necessary to make Maya work.

The Hypergraph is one of the easiest ways to see connections, because you can graph all of the connections of a selected node with the click of a button. Lines that go into the left side of a node in the Hypergraph are *inputs*, and lines that go out the right side are *outputs*. You can see the direction of a connection by the arrows that are drawn along the lines (the direction meaning a connection goes from the output of one node to the input of another). The Hypershade also graphs connections similarly. I created a very simple shading network and graphed it for you to demonstrate the similarity in Figure 9.3.

TIP

Connections Are Everywhere

You can actually see your connections in many different places in the Maya UI. For starters, all of the inputs and output connections of a selected node are normally displayed in the Channel Box on the right. Also, you can reorder and adjust connections by right-clicking on an object and choosing either Inputs or Outputs. Even though the Hypershade is most often used for creating materials, you can graph any type of node network in the work area as well. In the Connection Editor, loading two nodes that have connections will change the display of the connected attributes to italicized text. There are more ways to view connections, but suffice it to say you will never be at a loss finding connected nodes.

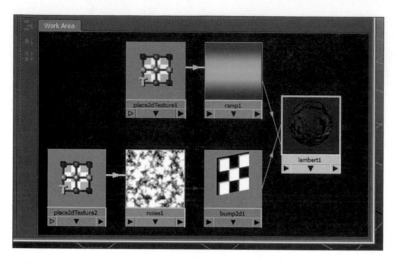

FIGURE 9.3
The Hypershade is very much like the Hypergraph in the way it displays connected nodes.

This is a simple shading network, showing all of the connections Maya creates automatically. The Ramp texture was created by simply clicking on the texture button to the right of the color channel. Maya created the correct connections when I chose the Ramp.

Creating Connections

To create connections, all you have to do is use Maya's top-level tools and Maya will do the rest. When you want to explicitly connect nodes and create a relationship, you have several ways to do so. You can type in the MEL command to connect attributes, you can drag and drop nodes in the Hypergraph, but probably the simplest and most straightforward way to connect a node is to use the Connection Editor.

The Connection Editor

Indeed, the Connection Editor even presents itself when making anything other than a default connection in the Hypershade or Hypergraph anyway. You may as well open it up and become comfortable and familiar with the interface. Make a new Maya scene and then click on Window, General Editors, Connection Editor. The Connection Editor will appear as it does in Figure 9.4.

To make a connection in the Connection Editor, click on any attribute in the left panel (Outputs) and click on one or more attributes in the right panel (Inputs). You can have a single output connect to more than one input, but you cannot connect multiple outputs to the same input. Let's load some attributes into these panels so we can start creating connections.

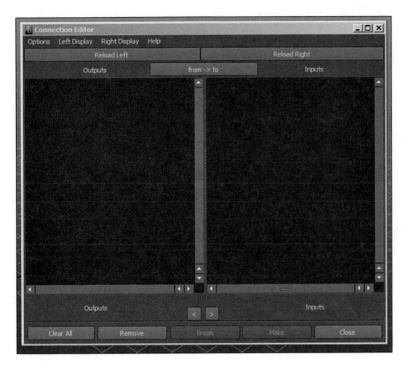

FIGURE 9.4
The Connection Editor has a simple interface: outputs on the left, inputs on the right.

NOTE

Auto-Load

Maya will automatically load the attributes of the selected object into the left pane of the Connection Editor. We opened this editor in a blank Maya scene, so nothing showed up.

Create a polygonal sphere by clicking Create, Polygon Primitives, Sphere. In the Connection Editor, click at the top left where it says "Reload Left." You will see that all of the potential outputs have loaded into the left pane, as in Figure 9.5.

Click on "Reload Right" on the top right and see the attributes load in the Inputs pane, as in Figure 9.6.

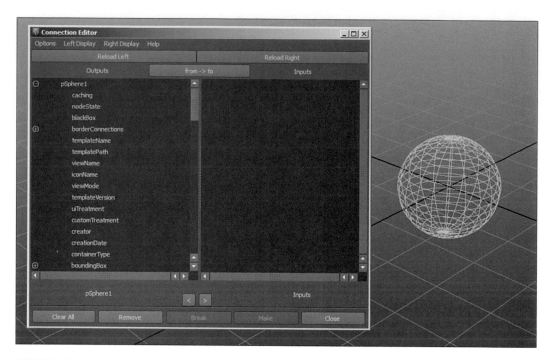

FIGURE 9.5
The sphere's attributes are loaded into the left pane. These can all be selected as outputs.

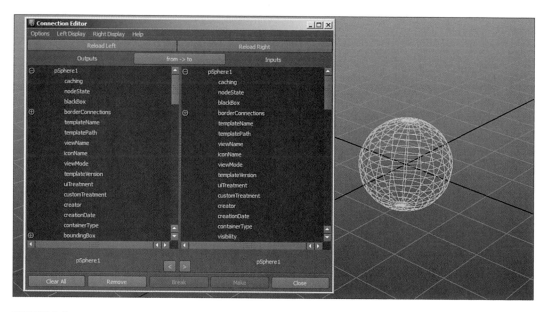

FIGURE 9.6
With the sphere's attributes loaded as outputs and inputs, we can make connections.

Selecting an attribute on the left makes it so Maya will use the output of this attribute as the input of one or many attributes on the right. Remember what was said in about compatible data in Hour 7, "Creating Node Networks in the Hypershade"? You can only connect an attribute that outputs compatible data to your desired input. Maya gives you visual feedback by graying out any input that is incompatible with the selected output. Let's see this in action. In Figure 9.7, you can see that if we select the "caching" attribute, Maya grays out most of the inputs on the right because they do not use the same type of data.

FIGURE 9.7
Maya will only let you connect compatible attributes. So, for instance, you cannot connect an RGB output (data in the format [x,x,x]) to a visibility input (data in the format [on/off]).

We will now connect an attribute that *is* compatible and see the result. On the left pane, click on the + sign next to Translate and then click on translateZ. On the right pane, click on the + sign next to Scale and then click on scaleY. Maya has connected these two attributes. You will notice that like in Figure 9.8, the sphere has completely flattened. This is due to the fact that the current translateZ value is 0.

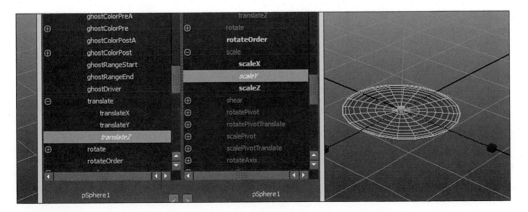

FIGURE 9.8
The sphere has flattened due to receiving an input value of 0 on its scaleY.

Open the Channel Box on the right of the screen and look at the channels for the sphere. The translate Y attribute is highlighted, which is Maya's way of showing you that an attribute has a connection. As you see in Figure 9.9, Maya does not show you the output connection on Translate Z (the attribute that is controlling Scale Y); only the input channel is highlighted.

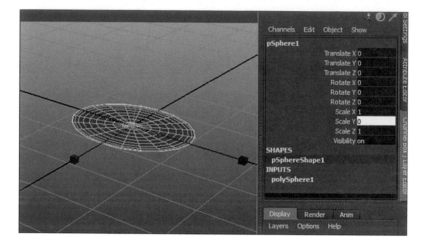

FIGURE 9.9
The Scale Y channel is highlighted, which means that it has an incoming connection.

Now we're going to test the connection. In the Persp panel, select and move the sphere along the Z axis. Notice as you move the sphere, the height (scaleY) is changing to match the translateZ values, as in Figure 9.10. Also notice that the connection is in real time, and does not require any calculation. Later on you will see that certain types of Maya tools and commands update at different times, such as expressions and constraints.

NOTE

Care in the Connection Editor

Once you connect an attribute in the Connection Editor, that attribute will change to the new input—meaning if you have some customized values for attributes that you accidentally connect, these values will be overwritten even if you disconnect the attributes again. Therefore, you have to be careful when connecting attributes, or locking attributes, that you do not want to change (right-click on the attribute or channel and choose Lock Attribute or Lock Selected, respectively).

This connection is interesting, but it does not have much real-world application. Let's make a connection that might be made in a real-world application, one that will help us in Hour 10, "Basic Rigging: Preparing Objects for Animation," when we start creating basic rigs.

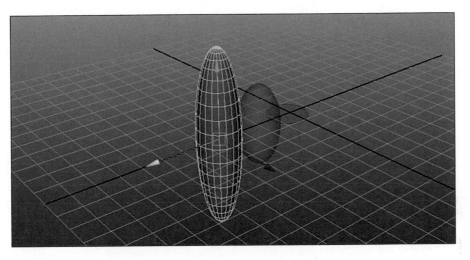

FIGURE 9.10
As you move the sphere along the Z axis, the Scale Y updates in real time.

Connecting New Attributes

Create a new Maya scene and then create a polygon sphere and a NURBS circle (click Create, Polygon Primitives, Sphere and then click Create, NURBS Primitives, Circle). Scale them to match mine, as shown in Figure 9.11.

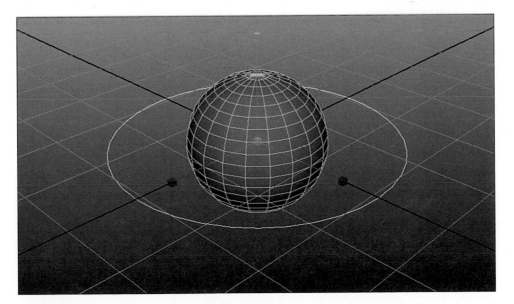

FIGURE 9.11
The sphere and circle scaled the way they might be in an animation rig.

With the objects scaled nicely, we will create a connection between a custom attribute on the NURBS curve and an attribute on the sphere. Select the circle and open the Channel Box. At the top of the Channel Box, click on Edit, Add Attribute, as shown in Figure 9.12.

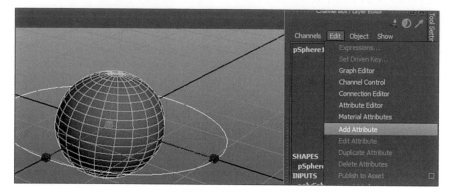

FIGURE 9.12
The align attribute enables you to left justify, right justify, and center text.

Now in the resulting menu that opens, we are going to create a new attribute that will later control the sphere material's transparency. In the Long Name attribute, type in "transparency." Leave the Data Type on "float" and make the Minimum 0, the Maximum 1, and the Default 0, like I did in Figure 9.13.

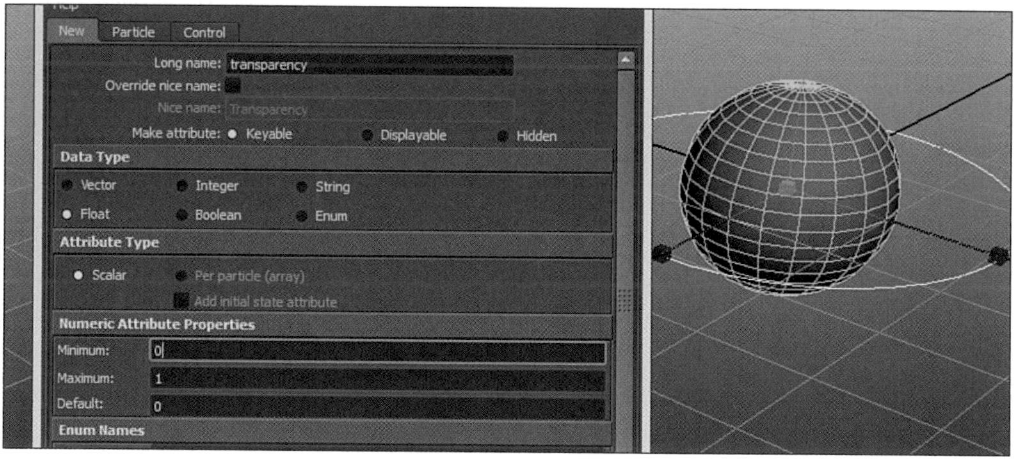

FIGURE 9.13
The correct settings to add our attribute to the sphere.

Click Ok, and you will see a new attribute called "Transparency" has been added to the Channel Box. Now we will connect this attribute to lambert1's transparency channel. With the circle still selected, open the Connection Editor. Its attributes should be loaded on the left. Your custom attribute of "transparency" should be all the way on the bottom of the list on the left. Now open the Hypershade (click Windows, Rendering Editors, Hypershade). Select lambert1 and in the Connection Editor click on Reload Right. The attributes of lambert1 should all load into the right pane. Now we will make the connection. Scroll down all the way in the left pane and find "transparency." Click on it and then find "transparency" in the right column as well. Click on the + symbol to expand its attributes and then click on transparency R, G, and B. If done correctly, it should look like Figure 9.14. The circle's custom attribute is now doing what is commonly called "driving" the transparency of lambert1.

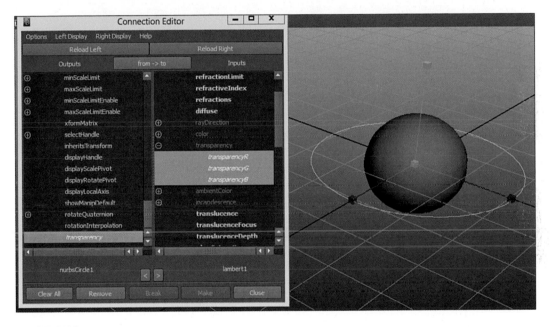

FIGURE 9.14
The new transparency attribute connected to the transparency R, G, and B attributes of the lambert1 material.

NOTE

Relationship Terms

Maya has a few different ways to connect attributes, but in general we use the term "driving" to indicate that attributes are connected, and to also indicate which attribute is the output and which attribute is the input. The output "drives" the input. This is worth mentioning because Maya also has something call "driven keys," which we will talk about in a bit.

Select the circle in the Persp panel, and in the Channel Box, click on the Transparency attribute and MMB drag back and forth to test out the connection. If working properly, the attribute will make it possible for you to control and animate the transparency of the material directly. In Figure 9.15, I have adjusted the attribute to .5, which is giving me a 50% transparent material.

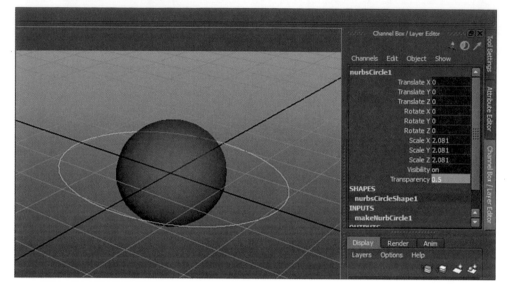

FIGURE 9.15
The connection is working properly; I have my attribute set to .5, and the sphere's material is showing a 50% transparency.

Other Relationships

There are more ways objects and attributes can relate to each other in Maya than simply being connected. This section details some of these ways.

Expressions

Expressions are small pieces of code that are executed as a scene updates. You can create expressions in the Script Editor, or you can create them in the Expression Editor. The syntax looks very similar to what you would expect from MEL script. For instance, to create the same functionality of the Translate Z driving the Scale Y of a sphere, you would type the following into the Expression Editor (click Window, Animation Editors, Expression Editor):

```
pSphere1.scaleY = pSphere1.translateZ
```

This is simply telling Maya that when it evaluates the transformations of pSphere1, to make the Scale Y equal to the Translate Z value.

Although there is really no limit to the functionality you can achieve with expressions, it should be noted that expressions are very high level, and as such are evaluated late in the process of a scene update and can slow down a scene considerably depending on what the expression is doing. There are many low-level nodes that are very fast and can offer the same functionality as an expression in most cases, and are not affected by the same problems, such as scene updating and the order of operations. Still, we will talk more about creating expressions in Hour 13, "Animation: Adding Movement to Your Scene."

Driven Keys

Driven keys are yet another way to make one node's attributes affect another's. This menu is found in the Animation menu set (press **F2**) by clicking Animate, Set Driven Key. The way it works is Maya allows you to have an attribute drive other attributes by using keys or points on a graph. For instance, you would set a key (make a graph point) at 0,0 by "keying" the transparency attribute at 0 while the transparency RGB is also at 0,0,0. Then key (make another graph point) at 1,1 by keying the transparency attribute at 1 while the transparency RGB is also at 1,1,1. Maya then interpolates the values in between, depending on the shape of the curve. I went ahead and keyed the same relationship I just described, and it looks like Figure 9.16.

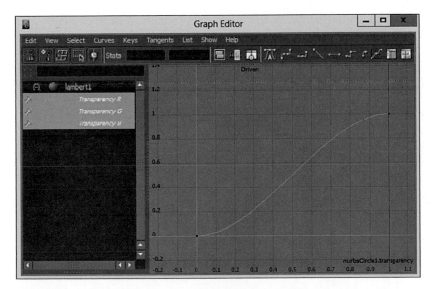

FIGURE 9.16
Driven keys provide a way to set up a relationship with fine control over the way the connected attributes behave. We will look closer at this type of relationship in Hour 13.

Driven keys have the benefit of working very well and updating in real time, but have the drawback of being very high level and, as such, cause scene slowdown. They might give a lot of control but they are not the most computationally inexpensive way to create relationships between nodes. We will go over driven keys in more depth in Hour 13.

The Relationship Editor

Now that we have seen the ways Maya offers to connect attributes, we should look at the Relationship Editor. This menu allows you to connect nodes in predefined ways to allow Maya to apply the correct effect, calculation, render, tool, and so on. Open the Relationship Editor by going to Window, Relationship Editors, Sets.

NOTE

One Relationship Editor

It's a little confusing the way Maya shows many different Relationship Editors when you go looking for the menu. There is really only one editor, but Maya offers the choices so that when you open the editor, it will display the correct nodes for you to connect.

Figure 9.17 shows the Relationship Editor open, with the Sets menu set loaded within it. Note that we will always choose what type of node we want to connect in this editor by using the drop-down box in the top left instead of opening a new Relationship Editor window through Maya's main menu.

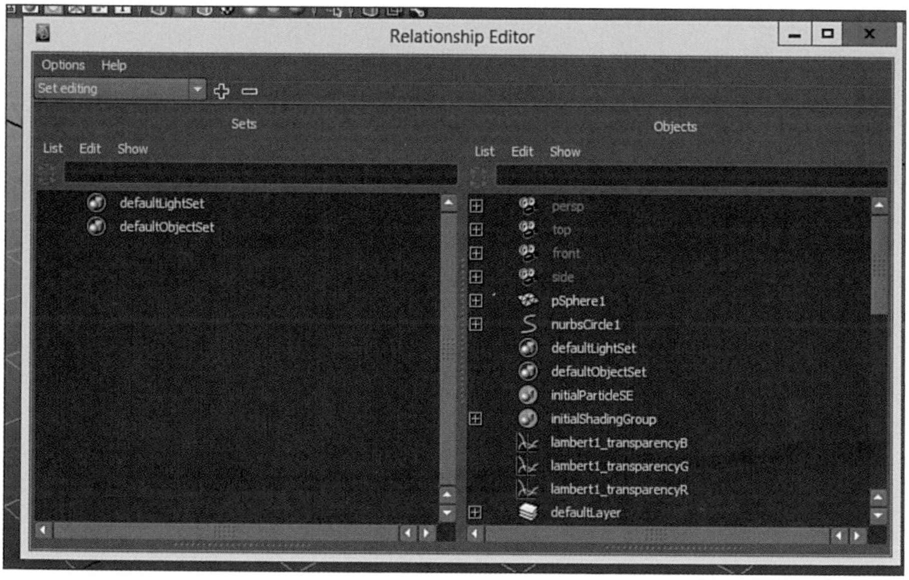

FIGURE 9.17
The Relationship Editor. Notice the drop-down box in the top left is where you can choose the menu set for the Relationship Editor only.

We used the Connection Editor first so that you would have some familiarity with the paradigm of choosing attributes on the left and connecting them on the right. This is the same thing. On the left pane, Maya displays all of the possible nodes you can use to create a relationship, and in the right pane, all of the possible nodes that can be included in that relationship. To create a relationship, or to include a node in a set, simply select the correct node on the left and then select the node you want to add on the right. Maya has this special editor because the tasks to create the relationships manually would be very tedious. Suffice it to say, this editor makes it very easy to include or exclude objects from a set you've created, make lights affect certain objects and not affect others, or choose what UV set a texture uses when it is applied to a mesh.

TRY IT YOURSELF ▼

Create More Relationships

Create a scene filled with connections and relationships to get some practice working with nodes and attributes.

1. Create a new Maya scene and create a handful of primitive objects.

2. Also create some materials and experiment with connecting some of the meshes' attributes to material attributes, such as the scale of an object connected to its own transparency.

3. Keep on practicing making connections and relationships until you are comfortable finding any object or node's attributes and connecting them in a desired way. Pay specific attention to the data type you are trying to connect and see which nodes are compatible for connecting.

Choosing the Right Relationship

In order to know how to connect nodes, you first need to decide what the functionality is supposed to be. If the connection is very simple, it is probably best to just connect the two nodes using the Connection Editor. For instance, if you want a sphere's Scale Y to be driven by its Translate Z, as we did in our example, then connecting the nodes is the simplest and fastest way to do that. When you start to need some more functionality, you still want to see if you can get the functionality out of a straight connection, because it is the fastest and lowest-level way to make nodes affect one another. For example, if you want a sphere's scale Y to equal *half* of its Translate Z, that is still possible with connections. Maya has a node (accessible in the Hypershade) called Multiply/Divide. This node allows you to input values and either multiply or divide them. In Figure 9.18, I connected the sphere's Translate Z attribute as the input into a Multiply/Divide node, which is set to multiply all values by .5, and then connected the output back to the sphere's Scale Y. This gives us the functionality we want using only connections that calculate quickly, update in real time, and are easier to modify and see than the other relationship types. You are not expected to know where to find these nodes or to be able to create this relationship type after only a few hours of exposure to Maya, but I've saved the file in this Hour's source files folder for you to see, as scale_Multiply.ma.

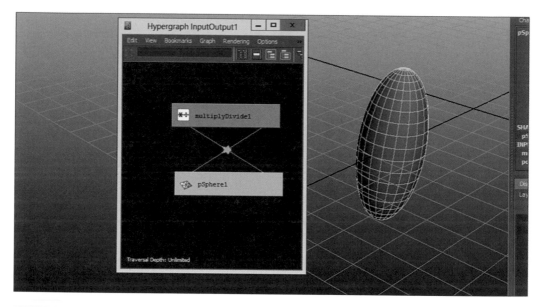

FIGURE 9.18
The Multiply/Divide node has both an input and an output connection. As you will see when you open the file, the Scale Y is exactly half the value of the Translate Z. Utility nodes like this one extend the functionality of connections and make a huge amount of control possible.

Now, the same type of functionality is possible with expressions. If we wanted this functionality with an expression, we would type the following in the Expression Editor:

```
pSphere1.scaleY = .5 * pSphere1.translateZ
```

As you might guess, the more complicated the relationship, the more difficult it can be to find the correct nodes to connect. Expressions might need to take over as the complexity goes too high to build the right node network for the result you desire. Finally, if control is really important, and you are going for an intuitive relationship, a driven key is a great idea. We will go over them in depth in Hour 13, but know that they offer an intuitive way to control the effect one node as on another—effects that could be extremely cumbersome to create with connected nodes, or require a very high level of math knowledge to achieve with expressions.

Depending on what you are looking for, choosing the right relationship to create normally starts with connections and then goes to expressions or driven keys as the complexity and/or control goes up.

VIDEO

Making Common Connections

In this video, I demonstrate some common connections artists make in Maya. I show some of the relationships that are made by default when you create objects in Maya, and how they are manipulated in real-world applications. We also view these connections in different editors.

Summary

We can view relationships in the Hypergraph and Hypershade, but also see what nodes are connected in many different editors and menus, including the Attribute Editor, the Channel Box, even RMB clicking on an object. To create connections, the easiest way is to use the Connection Editor. We tried a few connections ourselves and saw this functionality in work. There are a few different ways that nodes can be connected—be it with connections, driven keys, expressions, or in very low-level ways that Maya wants to handle, ways that we can modify using the Relationship Editor. This all-in-one editor holds the information regarding many relationships within Maya, ranging from light sets to character sets and UV sets. Last, to decide on how to create the right relationship, you should think about functionality and how complex the relationship needs to be, and then decide between a connection, expression, or driven keys, or if your relationship is one of the types Maya handles through the Relationship Editor.

Q&A

Q. Why can't I connect two attributes in the Connection Editor?

A. They are not compatible! You must make sure that the data you want to drive another attribute comes in the same format that the attribute reads. For instance, a color swatch reads data in the format [r,g,b], with each value being between 0 and 255. You can't simply connect a translation value to it; Maya doesn't know what to do with data coming in a different format.

Q. What is the fastest way to delete a connection?

A. If you want speed, the fastest way is to right-click on the attribute in either the Channel Box or Attribute Editor and choose Break Connections. This is break *all* of the connections on that attribute, though. If you have more than one connection, you may instead want to select the connection in the Hypershade or Hypergraph and delete it, or deselect the node in the Connection Editor.

Q. Why can't I change the value of a connected attribute?

A. You probably created the connection in the wrong direction. An attribute becomes basically locked when it has an input connection. You can only change the value of the attribute driving the connection, so check and see if you have the nodes switched in the Connection Editor.

Q. Why does the Relationship Editor not show any attributes?

A. The Relationship Editor connects nodes in predefined ways. For instance, it allows you to connect a UV set with a texture. This is a common task that in order to do manually through other editors would be cumbersome. Maya gives you this editor so that you can quickly create a small number of relationships that are common and essential to Maya. However, Maya can't predict the other *infinite* connections you can create with the Connection Editor, which is why it is totally open.

Workshop

The workshop contains quiz questions and exercises to help you solidify your understanding of the material covered. Try to answer all questions before looking at the "Answers" section that follows.

Quiz

1. Where is the Connection Editor found?

2. What does it mean that an attribute is "driving" another?

3. Which type of connection allows you to create keyframes that act as grid points to control a connection?

4. What are the drawbacks of using expressions to connect attributes?

5. How many different Relationship Editors are there?

Exercise

Try connecting many different attributes and see if you can create some interesting results. Explore the Hypershade's nodes, specifically the Utility nodes, and create some unique effects.

Answers

1. In Window, General Editors. For some reason, Maya does not centralize the Connection Editor, Expression Editor, or driven keys.

2. An attribute whose output is connected to the input of another node is "driving" that node.

3. Driven keys are relationships that are edited on a grid called the Graph Editor.

4. Expressions are calculated at a high level and therefore can be buggy and not evaluate correctly in a complex scene. They also can cause scene slowdown.

5. There is only one Relationship Editor. Maya breaks up the more common relationship types into different menus so that when you open the Relationship Editor, you are immediately presented with the correct menu set.

HOUR 10

Basic Rigging: Preparing Objects for Animation

What You'll Learn in This Hour:

▶ What a rig is and what should be rigged

▶ How to prepare an object to be rigged

▶ How to create a simple hierarchy

▶ What a rig's functionality should be

The objects that you've modeled so far have been at their very simplest polygonal and NURBS objects—basically, shape nodes contained in a transform node. Remember that a transform node is almost like an invisible box that holds the geometry and moves it around in space. For the purposes of animating objects, we have to create at the very least a simple hierarchy, and at most a fully deforming rig.

CAUTION

Setting the Project Before Starting

When we start working with rigs, no matter how simple they are, it is important to set your Maya project correctly. Without properly setting your project, you may run into many problems later referencing your files. Set your project to this Hour's files by going to File, Set Project... and then choose the folder where you've saved this Hour's files.

In this hour, you find out how to correctly set up an object with a simple rig. It will contain some interesting features even though it is still very basic. The most important thing to learn from this Hour is the steps you must take to make sure an object is ready for animation. Quite often, CG artists get lazy by the end of a project and just import geometry and try to move it around. This can lead to many headaches and having to redo work. Let's learn to avoid these problems.

What Is a Rig?

A *rig* is a control and deformation system created from curves, joints, groups, and other nodes to give animators the tools they need to create the movement desired. A rig is a complete system that contains all of the functionality that object will require. For instance, a very common rig is a "bouncing ball" rig. This rig needs to have movement controls for the ball mesh, squash, and stretch controls so that when the ball bounces, it looks realistic, rotation controls that allow the ball to roll along the ground, and perhaps even some extra added deformation controls so that an animator can make the ball look like it is performing anthropomorphized actions (looking, breathing, and so on). The most common rigs use NURBS curves exclusively for their controls systems. We will be looking at basic rigging principles in this Hour, and next Hour we'll rig the character we modeled in Hour 8, "Character Modeling."

NOTE

Environment Objects vs. Props

Not *everything* needs a rig to be used in a scene. You do not have to rig objects that are unmoving or are placed once in an environment. For instance, it is probably a good idea to have a chandelier model be separate from a living room model so you can work on them separately, and neither needs a rig if you are just going to be placing the chandelier in position when it's done. However, if a character in the scene is going to swing from the chandelier, now you need a rig for it as well.

Why We Rig

The most basic question about the necessity of creating rigs even for simple objects has many answers. Here are a few:

▶ Creating a rig for an object allows you to give an animator greater control over how the object moves.

▶ Creating a rig commonly entails adding extra deformation to an object, giving animators the ability to manipulate the geometry.

▶ Using a rig with common naming conventions allows for animation to be copied or retained from scene to scene.

▶ Geometry can be added or subtracted from a good rig, making it so that the modeling and the rigging can frequently occur at the same time by different artists.

▶ In order to create some complex systems such as constraints in the animation scene, it is necessary for an object to have more than one point of control, so we add them as we rig.

▶ Having one set rig for an object means that you do not have to redo work each time you start a new animation scene.

▶ Rigging an object signifies it is ready to be animated.

There are some other reasons, but these are the most common and important reasons to create rigs for objects you want to move and deform. Sure, you can add deformations in your animation files later, but you wouldn't want to re-create all of the controls on an object each time you want to animate it.

Preparing Your Mesh

The first thing we need to do is prepare the mesh to be rigged. Open hammer_Prep.ma in this Hour's folder. Frame the hammer in the Persp panel and change to the Persp/Outliner saved layout, like in Figure 10.1.

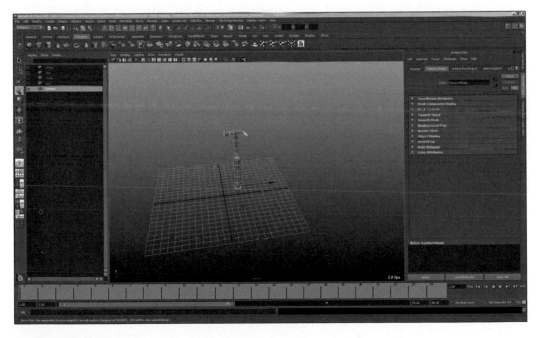

FIGURE 10.1
The Outliner is an essential window for creating rigs, because it shows the scene objects in hierarchy format.

Now select the hammer model. In the Channel Box, you will see some history and some transformations on the model, like in Figure 10.2.

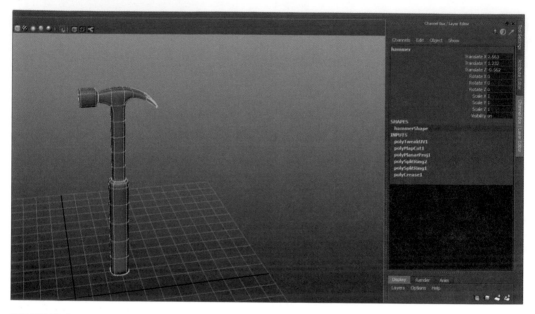

FIGURE 10.2
The Channel Box shows some history and transformations on our hammer model.

Delete the history by going to Edit, Delete by Type, History, or by pressing **Ctrl+Shift+D**. Before we remove the transformations on the model, we should center its pivot. The advantage to centering the pivot of an object is that the transform handles always center themselves at the pivot, which is more convenient. Because we are not going to ever animate the hammer model directly anymore (only using the controls we will set up now), the fact that an object also rotates and scales from its pivot doesn't affect the hammer. However, we will be making sure pivots are where we want them to be for our controls as we build our rig. Center the pivot of the hammer by going to Modify, Center Pivot. The pivot snaps to the average center of the vertices in the object. It should be in the middle of the handle of the hammer, as shown in Figure 10.3.

Now let's place the object at the world origin. Select the hammer, switch to the Move tool, and while holding down the **X** key (default for snapping to grid line), MMB drag the hammer to the center line in the grid, like in Figure 10.4.

This is important because we always want a value of 0,0,0 for the position of an object and a scale of 1. Objects that are scaled and transformed within a rig are considered messy and can misbehave when we try to animate or apply constraints to them. We now remove transformations by clicking on Modify, Freeze Transformations. After that is done, the Channel Box should have no transformations showing, as in Figure 10.5.

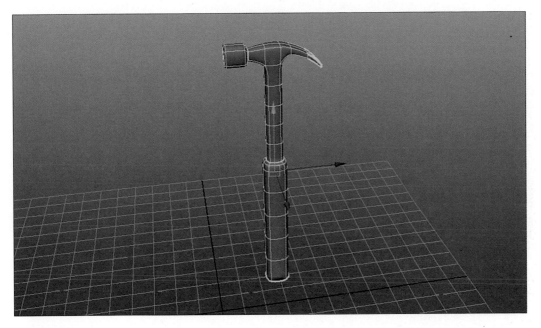

FIGURE 10.3
The pivot is now centered on the hammer.

FIGURE 10.4
The hammer has been moved to the world origin. This is helpful because now at a glance we can see if the hammer has transformations on it or not, which is essential for proper rigging.

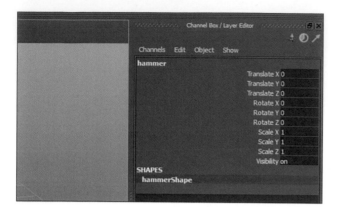

FIGURE 10.5
The channels are all zeroed, signifying the hammer now has its origin at the world origin. Again, this is all good workflow for rigging.

NOTE

Long List of Errors

The steps we've taken to conform the mesh to a good start for rigging are the minimum that may be required. There may be multiple errors in the model itself—from flipped normal, open edges, and multiple faces on top of each other, to name a few. The steps to center the pivot, remove transformations, and return an object to the world origin should be done after you are sure your mesh doesn't contain any other errors. The hammer model we are using is free from errors. To see if your model is suffering from some of the errors I mentioned, you can switch to the Polygons menu set by pressing **F3** and clicking on Mesh, Cleanup.... This tool will diagnose your mesh, but know that there are many errors beyond what this tool can diagnose. Maya gives you immense freedom and power when creating objects, but that comes with the possibility to create some messy geometry. Work methodically and carefully to avoid most problems.

Simple Hierarchy

Now that the mesh is conformed, we are ready to build some controls into it. Notice in the Outliner that the hammer doesn't have any hierarchy; it exists in world space on its own. Figure 10.6 shows the Outliner of our scene and the lone hammer mesh like I described.

A good prop rig starts with creating a few nested groups. This simple hierarchy is in place to separate the geometry and the control system of a rig. Follow the next few steps to get this hierarchy started:

▶ Select the hammer and press **Ctrl+G**.

▶ This creates a group holding the hammer.

▶ Rename the group to hammer_Geo_GRP by double-clicking on the name in the Outliner or in the Channel Box.

▶ In the Outliner, select hammer_Geo_GRP and press **Ctrl+G** again.

▶ Rename the new group hammer_Rig.

FIGURE 10.6
Our Hammer model is sitting alone in the Outliner. There is no hierarchy yet.

Now you should have a hierarchy that looks like the one in Figure 10.7.

FIGURE 10.7
The beginnings of a hierarchy. The geo group provides us some very useful functionality, described in the next section of this Hour.

The Geo Group

The purpose of creating the hammer_Geo_GRP is two-fold. First and most simply, a geo group organizes your objects into categories. It is a good idea to keep your scene organized, and even if you were not creating a rig, it is recommended that you use groups to do so. Secondly, one of the most advantageous benefits of rigging even simple props is that you can often apply modifications to the entire group itself. Doing so makes it so that if you want to add or remove geometry from a rig, you need only place the object into the group. Of course, some functionality is more complex than this, but for simple, non-deforming rigs this is actually enough to get the functionality you need.

Adding Controls

Now that we have the basic hierarchy, let's add a control. Follow these next steps to get a NURBS circle in position to act as a control:

▶ Create a NURBS circle by clicking Create, NURBS Primitives, Circle.

▶ Create the circle by clicking and dragging anywhere on the grid near the hammer, releasing when the circle is about three times the diameter of the handle.

▶ Rename the circle to hammer_CTRL.

▶ Move the circle to the origin by switching to the Move tool (**w**) and holding down the **X** key as you MMB drag the circle to the world origin.

▶ Move the circle downward until it sits in the middle of the hammer's handle.

▶ Click on Modify, Freeze Transforms to remove all transform information from the NURBS circle.

▶ Press **Ctrl+G** to make a group containing this circle.

▶ In the Outliner, rename this group to hammer_Ctrl_GRP.

▶ In the Outliner, select hammer_Ctrl_GRP and Ctrl+click on hammer_Rig, and press **P**. This parents the new group under the rig group. Alternatively, you can MMB drag a group onto another to parent it.

Your Outliner should now look like the one in Figure 10.8.

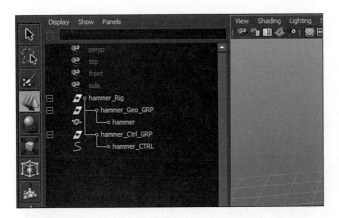

FIGURE 10.8
Our Outliner is starting to fill up. The control group holds rig controllers we will use to manipulate the geometry.

With the control group created and parented underneath the main rig group, it is now time to make sure the control is actually controlling the motion of the geometry. Follow the next few steps to create this relationship:

- ▶ In the Outliner, select hammer_CTRL and Ctrl-click on the hammer_Geo_GRP.
- ▶ Press **F2** to change to the Animation Menu set.
- ▶ Click on Constrain, Parent. The default options will suffice.
- ▶ Click on Constrain, Scale. The default options will suffice.
- ▶ Save your scene.

Test your new functionality. Select the hammer_CTRL and move, rotate, and scale it. You now have a control that is easy to see, easy to manipulate, and can transform anything that is placed inside the geo group. Let's test that theory:

- ▶ Return the control back to its starting position by clicking on Modify, Reset Transformations.
- ▶ Create a primitive sphere anywhere near your hammer.
- ▶ Select the sphere and the hammer_Geo_GRP by Ctrl-clicking in the outliner.
- ▶ Press **P** to parent the sphere in the geo group.
- ▶ Move and rotate the hammer_CTRL and see the sphere "riding" around with the hammer, as in Figure 10.9.

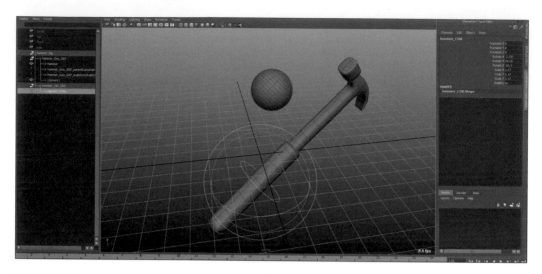

FIGURE 10.9
The sphere "rides" around in the geometry group nicely. We will take advantage of geometry groups frequently with character rigging.

Reset Transformations on your hammer_CTRL once again and select and delete the sphere; we no longer need the sphere because it won't be a part of our actually hierarchy.

Adding Functionality

We now need to decide what the functionality of this rig should be. Should the hammer be able to squash and stretch, should it be able to bend and twist? All of these questions should be answered by what you need the hammer to do in the animation scenes you have planned. The determining factors will be:

▶ Is the animation cartoony or realistic?

▶ Is the object going to be picked up and passed around a lot?

▶ Is the object going to attach to several different things over the course of a single shot?

And many more. For our purposes, let's assume that our scenes are going to be slightly cartoony, and so we'll want to add a little bit of bending to the hammer so that as a character swings the hammer, it can bend a little bit in air. This effect will give more impact to a fast swing, and is easy to set up.

Creating the Bend

Maya is packed with powerful deformation tools. Creating a bend control for the hammer is actually quite easy. Follow these steps to do so:

▶ Select the hammer geometry.

▶ Switch to the Animation menu set by pressing **F2**.

▶ Click on Create Deformers, Non Linear, Bend.

▶ Move the bend so that its center is at the point where the top of the hammer handle meets the shaft.

▶ In the Channel Box, click on "bend1" under Inputs.

▶ Change Low Bound to 0.

▶ In the Outliner, select bend1Handle and Ctrl-click on hammer_Geo_GRP.

▶ Press **P** to parent the bend handle under the geo group. The bend will now follow the movements of the group.

We're almost done. We want to control the amount of bend with the one control we've created. These next steps will make it so our hammer_CTRL will control the amount of bend in the hammer:

▶ Select the hammer_CTRL.

▶ In the Channel Box, click on Edit, Add Attribute.

▶ Make the long name "Bend," make the Minimum –8, the Maximum 8, and the default 0. Leave everything else the same and click Add.

▶ Click on Windows, General Editors, Connection Editor.

▶ The control's attributes will load on the left automatically. Click on bend1 in the Channel Box, and in the Connection Editor, click on Load Right.

▶ In the left pane of the Connection Editor, scroll to the bottom and click on "bend."

▶ Scroll down in the right pane of the Connection Editor until you find the "curvature" attribute and then click on it.

Now the hammer_CTRL's "bend" attribute actually controls the amount of bend in the hammer. Test it out by selecting hammer_CTRL and MMB dragging the "bend" attribute back and forth in the Channel Box. You should get results like Figure 10.10.

FIGURE 10.10
The bend deformer being controlled by the hammer_CTRL. Everything is working as expected. You now have a bending hammer rig!

▼ TRY IT YOURSELF

Create Some Practice Rigs

Take some completed prop models and create basic rigs for these objects. If you don't have any models, there are some extras included in the Bonus folders for Hour 4, "Modeling with Polygonal Geometry" and Hour 5, "Modeling NURBS Curves and Surfaces."

1. Conform the geometry by freezing transforms, deleting history, and checking that the models are created cleanly.

2. Create simple controls out of NURBS curves and constrain the geometry groups to the controls.

3. Try adding custom attributes to the controls, and connecting these attributes to deformers found in the Animation Menu set (found by pressing **F2**).

VIDEO

Good Prop Rigging Workflow

In this bonus video, I demonstrate rigging a prop for animation. We will walk through all of the important steps, and you will get to see a good workflow in practice. In particular, note how meticulously I pay attention to issues such as freezing transforms, making neatly organized groups, and using a naming convention.

Summary

It is highly recommended you put the time in to create controls rigs for your animated objects. A rig will give you many added benefits over simply manipulating the geometry—most notably the ability to reuse modifications to a mesh across multiple scene files. You must first prepare your mesh for rigging, by removing history and centering the object in the scene. Next, create a few nested groups that will contain the different types of objects contained in a rig. This is done for organization, as well as for the functionality of being able to freely add objects to the geometry group. Last, add your controls in the form of NURBS curves and set up the relationships. Decide on extra functionality you need and add this functionality in the form of extra attributes to your rig.

Q&A

Q. Why is my pivot outside my object when I center it?

A. When you center your pivot, Maya averages the position of all of the vertices and places the pivot where that average is. For some meshes, that means it will be outside the shell of the polygons. A torus, or donut shape, for example, has a pivot centered where there is no geometry encasing it.

Q. I have seen NURBS curves in very different shapes on rigs in the past. How do I make those?

A. Any NURBS curve is acceptable for a controller. You can download many tools online that provide free controllers for use in rigging, or you can create them yourself. Using the EP Curve tool, you can try drawing some shapes in panel that indicate what a controller is used for. For instance, it's common that eye controllers are shaped like eyeballs.

Q. Why do we need so many groups?

A. Three groups is nothing! Groups offer a lot of functionality. First, they let you organize your objects. They also act as "containers" for your objects, allowing you to manipulate more than one object at a time. Complex rigs might have dozens of groups for the sole purpose of giving fine control over objects.

Q. I can scale both the hammer_Rig and the hammer_CTRL. Which one should I use to scale the hammer?

A. You have stumbled across a common issue in rigging. Sometimes more than one control offers the same functionality. If it is a good rig, you need only choose the control that makes sense to you and stick with it. Most often, though, you want to do all of your animation with the controls that have been specifically created to perform a function; look for NURBS curves provided for you and use those over using groups in the Outliner.

Workshop

The workshop contains quiz questions and exercises to help you solidify your understanding of the material covered. Try to answer all questions before looking at the "Answers" section that follows.

Quiz

1. What is the hotkey for creating a group?

2. Clearing transforms and setting an object's current position to 0,0,0 and scale to 1 is called doing what?

3. All controls on a proper rig are made from what type of geometry?

4. What group would you add an object to in order for it to be moved by the hammer_CTRL?

5. Adding an attribute to a controller is best achieved through which panel?

Exercise

Try creating a rig for another prop you have modeled. Don't forget to spend a little time preparing the model for rigging by removing history, centering the object, and freezing transforms. Follow the same protocol we used to rig this hammer, and think ahead in terms of what kind of functionality your object will need. Should it squash, stretch, twist? Start simple and don't get ahead of yourself; we'll move onto more complex rigs in the next Hour.

Answers

1. **Ctrl+G** creates a group, and will place selected objects into that group. If no objects are selected, Maya creates an empty group (which is just a transform node).

2. This is called "freeze transformations," and is accessible by clicking Modify, Freeze Transformations.

3. A good rig has only NURBS curves as controllers. They are easy to see, do not render, and are simple to manipulate.

4. "hammer_Geo_GRP" is constrained to the control, so all objects within this group move with it.

5. The Channel Box is the simplest panel to use. Click on Edit, Add Attribute to add any custom attribute to any selected object.

HOUR 11

Character Rigging: Articulating Characters

What You'll Learn in This Hour:

▶ How to create skeleton systems for characters

▶ How to use curves as controls

▶ How to connect the curves to your skeleton

▶ What other types of controls there are on a character rig

To create realistic and engaging character performances, 3D artists must first create all of the articulation in the model. The limbs must be able to bend, the body must be able to deform, the mouth must open and close, and so on. We've created a simple rig for your hammer prop; now it's time to see how skeleton systems work. We will use a combination of joints and deformers to make a rig for our character.

TIP

Track Your Progress

Rigging can be finicky in Maya. It is also cumbersome to remember the steps you have taken in your rigging process, no matter what program you are using. Especially if you are taking multiple work sessions to complete a rig, you should keep a log of what you have done. Then, when you sit down to work further on your rig, you will not be lost as you stare at a half-completed rig. Also, this log will serve as a record of what is working and what is not, allowing you to troubleshoot the rig as it is created.

In this hour, you will create a character rig for our character, Sam. In doing so, you will be exposed to skeleton systems in Maya and how to correctly place and order joints. When you are finished with the joints, you will create controllers and deformers that give the character extra articulation, which in turn allows an animator to create richer, more entertaining performances.

Joints

Skeleton systems in Maya are made up of connected objects called joints. It can be a little confusing at first to say "joint" when you mean a bone, but the confusion quickly subsides when
you realize that the only information that is really essential to a joint is the rotation of its pivot.
Therefore, we are really only concerned with the actual joint itself, because it tells us the orientation of the bone it is connected to. Don't worry if it *still* seems hard to grasp because we'll create
some joints and see exactly what it means to connect them. Do as follows:

- Create a new scene in Maya.
- Switch to the Animation menu set (**F2**).
- Click on Skeleton, Joint Tool.
- In the Persp panel, click anywhere on the grid to place your first joint; then click two more
  times to create a simple skeleton, like in Figure 11.1
- Exit out of the Joint tool by pressing **E** to switch to the rotate tool; we'll rotate the joints
  later on, but for now let's discuss what was created.

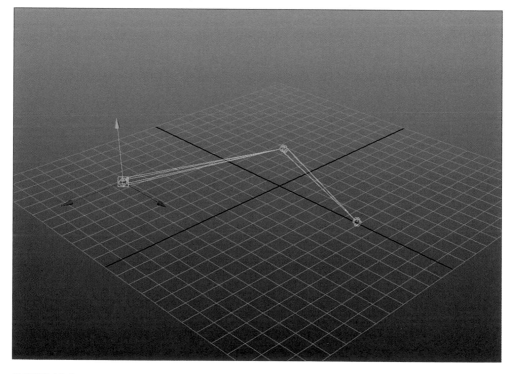

FIGURE 11.1
A simple skeleton containing three joints. It sort of resembles an elbow, doesn't it? These joints contain
rotational information that will be used to deform our character later.

Our simple skeleton contains three joints. If you look in the Outliner (Window, Outliner), you will see that the joints are automatically created in a hierarchy according to the order they were created. That's because a skeleton is, by definition, a hierarchy—joints that rotate their children, which rotate their children, and so on. Think of your arm: Your shoulder rotates your whole arm, the elbow rotates just the forearm, the wrist rotates just the hand. Just like in real life, a joint in Maya rotates all of the joints below it. This relationship is called Forward Kinematics.

Forward Kinematics Versus Inverse Kinematics

Any simple joint chain is considered an "FK Chain." Forward Kinematics (FK) means that each joint moves and rotates its children. In our case, Joint 1 rotates Joints 2 and 3, Joint 2 only rotates itself and Joint 3, and so on. The other type of motion you can apply to a skeleton system is called inverse kinematics (IK). This type of motion allows a child joint to dictate the orientation of the parent joints. However, this type of motion also requires a solver (a small calculation running in the background of Maya) to work correctly. To see the difference between FK and IK, follow these simple steps. (Make sure there is nobody standing next to you, or they might get whacked!)

▶ Hold your right arm out to your side.

▶ Place your left finger in the bend of your right elbow, and bend just your elbow. Imagine that in Maya you have selected the elbow joint and are rotating it.

▶ Notice that when you bend just your elbow, your hand moves with your forearm. This is Forward Kinematics. All of the child joints of the elbow are "along for the ride."

▶ Now grab your right wrist with your left hand.

▶ Relax your right hand so that the left hand is holding 100% of the weight of the arm.

▶ Move your right wrist around with your left hand.

▶ Notice how your shoulder *and* elbow both bend so that you are *able* to move your wrist where you want it.

▶ Imagine in Maya you are grabbing the wrist controller and are placing it where you want it to be, and the elbow and shoulder joints are automatically "solving" to give you the result you want. This is Inverse Kinematics.

We will build a skeleton that can utilize both FK and IK in our rig, as certain character movements require access to either FK or IK motion.

Starting a Rig

A little bit of cleanup is necessary before you start a rig. Open sam_Rig_Start.ma in this Hour's source files. As you can see in Figure 11.2, Sam has been positioned so he is "standing" on the ground, and his pivot repositioned to the world origin. This makes things easy to see if you are creating the rig in the correct position.

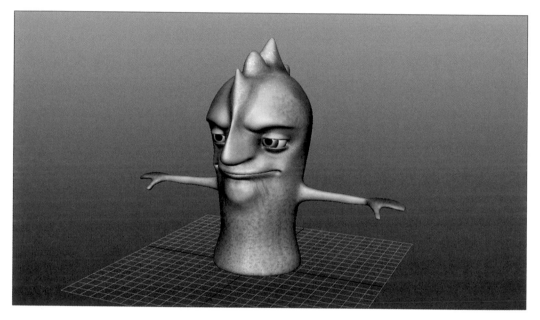

FIGURE 11.2
The character model is zeroed and ready to be rigged.

I have also deleted history on the model and created a simple texture for our character. Texturing can be done at any point after UVs are created.

CAUTION

Changing the Model

It is quite cumbersome to change topology of a character after it is skinned (attached to a rig). However, at this point, the position of the model is all that we are concerned with. It is typical for riggers to start a rough rig at the same time modeling is being completed, all while the texture artists are developing the look.

Placing Joints

We will first place the joints that will serve as the spine. Follow these steps:

▶ Activate the Joint tool by going to Skeleton, Joint Tool.

▶ In the front panel, press and hold the **X** key to snap to grid lines and then click on the world origin. A joint will appear.

▶ Still holding **X**, place two more joints above the first, spaced every other grid line, as in Figure 11.3.

▶ When you are done, press **Enter**.

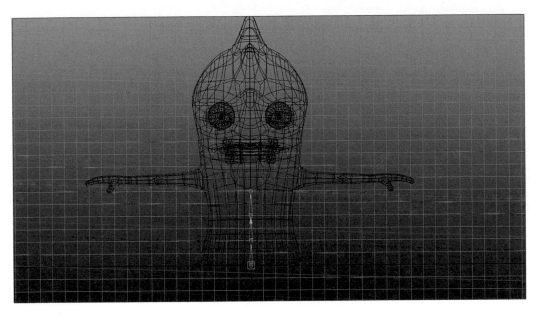

FIGURE 11.3
The three joints of the spine. We snapped to the grid lines because we want our skeleton directly in the middle of the rig.

Let's keep going:

▶ Select the Joint tool again or press **Y** to activate the last tool.

▶ In the front panel, click on the top spine joint to connect newly placed joints to this chain. Place a joint just to the right of the top spine joint. This joint will be connected to spine4.

▶ Click again at the root of the shoulder to place a joint there.

▶ Place a joint at the center of the elbow.

▶ Place joints on the wrist, the first knuckle, and the second knuckle. When you are done, press **Enter**, and your joints should look like Figure 11.4.

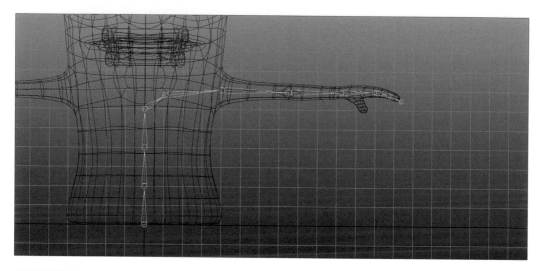

FIGURE 11.4
The arm joints are placed in the front panel. We only need two knuckles in a "mitten" type of hand because it doesn't have the resolution or detail of a realistic hand.

▶ Starting with the first bone, select the bones you've created, one at a time, and in the Channel Box, rename them to Spine1, Spine2, Spine3, l_Spine4, l_Shoulder, l_UpperArm, l_ForeArm, l_Wrist, l_Knuckle1, and l_Knuckle2, respectively.

▶ In the top panel, move the arm joints into correct position, as shown in Figure 11.5.

▶ Choose the Joint tool again or press **Y**. In the top panel, click on the l_Wrist bone to connect newly place joints to this chain.

▶ Create three joints that represent the thumb, as in Figure 11.6.

▶ Remember to use the Move tool and not the Rotate tool when positioning the joints.

▶ Press **Enter** when you are done and then rename the joints l_Thumb1 and l_Thumb2.

TIP

Joint Display

Joints have their own scale that is separate from their display size. Maya does this so that you can make joints of any length and not be confused as to the scale of the joint when looking at a skeleton. To make our joints an appropriate size for the model we are using, go to Display, Animation, Joint Size.... In the dialog box that opens, change the size to .5 and press **Enter**.

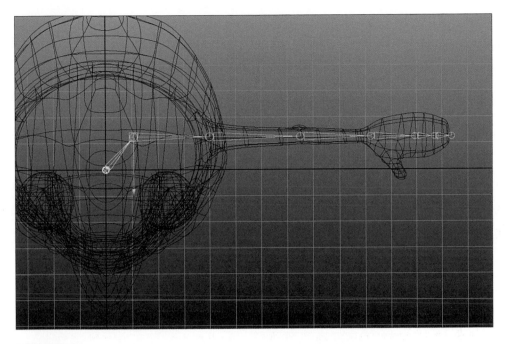

FIGURE 11.5
The joints we just created need to be lined up with the arms, like shown.

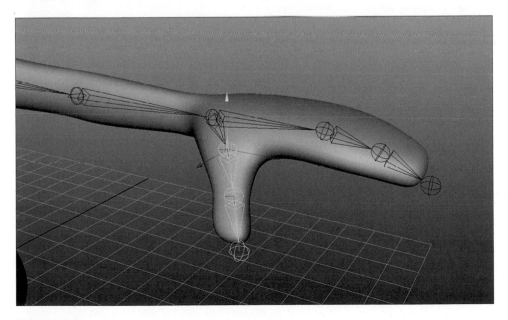

FIGURE 11.6
The thumb joints are added. Do not rotate the joints when placing them; instead, use the Move tool. The reason is you want your joints to have zero rotations when you attach the geometry (skinning).

Mirroring Joints

We do not want to attempt to re-create the arm joint chain on the other side of our character's skeleton. Fortunately, Maya has simple commands that allow you to mirror a joint across the world center axis. We will do this to get his right arm joints in place, as follows:

- ▶ Select the l_Shoulder joint. In the Animation menu set, click on Skeleton, Mirror Joint and the options box □.

- ▶ In the options box, choose the YZ.

- ▶ Mirroring has the option to rename joints based on a search string. This is handy so you don't have to spend a lot of time renaming joints. In the top field, enter **l_** and in the bottom field, enter **r_**.

- ▶ Click on Mirror.

- ▶ You will see your left arm joints are now mirrored into the right arm, as in Figure 11.7.

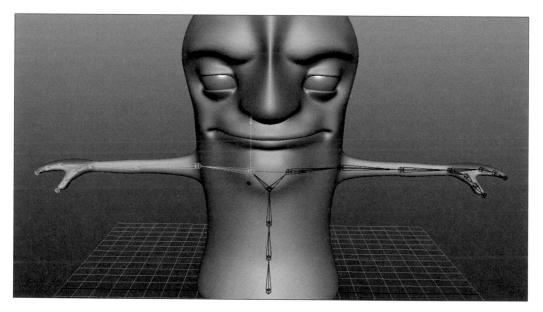

FIGURE 11.7
The arm joints have been mirrored across the center axis. You will also note that the joints have been renamed with the corresponding right-side prefix of "r_".

Finishing the Joint Chain

We will now place the last few joints to complete this skeleton. Follow these steps:

- ▶ Load the Joint tool again and in the front panel, while holding **X**, click on the spine4 joint.

- ▶ Click and place a joint on the center axis one gridline upward in Y.

- ▶ Place another joint one more gridline upward in Y.

- ▶ Place a final joint on the gridline that intersects the top of his head and then press **Enter**.

- ▶ In the Persp panel, move the joints back in Z until they are relatively centered in the character's head, as shown in Figure 11.8.

- ▶ Rename the two new joints "neck" and "skull."

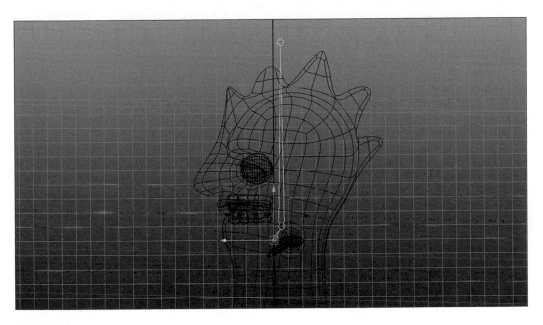

FIGURE 11.8
The rest of the spine (neck and head joints are considered part of the spine) added and moved into the center of the character's head.

CAUTION

Extra Joints

Maya draws a visual helper ("bones") between two joints, so the result of creating a single visual "bone" is actually two joints—one that is the joint you are actually rotating and another to determine the length of the "bone." Even though for visual reference it is nice to have a "bone" that goes through the geometry, in reality, the very last joint you create will always be useless. Take a look at the joints at the end of the fingers, the thumb, and the head. They all will be excluded from our deformations. Rename all of them to nullJNT1, nullJNT2, and so on.

Jaw Joint

The ideal placement for the jaw is such that the point of rotation will mean that the chin and lower lip geometry won't shear or intersect into the body too quickly. On a human character, the rotation point would be in front of the ear. On our character, the rotation point should be lower down so that the jaw doesn't rotate into the body very much. Don't forget to rename the end joints on the jaw and the head to "null."

Add the jaw joints, as shown in Figure 11.9.

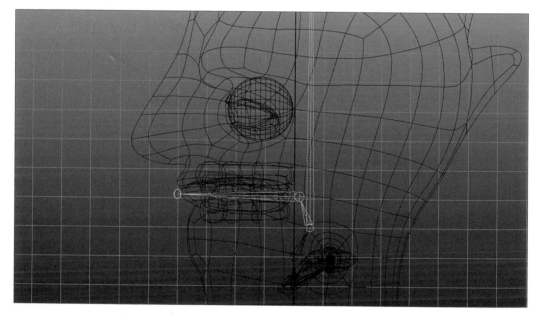

FIGURE 11.9
The jaw joint placed properly. Remember that the joint on the end of the jaw is a null.

Joint Orientation

It is good to be in control of the orientation of your joints (in other words, the axes that each joint will use to rotate locally). Selecting the spine1 joint and switching to rotate (press E) shows that locally, the joint wishes to rotate in its Y axis when in actuality it is rotating in the world X axis. This may differ slightly from what you have created, because Maya chooses orientation at creation based on factors such as if the child joint is lined up perfectly along an axis with its parent. It is generally accepted that Y should always point "down" the bone. In Maya, we call this the "primary axis." We will reorient the joints we've created to make sure they have the correct axes. Do as follows:

- Shift-select all of the joints in the spine, starting with spine1 and going all the way up to the null joint on top of the head.

- Go to Skeleton, Orient Joint and click the options box □.

- In the box that opens, choose Orient Joint to World and then click Apply.

- The joints in the spine should be oriented to the world axis now.

Because many factors affect the orientation of your joints, the rest of the joints you've created may not look like the ones created for this book. Therefore, it will take some experimentation with the Orient tool to make sure your joints are oriented properly. To fast forward to a finished, oriented joint chain, open sam_Rig_Orient.ma. You will see the joints have been all oriented so that the Y axis points "down" the joint and that the most common axis of rotation is the X axis. We can add some controls to this chain.

Adding IK to the Arms

We will add an IK handle to the arms to allow you to move them using an IK solver. Therefore, instead of having to rotate the shoulder, elbow, and wrist in that order to attain a certain arm pose, you can simply position the wrist, and the elbow and shoulder will rotate to compensate.

We first need to make sure the arms are going to give the IK solver the correct start orientation. The IK solver will make the elbow bend in the direction that is parallel to the alignment of the joints. Therefore, because we want it to bend in Y, the joints need to be aligned in Y. Do these steps:

- Select the shoulder, elbow, and wrist joints in both arms.

- In the front panel, hold down **X** and translate them in Y to the nearest gridline to snap them all to the same Y height.

- Let go of **X** and move just the shoulder joints back into position in the middle of the arms.

- Now in the top panel, select both of the elbow joints and move them *slightly* backward in Z. A tiny little bit will do.

Follow these few steps to add the IK handle:

- In the Animation menu set, click on Skeleton, IK Handle Tool, and the options box □.

- In the Tool Settings, under Current Solver, choose ikRPsolver. This is a solver that allows you to create a "pole vector," or an object that the elbow points at.

- Click on the joint l_UpperArm and then click on the joint l_Wrist.

- ▶ Maya will create an IK handle on the wrist and exit the tool.

- ▶ Press **Y** to activate the last tool again, and repeat the process on the right side of the character rig.

- ▶ With both IK handles created, your rig should look like the one in Figure 11.10.

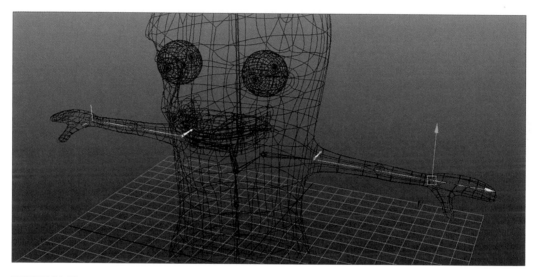

FIGURE 11.10
The IK handles added to our aligned arms.

- ▶ Select the IK handles and move them to test the motion you are getting. Press **Z** (or undo) to reset their positions back when you are done moving them.

- ▶ Now we will create the pole vector objects. Click on Create, Locator.

- ▶ Move the locator while holding down the **V** key so it will snap to the center of the left elbow joint. Once it is in position, press **Ctrl+D** to duplicate this locator.

- ▶ Repeat on the right side. Select both locators and move –5 units in Z, like in Figure 11.11.

- ▶ Click Modify, Freeze Transformations.

- ▶ Name them l_Elbow_PV and r_Elbow_PV, respectively.

- ▶ Select l_Elbow_PV and Shift-select the left wrist's IK handle. Click on Constrain, Pole Vector. The elbow will now point toward this locator so you may use it to adjust the angle of the arm pose.

- ▶ Repeat the constraint on the other side of the mesh.

- ▶ Test the results by moving the IK handles, and subsequently moving the pole vector locators.

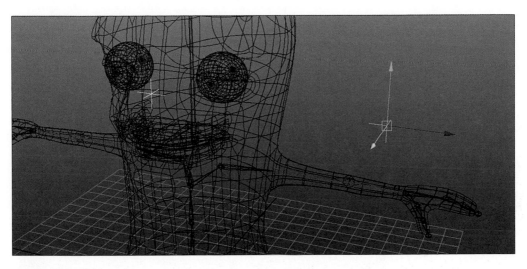

FIGURE 11.11
These locators will be our elbow pole vectors. Here, they are positioned directly behind the elbows so that when they are constrained, the joints will not reorient in any way.

Adding Controls

We will add NURBS curves to our character to serve as controllers on this rig. Commonly the controls will move the joints using constraints. Sometimes controls will be added to edit attributes on nodes connected to the rig. They may even control deformers added on top of the skeleton system.

Open sam_Rig_Controls.ma. This scene has some NURBS controls created for you, as you can see in Figure 11.12.

We now will position the main controller for our character, normally referred to as the "Master":

▶ Move the large four-pointed arrow object to the world origin by moving it while holding down X.

▶ Rename it master_Control.

▶ Click on Modify, Freeze Transformations.

NOTE

Freezing Everything

When you are creating controls for a rig, you want to freeze transformations on all controls when you have sized and positioned them correctly. This is because you want to be sure if an animator selects all of the controls and resets the transformations to zero, that the rig will be in its "start" position.

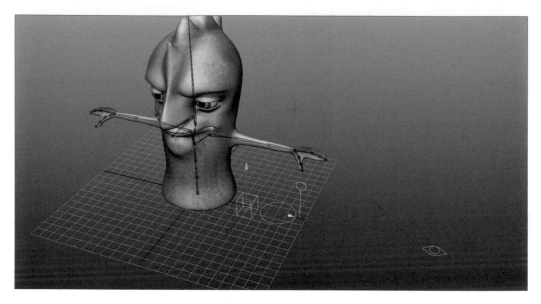

FIGURE 11.12
I've gone ahead and loaded some controls into the scene so you do not have to spend time creating these shapes out of NURBS curves.

▶ Select the circle NURBS object that is on the ground.

▶ Press **Ctrl+D** to duplicate it.

▶ Move the new circle to the spine2 joint by holding down **V** as you move it. It will snap to vertices as well as joints, so take care in making sure you are snapping it to the right one.

▶ Scale it up so that the curve is a good size outside the mesh of the character.

▶ Duplicate this curve again by pressing **Ctrl+D** and position the new curve on the spine3 joint. Size it accordingly.

▶ Repeat duplicating, positioning, and scaling until you have controls for all of the joints of the spine (including the head and neck).

▶ Once you have positioned (don't forget to snap by holding down **V**) and scaled the controls, select them all and click on Modify, Freeze Transformations.

▶ Rename these curves to their respective joints. For instance, the curve position at the spine2 joint would be called spine2_CTRL. The abbreviated, uppercase suffix is a good way to distinguish your controls from other NURBS curves you may have in the scene (for modeling purposes or other reasons).

▶ When you are done, your scene should look like Figure 11.13.

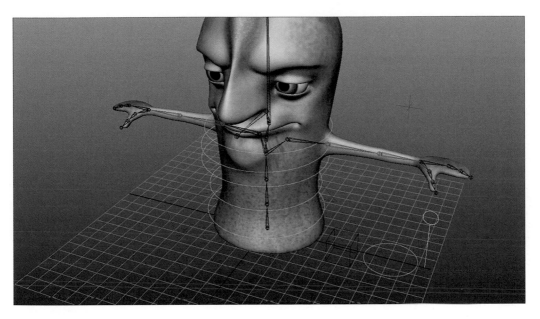

FIGURE 11.13
The controls for the spine are in place.

▶ Now move the cube control that is on the ground to the lWrist joint by holding **V** while moving. (You generally want to use different control shapes for different functionalities. In this case, the circle represents FK rotations, and the cube represents IK movement.)

▶ Scale it to be an appropriate size.

▶ Freeze Transformations on the cube.

▶ Duplicate it by pressing **Ctrl+D**.

▶ Move it to the rWrist joint by holding down **V** while moving.

▶ Freeze Transformations on this new cube.

▶ Rename the two cubes lWrist_CTRL and rWrist_CTRL, respectively.

▶ Select lWrist_CTRL, duplicate it, and move it to the position of lElbow_PoleVector.

▶ Scale it down, freeze transforms, and then repeat the duplicate+freeze process for the right pole vector. (We want all controls to be NURBS curves, remember? We'll have to replace the locator with this cube.) It should look like Figure 11.14.

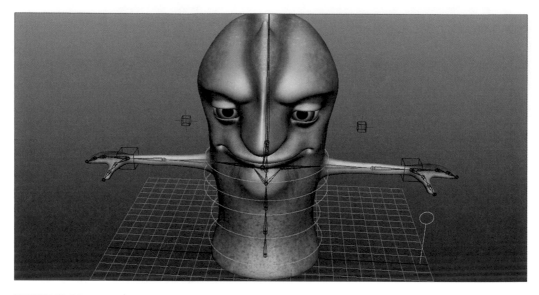

FIGURE 11.14
The controls for the arm are now in place.

Remember, Forward Kinematics means that a parent joint will move its child joints, which in turn will move its child joints, and so on. We added an IK handle to our character's arms. Therefore, the arms will be controlled by translating the wrist controls and then positioning the elbow using the elbow pole vector.

NOTE

FK/IK Switches

Commonly, rigs are made so that you can switch between FK and IK control on the limbs. Although this is a great trick to know, it would take too many pages to include in this hour. The basic concept is you use the ikBlend attribute on an ikhandle to change between FK and IK on an IK chain. You need to constrain controls for FK rotations to each joint in addition to constraining an IK control for the IK movement. You can give it a try if you'd like, and look at the finished rig included with this Hour's extra files to see this switch in action.

I have taken the liberty of adding the controls on the fingers. I did this because we needed to parent the finger controls under a group that has been rotated to be aligned with the joints of the fingers. In the next section, you will start from this file.

Connecting Controls

The final step of adding controls is connecting them to the joints. In most cases, we will use constraints to connect the controls. Open sam_Rig_Controls_Done.ma and see the controls in the correct positions. There is also a world_Mover_CTRL that is added to give us the ability to position and scale the entire rig before creating animation. Follow these steps to connect the controls:

▶ We first need our controls to be in the correct hierarchy before we connect the joints. Select head _CTRL, Shift-select neck_CTRL, and then press **P**. The head is now a child of the neck.

▶ Select neck_CTRL, Shift-select spine4_CTRL, and then press **P**.

▶ Repeat these steps until you have created the hierarchy of the spine all the way down to master_CTRL, which should be the uppermost parent node.

▶ Don't forget to add jaw_CTRL by parenting it to head_CTRL.

Normally, IK hands stay completely independent of the spine hierarchy so they can be placed on an object and stay still as the rest of the body moves. We'll leave them out of the spine hierarchy, but we'll make them part of world_Mover_CTRL's hierarchy so they scale and move with the entire rig if you want to position Sam in your scene. Select both instances of wrist_CTRL and both instances of elbow_PoleVector and then Shift-select world_Mover_CTRL and press **P**. Parent eye_Target_CTRL to world_Mover_CTRL as well. Now we'll connect the joints to these controls:

▶ Select master_CTRL and Shift-select the spine1 joint.

▶ In the Animation menu set (**F2**), click on Constrain, Parent, and the options box □.

▶ In the options box, click on Edit, Reset Settings and then click Add.

▶ With the control and the joint still selected, click on Constrain, Scale and the options box □.

▶ In the options box, click on Edit, Reset Settings. Then click on Maintain Offset. Click Add.

▶ You do not need to change these settings anymore; once will do.

▶ One by one, select a control in the spine and then Shift-select its corresponding joint. Create a parent constraint and then a scale constraint.

▶ Move all the way up the spine to the jaw creating these constraints.

▶ When you get to spine4_CTRL, you should create the parent and scale constraint for not only the spine4 joint, but also both the left and right shoulder.

▶ You should also parent and scale constrain the null joints on the top of the spine and the end of the jaw to their respective controls. This solves common scaling issues.

The arm joints are always going to get their position information from the IK Solver, but they need scale information from somewhere if they are going to scale with the rest of the rig correctly. Use the Connection Editor to connect the scale of the lShoulder joint to the scale of the lUpperArm and lLowerArm joints, and the same for the right side. You have to create each connection individually; you cannot batch-create these connections. Remember to load the shoulder joints on the left side of the Connection Editor because they are the nodes "driving" the attributes on the right.

Connecting the IK Hand Controls

Now we connect the controls for the arms to the IK handles and pole vectors. Follow these steps:

- ▶ Select lWrist_CTRL and Shift-select the left IKHandle.
- ▶ Click Constrain, Parent. (IKHandles do not need scale information.)
- ▶ Click lElbow_PoleVector_CTRL and Shift-select the locator called lElbow_PV.
- ▶ Click Constrain, Parent. (Pole vectors do not need scale information.)
- ▶ Repeat these constraints on the right side.
- ▶ I created groups to hold the finger controls, so these need to be parented to the wrist controls. In the Outliner, select the group lFinger_Ctrl_GRP, Shift-select lWrist_CTRL, and press **P**.
- ▶ Repeat the same on the right side.
- ▶ Parent and scale constrain the controls of the hand to the joints of the hand, starting with the wrist and going to the ends of the fingers and thumb. Remember to parent and scale constrain the null joints as well.

Other Controls

So far, our controls are primarily translation and rotation controls. These controls are essential to make the character move, but what about making the character change facial expressions, employing extra articulation, or simply looking at the control we built for him already? There are other categories of controls than the simple transformation controls. Primarily, these controls edit other attributes such as BlendShapes, material attributes, dynamic channels, and so on. We will first create a control that will house all of our BlendShape channels so they are easily accessed when we're working with the character in panel. We will then create an Aim Constraint for Sam's eyeballs to eye_Target_CTRL so an animator will be able to control the direction of his eyes.

NOTE

Placing Switches

As mentioned before, most production rigs allow the animator to switch between FK and IK movement on certain parts of the character—normally the arms, legs, and spine. You would normally place the switch close to the limb that is being switched, but it is also common for there to be a single master switch control that holds all of the channels for switches in the rig. Either is fine, but make sure the control shape is unique to the switch so you do not visually clutter your rig with controls that are indistinguishable from each other.

BlendShape Control

Sam will have facial performance animated via BlendShapes. This deformer type in Maya allows the animator to blend between different poses of the face (covered fully in Hour 15, "Making Diverse Shapes with BlendShapes"). However, like most deformers, the attributes for a BlendShape node are difficult to access while performing other animation tasks such as transforming controls and editing keyframes. It is therefore very common to create a control that has attributes connected to the BlendShape attributes. Follow along to create this control:

▶ Import the face control by clicking File, Import. Navigate to this Hour's files, choose face_CTRL.ma, and then import.

▶ The face_CTRL loads into the scene next to Sam's head. You will notice the transforms are locked.

▶ Select the face_CTRL curve (the one that is the shape of the head). Shift-select Sam's skull_CTRL and press **P**.

▶ Now the control is parented under the skill control.

▶ We will be using the curves in this control group to manipulate the BlendShape attributes.

Eye Target

The eye_Target_CTRL is present and accounted for, but it does not control his eyes yet. To make this connection, we are going to use a type of constraint we never have before, called an "aim constraint." This type of constraint does exactly what the name says: It makes one object "aim" at another, by rotating the object to face the other along a certain axis. Follow these instructions to get the aim constraint set up:

▶ Select lEye_CTRL (the eye-shaped curve that is within the box-shaped curve floating in front of Sam's face).

▶ Now Shift-select Sam's l_Eye_GEO.

▶ In the Animation menu set, click Constrain, Aim and the options box ☐.

▶ In the settings box that opens, click on Edit, Reset Settings.

▶ Now make sure Maintain Offset is checked on.

▶ Click on Apply.

▶ Now select rEye_CTRL and Shift-select r_Eye_GEO.

▶ In the settings window for the aim constraint that is still open, click on Add.

▶ The settings box will close and you will be able to check to make sure it worked by select-ing eye_Target_CTRL and moving it around and seeing if the eyes follow the movement, as in Figure 11.15.

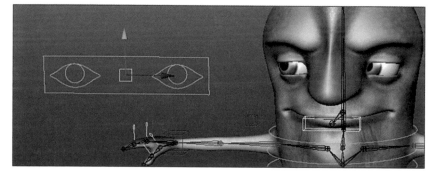

FIGURE 11.15
The aim constraint is working; the eyes are aiming at eye_Target_CTRL.

Final Cleanup

There are just a few tasks to complete before this rig is ready for skinning. We should make groups for the different objects, make display layers, and hide objects we are not going to ever touch. To do so, follow these steps:

▶ Select both IK handles and both pole vector locators.

▶ Press **Ctrl+G** to group these objects. Rename the group sam_DNT_GRP. (DNT stands for do not touch.)

▶ Select this new group and then Ctrl-select the group sam_Rig_GRP in the Outliner.

▶ Press **P**. The DNT group is parented under the main rig group.

▶ Select joint1. Press **Ctrl+G** to group the joint, and then rename the new group sam_Skeleton_GRP.

▶ Parent this under the main rig group as well.

▶ Select world_Mover_CTRL. Create a new group for this as well, rename it sam_Ctrl_GRP, and parent it under the main rig group.

▶ Hide the DNT group. Your Outliner should look like Figure 11.16.

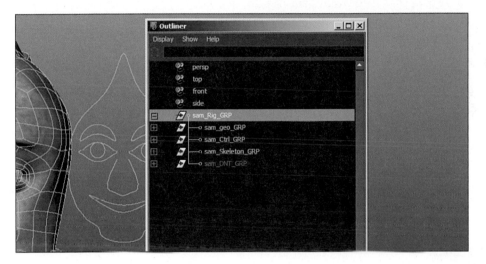

FIGURE 11.16
The Outliner with all of the controls, joints, geometry, and extras grouped nicely.

▶ Select the group sam_geo_GRP and in the Channel Box, Layer Editor (at the bottom right of your screen), click on Layers, Create Layer from Selected.

▶ Rename this new layer sam_Geo_LAYER.

▶ Select the group sam_Ctrl_GRP and click on Layers, Create Later from Selected.

▶ Rename this new layer sam_Ctrl_LAYER.

▶ Create another layer from sam_Skeleton_GRP and name it accordingly.

▶ Your Layer Editor should resemble the one in Figure 11.17.

This file has been saved for you as sam_Rig_Final.ma.

Now that we have cleaned up our scene, we are ready to make our rig deform our geometry using the Skin deformer. We are going to have a lot of fun attaching Sam's geo to this rig, especially when we are able to start animating him around and bringing him to life!

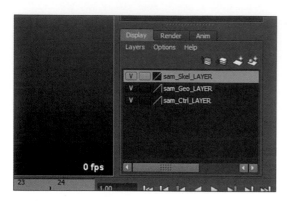

FIGURE 11.17
The Layer Editor properly configured with our display layers. Now we can move on to skinning!

VIDEO

Advanced Rigging Techniques

In this video, I show off some of the more advanced features of the Sam 2.0 rig, which also ships with this book, and how to create some of these features, such as FK/IK switches, deformation in the spine controls, and more.

Summary

Simple object rigs are a combination of groups, constraints, and controls. When you start creating character rigs, joints are added into the mix. You should be aware that joints are not used solely for organic characters. In fact, car rigs, spaceship rigs, and many other mechanical or non-living objects typically make use of joints in production. We created a skeleton and took advantage of mirroring. We set up the controls in the right place and then created the hierarchy and constraints to make them move correctly. We then added a few extra controls to round out our character rig.

Q&A

Q. I'm creating a character with legs. Is the IK solver still the right way to go?

A. Yes, you will mainly be using IK with legs. However, some of the properties of a foot need to be worked out in advance, such as the ability to lift from the toe. Google "reverse foot rig" to find out more.

Q. **I can't seem to create joints that start from the end of my last joint. Maya just creates a new joint on top of the old one. What's wrong?**

A. Most problems in Maya are resolved by a restart of the program. This is one that pops up sometimes.

Q. **Why use constraints for making the joints follow the controls instead of parenting?**

A. We will go over constraints in detail in Hour 13, "Animation: Adding Movement to Your Scene." The short answer is that parenting the joints under the controls would change the hierarchy of the joints, which we do not want to do. Also, constraints can be dynamic, meaning in advanced rigging we can adjust how the controls actually move the joints.

Q. **When I tried to orient my joints, I did not come up with the nicely oriented joints that you did. Why?**

A. As mentioned, orienting your joints is a trial-and-error process, and you may not get the results you are looking for on the first try. Also, be careful; there is an option to reorient the child joints of the selected joint when you orient. This can mess up correctly oriented joints easily.

Workshop

The workshop contains quiz questions and exercises to help you solidify your understanding of the material covered. Try to answer all questions before looking at the "Answers" section that follows.

Quiz

1. Why are the "bones" in Maya called joints?

2. What do FK and IK stand for?

3. What type of movement did we create in our character spine: FK or IK?

4. What do we call the extra joint at the very end of a joint chain?

5. What is the name of the constraint that makes an object rotate to face another object?

Exercise

Take a look at the Maya file sam_Rig_v2.0.ma. This rig has some cool additions to the rig we created in this Hour. Although rigging to this level is outside the scope of this book, you should be able to open up the Outliner and Hypergraph and see how the objects are connected. After watching Video 11.1, see if you can reconstruct some of the more advanced rigging concepts we went over in the video. In particular, you might want to try making an FK/IK switch on your version of Sam's rig. Create circle controls on his shoulder, elbow, and wrist, and constrain the joints to these controls in addition to the IK wrist and pole vector controls you've already made. Adjusting the IKBlend attribute on the IKHandles will make the bones either snap to the IK solver position or back to the position of the FK controls you've made. Giving good switches on rigs is a top priority for most animators.

You may even want to try creating a rig for a very simple character such as a flour sack using the concepts we talked about in this Hour. Just remember to work slowly and log your progress.

Answers

1. Simply because we are constantly using the rotational information from a bone; therefore, the pivot point, or "joint," is the logical choice.

2. FK stands for "Forward Kinematics" and IK stands for "Inverse Kinematics." FK is when the parent joint controls the child's movement, and IK is when you position the child and the parent joints rotate to accommodate, or "solve," this new position.

3. We used an FK spine for Sam.

4. We rename those to Null so that when skinning, we can disregard their influence on the geometry. You should always remember to include them, however, in the constraining of controls so that scale works properly.

5. An *aim constraint* makes an object rotate to face, or point at, another object. We used this constraint on the eyes of Sam.

HOUR 12
Skinning: Attaching Geometry to a Rig

What You'll Learn in This Hour:

▶ How to attach geometry to joints using skin deformers

▶ How to decide on rigid binding or smooth binding

▶ How to paint weights and refine your smooth bind

▶ How to add more deformations to your skinned model

After your joints and controls have been created, the task of "skinning" your character may begin. Although it sounds like the opposite, skinning is the act of applying the mesh to the rig you have created so it can move along with the controls you have created.

NOTE

Sam 2.0

In this Hour, we will continue with our character Sam. However, we will start from the 2.0 version of the character rig I created and not the simpler rig you made in the last Hour. If you like, however, you can still use your rig to follow along in this Hour. I recommend that you use the Sam 2.0 rig to see some more dynamic rigging and skinning techniques in action.

In this Hour, you find out how to make your models deform using joints by investigating Rigid Binds and Smooth Binds. We will then attach our character Sam to the control rig we created last Hour. You will see how to clean up the blending between the joints by painting weights, as well as some good methods for smoothing out problem areas in our rig. We will also look at some helpful deformers that provide us with added versatility in the function of our rig.

The Skin Nodes

Maya deforms meshes to move with joints with two different types of "binds": Rigid Binds and Smooth Binds. Rigid Binds make your geometry behave almost like it is parented to the joint. Smooth Binds make your geometry bend smoothly across joints. Whichever skin node you are using, first it is important to realize the distinction between parenting and skinning. *Parenting* means that the transform node of an object is a child of the joint, and therefore actually moves with the joint through space. The object's position changes with the parent's position. *Skinning*, on the other hand, is actually a deformer, meaning the object being skinned technically *does not move*. The vertices of the object deform as the joints move, but if you select the mesh even after doing complex adjustments to its rig, you will see the object's transforms are still all at 0. This distinction is good for us because it allows us to layer deformers on top of each other without worrying about multiple transformations affecting the object itself. The ordering of the deformers is important, though, and in Hour 15, "Making Diverse Shapes with BlendShapes," we will make some adjustments to the order of deformers.

Rigid Bind

The first type of bind is called a Rigid Bind. The way Rigid Bind works is that a certain joint can only influence a vertex 100% or 0%—meaning there is no real blending of the influence, or "weight" of a joint on a mesh. Why would you use a deformer that has no weights? Rigid Binds are commonly compatible with most game engines, and sometimes offer a better alternative to parenting for rigid objects. As you will see as we add deformers to a skinned mesh, keeping mesh transformations and deformations separated is important to keep things from getting overly complex; you can quickly create some very undesirable results if you are not careful mixing deforms and transforms.

Open rigid_Skin.ma in this Hour's files. This is a basic file that has some geometry positioned over joints, much akin to a robot arm. Rigid Binds are commonly used for skinning rigid objects such as robots and cars (yes, even cars have rigs).

As you can see in Figure 12.1, the geometry is placed exactly where it should be. Rigid Binds are much like parent constraints in that the position of the mesh relative to the joint cannot be changed once it is skinned. If you are looking for additional control over the position of the mesh relative to the joint, perhaps a constrained group (as in Hour 9, "Relationships and Making Nodes Work Together") or a parent relationship is more appropriate.

Using Rigid Bind means that the joints will actually *deform* the vertices of the mesh that is bound to them. Remember this important distinction: An object that is transformed has a position that changes in world space, found at that object's pivot point. On the other hand, an object that is skinned will seem to move through space as the joints move, but its pivot will not move at all. Only the vertices will move. Let's Rigid Bind this arm and test this theory:

▶ Select the joint labeled upper_Arm. Shift-select the mesh labeled upper_Arm_GEO.

▶ Press **F2** to switch to the Animation menu set.

► Click on Skin, Bind Skin, Rigid Bind and then choose the options box □.

► Change the Bind To option to Selected Joints and click Bind Skin.

► Repeat this process for the forearm joint and forearm geometry.

FIGURE 12.1
The robot arm geometry is positioned over the respective joints.

Once the meshes have been skinned using Rigid Bind, select and move the IK handle around in the scene. The meshes follow the movement of the joints. But let's see the difference between parenting and binding geometry. Select the hand geometry. You will see the hand geometry's pivot point moves along with the wrist joint. This is because the object's transform node is being moved as a child of the joint. Now select the forearm geometry. Notice how the pivot point is always at the world origin, no matter what pose the arm skeleton takes. As in Figure 12.2, no matter how you manipulate the IK handle or rotate the joints, the forearm and upper arm geometry will have a pivot that remains still.

Imagine the vertices are being glued to the joint, but the transform node that acts as a container does not move at all. Remember, Rigid Bind is useful for game engines and rigid geometry.

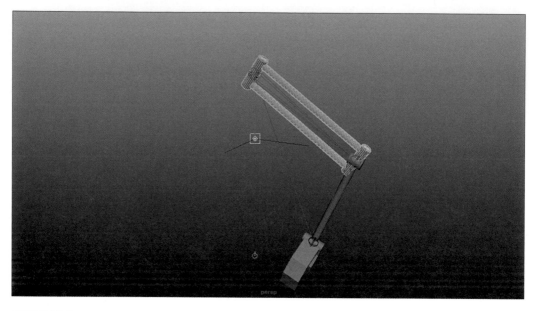

FIGURE 12.2
Because the geometry is bound, and not parented, the vertices are being "deformed" into position by the joints, not translated. Notice the pivot is still in place because the transform node hasn't moved.

Flexors

If you need extra deformation, Flexors allow you to create custom shapes at the intersections of joints, leading to more smooth transitions between joints. Flexors are easy to create. Follow these steps to add one:

- ▶ Open flexor.ma in this Hour's files.

- ▶ We have a tube that is skinned to the joints using Rigid Bind. Select the joints and rotate them a bit to see the harsh, jagged bind.

- ▶ Click undo to get the joints back to their start position.

- ▶ Switch to the Animation menu set by pressing **F2**.

- ▶ Select the forearm joint.

- ▶ Click on Skin, Edit Rigid Bind, Create Flexor....

The three different types of Flexors are Lattice, Sculpt, and Joint Cluster. The Lattice type creates a lattice around the joint that will allow for smoother blending. The Sculpt type creates a manipulator that will affect the geometry by scaling and bulging. The Joint Cluster type creates a cluster at the joint that has a falloff allowing for smooth bends, much like the Lattice.

▶ Make sure the type is set to Lattice and click Create.

▶ Bend the joints again and see how the Flexor makes it so there is a smooth transition between the joints.

Deform vs. Transform

We've brought up the importance of distinguishing between deforming and transforming a few times. The main reason we should be careful is because of the way that Maya handles adding more than one deformation to the same model. The order of the deformations makes a big difference. For instance, in Figure 12.3, you can see the difference between first applying a Twist and then a Bend deformer, and the result if the order is switched.

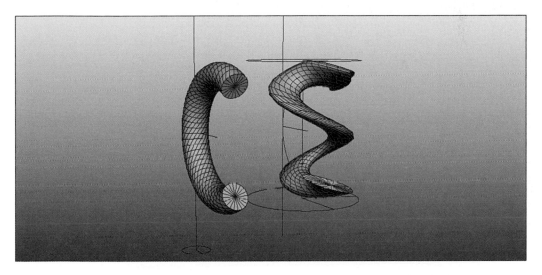

FIGURE 12.3
On the left is a tube that has a Twist and then a Bend deformer applied. On the right is the same tube with the deformer order switched. Deformer order matters, and mixing transforms and deforms together can have even more unpredictable results.

As you can clearly see, the order of deformations makes a huge difference. This is pertinent to the discussion of deform versus transform because when you transform geometry, you are effectively moving the "container" (transform mode) that holds the shape. Moving this container also moves the vertices in the shape node, and can result in very undesirable results. In Hour 15, we will go over BlendShapes, the most common deformer used in conjunction with skinning. Deformation order will play a big role there as well, and we will show how mixing transforms and deforms can get messy.

Smooth Bind

The other type of bind is called a Smooth Bind. When it comes to characters, you will use the Smooth Bind tool to get your meshes skinned to your rigs. Remember, we are going to be using the Sam 2.0 rig that I've created so as to have even better control than the basic rig created in the last Hour.

When you create a Smooth Bind, you are essentially creating a Skincluster deformer. This deformer allows you to bind the vertices of a mesh to a joint or group of joints. The weight of the bind is controlled by painting the weight in panel, with zero being zero influence, and white being full influence. Let's get started on Sam.

Skinning Sam

Open sam_Skin_Start.ma in this Hour's files. This file contains the final Sam model and the final Sam Rig v2.0. We will skin this mesh and adjust the skin weights once finished. Actually applying the Smooth Bind is a simple process. Follow these steps to get the initial bind:

- ▶ Select Sam's body geometry.

- ▶ Switch to the Animation menu set by pressing **F2**.

- ▶ Click on Skin, Bind Skin, Smooth Bind and the options box ☐.

- ▶ For the options, match my settings as shown in Figure 12.4.

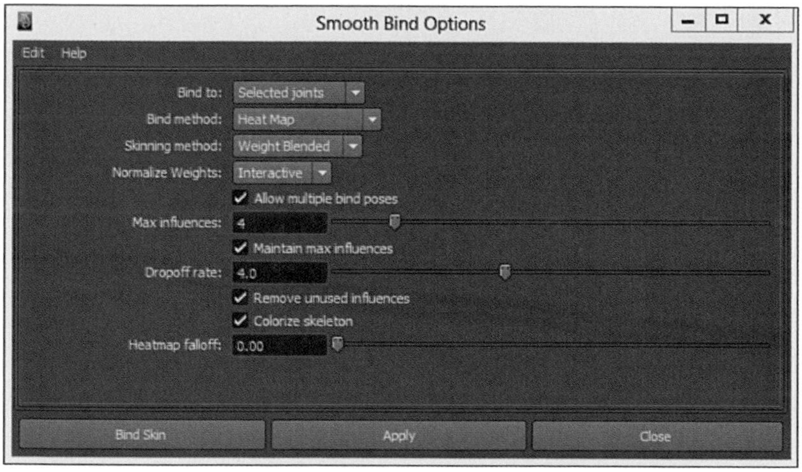

FIGURE 12.4
Copy these settings to get a good baseline for a Smooth Bind.

NOTE

Null Joints and Skinning

Because we are going to only use "Selected Joints" for our skinning, we need to select all of the joints that are going to be used for the skin weights. This is why it is important to know about, label, and keep track of the Null joints in a rig. They are included in the skin weights if you simply select the root joint and choose Hierarchy in the Smooth Bind options. Having these null joints interfere with the skinning is problematic.

▶ Select the following joints by holding Shift while you LMB click on them. We select them in reverse hierarchical order because when you select a parent, the child joints are drawn as selected, too. This way, we can see exactly which joints we've selected: lKnuckle2, lKnuckle1, lThumb2, lThumb1, lWrist, lForearm, lUpperArm, lShoulder, rKnuckle2, rKnuckle1, rThumb2, rThumb1, rWrist, rForearm, rUpperArm, rShoulder, skull_JNT, jaw_JNT, neck_JNT, spine4, upperSpine_Shaper_JNT, lowerSpine_Shaper_JNT, and Spine1.

▶ In the Smooth Bind options box, click Smooth Bind.

▶ A skincluster node is added to the geometry, the transformations are locked, and the controls will now move the character, albeit roughly.

▶ Select some of the controls and make sure they are moving the character.

Painting Weights

If the act of skinning a character seemed too easy, that's because the work has just begun. We now have to make sense of the skin weights and start smoothing them out. We achieve this by doing what is called "painting weights." This is the process of using a brush to paint values of color on the surface of the model to distinguish which areas are affected by the joints in our skeleton. Carefully painting smooth values in turn gives us smooth deformation in our model. Painting skin weights is as much an art as a science. Let's take a look at a few techniques.

Painting

Select Sam's body geometry and click on Skin, Edit Smooth Skin, Paint Skin Weights Tool. The resulting box looks very similar to all of Maya's painting windows. The simple workflow is to select a joint in the Tool Settings box and then use the paintbrush to paint the influence of that joint on the body mesh. The whiter the mesh is, the higher the influence. Because Maya creates a default weight mapping for you when it creates a smooth bind, the majority of your time when skinning is spent *fixing* weights. Let's put this to practice:

▶ In the Paint Skin Weights tool settings, scroll down in the Influences box until you find Jaw_JNT and select it.

▶ Notice how, like in Figure 12.5, the mesh displays the weight of the joint on the skinned mesh.

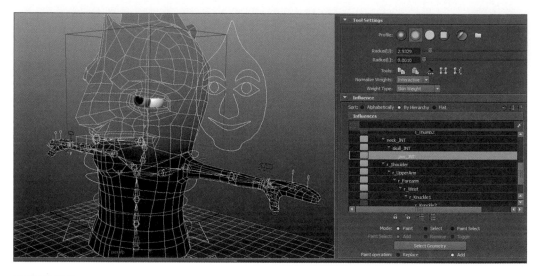

FIGURE 12.5
The selected joint displays its influence on the skinned geometry. The default skinning of the jaw joint has far too much weight on the head.

▶ We need to move the joint to see just how much weight smoothing needs to be done, so select jaw_CTRL and rotate it down in X about 35 degrees.

▶ As you can see from Figure 12.6, the jaw JNT is influencing the geometry of the head far too much.

▶ Select the body mesh again and press **Y** to enter the last tool, which should be the Paint Skin Weights tool.

▶ In the Tool Settings box, select jaw_JNT again under Influences.

▶ Now move your mouse over the body mesh to see your paintbrush. You can scale the brush by holding down the **B** key and LMB clicking and dragging while in any brush tool.

If you look in the Tool Settings underneath the Influences, the Mode, Operation, and other brush options are available. When we are painting influence, we keep the mode on Paint. The paint operations are as follows.

Replace

This paint mode makes the weight on the painted vertices exactly what the "value" is set to in the tool options by just replacing the weight.

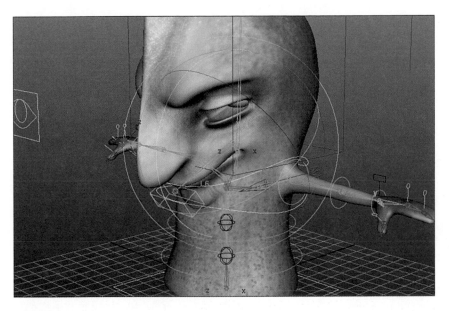

FIGURE 12.6
The jaw JNT is pulling the vertices of the head downward with it. We will have to clean up these weights by using the Paint Skin Weights tool.

Add

This is an additive brush that will "build" weight as you paint over an area more and more. Similar to an airbrush.

Scale

This is a subtractive brush that will scale the weight on the painted vertices by the value you have set in the tool options (.5 = 50% and so on).

Smooth

This brush simply smooths the weights as you paint over the vertices. You should note that holding down the **Shift** key makes any of the other paint operations switch to smooth temporarily.

Other Options

The rest of the tool options can be investigated on your own; most are self-explanatory. Make sure before you start painting weights, however, that the Normalize Weights setting is set to Interactive at the top of the tool settings window. This makes it so that the weights are always kept so that the cumulative weight of all the influences of a vertex are 1.0. Follow these steps to start painting weights on Sam:

▶ Switch to the Scale operation in the Tool Settings window, and change the Value to .85.

▶ Use the paintbrush to reduce the weight of jaw_JNT on the face by painting with the LMB across the head, nose, and upper lip.

▶ Your results should start to look like Figure 12.7 as the weight of the jaw starts approaching a more correct value on the vertices of the head.

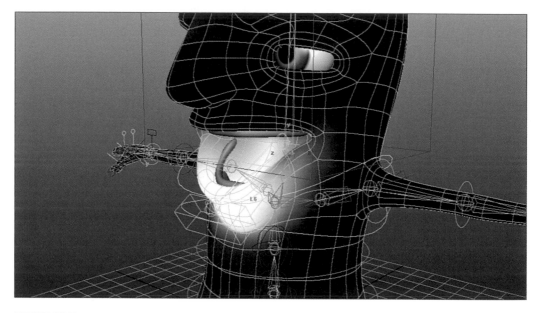

FIGURE 12.7
The weighting on the jaw is getting much better.

▶ If you mess up an area, you can undo by pressing **Z**. If you need to add weight back again, simply switch to the Add operation. Note, however, that adding .85 is extreme; you have to constantly adjust the value of the brush when switching back and forth between Add and Scale.

Continue to paint the weight on the jaw. Rotate the jaw control in different directions to get a sense of how the joint is deforming the mesh, and adjust the weights to smooth the deformations.

Prune Small Weights

Sometimes a joint has a very small influence on a vertex far away from it that is difficult to see in the panel. You can use the Prune Small Weights tool by clicking Skin, Edit Smooth Skin, Prune

Small Weights. This tool will remove weights under a certain threshold, making it so that you need not worry about missing tiny areas on your mesh when painting weights.

Locking Weights

Once you have finished painting a weight and you are happy with it, you can lock it by clicking on the lock icon located just under the Tool Settings window. You can still paint the weight of a locked influence as long as it is selected, but if you are painting weights on other influences, you cannot change the weight of a locked influence. Be careful painting weights with too many locked influences; you can get some undesirable results if you paint large areas covered by locked influences when the weights have "nowhere to go."

TRY IT YOURSELF ▼

Paint Weights on the Rest of Sam

The best way to learn how to paint weights is to practice:

1. Traverse the entire skeleton chain in the Influences tab of the Tool Settings pane, painting weights as you go.

2. Don't forget to move the controllers so that you can see which joints are wrongly affecting vertices elsewhere in the body.

3. Use the Smooth brush or hold **Shift** as you paint to smooth the weights as well.

4. The spine is tricky because Sam 2.0 has joints that "float" in the middle of his spine and that automatically squash and stretch when you move the spine controllers. You will have to put his spine in a variety of poses to be able to correctly paint the weights on his middle.

5. A good tip is to make sure that the spine1 joint has 100% (all white) influence on all of the vertices on the bottom of Sam's body, and the first row of vertices as you go up the spine. This will make it so he has a solid platform that can be placed predictably by the master_CTRL.

6. Save often! Painting weights sometimes does not Undo correctly, and can also crash.

VIDEO

Skinning Tips

In this video, I show off some techniques that are helpful to the skinning process, including selecting hierarchies, locking paint weights, and more.

Adding More Deformation

The Sam 2.0 rig has some interesting automatic deformations that happen to his spine as you stretch and move him around. Take a look at the finished skin weights in sam_rig_v2.ma in this Hour's files. We can add some more deformation to this rig to make things even more interesting.

Sam has these spikes on his head that might be fun to wiggle around when his head is moving quickly. Let's add some clusters to these points and get a little bit of experience with deformation order at the same time. Follow these steps:

▶ Import wobble_CTRLS.ma from this Hour's source files into your scene by clicking on File, Import and choosing the file. Five controllers appear on the top of Sam's head.

▶ RMB click and drag to the left on Sam's geometry to switch to the vertex component mode.

▶ Select the vertices that make up the first spike, as in Figure 12.8.

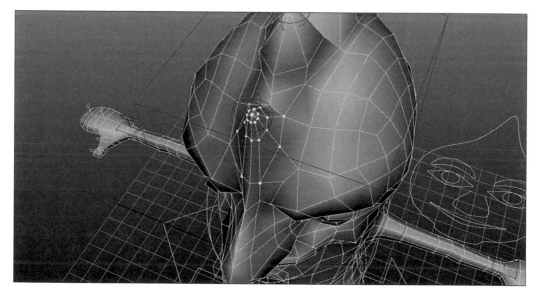

FIGURE 12.8
The vertices of the first spike are selected.

▶ Switch to the Animation menu set by pressing **F2**.

▶ Click on Create Deformers, Cluster. A "C" will appear in the panel, indicating the cluster is created.

▶ Select wobble_CTRL1 and then head_CTRL and parent it by pressing **P**.

▶ Select wobble_CTRL1 again and open the Connection Editor by clicking Window, General Editors, Connection Editor.

▶ Note that wobble_CTRL1 is loaded into the left panel already. Now select the cluster that was created and in the Connection Editor, click Reload Right.

▶ In the left column, select the "translate" attribute. In the right column, also select the "translate" attribute to connect the translation of the control to the cluster.

▶ The last thing we need to do is make sure the deformation order is correct. Rotate head_ CTRL and then select and move wobble_CTRL1 and see the result. As you can see in Figure 12.9, the results are not what we are going for.

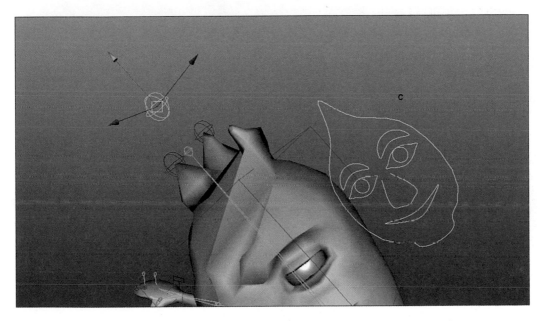

FIGURE 12.9
Because the cluster is *after* the skin deformer, Maya is moving the vertices in the spike In the wrong direction when we adjust the controller. We want the evaluation of the cluster to happen *before* the skin deformer so that the spike moves in a predictable way.

▶ Undo these movements or return the transformations and rotations of wobble_CTRL1 and head_CTRL to zero.

▶ RMB click and hold on Sam's geometry until the marking menu appears. In the center-bottom column that appears, click on Inputs, All Inputs.

▶ This menu shows you all of the inputs on a node. As you can see, the Cluster deformer is above the Skin deformer. We want it below. To do that, MMB click and drag the Cluster node on top of the Skin Cluster node. They should switch order.

▶ Repeat the test of the rotation of the head and the transformation of the wobble control. It should move predictably now. To get just a little bit cleaner falloff on the cluster that affects the spike, we are going to smooth the cluster weights. Click on Edit Deformers, Paint Cluster Weights Tool.

▶ This tool is exactly like the Paint Skin Weights tool, so you should be familiar with it.

▶ Use the tool to smooth the influence at the bottom of the spike, like in Figure 12.10.

FIGURE 12.10
By default, all the vertices of a cluster made from selected geometry will have a weight of 1. We used the Paint Cluster Weights tool to smooth out these weights to give us a more appealing shape when animating wobble_CTRL.

▶ Repeat all of these steps for each one of the spikes until all five have their own controller.

▶ When you are finished, put all of the clusters into the group sam_DNT_GRP.

Maya's deformations are limitless. Because you are only bound by your imagination, sometimes it is best to see what kinds of deformation you need in animation before you get too carried away adding bells and whistles to a rig. There are issues of unnecessarily slowing down your scene by adding many layers of deformation that may never been used by an animator. We're going to leave off here with the deformation for now; maybe more control will be needed in the future.

Summary

We first took a look at Rigid Bind to see how geometry is deformed by a bone in a rigid way. This type of skinning is useful for solid objects that may need other deformations added on top of them. Even automobiles make use of rigid binds, and they are universally compatible with game engines. Deformation order is an issue with skinning, so we took a brief look at the way that the order of deforming a mesh seriously impacts the outcome. We then added a Smooth Bind to Sam, finally skinning his geometry to the rig we've worked so hard on. The default skin weights are almost always mediocre, so our job as artists is to fix the weights by using the Paint Skin Weights tool. After you painted the weights and tested the rig in different poses to affirm your weights, we added more deformations to the character. These clusters were added after the skin cluster node, so we had to reorder each cluster node in the "inputs" menu each time we created one. When that was done, the new deformation order had our wobble controls working perfectly.

Q&A

Q. I'm having a lot of trouble painting weights on the character. Is there any easier way?

A. It's a time-intensive process. Although it is possible to type in weights on vertices, and although a host of skinning scripts are out there that can speed up the process, skinning will always be laborious. Practice makes perfect.

Q. My model deforms oddly when I move the controls. Any tips for smoothing the deformations?

A. It is always a good idea to move the controls into very extreme poses to exacerbate any weighting issues you are having. For instance, stretch spine3_CTRL way up, down, side to side, and *then* move the arm controls around. If you see small areas that are "tweaking" when you move the arms, it means you have to continue to paint weights.

Q. I see the null joints in the list of influences. Why?

A. When you applied the Smooth Bind, you had Joint Hierarchy selected to apply the skin to and not Selected Joints. Go back to that step and make sure you copy my settings as in Figure 12.4.

Q. Can I apply any deformer to the model?

A. Yes, you are not limited in what kinds of deformation you add to the model. You could add a Squash deform to the body or a Twist to the head.

Workshop

The workshop contains quiz questions and exercises to help you solidify your understanding of the material covered. Try to answer all questions before looking at the "Answers" section that follows.

Quiz

1. How can you tell if geometry is transforming or deforming?

2. Which form of bind is used for inorganic objects such as robot arms and cars?

3. What key can you press to switch the current paint operation to Smooth?

4. When you're painting weights, there is an add operation but no subtract operation. Which operation do you use to remove weight from a vertex?

5. How do you access the menu that allows you to reorder deformations?

Exercise

Continue practicing painting weights and creating smooth deformation in a rig. Open up sam_Rig_v2_Final.ma and see if you can get your skin weights as smooth as this file. Try to create a simple rig for other objects using the skills learned in Hour 11, "Character Rigging: Articulating Characters," and then skin them smoothly. The original sam_Rig we created in Hour 11 can be used for practice as well, because the skeleton is much simpler than v2.

Answers

1. Geometry that is transforming can be seen as doing so because its position (pivot) moves as it is being transformed. Geometry that is being deformed stays in place while the vertices move *within* the transform node.

2. A Rigid Bind is useful for deforming rigid objects, as opposed to transforming the geometry.

3. The **Shift** key changes the current operation to smooth. It is useful to adopt a rhythm of painting and smoothing.

4. The Scale operation is the equivalent of subtract, in that it reduces the weight on the painted vertices by scaling the value.

5. The inputs menu is accessed most easily by RMB clicking and holding until a marking menu appears. Click on Inputs, All Inputs to access the deformers and reorder them as needed.

HOUR 13

Animation: Adding Movement to Your Scene

What You'll Learn in This Hour:

▶ How to create keyframes and work with the Timeline

▶ Which animation editors should be used and for what purposes

▶ How to create and manage constraints in animation

▶ What other tools can be used to create animation

Animation, or creating the illusion of movement through the rapid display of successive frames in a sequence, is Maya's forte. Well, to be fair, Maya has many fortes. But truly, the animation tools in Maya are fantastic, and contribute greatly to the reason why Maya is the de-facto standard animation program used by feature animation studios and visual effects firms worldwide. Although lauded as the toughest skill to master in all of CG, animation is actually based on some very simple principles. It is the combination of these principles in conjunction with skillful application of Maya's keyframe and dynamic animation tools that makes a true animator shine.

NOTE

Artistry Versus Technique

Animation is truly the most challenging aspect of CG. Animators train for years before they are trusted with the scenes you see in your favorite animations and visual effects. If you are serious about becoming an animator, you should find artistic support in the form of books, online forums, or even school. This book will teach you how to operate Maya's animation tools, but cannot make up for the kind of artistic information you will need to create engaging performances.

In this Hour, you find out how to use Maya's animation tools to create motion in a scene. You will learn the different animation editors and get some exposure to manipulating animation. You will also have some practice animating constraints and see other tools that Maya offers in animation.

The Principles of Animation

Although this book offers a technical walkthrough of Maya's animation tools, no section on animation in any book would be complete without discussing the following principles of animation. These 12 principles, developed and refined by the "Nine Old Men" of Disney, have survived and persisted through history to inform even the most cutting-edge animators from movies to games and everything in between. These principles will never be lost, only built upon, expanded, and taken to the next level by generations of animators... maybe starting with you!

Squash and Stretch

This principle dictates that bodies and objects tend to squash and stretch as they go from extreme poses. For instance, a ball squashes when it hits the floor and stretches out as it goes into the air. A cat squashes into a small form before it stretches out, leaping forward. The application of this principle in animation can lead to some very cartoonish animation very quickly.

Anticipation

This principle says that before any action, a body or an object will first move in the opposite direction to build energy for the action. Before you jump off of the ground, you bend your legs and swing your arms backward. This principle not only helps us understand the motion of an object, but it also allows the audience to follow along better, because their eyes can much more easily track an object that gives warning of its movements.

Staging

Staging deals with the "setup" of your entire scene—the position of the characters, the position of the set and props, the camera angle, and the plan to have the action execute in a way that the audience will understand what is going on. Think of staging as the *clarity* of your idea of what you would like to animate, in terms of the visual setup of the scene. If you have one character punching another, it is hard to see what is happening if the camera is behind one of them. You would probably *stage* that action in profile, so we can see both characters the whole time.

Straight-Ahead Action and Pose to Pose

This is not so much a principle as it is the two techniques you can use to create character performances. Straight-ahead action is action in which it is easier to create keyframes in sequence, moving forward in time and making a small change to the rig and then moving on again. This method is akin to animating stop motion or clay animation. Pose to pose, on the other hand, is the process of determining a group of strong poses you would like to see the character strike, and then timing those poses individually on the timeline. When you are done creating the poses, you then begin smoothing and interpolating the movement to give a seamless performance.

Follow Through and Overlapping Action

Follow through and overlap deal with the way objects that are jointed or connected move. Follow through is basically the idea of inertia; an object in motion tends to stay in motion. So when a character is running and comes to a stop, the feet, spine, and waist all "overshoot" their rest position before they settle back into the rest pose. Follow through is what determines how far past the end pose an object will travel. Overlapping action is kind of like the opposite of follow through; think of it like "drag." If you swing a bat, the end of the bat is going to "lag" behind the motion of your body and arms in the beginning of the action. That is overlap.

Slow In and Slow Out

This fundamental describes the tendency of objects to come to gradual stops and have gradual starts. Only mechanical objects such as robot arms can accelerate instantly. Humans and other natural characters should have a bit of ramp-up time to their movements, and should gradually change directions as well.

Arcs

In nature, almost all motions follow curved trajectories. This is due mostly to the fact that our joints are rotational joints; therefore, we move in arcs as we move our limbs. To avoid mechanical motions, move all of your motions on arcs, if possible, even such things as head turns, walk cycles, and so on.

Secondary Action

Secondary action is action that contributes to the main action of a scene, without being so prominent that it distracts from the main action. A character fiddling with his buttons nervously as he talks to his boss would be a good example of secondary action. Secondary action is great for making a scene feel much more "full" and natural. It also allows the audience to see a subtle layer of a character's performance, in the way that the secondary action is executed.

Timing

Timing is another one of the fundamentals that is not as much a fundamental as much as it is a part of animation itself. Timing deals with experimenting with different ways to execute an action in an interesting way—breaking physics and mechanics to show the audience something they've never seen before. An experimental attitude is easy with Maya's many timing tools.

Exaggeration

In animation, we have the opportunity to create fantasy, so although everything should not be exaggerated, a little bit of emphasis goes a long way. You should look out for chances to embellish what would normally be a boring, run-of-the-mill animation with some flair.

Solid Drawing

This fundamental is slightly antiquated in the digital age. It deals with drawing the characters with volume, and respecting the construction of a model. It still has some application in the 3D medium, though; in Maya, working with models that can break if you stretch the rigs too far means that respecting the physical structure of a model plays a large role in animating. Solid drawing deals with knowing the limits of the characters you are working with, and still getting great animation.

Appeal

Appeal is one of the most important fundamentals, but alas one of the most difficult to describe, or attain for that matter. Appeal means that your animation is interesting and engaging. In terms of characters, even villains, they are fun to watch. No matter how evil a character is, they should still be designed and move in an appealing way. Your goal should always be to engage your audience!

Now that we have briefly familiarized you with some of the fundamentals and guidelines of good animation, let's see how to technically achieve this in Maya.

Time in Maya

Since the dawn of animation, we have depended on the rapid display of successive frames to give the illusion of movement. Maya handles time in just this way; by breaking 1 second of time into 24ths, you are manipulating "frames" that will display at 24 frames per second (24fps). When you watch the frames at this speed, smooth motion occurs. Other time formats are available as well. Some common time formats are 12fps and 30fps. These formats help us match stop-motion animation and television display formats, respectively. Regardless of what time format you are using, you should know that even though a frame displays for a fraction of a second, Maya actually calculates time with near-infinite precision. Even though we are playing the animation at 24fps, in between those frames there is transformation information being calculated in fine detail. You are going to become very familiar with this calculation when we start working with "interpolation" in Maya. So rather than think of a frame as a photo, think of it as the positions and orientations you've chosen for the objects in your scene at a given point in time—and only the *playback* of those positions displays at set intervals (12fps, 24fps, and so on).

The Timeline

Remember from our discussion of the Maya UI in Hour 2, "Menus and Navigating the Maya UI," that the bottom area holds the Timeline and Range Slider. As you can see in Figure 13.1, the default Maya UI displays the Timeline prominently.

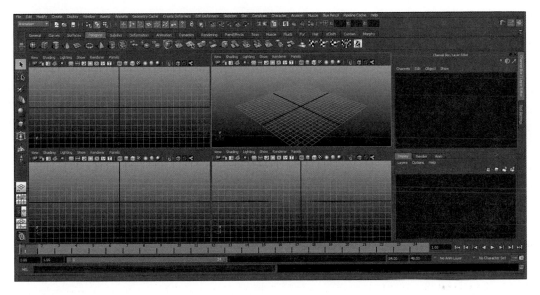

FIGURE 13.1
The Timeline and Range Slider occupy the bottom of the Maya UI.

The controls to the right of the Timeline are standard VCR controls, such as play forward, play backward, frame forward, and frame backward. You can also advance to the nearest keyframe forward or backward as well. Truthfully, once learning the hotkeys, most Maya users do not use the buttons to play animation or advance frames. Let's learn them quickly:

▶ To play animation, press **Alt+V**. **Esc** or **Alt+V** will stop playback.

▶ To advance one frame, press **Alt+.** (period). To reverse one frame, press **Alt+,**.

▶ To advance to the next keyframe, simply press the period key. To reverse to the previous keyframe, press the comma key (,).

The Timeline displays the current time by drawing a shaded box with a white frame label. Click anywhere on the Timeline and notice that the box moves to that time. You can see the frame labels on the Timeline, and by default you will have 24 frames in your scene. Let's change that.

The Range Slider

The Range Slider allows us to change the number of frames in our scene, or view only a portion of the frames for editing animation in a more detailed way. The Range Slider sits just below the Timeline. Follow these instructions to change the frames of your scene:

▶ Start a new Maya scene.

▶ Notice the left and right sides of the Range Slider have two boxes. The far-left and far-right boxes are the scene range—how many frames are in your scene. The near-left and near-right boxes are the playback range—the frames that will display if you play the animation.

▶ Change the far-right (scene end time) box's value to 100.

▶ Notice you still have 24 frames in your timeline, but that the Range Slider bar is now smaller. This is because you are displaying a smaller amount of frames relative to the total scene length.

▶ To display a different range of keys, drag the slider in the middle of the Range Slider back and forth. You will see the Timeline update as you move it back and forth.

▶ To display all the frames in your scene, you can either make the values in the playback range boxes the same as the scene-start and scene-end range boxes, or simply drag the square handles on either end of the Range Slider to expand or contract the playback range.

Now that you have adjusted the scene length and the playback range, you are ready to add key-frames to the timeline.

What Is a Keyframe?

In hand-drawn animation, a keyframe was a drawing done by an animator that defined an important moment in the scene. It could be the extreme pose of an action, the dramatic wind-up of anticipation, and so on. An "in-betweener" would then gather the keyframes drawn by a lead animator and then fill in the drawings in between (hence the name) the keyframes. In Maya, a keyframe is when you define an explicit position for an object at a specific time. This is akin to a keyframe in hand-drawn animation in that you are assigning a certain amount of importance to this frame. However, remember that the idea of a frame is arbitrary; in between the displayed frames, there is still movement occurring. When you "set a key," you are telling Maya that at a certain point in time, you want an object to be positioned and oriented in a certain way. You can also set keys on many attributes. Doing so also tells Maya that at a certain point in time, you want the value of the attribute to be whatever you decide. Keyframes are also referred to as simply "keys." A keyframe is represented by a red line on the timeline, as seen in Figure 13.2.

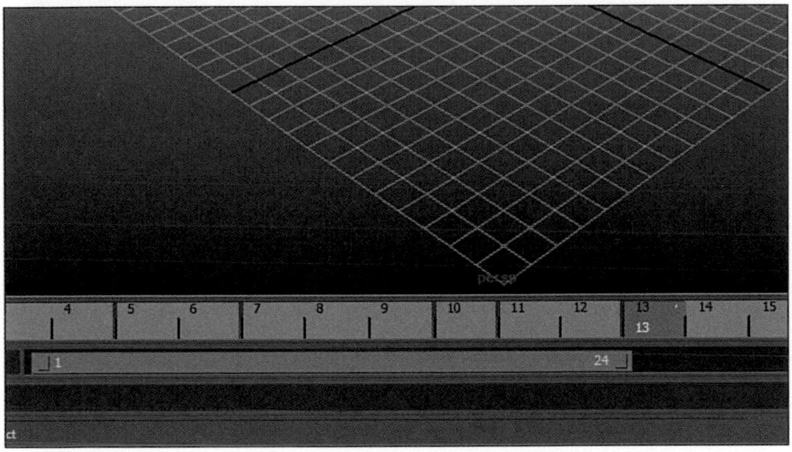

FIGURE 13.2
The Timeline shows keyframes for any selected object or node. Keys are displayed as red tick marks.

To make sure your keys are displaying on the Timeline in a clearly visible way, let's increase the Timeline height and increase the Key Tick size. Click on Window, Settings/Preferences, Preferences. In the Time Slider menu listed under the Display category on the left side of the Preferences window, change Time Slider Height to 2, change Key Tick Size to 4, and then click Save.

Creating Keyframes

To create a keyframe, you simply press the **S** key with any object selected. By default, a key will be set on all the channels that are active in the Channel Box. If you want to set a key on only specific channels, you can change your preferences to do so. However, the default functionality of Maya is what most animators use. Right-clicking on almost any attribute or channel in almost any editor will bring up a marking menu that allows you to set a key as well. Let's try:

▶ Open key_Test.ma in this Hour's files. There is a sphere sitting in the middle of the scene.

▶ Select the sphere and go to frame 1 by clicking on frame 1 on the Timeline.

▶ Press **S**. All of the channels in the Channel Box should turn a bright pink, and a key is set on frame 1, as in Figure 13.3.

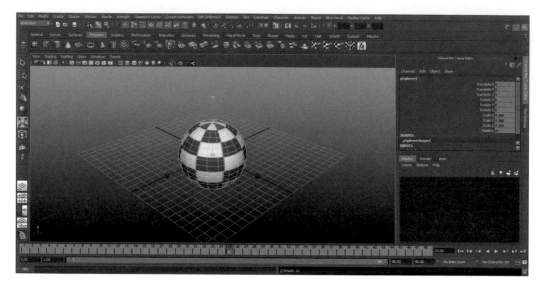

FIGURE 13.3
When you set a key, it will appear on the Timeline and all channels in the Channel Box will turn pink.

NOTE

Key Feedback

You can tell that you have "keyed" (vernacular for creating a keyframe) all channels by looking at the Script Editor bar. Notice how it says "//Result: 10." This is telling you that 10 channels have just received a keyframe. Counting the number of channels on the sphere's transform node confirms this. Whenever you are not sure if you have set a key, look for the "Result" to confirm that you have.

We've created a single keyframe on the sphere; now let's create animation:

- ▶ Select the sphere.

- ▶ Click on frame 50 on the Timeline.

- ▶ Press **W** to switch to the Move tool. Move the sphere along the Z axis about 10 units.

- ▶ Press the **S** key.

- ▶ Play back the animation by pressing **Alt+v**.

Notice how the sphere is now moving from the origin to the end position over 50 frames. Also notice that the sphere does not simply "pop" to its new position on frame 50, meaning that new keyframe is not really akin to a drawing. Instead of being a new "frame," that keyframe represents the position the sphere needs to be in at that specific time, and Maya *interpolates* the in-betweens for you. We will look even closer at interpolation in a bit.

Using AutoKey to Set Keys

You have created some animation now, but it can be cumbersome to have to hit **S** every single time you want to create a key. Maya has a feature called AutoKey that satisfies this problem. When AutoKey is turned on, any change to a channel that has at least one keyframe set on it will automatically create a new key on that frame. Many professional animators rely on AutoKey to save time when animating. Let's turn on AutoKey and do some testing with it:

▶ In the bottom-right corner of the Maya UI, click on the small button with a picture of a key on it that looks like this:

▶ Once it is toggled, AutoKey is now active. Any change to any channel that is already keyed will set a new key on the current frame.

▶ Click on Frame 75 on the Timeline.

▶ Select and move the sphere upward in Y about 10 units, or as high as you'd like.

▶ Notice that on frame 75, even though you have not pressed **S**, there is a new keyframe on the Timeline.

NOTE

AutoKey and Channels

AutoKey only sets a key on the channels that are affected! This means that because you have only moved the sphere upward in Y, only the TranslateY channel has a keyframe on it. This is important to remember as we create animation, because sometimes you will actually want to press **S** to set a key on all channels at the same time; other times, you will only want translate keys or rotate keys.

TRY IT YOURSELF ▼

Set Multiple Keys on the Sphere

Change the time to many random frames and translate, rotate, and scale the sphere.

1. Notice that with AutoKey ON, only the transforms you change set keys automatically.

2. Use the **S** key to set keys on all channels and see how it affects keys that were set with AutoKey.

3. If you want to delete the animation on a channel, right-click on the channel in the Channel Box and choose "delete selected."

Manipulating the Timeline

We are going to manipulate the Timeline to practice moving and scaling keys. Start from the scene you are currently working on, making sure a good number of keys is spread across the entire Timeline. Do as follows:

▶ To select a range on the Timeline, **Shift**+LMB click and drag the range you would like to select. It will turn red, as in Figure 13.4.

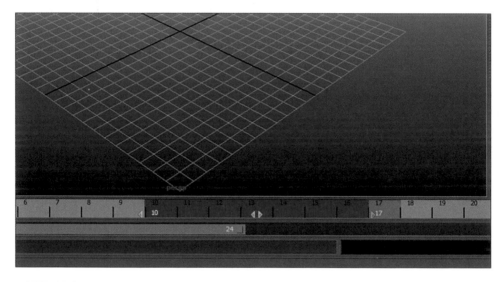

FIGURE 13.4
A range of frames has been selected using the Shift+LMB method.

▶ To deselect a range on the Timeline, click anywhere outside the range you have selected.

▶ To select the entire Timeline, double-click with the LMB on the Timeline.

▶ To scale a range of keys on the Timeline, use the arrow manipulators on the left and right sides of the selected range.

▶ To move the selected range of keys, use the double-arrow manipulator in the center of the selected range.

Animators frequently will select a single frame with the intent of moving one key. **Shift**+LMB clicking on one frame will work the same as selecting a range of frames, and the manipulator handles the function the same as well.

Copying and Pasting Keys

There are many methods of copying and pasting keys in Maya. One of the quickest ways is to select a range on the Timeline, right-click and choose Copy, and then click on a new frame. This frame will act as the start frame for the pasted animation. Right-click on the new frame and choose Paste, Paste.

Another method involves using the Copy Keys tool in Maya. This is an underused tool because it allows you copy animation between scenes by using the Windows clipboard. Follow along and you will see:

▶ Save your scene as copy_Test.ma.

▶ Select the sphere.

▶ Click on Edit, Keys, Copy Keys and the options box □.

▶ Copy the settings shown in Figure 13.5 and click Copy Keys.

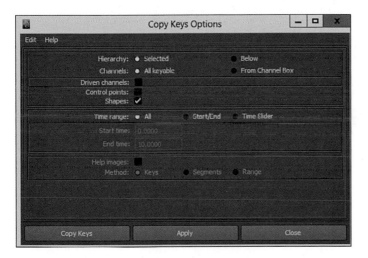

FIGURE 13.5
The settings for copying your keys on the sphere.

▶ Now open key_Test.ma.

▶ It is the same scene you started with, except with no keys on the sphere.

▶ Select the sphere.

▶ Click on Edit, Keys, Paste Keys and the options box □.

▶ Copy the settings shown in Figure 13.6 and click Paste Keys.

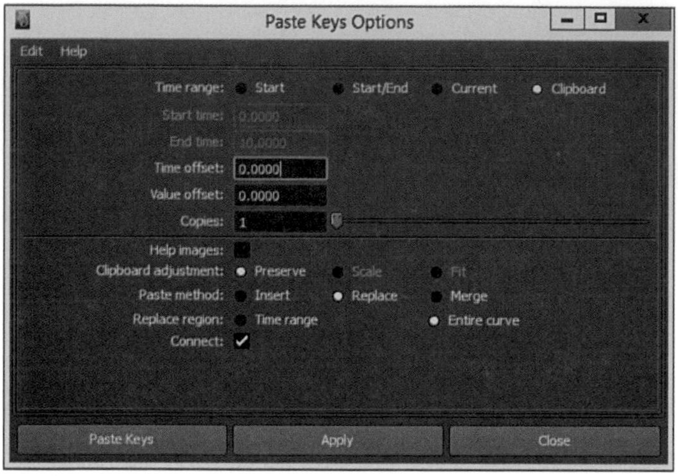

FIGURE 13.6
The settings for pasting keys from the clipboard. Copy these settings and click Paste Keys.

▶ If you copied my settings correctly, your animation should be pasted into this blank scene as it was in the copy_Test.ma scene.

▶ Play back the animation by pressing **Alt+v**.

A commonly used method for copying keys is executed on the Timeline. It is not strictly a method for copying keys as much as it is a method for copying the current "state" of the Channel Box. In other words, it will copy the current values of all channels of a selected object or node for you to paste somewhere else on the Timeline. Let's give it a try:

▶ In your animation scene, click on frame 1.

▶ Take note of the position, rotation, and scale of the sphere.

▶ Now MMB click and drag from frame 1 to frame 24 on the Timeline.

▶ When you release the MMB, nothing will appear to happen, but what Maya has done in the background is actually copy all of the values in the Channel Box on frame 1 into the clipboard. Also notice that the sphere did not move to where it actually is on frame 24; it is still in its frame 1 position.

▶ Set these values on frame 24 by pressing **S**.

▶ Play back the animation and notice that you have successfully copied the sphere's information from frame 1 to frame 24.

Remember, the MMB-drag trick does not require there to be a keyframe on the frame you are copying. Try it a few more times on frames that do not have keys on them. You will see that you can copy the "state" of an object anywhere on the Timeline.

The Graph Editor and Editing Keys

The most powerful animation editor and arguably the longest to master is the Graph Editor. This editor displays the mathematics behind the motion, in the form of what are called *animation curves*. If you are familiar with algebra, you will know that a graph displays the relationship between two different variables. In Maya's Graph Editor, the relationship on display is that between *time* and *value*. Click on Window, Animation Editors, Graph Editor to open the Graph Editor and begin to see its functionality. It will look like Figure 13.7.

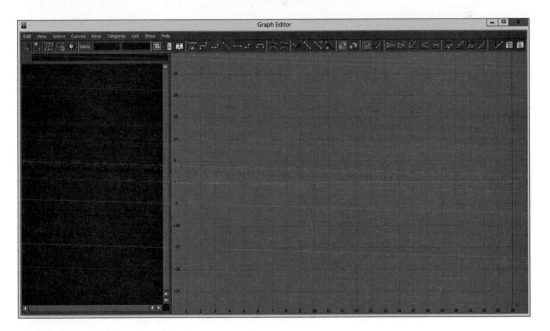

FIGURE 13.7
The Graph Editor is a powerful editor for animation. Learning to work with this editor is essential to creating lifelike and engaging animation.

At the top of the window are the menus for editing the different components of animation: Curves, Keys, Tangents, and so on.

Select your sphere. You will see that all of your animation curves load automatically into the Graph Editor, as in Figure 13.8.

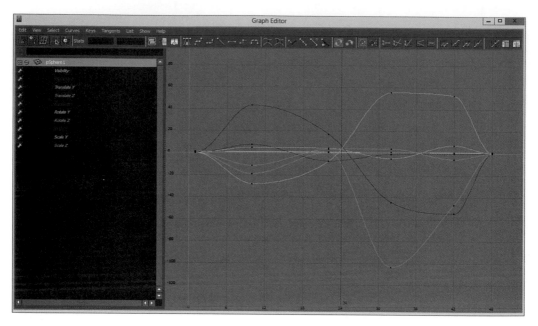

FIGURE 13.8
The Graph Editor will display animation curves on selected objects.

Look closely at the two axes in the Graph Editor. Along the bottom of the window, the frame numbers are displayed. Along the left side of the graph, values are displayed. So, as time goes by, the values change, and you can see what a value will be on any given frame. See this in action by pressing **Alt+v** and the red vertical line representing the current time moving across the graph.

Working with the Graph Editor

The Graph Editor is used primarily for polishing your animation. You will work by assessing the smoothness of the curves and then selecting and moving keys and adjusting tangent handles (described next) to take your animation that last 10% of the way. All of the black dots represent keys, and the colored lines represent the animation curves of your channels. Let's click on a few of the tools and menus to see what they do:

▶ Select any of the black dots that represent keys.

▶ You can move a key by pressing **W** and then MMB dragging it. Dragging left or right changes the frame that the key falls on. Dragging up or down changes the value of the key.

▶ LMB dragging while near a key will move the key, too. The Rotate tool does not work in the Graph Editor, but the Scale tool does.

▶ Select a group of keys.

▶ Switch to the Scale tool.

▶ MMB dragging up and down scales the values, and MMB dragging left and right scales the time. Notice that the center point of the scale is wherever you initially click on the Graph Editor.

▶ Select any one of the channels on the left side of the window. You will see that only that channel's animation curve displays when it is selected. You can return to viewing the entire object's channels by selecting the object in the left side of the Graph Editor.

Interpolation and Tangents

You may notice that when selected, a key has a handle attached to it. This is called a *tangent handle*. Manipulating this handle will adjust the animation curve as it passes through the key, and the handle will always stay tangent to the curve itself. Manipulating tangents is the primary method of smoothing animation using the Graph Editor. You will see all of the different tangent types as buttons along the top of the Graph Editor, as in Figure 13.9.

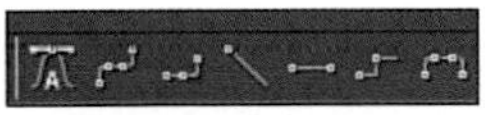

FIGURE 13.9
The different tangent and interpolation types that Maya offers.

The terms "tangents" and "interpolation" are generally interchangeable in Maya, as you use the different tangent types to access different types of interpolation between keys.

We call the animation curves between keys "interpolated" frames. Maya has some default interpolation types, but really all they determine is the angle of the tangents. When you use keyframes sparingly and use the tangents to get the animation curve that you want, you are using good keyframe economy, but on the other hand, you may have to do a lot of serious tangent polishing to get your scene to look finished. Let's look at some of the interpolation types:

▶ Open graph_Editor.ma.

▶ Select the sphere.

▶ Open the Graph Editor.

▶ Click on the RotateY channel on the left and see just that channel's animation curve load.

▶ Press **F** to frame the curve in the Graph Editor.

▶ Your Graph Editor should look like mine in Figure 13.10.

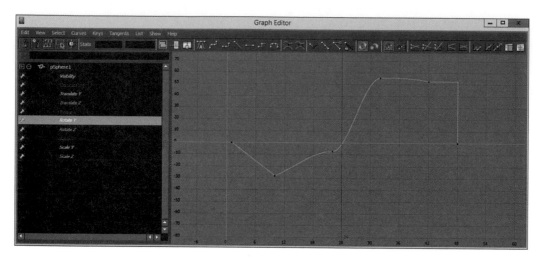

FIGURE 13.10
The RotateY animation curve has all the different types of interpolation on it for us to see.

There are actually only three different types of interpolation, even though there are seven different tangent types. The three interpolation types are linear, spline, and stepped. The seven tangent types are Auto, Spline, Clamped, Linear, Flat, Stepped, and Plateau. The two I did not specifically build into this animation curve are Auto and Spline, because Auto tangents simply try to anticipate the smoothness you are trying to create and will use a combination of the other tangent types. Finally, with Spline tangents, Maya will always try to make your animation curves as smooth as possible, no matter what you intended the shape to be. Next we'll discuss each one of these tangent types:

▶ The very first keyframe uses Linear interpolation. This means Maya will move all of the objects linearly between keys. This type of movement is considered mechanical and boring.

▶ The second key has Linear as well.

▶ The third key has Flat tangents. This is a form of spline interpolation, where the tangents have Slow In/Slow Out applied to them. As the time advances toward the key on frame 22, the rotation in the Y axis comes to a temporary stop, before it accelerates out of that key again.

▶ The fourth key is Flat as well, but it was generated by using the Plateau tangents. Plateau tangent types gives you Flat tangents between two keys that have close values, and Smooth tangents between keys that have large change in values. The only difference between Plateau and Clamped tangents is that Plateau will also create Flat tangents at the beginning and end of your animation, and Clamped will make them Smooth.

▶ The fifth key is Stepped interpolation. This type of interpolation is akin to stop-motion animation. A key with Stepped interpolation will hold the value until the next keyframe, no matter how much time passes. This tangent type is commonly used in the very early block-ing stages of animation, because it is easier to view your animation with no interpolation than to try to imagine your animation with rough interpolation removed.

Now that you have seen the different interpolation types, let's see a few of them in practice in an animation scene with a little more practical application:

▶ Open bouncing_Ball.ma in this Hour's files.

▶ Play the animation by pressing **Alt+v** to see the ball bouncing.

▶ Stop the animation by pressing **Esc**.

▶ Select the sphere and open the Graph Editor.

▶ Select the Translate Y channel in the left panel of the Graph Editor and press **F** to frame the curve in the window.

▶ Notice how the shape of the animation curve resembles the motion of a bouncing ball itself. As you learn to animate, you will begin to notice patterns like this in the Graph Editor, and motion becomes easier to manipulate and smooth.

▶ Select any one of the keys at the bottom of one of the bounces.

▶ It has a tangent that is "broken," as in Figure 13.11.

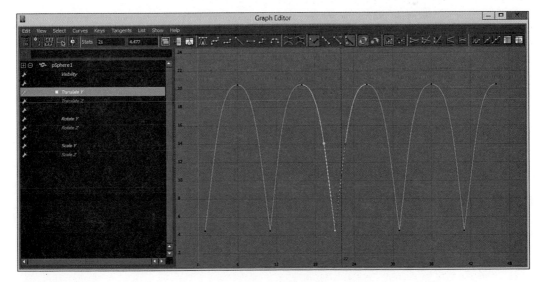

FIGURE 13.11
As you can see, the tangents on this key are not in a line, but broken in the middle.

To get the sharp impact on the floor, the tangent handles needed to be broken. You can do that by pressing the button with the folded tangent handles in a "V" shape in the middle of the row of buttons at the top of the Graph Editor. Once you have broken a tangent handle, you can individually manipulate either side to give any shape you like.

What does the tangent look like at the top of the bounce? If you said "flat," you are correct. We need a Slow In/Slow Out motion at the top of the arc of a bouncing ball because that is how gravity affects an object in air. However, those tangents are not just flat, they are *weighted*.

▶ Select any of the top keys on the Translate Y animation curve in the Graph Editor.

▶ Notice how the circles at the end of the handles are not solid like normal tangents, but hollow. This is because they are weighted tangents. Weighted tangents can be stretched to give greater or lesser influence on the animation interpolation between keys.

▶ With one of the keys at the top of the curve still selected, click on Curves, Non Weighted Tangents.

▶ You will see the curve goes back to the default tangent that you are used to.

▶ You can use the Curves menu in the Graph Editor to make any key, or to make any selected curve, use Weighted or Non Weighted tangents. Your default tangent types can also be set by clicking Window, Settings/Preference, Preferences and then adjusting the options in the Animation tab in the preferences window.

Buffer Curves

Buffer Curves is a tool in the Graph Editor that allows you to switch between two different "snapshots" of an animation curve. Follow along to learn how to use these curves:

▶ Let's pretend we want to try a version of our bouncing ball scene in which the ball travels twice as high. Select the Translate Y animation curve by clicking anywhere on the curve that is not on a keyframe.

▶ Click Curves, Buffer Curve, Snapshot. You have just made a Buffer Curve snapshot, which you will be able to snap your animation curve back to at any time.

▶ We are not viewing Buffer Curves yet, so click on View, Show Buffer Curves.

▶ Now select all of the keys at the top of the bounces, and MMB drag them upward, like in Figure 13.12.

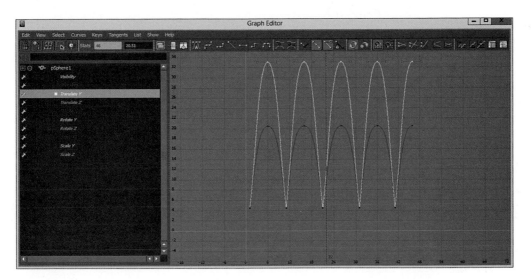

FIGURE 13.12
The keys at the top of the bounces moved upward in the Graph Editor, revealing the Buffer Curves beneath them.

The Buffer Curves are the dark gray curves that are left behind as you adjust the animation. This snapshot can be used to "undo" your animation back to the previous snapshot with a single click.

▶ Let's now pretend that you don't like the new animation. Click on Curves, Swap Buffer Curve.

▶ The animation curves swap back to the snapshot that you first made, and a new snapshot is left behind in their place.

Buffer Curves save into a Maya file, can be swapped an infinite number of times without messing up the animation, and best of all, are outside the normal Undo queue and therefore will not be affected by you undoing actions in the scene. This is a very handy tool for viewing multiple versions of an animation, comparing ideas, and saving revisions for review later.

NOTE

Graph Editor Use and Scene Lifespan

As you create a scene in Maya, it is typical to work less and less in the panels and more and more in the Graph Editor. At an advanced stage, an animated scene will have hundreds of controls, each with dozens of animation curves in the graph editor. However, problems in the panel such as unsmooth animation and jerky motion are still easier to diagnose from looking at your animation curves than to fix in panel. A scene that is ready for final polish will normally be finished by working about 75% in the Graph Editor and 25% in panel, checking results.

The Graph Editor has many more tools for retiming animation, manipulating keys, and working with animation curves. Use Maya's help to explore the buttons and menus.

The Dope Sheet

Another useful animation editor is the Dope Sheet. This editor looks and behaves like a spreadsheet, in which keyframes are designated by colored cells. You can move and scale ranges of cells, but you cannot change the values of any of the keys. In this way, the Dope Sheet is used for gross retiming of your animations. Let's use it in this way to retime an animated scene:

- ▶ Open bouncing_Ball_Squash.ma in this Hour's files.

- ▶ This is the bouncing ball scene we've been looking at, but with Squash and Stretch applied to the ball. However, the timing is totally off. We will retime this with the Dope Sheet.

- ▶ Click on Window, Animation Editors, Dope Sheet.

- ▶ The Dope Sheet will open, like in Figure 13.13.

- ▶ Play back the animation and see how poorly timed the Squash and Stretch effect is applied.

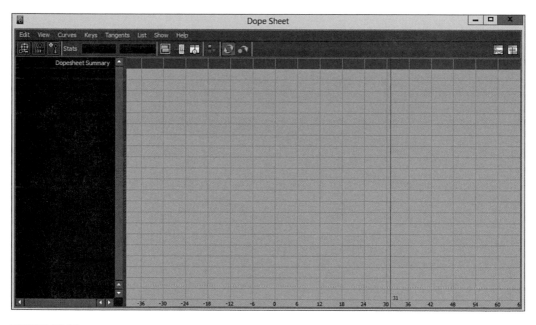

FIGURE 13.13
The Dope Sheet looks like a spreadsheet. It is useful for gross retiming of animation.

If you are using a pose-to-pose method of creating animation, the Dope Sheet is useful in the early blocking stages of your shot. You can have at-a-glance feedback on the timing of your keys, as well as access all of the keyframes in the scene without having to make complex selections. Let's fix the timing now:

▶ In the Dope Sheet, click on View, Scene Summary. This turns on the display of all of the keyframes in your entire scene. This is valuable for very high-level retiming of an animation.

▶ We want to retime the Squash and Stretch keys only, so we will need to display them.

▶ On the left side of the Dope Sheet click on the plus sign (+) next to the Scene Summary to expand it. All of the names of all of the animated channels will appear. You will see "Squash" is one of them.

▶ Click on the Squash channel.

▶ The keys of the Select channel will turn yellow to indicate they are all selected.

▶ Use the MMB to drag the keys in the Squash channel three frames to the left (earlier in time).

▶ The Squash keys will line up much better with the rest of the animation, as in Figure 13.14.

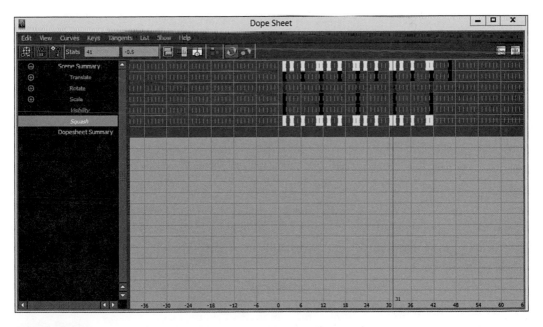

FIGURE 13.14
The "squash" keys have been moved in the Dope Sheet to be in better timing with the rest of the keys.

▶ Now play back the animation, and see the keyframes are timed much better than before.

▶ As an alternative to using the Scene Summary view to see all of the animation channels in a scene (particularly when a scene contains many animated controllers), the Dope Sheet will load the channels of any selected object.

The Dope Sheet has menus and options for manipulating keys similar to the Graph Editor. Explore the menus and use the Maya Help to get you started learning this powerful tool.

Editing Motion with the Trax Editor

Maya allows for nonlinear animation. You can import, export, copy, and paste animation "clips" and arrange them in a window called the Trax Editor. This view is analogous to video-editing software; layers of clips can be arranged as well, and the resulting animation will be added together. You can even do some retiming in this view. You will see how to simply import and apply clips to an object and from there you can experiment with retiming and editing the clips. Follow these steps to familiarize yourself with using the Track Editor:

▶ Open trax_Start.ma.

▶ This scene contains just our bouncing ball rig but no animation. Let's import some animation clips onto this ball.

▶ Click on Window, Animation Editors, Trax Editor.

▶ The Trax Editor opens and it will be blank, as in Figure 13.15.

The Trax Editor functions similar to any nonlinear editing program; you can import clips and move them anywhere you want in time, and even copy and paste multiple clips into new layers. Let's try something a little simpler to start:

▶ Select the sphere.

▶ In the Trax Editor, click File, Import Animation Clip to Characters.

▶ Navigate to this Hour's source files and choose bouncing_Clip.ma.

▶ Play back the animation. The ball bounces a few times and then comes to a sudden stop.

▶ Select the sphere again and in the Trax Editor, click File, Import Animation Clip to Characters.

▶ Choose rolling_Clip.ma.

▶ You should have two clips in your Trax Editor, as in Figure 13.16.

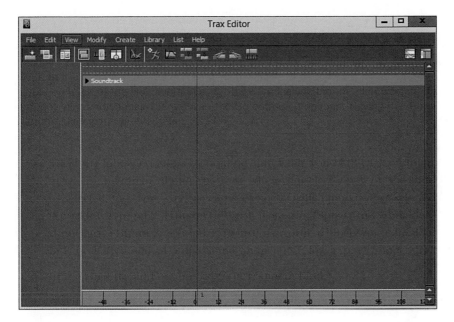

FIGURE 13.15
The empty Trax Editor before we import animation clips.

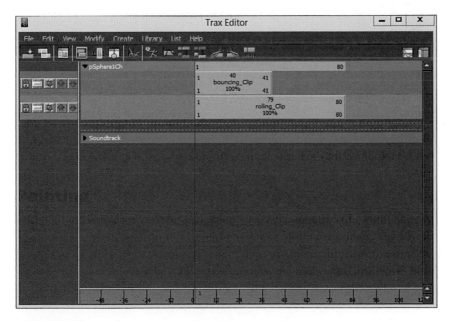

FIGURE 13.16
The two clips are loaded into the Trax Editor.

- ▶ Now select and drag rolling_Clip so that the start frame is on the last frame of bouncing_Clip.

- ▶ Play back the animation and watch the ball bounce, stop, and roll a bit to the side.

- ▶ Experiment by importing more copies of both clips and assemble the animation in a unique way in the Trax Editor.

- ▶ Remember that the layers are additive, so you can have some unpredictable results if you blend animation that was not created to be blended.

- ▶ To export animation clips, you can simply click on File, Export Animation Clip in the Trax Editor and it will export all of the animation on the currently selected channels or objects as a clip for you to use later.

The Trax Editor offers the ability to layer and edit animation clips in an intuitive way. Create your own animation clips and assemble them in an interesting way using the Trax Editor.

Constraints and Animating

One of the biggest concerns of animators is making objects "stick" to one another when animating. A character holding a prop, for instance. This comes up so often that we had to include a section on constraints in this Hour so as not to be remiss in our duties.

Constraint Versus Parent

You've seen the use of constraints already, so you know that they function similar to parenting or grouping. What constraints offer above and beyond parenting is the ability to turn the relationship on and off, and to even animate this ability. Using constraints, you are able to create an animation of a character picking up a hammer and even putting it down again. What you need to remember, however, is that the relationship of the object constrained to another cannot be animated, only the strength of the constraint. In other words, once an object is picked up, it cannot be moved around within the hand that is constraining it; it is "locked" into the position that it is constrained in. However, we have a simple workaround for this problem: using locators and/or groups as our constraining objects, thus leaving our props free to animate even when their parent is constrained.

We'll take a look at this relationship now. To begin, open constraints_Start.ma. The familiar robot arm from Hour 12, "Skinning: Attaching Geometry to a Rig," is in this scene, and it is rotating around in a circle. When the arm comes to a stop, the cup on the conveyor belt arrives in the robot's claw. We want the claw to pick up the cup and move it over the barrel, then release it. We already have a rig set up that is built for this kind of action. Both the claw and the ball have locators that will serve as the constraint points:

▶ Play the animation back. The cup rolls to the end of the conveyor belt but is not taken by the robot arm.

▶ Select cup_CTRL. It is the box that is around the cup itself, not the locator.

▶ Move it around to see that cup_CTRL is parented under the locator and can freely move around. Undo your movements to get the cup back to its original position.

▶ Go to frame 50 by clicking on it on the Timeline.

▶ In the perspective panel, select the locator called claw_Locator.

▶ **Shift**-select the locator called cup_Constrain_HERE.

▶ Switch to the Animation menu set by pressing **F2**.

▶ Click on Constrain, Parent.

▶ Press **S** to set a key on frame 50 on the locator.

▶ Change to frame 49 by pressing **Alt+,** on your keyboard.

▶ Select the cup_Constrain_HERE locator and in the Channel Box, change the value of the Blend Parent channel to 0. Scroll down until you see the input called cup_Constrain_HERE_ parentConstraint1. Change the channel marked "Claw Locator W0" to 0 and set a key by right-clicking on the channel and choosing Key Selected. We just turned off the parent constraint so that the cup is free to move in the frames leading up to frame 50.

▶ Click on frame 80 on the Timeline.

▶ Select the cup_Constrain_HERE locator and press **S** to set a key. Also, right-click on the Claw Locator W0 channel and choose Key Selected.

▶ Click on frame 81 on the Timeline.

▶ Select the cup_Constrain_HERE locator and in the Channel Box, change the value of the Blend Parent channel to 0. Scroll down until you see the input called cup_Constrain_HERE_ parentConstraint1. Change the channel marked "Claw Locator W0" to 0 and set a key by right-clicking on the channel and choosing Key Selected. The constraint is "off" again, so we can now freely animate the cup.

▶ Click on cup_CTRL and press **S** to set a key.

▶ Click on frame 100 on the Timeline.

▶ In the Persp panel, select and move cup_CTRL down in Y until it is inside the barrel.

▶ Press **S** to set a key.

▶ Play back the animation. The cup should roll down the conveyor belt, get picked up and move over the barrel, and then be dropped into the barrel, as in Figure 13.17.

FIGURE 13.17
The animated scene, with the cup being brought to the barrel and then dropped.

I have saved the final version of this animation as constraints_Finish.ma. Open the scene and make sure your version matches the animation I created. You should have a nice loop of animation of the cup appearing and then disappearing into the barrel. Constraints offer the functionality of a parent/child relationship, but with the added ability to turn the relationship on and off. Remember, you cannot change the positioned of a constrained object; try to move the locator cup_Constrain_HERE in any of the frames between 50 and 80. It will move, but then will snap back to its constrained position. The cup_CTRL, however, is free to move because it is simply parented to the locator. This is the reason we always create a rig for props—to give animators a point to constrain to.

Using Other Animation Tools

As you can probably tell from the numerous menus in the Animation menu set, there are literally hundreds of methods of creating movement in your Maya scene. Take some time to explore tools such as Ghosting, Editable Motion Trails, and even animating some of the deformers on objects and characters. The Maya Help is very valuable for understanding the basic function of these tools.

Creating Dynamic Relationships with Expressions

The Expression Editor is listed under Animation Editors because the relationships you can create with it are dynamic and useful for creating scripted movements. Let's create a dynamic relationship to see this in action. To begin, open expression_Start.ma. You'll see a sphere that is animated moving up and down in Y. The cone is static. We are going to use an expression to make the cone animate based on the movement of the sphere:

▶ Click on Window, Animation Editors, Expression Editor.

▶ It will look like Figure 13.18.

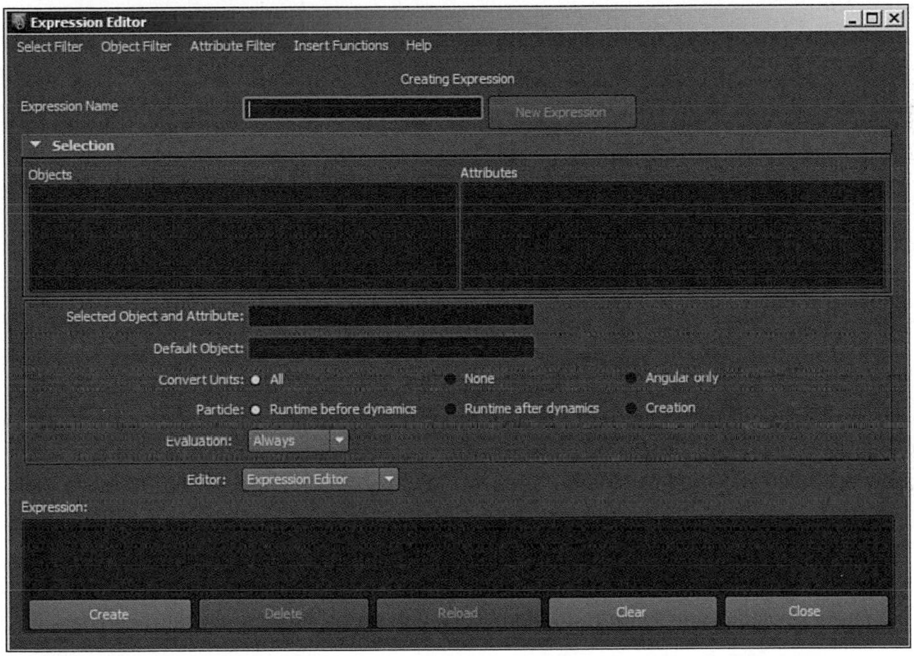

FIGURE 13.18
The Expression Editor. Objects load on the left, and attributes load on the right.

▶ The Expression Editor allows you to create links and execute equations by creating what are called "expressions" in the bottom of the editor. Select the sphere.

▶ Notice how the sphere's name loads in the left panel of the Expression Editor and its attributes load into the right side.

▶ Click on translateY on the right side.

▶ In the center of the Expression Editor, the name pSphere1.translateY appears in the box labeled Selected Object and Attribute.

▶ Copy this down into a Notepad window (if you are using Windows) or a text editor application of your choice.

NOTE

Copy Down Expressions

The Expression Editor is constantly refreshing depending on what is selected, so you can lose your place easily. It's best to copy down the attributes you want to use so you don't lose them when the Editor loads newly selected objects.

▶ Now select the cone.

▶ In the right side of the Expression Editor, select the scaleY attribute.

▶ Copy the result from the center of the Expression Editor, which should be pCone1.translateY in your notepad as well.

▶ Now we will create the expression. Using your notepad to copy and paste the correct attributes, put the following into the bottom box of the Expression Editor, labeled "Expression":

```
pCone1.scaleY = pSphere1.translateY * 2
```

▶ Press **Enter**.

▶ Play back the animation. You will see that the cone now scales in the Y axis along with the movement of the sphere.

Hundreds of commands and functions are available to you in the Expression Editor, but our simple math function serves nicely as a demonstration of the power of expressions. You can create a dynamic connection between any two attributes in Maya using this tool, which makes it an impressive part of the software's animation offering.

Creating Animation on a Path

Motion paths offer a wide array of uses. From camera animation to animating particles, to animating a roller coaster on a track, paths serve many purposes. They are quick to set up as well. Let's create a simple path animation using these steps:

▶ Open path_Start.ma. There is a sphere and a NURBS curve created by randomly clicking the EP Curve tool. You can also use any NURBS shape that you want, such as a line or a NURBS circle.

▶ Select the sphere.

▶ **Shift**-select the curve.

▶ Switch to the Animation menu set by pressing **F2**.

▶ Click on Animate, Motion Paths, Attach to Motion Path.

▶ The sphere now follows the path of the curve.

▶ It is moving very fast, though. Let's change that. Open the Graph Editor by clicking on Window, Animation Editors, Graph Editor.

▶ Select the sphere in the Persp panel.

▶ The animation curve for the motion path is labeled "u value." Select the key on frame 24 and **Shift+MMB** drag it to the right until the key sits on frame 72.

▶ Type **72** into both the playback range end and the scene end boxes in the Range Slider.

▶ Play back the animation, and like in Figure 13.19, the sphere should now only finish the path animation by frame 72.

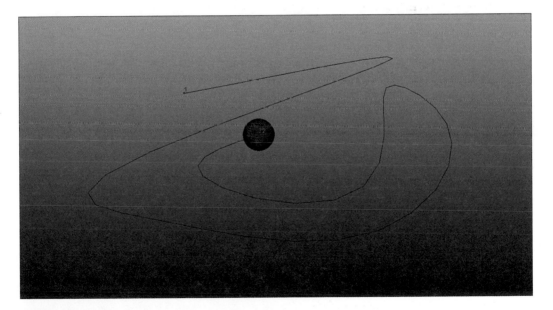

FIGURE 13.19
The sphere following the path from frame 1 to frame 72.

Motion paths have some interesting features, such as the ability to change which direction the object faces (and to animate that attribute) and to have the object automatically bank on turns. Explore the attributes of the motion path by selecting the sphere, going into the Attribute Editor (**Ctrl+A**), and looking at the "motion1" tab.

Driven Keys

Driven Keys made their debut in Hour 9, "Relationships and Making Nodes Work Together," and they are definitely a good tool to know in terms of creating relationships. They are also a good animation tool. For instance, if you want to make a wheel automatically roll when you move it along the ground, a Driven Key makes that possible. Follow these steps to familiarize yourself with Driven Keys:

- ▶ Open driven_Start.ma. We have a wheel sitting on the ground, ready to animate.

- ▶ Switch to the Animation menu set by pressing **F2**.

- ▶ Select the wheel.

- ▶ Click on Animate, Set Driven Key, Set.

- ▶ The Set Driven Key window will open, and the wheel is loaded as the Driven Object. Click on Load Driver.

- ▶ In the Driver section (top section) of the Set Driven Key window, click on Translate X. In the Driven section (bottom), click on Rotate Z.

- ▶ Click Key.

Because we know that the circumference of a circle is pi times the diameter, we will use that equation to make the right amount of rotation on the wheel as the wheel moves. Let's apply this knowledge to a Driven Key setup:

- ▶ Select the sphere and in the Channel Box, type **6.28** in the translateX channel and press **Enter**. (That's pi times the diameter of the wheel, the diameter being 2.)

- ▶ Type **-360** in the Rotate channel and press **Enter**.

- ▶ Back in the Set Driven Key window, click on Key.

- ▶ Open the Graph Editor by clicking Window, Animation Editors, Graph Editor.

- ▶ Select the wheel, and when the animation curve for the Driven Key appears, select it. Your window will look like Figure 13.20.

- ▶ In the Graph Editor, click on Curves, Post Infinity, Linear. Click on Curves, Pre Infinity, Linear. You just made it so that all ranges to infinity will have the same rotational relationship.

- ▶ Close the Graph Editor and the Set Driven Key window and then select and move your wheel. Notice how the wheel rotates realistically no matter which direction you move it, and no matter how far in either direction it moves.

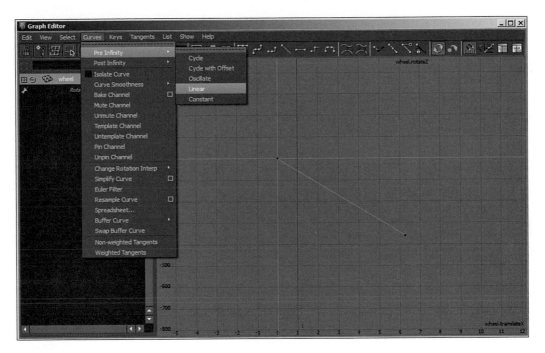

FIGURE 13.20
By setting our Pre Infinity and Post Infinity types to linear, the wheel will always have the correct rotation value no matter the translate value.

Driven Keys are not only a great way to set up relationships, they are very helpful when you need to automate some animation. You can create some very interesting movements by chaining together multiple Driven Key systems. In fact, some very complex animated relationships that you've seen in major feature films, such as the metal panels shifting as a car transforms into a robot, are controlled and animated using Driven Keys.

An Animated Scene

Even though teaching an entire character animation pipeline would fill a book twice the size of this one, I wanted to include some animation so you can see all of the principles and the technical animation tools in Maya in action. Therefore, I've created a scene with Sam and did a little bit of animation on him.

BONUS

Sam Animated

I've included a scene with Sam doing a simple motion for you to open and play with. It is called sam_Greeting.ma. Although character animation is outside the purview of this book, hopefully you will be inspired to create some animation with Sam after seeing this scene. Open the scene and look in the Graph Editor as you select his different controls and see how I've dealt with the tangents. Look at the controls on the hammer prop and see how I've set up the constraint. Click around and view the different keyframes I've placed on the character and learn about how they work by making your own little adjustments to the animation. Only by practicing daily will you learn to move characters in a convincing, engaging way.

Summary

Animation, or creating the illusion of movement, is easy to do in Maya. However, just because you can create keyframes with the click of a button doesn't mean your animation will be engaging or appealing. You must first master the use of the animation tools and become intimately familiar with the many animation editors if you want to advance to the level of a true animator. Start with small, simple animation tests like the ones shown in this book (bouncing ball, robot arms, and so on). Then move on to doing very simple gestures with the Sam_v2 rig I've provided for you. Only after you have created some very detailed and dynamic (yet simple) scenes using our character rig will you be ready to tackle even more difficult scenes. Scenes with complex character rigs (believe it or not, Sam is *very* simple), scenes with dialogue and acting, and scenes with multiple characters should only be *attempted* after at least a year of practicing. Trying to create these very complex animations too soon can be very discouraging to a learning animator. Luckily, Maya makes the tools simple to use and easy to learn; the rest is up to you.

Q&A

Q. My animation does not play back at 24fps. Why?

A. To set your playback to 24fps, click on Window, Settings/Preferences, Preferences. Then in the Time Slider section, find the Playback Speed drop-down box and choose 24fps.

Q. My objects are moving all over the scene but I never set any keys. Why?

A. Is AutoKey turned on? Look in the bottom-right corner of the Maya UI. If the button that shows a key is highlighted, you are setting keys any time you make a change to a channel (or, in this case, move an object that has been keyed already). Most animators like AutoKey, yet many work without it.

Q. **My Graph Editor doesn't show any animation curves. Why not?**

A. By default, the Graph Editor shows the animation curves for only selected objects. If you find it cumbersome to have to select the objects you are animating (if you are only animating one object in a scene, for instance), you can change the functionality of the Graph Editor by clicking on List, Auto Load Selected Objects. With that unchecked, you can load the objects you want to animate a single time.

Q. **Why is my constrained object still moving with the locator even though the Blend Parent is set at 0?**

A. You must animate two channels if you want to turn a constraint off. The first is the Blend Parent channel located underneath the object's channels in the top of the Channel Box. The second channel is the actual weight of the constraint, located in the inputs listed in the bottom of the Channel Box. The weight channel will be called something like Locator W0. These two channels need to be animated in concert to turn a constraint on or off.

Workshop

The workshop contains quiz questions and exercises to help you solidify your understanding of the material covered. Try to answer all questions before looking at the "Answers" section that follows.

Quiz

1. How do you set a key on all channels?

2. Which animation editor offers you quick access to keys for retiming?

3. The steepness or smoothness of an animation curve is controlled by a handle called what?

4. True or false? A constrained object can be animated and change position.

5. Why is it a good idea to copy objects and attributes names out of the Expression Editor and into a notepad or other text editor?

Exercise

I've provided several animation scenes you can peruse to learn how to move objects in a convincing (or at least technically correct) way. For your exercise, try to re-create one of these scenes from scratch, be it the bouncing ball or perhaps the robot arm. Use the Timeline to set your keys and the Graph Editor to adjust them. Manipulate the curves and adjust the tangent handles. When you are finished, you may want to save your scene for later use in the lighting and rendering hours!

Answers

1. The **S** key sets a key on all channels in the Channel Box.

2. The Dope Sheet offers at-a-glance viewing of the timing of all keys in a scene.

3. The smoothness of animation curves is controlled using tangent handles. These can be any of the seven built-in types that Maya offers, or they can be customized.

4. False. A constrained object has all of its channels locked while it is constrained. You can turn off the constraint to move the object once again—or better yet, you can apply your constraints to objects that are the parents of the actual object you want to be animated. This way, you can still animate the object within the parent.

5. The Expression Editor annoyingly refreshes with every single newly selected object. Once you have found the object and attribute name you are going to use in your expression, the best idea is to start a notepad that you can copy these long names into and avoid typing them out again.

HOUR 14

Creating and Adjusting Cameras

What You'll Learn in This Hour:

▶ How to create cameras

▶ What the different camera attributes do

▶ What the different types of cameras are used for

▶ How to properly animate a camera

Fundamentally, you are using cameras all the time when you use Maya. The Persp panel is indeed just a perspective camera that you have been flying around the scene, adjusting its position and rotation. In CG visual effects and in fully CG animation, however, knowledge of the many attributes of a camera and proper manipulation of those attributes are paramount.

NOTE

Cameras and Panels

Any panel can display the point of view of any camera. In fact, more than one panel can display the same camera. You should note that a panel's display is independent of the camera. In other words, if you have a panel that is displaying the Persp camera and everything is in wireframe mode, with NURBS curves hidden, and another panel also showing the Persp camera, it can be in shaded and textured mode with all objects displaying. A panel is merely a window through which you can load any camera, and each panel has its own display settings.

In this Hour, you will see how cameras are created and adjusted to bring the best result to the shot. You will see some of the attributes in action and their effect on a camera's point of view. We will take a brief look at the different types of cameras Maya offers, and also use a simple rig to give our camera some animation.

Creating Cameras

Maya's cameras are all created through the Create menu. Follow these short steps to create a simple camera:

- ▶ Click on Create, Cameras, Camera □.

- ▶ In the options dialog box that opens, leave all the settings at their default, but change the Focal Length setting to 50.0.

- ▶ Click Create.

TIP

"CG" Camera

Because Maya and nearly all other 3D programs create a 35mm camera by default, when you don't change the focal length, your work will stick out as "CG." Audiences (and CG recruiters) have an eye for the default camera, so you want to avoid using a 35mm focal length as much as possible. One nice trick is to change the default camera's Create settings to have a focal length of 50. This is a slightly more "zoomed" lens—one that is a standard lens for photography and does not seem so "wide" and "CG" looking.

There should be a camera created at the world origin, as in Figure 14.1.

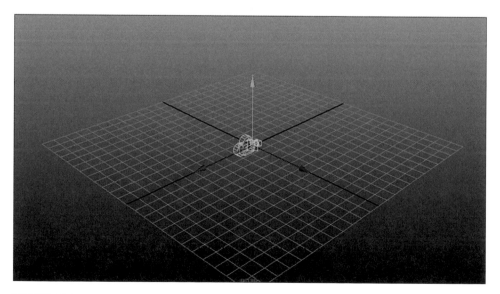

FIGURE 14.1
The camera created at the world origin.

But now that you have a camera, how do you see through it? There are a few ways to change to a camera's view:

▶ Select the camera, and in any panel that you would like to switch to this camera's view, click on Panels, Look Through Selected.

▶ Select the camera, and in any panel that you would like to switch to this camera's view, click on Panels, Perspective, camera1.

▶ MMB-drag a camera from the Outliner onto a panel window, and it will switch to that camera's view automatically.

Let's load a panel configuration that allows us to see the camera and the camera's view simultaneously:

▶ In the Toolbox (left side of screen), select the Four View layout. Alternatively, you can click in any panel on Panels, Layouts, Four Panes.

▶ Now in the top panel, select camera1 and click on Panels, Look Through Selected.

Your layout should resemble the one in Figure 14.2.

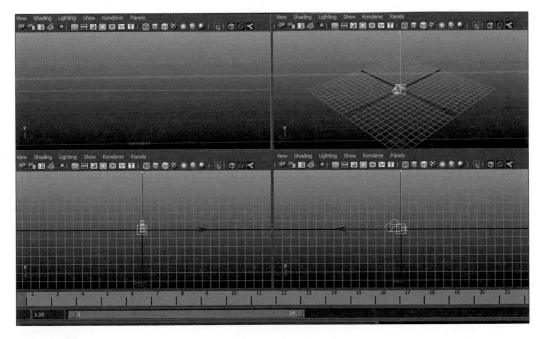

FIGURE 14.2
This is a common Maya layout—a perspective panel, a few orthographic panels, and a camera panel ready for animation.

Now that we can see what is going on, let's manipulate the camera a bit.

First, in the camera1 panel, use the camera dolly, track, and orbit controls and watch the resulting movement in the Persp panel. You will be able to confirm that although **Alt**+RMB is commonly called "zooming" by artists and books alike, it is in fact "dollying." There is no change in the focal length (zooming), only movement of the camera in the local Z axis.

Select the camera in the Persp panel again, and use the Move and Rotate tools to manipulate the camera's position and rotation. You will notice that translating the camera is akin to tracking within the camera view (**Alt**+MMB), but that rotating the camera actually rotates the camera in place, whereas orbiting the camera in its panel rotates the camera around a point in space in front of it called the "point of interest." This is not just rotating it but applying translations as well.

TIP

Orbiting and Rotating

When you start animating cameras, you will see how dangerous it can be to use AutoKey while you orbit a camera. Because the camera is rotating around a fixed point in front of it, all of the rotation channels are being changed in unpredictable ways, even during very simple camera moves. It is always better to use the Translate and Rotate tools on the camera in a Persp panel than to use the camera-moving tools within the camera panel. Better still is to have a camera rig for controlling animation.

▼ TRY IT YOURSELF

A Look at Camera Curves

Create some animation on a camera to see the unpredictable animation curves it creates:

1. Create a new camera and press **S** to set a key. Then change one of your panels to display this new camera. Scroll forward on the Timeline and use just **Alt**+LMB to orbit the camera around its center of interest. Scroll forward again and do some more camera orbiting in panel.

2. Open the Graph Editor by clicking Window, Animation Editors, Graph Editor. With the Camera selected, look at the tangle of animation curves that result from using the Orbit tool. The camera is rotating *and* translating, and the curves do not look organized at all.

We will look at how to better manipulate the camera in scene and create predictable animation in a little bit. Now let's look at the attributes of a camera.

Common Camera Attributes

Cameras come with hundreds of attributes, many of which you will not touch, even if you are working in a high-end production. Many of the attributes deal with calculations or output methods that are very specific, such as matching a certain camera that was used to capture footage for a visual-effects shot. To get up and running in Maya, though, you should know what the following attributes do and how to control them. Create a new scene and create a camera (Create, Cameras, Camera). Select the camera and press **Ctrl+A** to open the Attribute Editor, like in Figure 14.3.

FIGURE 14.3
The Attribute Editor with a camera selected. Notice how many different sections there are for a camera's settings.

Now open the first tab, labeled Camera Attributes.

Camera Attributes

Because they have to match real-world cameras, Maya's cameras are loaded with attributes. These many settings give artists the control they need to create impressive imagery or to match footage shot in real life.

Controls

This attribute allows you to change your camera's control set to a different type after creating the camera. You may use this if you are having trouble making your camera behave like you want it to.

Angle of View

This attribute is automatically determined by the film back and focal length ratio. You normally do not need to adjust this attribute because your focal length will determine your angle of view for you.

Focal Length

This attribute is the most commonly adjusted attribute for a camera. Focal length is otherwise known as "zoom." Simply put, the more "zoomed in" a camera is, the smaller the angle of view; therefore, less perspective is shown in a scene. The lower the focal length, the higher the angle of view; therefore, more perspective is shown. A low focal length is called "fisheye," and a high focal length is called "telephoto." Follow these steps to familiarize yourself with focal length:

▶ Open focal_Test.ma in this Hour's files. There are two spheres. One is smaller than the other.

▶ Create a camera and change the Focal Length attribute to 15.

▶ Switch to the camera's view in a panel and then move the camera back in Z until the panel resembles the view in Figure 14.4.

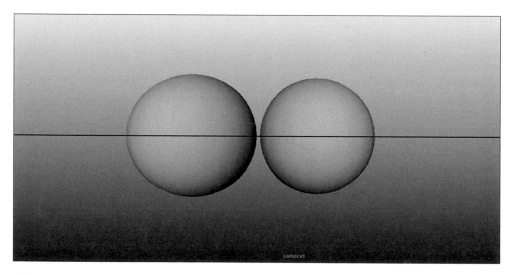

FIGURE 14.4
The two spheres in the camera1 view, with a Focal Length setting of 15.

- ▶ Now create another camera. This time set the focal length to 120.

- ▶ Change another panel's view to look through this new camera.

- ▶ Move the second camera back in Z until the view looks like the one in Figure 14.5.

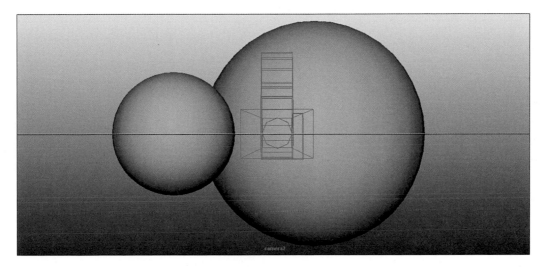

FIGURE 14.5
The same two spheres as seen through camera2, at a focal length of 120.

As you can see, the front sphere is relatively the same size in both views. The rear sphere, however, has radically different sizes. This is due to the fact that the camera with the low focal length of 15 has a very wide field of view that really displays the effect of perspective.

Focal length can be animated to make the camera zoom in and out.

Camera Scale

This attribute is not used often; it affects the relationship between the camera focal length and the scene. It is therefore used only in matching live-action cameras—and then only infrequently.

Auto Render Clip Plane

Checking this box means that at render time, Maya will determine what the closest point and the furthest point to be rendered will be, based on the objects that exist in the scene.

Near Clip Plane and Far Clip Plane

With Auto Render Clip Plane unchecked, you will set the near clip plane and the far clip plane with these two attributes. Anything closer to the camera than the value in Near Clip Plane, and anything further from the camera than the value in Far Clip Plane, will not render.

TIP

Clip Plane Display

Even though the Auto Render Clip Plane box is checked and Maya will determine the clip planes at render time, you will still see the effect of the values in the near and far clip planes in a panel. Also, if the value of Near Clip Plane is too low, sometimes Maya will have errors when displaying geometry that is close together. To alleviate such display errors, change Near Clip Plane to a higher value.

Film Back

The next set of attributes gives you control over matching your Maya camera to a real-world camera from which you have captured footage. We will cover these attributes in depth in Hour 22, "Working with Film."

Depth of Field

These attributes control the depth of field, or the focus of an image. When applying depth of field, you should remember that the more blurry an image is, the longer it takes Maya to render it.

Depth of Field

The first check box turns depth of field on or off for this camera. You still have to enable depth of field in Maya's render settings for it to render correctly.

Focus Distance

This is the distance from the camera that will be in focus. Objects at this distance will be clear and crisp.

F Stop

This attribute is similar to the F Stop on a camera. Because it can be very confusing even to photographers how F Stop relates to exposure, focal length, and the like, we will simplify it for you here. In very general terms, a higher F Stop in Maya means that there will be a large depth of field (that is, more in focus). A low F Stop conversely means that there will be more blurring, and the blurring will encroach even closer to the focus distance.

Focus Region Scale

This attribute scales the focus distance. This attribute and most other scale attributes are normally only useful in cases where you do some scene-wide scaling.

Output Settings

These attributes control the output of the camera. They are commonly kept at their defaults because most of the settings here can be overwritten at render time by the renderer. We will look at these settings more in Hour 21, "Rendering Final Imagery."

Environment

These attributes control the "background" of the camera's rendered image. Changing these settings does not actually create or adjust an environment in your Maya scene, however.

Background Color

This is the actual color of any "blank" space in your rendered image. If no geometry or image planes are loaded, this color will show. Because of how objects are anti-aliased (the fuzzing of the edges of an object to remove jagged pixelated lines), you should be aware that this color "bleeds" into the periphery of a rendered object.

CAUTION

Background Color and Premultiplying

In basic terms, "premultiplying" is when a pixel's brightness value is calculated respective to the background color it is on. This greatly affects the periphery of an object that is rendered against a colored background, even black. In compositing programs, you must normally tell the program what color was used to generate the premultiplied image with an alpha matte. Not doing so, or skipping this step, will mean you will see the color bleeding into the transparent areas, or a halo effect around the perimeter alpha. Again, even black is a color and behaves this way; do not think keeping the background color black means no color is chosen. If you are planning on using a compositing package to put your images together, make note of the background color for setting it correctly when the compositing package asks for the premultiply color.

In general, a background color should be black even if you are planning on using another color later; premultiplying everything with black saves the headache of trying to figure out what colors are bleeding into your transparent objects.

Of course, if you absolutely must use a background color, for whatever purpose, the color slider will give you the result you need.

Image Plane

An image plane is an image or a movie that displays as the background of a rendered camera. We have some experience with image planes, working with them for modeling in Hour 8, "Character Modeling." We will cover image planes and how to correctly use filmed footage as a background more in Hour 22.

Special Effects

This tab controls some of the more esoteric functions of a camera. However, by default, Maya's cameras only come with one attribute loaded here.

Shutter Angle

This is the only attribute listed in this tab. It controls the shutter angle for motion blur; essentially, a higher value means increased blurring in your motion blur.

Display Options

This section controls what visual feedback you get from your camera in a panel. These attributes can help you properly frame a shot, for example, or see if an action is falling within the area of screen that you want it to.

Display Film Gate

Essentially, this displays the entire area that is "filmable," as defined by your camera focal length and film back settings. Think of this as the piece of film in the back of the camera.

Display Resolution

The resolution gate is the actual area that will render at render time. If the film gate is the film in the back of the camera, the resolution gate is a piece of cardboard with a rectangular hole punched in it, at the aspect ratio of your render settings, that is placed in front of the film gate. How the film gate fits within the resolution gate is determined by attributes in the film back settings, which will be covered in Hour 22.

Display Gate Mask

The gate mask blocks the area of the panel that does not fall within the resolution gate and therefore will not render. The default setting is 70% opaque grey, which is adjusted by the two sliders that follow this attribute: Gate Mask Opacity and Gate Mask Color.

Display Field Chart

In traditional animation, fields were units of measurement used to determine the size of a drawing. The field chart in Maya is a remnant of those times and is useful only for matching 2D animation—and even then not very useful.

Display Safe Action

This setting draws a box in your camera panel to indicate where the action of the scene is "safe" to take place within. This is also a remnant of older times to a degree; CRT televisions did not display the same area of the screen from TV to TV, and therefore you might lose some of the action on the edges of the frame. Modern LCD and plasma screens displaying digital signals do not have the same issue.

Display Safe Title

Similar to Safe Action, "Safe Title" was an area even further from the edge of the screen where it was considered safe to write titles, logos, or any other text that was needed onscreen. Although losing pixels is not a problem these days, it is still considered good aesthetics to stay within Safe Title. If you are animating a company's 3D logo, for instance, normally you will want the final frame to display the logo as large as possible within Safe Title.

Display Film Pivot and Film Origin

Both of these settings have to do with matching very specific film camera specifications and are seldom if ever touched. More on these attributes in Hour 22.

Overscan

This attribute allows you to display more or less of the scene in a camera's view. It does not affect the render area; it only allows you to view the scene around your resolution gate.

2D Pan/Zoom

It is possible to move the camera view around within a panel, parallel to the camera's view, in a "2D" way. Applications of this function include wanting to look closely at an area of a camera's renderable area, but not wanting to change the camera's position or rotation.

Movement Options

This tab contains some of the options that control how your camera moves in Maya. Specifically, when you are dollying or tracking the camera, the following attributes affect your cameras greatly.

Undoable Movements

In general, you want to keep this option off. Maya has its own undo queue for the camera movements anyway, by pressing the [and] keys for undo/redo respectively.

Center of Interest and Tumble Pivot

This is the distance from the camera and the point in world space that the camera will orbit around when you **Alt+LMB** click in a panel. When you create a camera with an aim object, the aim object is connected to these attributes.

Orthographic Views

To change a camera into an orthographic view, simply click the check box and set the width of the view.

The Different Camera Types

Maya provides a few different camera types to give artists the versatility they need to create complex imagery. Each type lends itself to different uses, but all types are valuable.

Camera

The normal camera type has all of the attributes we just described and is treated like any other object in Maya. That is, it has a shape node and a transform node, is animatable and scalable, and can be connected to other nodes using the Hypergraph, Hypershade, Connection Editor, or the other myriad menus used to do so. This is the most common camera type used.

Camera and Aim

This camera type creates a target object along with the camera shape when you use it. The advantage to this camera type is that you can control the direction a camera is pointing explicitly. The disadvantage is that you have to constantly animate the aim target in order to make the camera seem like it's tracking freely, as if it's moving along a dolly track. This can get tiresome.

Camera, Aim, and Up

This camera type adds a control that keeps the camera upright. This is highly useful for complicated movements when the camera is likely to flip over trying to keep pointed at the aim target. Just like Camera and Aim, though, constantly having to animate these extra controls just to get free movement makes this camera type only a good choice for the specific shots that need it.

Stereo Camera and Multi-Stereo Rig

These camera types are used for creating imagery for 3D Stereo display. These cameras are only useful if you are working on a 3D project, so they will not be covered in this book.

Animating Cameras

We have seen the many attributes that a camera contains, and surely the level of control on a camera is impressive. Let's switch gears and look at a few ways to move cameras through a Maya scene.

Open camera_Anim.ma in this Hour's files. In this scene file, we have the Sam model with some cameras animated around it.

Keyframing

Let's keyframe camera1 to get some practice framing a shot. Follow these steps:

▶ Select camera1 and in any panel, click on Panels, Look Through Selected.

▶ Switch a different panel to the perspective camera by clicking on Panels, Perspective, Persp. Your layout should resemble Figure 14.6.

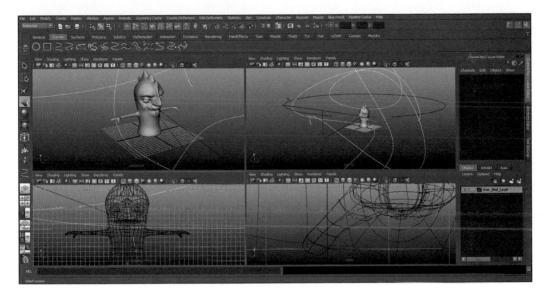

FIGURE 14.6
The layout of the Maya panels so we can watch the camera animation happen.

▶ Play back the animation, and you will see that camera1 moves past the character but that he does not stay in frame.

▶ Set the time to frame 36 by clicking on frame 36 in the Timeline.

▶ In the Persp panel, select and rotate camera1 so that it is facing Sam on this frame.

▶ Set the time to frame 72 and this time use the camera orbit tools inside the camera1 panel to frame Sam in the center, like in Figure 14.7.

▶ Remember, however, that using the Orbit tool actually moves the camera as well as rotates it; it *orbits* the center of interest. It just so happens that this camera has a center of interest that is close to itself, so the amount of translation is small.

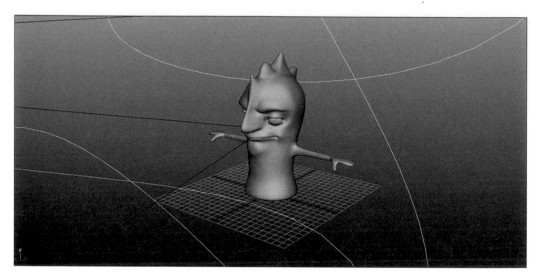

FIGURE 14.7
Sam is framed in the center of the camera view, using the Orbit tool like we are used to.

▶ Now select camera2. It has an aim, and we're going to take advantage of that by turning this camera into a turntable camera.

▶ Change the camera1 panel to display camera2 instead by clicking on Panels, Look Through Selected.

▶ **Shift**-select the NURBS circle in the scene.

▶ Switch to the Animation menu set by pressing **F2**.

▶ Click on Animate, Motion Paths, Attach to Motion Path and then the options box ☐.

▶ Uncheck Follow and then click on Attach.

▶ Play back the animation. The camera is now following the circular path around Sam, and because the Aim is placed in the center of his mesh, he stays framed neatly in the center of the camera.

NOTE

Aim Is Rotation

We had to uncheck Follow in the motion path options because a motion path gives rotation information to an object following it, making the front of the object point forward down the path. Remember that an Aim already creates a connection in a camera's rotation attributes and you cannot connect two outputs to the same input.

Now let's attach the last camera, camera3, to the crazy path in the scene. This path would surely mess up the rotations of any camera, even one with an Aim. First, we want the camera to always be oriented with the top facing upward, so let's constrain the Up point object to the movements of the camera. Doing so will make it so that it stays in position above the camera. Do as follows:

- Select camera3. **Shift**-select the Up control that floats above it.
- Click on Constrain, Point and then the options box □.
- Check Maintain Offset and then click on Add.
- Select camera3 and then **Shift**-select the twisted NURBS curve called "curve1."
- Click on Animate, Motion Paths, Attach to Motion Path.
- Play back the animation. Although the movement is extremely erratic, the camera stays pointed upright.

In general, moving cameras are keyframed, although occasionally they are attached to a path. When they are attached to a path, normally the free camera is parented under a group instead and the group is attached to the motion path. This allows the animator to get the path animation and to animate the camera "on top" of the path. Be careful when animating cameras using the camera movement tools *within a panel*; orbiting the camera translates *and* rotates the camera, and the dolly tool is commonly mistaken for "zooming" when in fact it does not change the focal length at all. Cameras with an Aim are great for turntable cameras or for shots where you need to keep the camera focused on a spot. They can be cumbersome to animate if the camera is supposed to feel "free," though. And adding the Up vector to a "Camera, Aim, and Up" variety camera indeed adds more control, with the tradeoff of yet another control that you must worry about as you create the camera animation.

TRY IT YOURSELF ▼

Build Your Own Camera Rig

Using your knowledge of constraints, groups, and attributes, create your own custom camera rig:

1. Start with a free camera and put it in a group. This way, if you want to attach it to a path, you can do so and are still able to move the camera freely.

2. Make a controller to rotate the camera; then add attributes such as Zoom and Center to this controller. Connect these custom attributes to the camera's Focal Length and Center of Interest attributes to offer access some of the common camera settings.

3. Perhaps use a camera with an Aim, but add a constraint from the camera to its own Aim that you can turn on or off, depending on whether or not you want the camera to be "free."

VIDEO

Complex Camera Rig

CG artist and fellow teacher Damon Lavenski has been kind enough to let us include his awesome camera rig in this book. Look in the Bonus folder in this Hour's files to find the Maya scene. You will immediately see upon loading the file that the level of control and sophistication on this camera rig is outstanding. Feel free to use this rig in all of your projects for fine-tuned camera control.

Summary

We saw how to create the various cameras Maya has to offer, and then went step by step through the many attributes all cameras have. We discussed the specific uses for the different camera types, and then we practiced animating cameras in a way that's similar to their common uses. In high-end production, most studios use a camera rig that simulates real-world camera movement, with specific controls for panning, dollying, craning, and so on.

Q&A

Q. My camera is flying all over the place when I try to orbit it. Why?

A. After a lot of use in a scene, sometimes the center of interest gets pushed far away from a camera. Just set the Center of Interest value to something small, and it should reset.

Q. How do I change the default attributes of a camera?

A. If you go into the Options for any camera, the settings you choose persist as long as you don't reset the tool. I make the default focal length for my cameras 50 just because I think a 35mm camera looks amateurish.

Q. Are Persp and normal cameras the same thing?

A. That is very astute of you. Yes, a Persp camera is just a normal camera; it's just created by default with a Maya scene. In fact, if you create a new Persp camera by clicking Panels, Perspective, New, yet another normal camera will be created named Persp1.

Q. I want a camera with an Up vector but not an Aim. How do I do that?

A. Just parent the Aim to the camera and it will be negated.

Workshop

The workshop contains quiz questions and exercises to help you solidify your understanding of the material covered. Try to answer all questions before looking at the "Answers" section that follows.

Quiz

1. Side, top, and front cameras are what kind of camera?

2. When someone talks about "zoom," what attribute are they talking about?

3. What is the gate called that shows the renderable area of a camera?

4. Which camera type is most commonly used as a turntable camera?

5. What is the attribute that determines how wide an "orbit" a camera has when the camera-movement tools within a panel are used?

Exercise

Using your new knowledge of cameras, try to reframe all of the animated shots you created in Hour 13, "Animation: Adding Movement to Your Scene," with more dynamic angles and focal lengths, and even add some camera animation. Experiment with the different camera types to create the right effect you desire. Create a turntable for your Sam model, or hand keyframe an interesting fly-by on your bouncing-ball animation. Remember that in animation, we can create as many cameras as we like and can view a scene from every angle. Use that to your advantage to find new methods of storytelling.

Answers

1. These are "orthographic cameras." In other words, they have no focal length or perspective.

2. Zoom is controlled by the Focal Length attribute.

3. The resolution gate will show you all of the renderable area of a camera.

4. Although all cameras can be used for turntables, the simplest way to make a camera circle a subject and keep the subject centered in frame is to attach a camera and Aim to a circular path.

5. The Center of Interest attribute determines the point that a camera orbits around when you are using the camera-movement tools within a panel. It is very important to remember that orbiting puts translation *and* rotation values onto your camera. If you only want to rotate a camera, you should do so by selecting and rotating it in a panel.

HOUR 15
Making Diverse Shapes with BlendShapes

What You'll Learn in This Hour:

▶ What a BlendShape is and how to create one

▶ How you can add articulation to characters with BlendShapes

▶ When it is a good idea to use corrective BlendShapes

▶ How to use BlendShapes for other purposes

Maya has a deformer called the BlendShape node. It requires special mention because of the wide array of uses it has. From being the literal backbone of facial animation, to being an alternative to many other deformers, the BlendShape node is a staple of animation in Maya.

NOTE

Clean Geometry

The BlendShape node, perhaps more than most other deformers, depends on your geometry being clean—that is, no history, a centered or zeroed pivot point, and all of the geometry edits finished. Making edits to a model with a BlendShape node on it is very taxing computationally, and very cumbersome.

In this Hour, you find out how to create a BlendShape deformer on a skinned model. You will see how to create a diverse range of BlendShapes for the model to give it the articulation in the face necessary to perform facial animation. You will create some corrective BlendShapes that adjust the model based on parameters you set. Finally, you will see that BlendShapes can serve other purposes, and in some cases offer a good replacement to other deformers. Once you start to explore the power of BlendShapes, chances are you will be using them for many functions in your Maya scenes.

BlendShape Node

The BlendShape node is accessed in the Animation menu set (**F2**). The function of this node is simple. Given two models with identical topology (same number of vertices, edges, and faces), the BlendShape node allows you to "blend" a model into another. It will move the vertices into their new position as you slide the BlendShape's channel from 0 to 1.

There are a few key things to remember when starting with the BlendShape node. First, and most importantly, a vertex's position is calculated relative to the object's pivot point. This is why it is important to have a model that is very clean, with transforms frozen, the geometry centered, and the pivot at the world origin. Two models that have the exact same topology, but pivots in different locations, will produce very unpredictable results when a BlendShape is applied.

The second thing to remember is that the blending of different models is additive. Any transformation on a vertex in relation to the pivot will be added on top of other transformations you have done with other BlendShapes applied to the same model. We will take a closer look at this.

Open BlendShape_Intro.ma in this Hour's files. You are presented with three spheres, as in Figure 15.1.

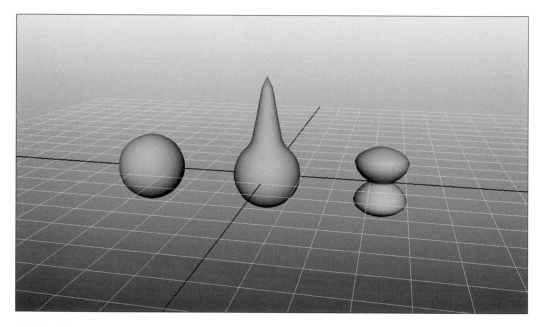

FIGURE 15.1
This scene will help you learn how to use BlendShapes. The two modified spheres will be added as BlendShapes to the default sphere on the left.

The three spheres all have different modifications to them, but they all have the same topology. They have the identical vertices, vertex numbers, edges, and faces. They also have pivots in the same position relative to the object.

CAUTION

Centered Doesn't Mean Zeroed

If you make a modification to a model to use it as a BlendShape, use great caution with the pivot point. The best rule is to make the modifications on a freshly duplicated copy of the original model. This normally rules out problems with the pivot. If you accidentally center the pivot on a model that has changes to the position of some of the vertices, then the new center will be calculated on the average of the new model. Therefore, vertices that have *not* moved will be in a different *relative* position to the pivot. Your results will be bad.

Applying a BlendShape

To apply a BlendShape node, simply **Shift**-select all of your source models and then click on the target model last (the target model is the one that will have the BlendShape node applied to it). When you are done selecting, click on Create Deformers, BlendShape.

Let's try this on our scene. Select the two modified spheres, then the base sphere, as in Figure 15.2.

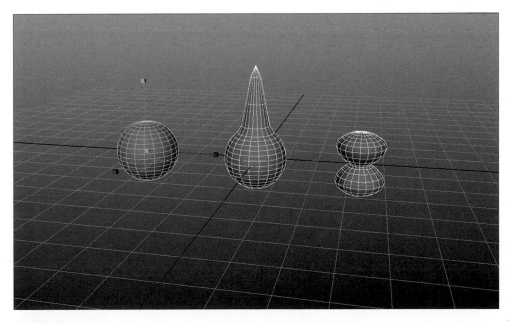

FIGURE 15.2
The spheres selected in the proper order. Note that the last object selected is always highlighted in green.

Now click on Create Deformers, Blend Shape. Select the base sphere and go into the Channel Box. As in Figure 15.3, you will see that there is a new BlendShape node on the sphere.

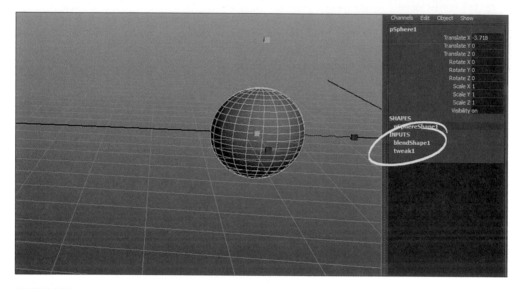

FIGURE 15.3
The base sphere now has a BlendShape node added.

Expand the BlendShape node in the Channel Box by clicking on it. The names of the modified spheres "spiky" and "bulgy" are listed with channels next to their names. A value of 0 means that there is no blending happening, whereas a value of 1 means that the base model will transform all of its vertices to match the target 100%.

Let's see some of this blending in action:

▶ Type in .5 in the "spiky" channel and press **Enter**.

▶ As shown in Figure 15.4, you will see that the base sphere is a 50% blend of its base model and the spiky sphere. You could say that it is exactly halfway "between" the two models.

▶ Type in 1 in the "spiky" channel and press **Enter**.

▶ Now the sphere totally matches the "spiky" sphere. All of the vertices have traveled to their new position relative to the object's pivot point.

▶ Type 0 into the "spiky" channel, type 1 into the "bulgy" channel, and press **Enter**.

▶ The base sphere is now 100% blended into the "bulgy" one.

▶ Now type in 1 in the "spiky" channel and press **Enter**.

▶ As shown in Figure 15.5, the two channels are *adding* together. The spike is protruding from the bulging top of the sphere.

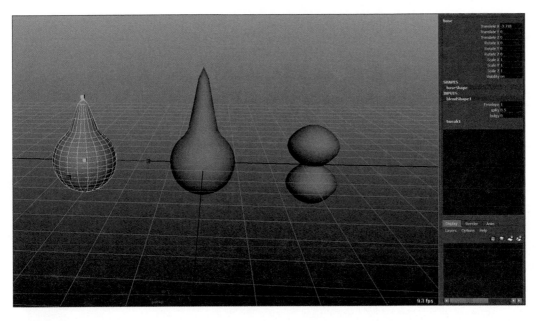

FIGURE 15.4
With the spiky BlendShape added at a weight of .5, the base sphere is a perfect blend between its own rest shape, and the shape of the spiky sphere just to its right.

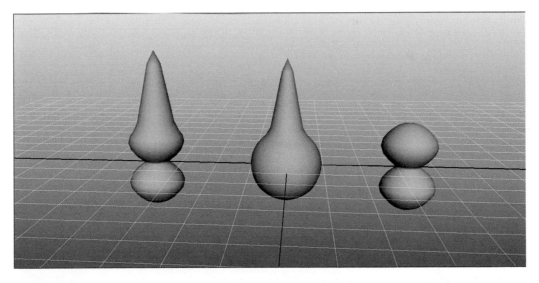

FIGURE 15.5
At 100% weight of both BlendShapes, the base sphere is now an even blend of both shapes. Notice how this effect is *additive*—both the bulging of the top of the sphere and the spike are shown.

As you just saw, the additive nature of BlendShapes can produce some interesting results. It can also produce some very bad results. In the case of character facial performances, animating too many BlendShapes together can make for some very unattractive facial poses.

Creating BlendShapes

You've seen how to apply the BlendShape node and how to access it in the Channel Box; now let's create some BlendShapes for our character to be used in facial animation.

Open sam_Blend_Start.ma in this Hour's files. You will see our character has a couple of BlendShapes created already, as in Figure 15.6.

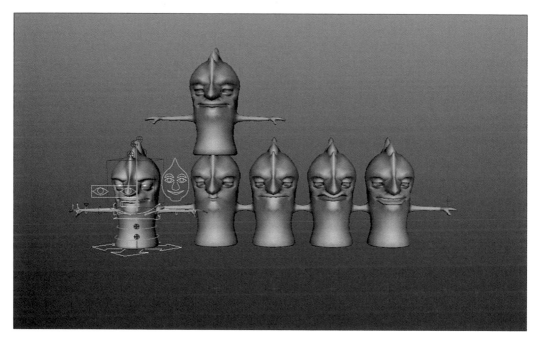

FIGURE 15.6
This file contains some BlendShapes that we've started for Sam.

These are some common *visimes*, or shapes of the mouth we see when speaking. We will use the Sculpt tool to make a happy face and a sad face to add to our BlendShape library on this character.

Sculpting Geometry

The first thing you may notice is that all of the BlendShapes are within a group called BlendShapes_GRP within the geo_GRP group. Stay organized when creating BlendShapes by having a separate group that contains all of the shapes you've created for your character.

Second, notice how there is a "base" model in the group. It has not had any modifications done to it. It is a good idea to have a clean model in this group because you can duplicate it at will without risk of messing up your skinned model.

We will take a look at the common tools used to "mold" a model like clay. Why do we use these tools when making BlendShapes? Many reasons:

- We cannot make topology changes to a model that is being used in BlendShapes. The tools we are going to employ merely "push" and "pull" the geometry around, the way that muscles would. For this reason, they are well suited to creating face shapes.

- The tools we use make use of symmetrical changes to the geometry. Much like mirroring your object when you are creating polygons, the sculpting tools we use will make congruent changes to both sides of your model.

- These tools are specifically designed to model the mesh like clay, with push, pull, and smooth tools built in. This sculpting paradigm makes a lot of sense when you think about the way muscles and skin works; we want our results to look like real face shapes, not "modeled polygons."

Let's begin making the first shape, which is the happy shape:

- Select the base model in the top-left corner of the displayed BlendShapes.

- Press **Ctrl+D** to duplicate this model.

- Rename the new mesh smile_BS in the Channel Box or the Outliner.

- Move it away from the rest of the shapes in an area where you can work on the model.

- Press **F** to frame the model in the perspective panel.

- Your Persp panel should resemble the one shown in Figure 15.7.

- With the smile_BS model selected, switch to the Polygons menu set by pressing **F3**.

- Click on Mesh, Sculpt Geometry Tool.

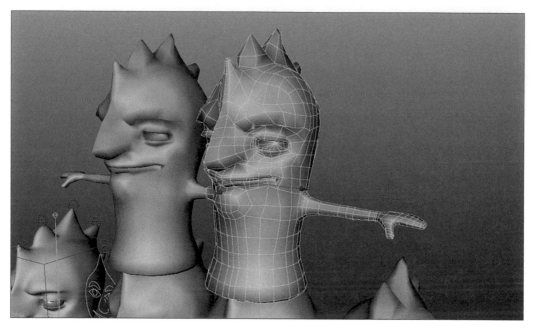

FIGURE 15.7
The newly duplicated model moved to the side and ready to be worked on.

Load the Tool Settings window by clicking on the Tool icon in the top-right corner of the screen or by going to Window, Settings / Preferences, Tool Settings. Let's point out a few of the features of the Sculpt Geometry tool so you can use it effectively.

The six different modes of this tool are Push, Pull, Smooth, Relax, Pinch, and Erase. They work almost exactly like you would expect them to. Each tool has an area of effect that can be grown or shrunken by hovering your mouse over the model, holding down the **B** key, and then LMB scrolling left or right. To increase or decrease the maximum displacement (basically the strength value), hold down the **M** key and LMB scroll left or right on the model. Follow these steps with the Sculpt Geometry tool to get the smile_BS face started:

▶ Turn on the symmetrical brush by clicking in the Tool Settings window on Reflection, found in the Stroke tab. The reflection axis should be the X axis.

▶ Change to the Push brush by clicking its icon, and then change the radius to 5 and the max displacement to .5.

▶ Push the character's cheeks out under his eyes with the LMB button to make them bulge a bit.

▶ Push the sides of the mouth out a little, too, as in Figure 15.8.

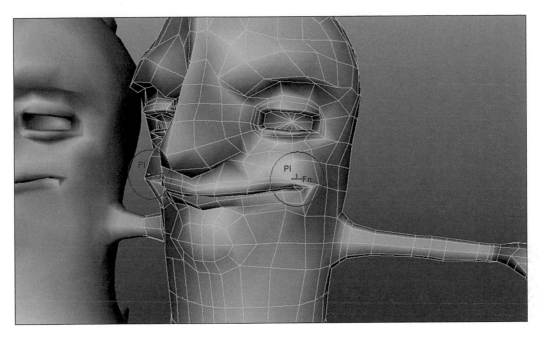

FIGURE 15.8
The cheeks are being sculpted to bulge a little bit with the Sculpt Geometry tool.

Now let's pull the corners of the mouth inward. To do this, we will use the symmetry function of the Move tool:

▶ Select the character model and RMB drag to bring up the component marking menu.

▶ Choose Vertex.

▶ Press **W** to switch to the Move tool and open the Tool Settings window once again.

▶ Under Soft Selection, check the box labeled Soft Selection and change the radius to 1.

▶ Now, under the Reflection tab, turn on reflection and make sure the axis is set to the X axis once again.

▶ Select the corners of the character's mouth and then translate them upward in Y and backward in Z.

▶ Hold down **B** and LMB drag to change the size of the Soft Selection falloff. Using the Move tool, create a very cheeky smile shape, like in Figure 15.9.

▶ Once you have a good version that you are fairly happy with, exit component mode by pressing **F8** twice, and switch back to the Sculpt Geometry tool.

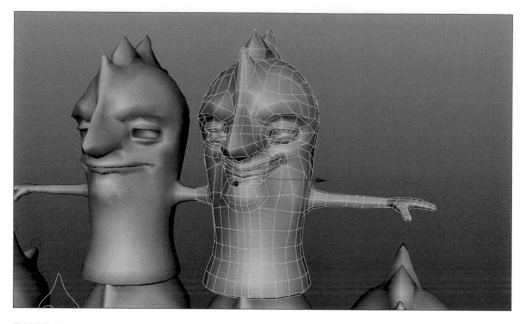

FIGURE 15.9
The finished smile BlendShape has a nice volume to the cheeks and the lips are pulled back.

▶ Hold down the **Shift** key to temporarily toggle the Smooth tool, and lightly smooth the corners of the mouth region.

▶ When you are satisfied, press **3** to see the smooth mesh preview. It should resemble the model in Figure 15.10.

▼ TRY IT YOURSELF

Make the Rest of the BlendShapes

Use the Sculpt Geometry and Move tools to create the rest of the BlendShapes for Sam. We need a sad face, an eye blink (on either side of the face), mouth BlendShapes for the "Ooh," "F," and "V" sounds, and many more. You can find a list of the appropriate shapes to create for Sam by searching for "visimes" or "facial BlendShape list" online.

1. Remember to duplicate the base model in the BlendShapes' group.

2. Make small adjustments; don't try to do everything with a single brush stroke. The Sculpt Geometry tool has an Erase tool that removes edits, but be careful because if you change tools and come back to the Sculpt tool, the eraser will not work.

3. Use the Move tool and Soft Selection to manipulate the model, and then smooth the rough parts out with the Sculpt Geometry tool when you are nearly finished.

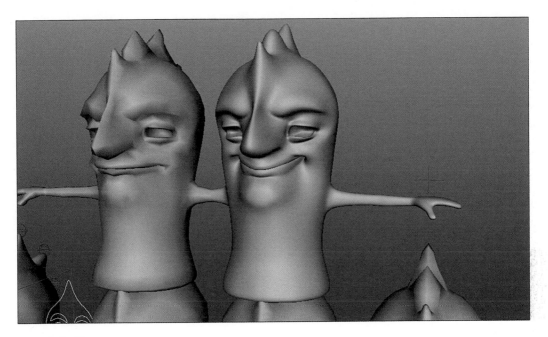

FIGURE 15.10
The finished BlendShape looks even better when smoothed.

Adding a BlendShape

We now need to add these new BlendShapes to the skinned character.

If you would like to add your own shapes, you can continue with your own Maya scene, or you can open sam_Blend_Add.ma to follow along from this point:

▶ Select the BlendShapes "smile_BS" and "sad," or any shapes you would like to add to the skinned model, and then **Shift**-select the skinned model last.

▶ In the Animation menu set (**F2**), click on Create Deformers, Blend Shape and then click the Options box □.

▶ In the resulting box that opens, type in **sam_BlendShape** in the Blend Shape Node box and then click Create.

▶ RMB click and hold on Sam's body and select Inputs, All Inputs.

▶ MMB drag the BlendShape node almost to the bottom of the deformer list, just above tweak1.

▶ Select the skinned model and open the BlendShape node in the Channel Box; you will see that all of the BlendShapes in the scene are added to the channel list.

Making Controllers

It is not enough to have a BlendShape node on the skinned model, because like everything else in a character rig, it is most useful to have a NURBS curve controller used to give animators control over an attribute.

We will now add these BlendShapes to the controller next to the character's head that is shaped like a face. You can use any shape for your controllers, but it is common to use controllers that resemble the body part they are controlling. Remember back in Hour 9, "Relationships and Making Nodes Work Together," you learned how to connect nodes. We are going to do the same for the BlendShape controls.

Select the face_CTRL curve and look in the Channel Box. There are already many channels added, but they are not connected to the BlendShape node yet. We will add the happy and sad shapes to this controller, too. Follow these steps:

▶ In the Channel Box, select Edit, Add Attribute.

▶ Make the Long Name "smile," the type "float," the Minimum 0, Maximum 1, and Default 0.

▶ Click on Add.

▶ The dialog box will not close, so we can add another attribute.

▶ Make the new attribute's Long Name "Sad" and keep all of the other settings the same.

▶ Click on OK to add this attribute and close this dialog box.

The two new channels "smile" and "sad" should be added to the controller's channels in the Channel Box. Now let's connect these channels to the BlendShape node's channels:

▶ With the controller select, click Window, General Editors, Connection Editor.

▶ Select the skinned character model.

▶ Open the Attribute Editor (**Ctrl+A**).

▶ Find and click on the tab labeled sam_BlendShape to load the BlendShape node's attributes.

▶ At the bottom of the Attribute Editor, click the button labeled Select. You have now selected just the BlendShape node itself.

▶ Back in the Connection Editor, click on Reload Right at the top right of the editor.

▶ The BlendShape's attributes load in the Connection Editor.

▶ In the right column, find and click to expand the attribute labeled "weight."

▶ Now, for every channel on the left that belongs to the NURBS controller, find the corresponding BlendShape weight channel. Click on the channel in the left column first, then the similar channel in the right column, as in Figure 15.11.

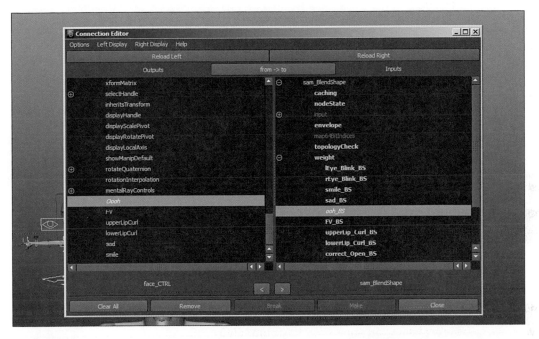

FIGURE 15.11
The familiar Connection Editor with the Oooh control connected to the ooh_BS BlendShape.

When you are done and the attributes are all connected, close the Connection Editor and select face_CTRL. In the Channel Box, test and make sure the channels are properly connected. You should be able to make some pretty interested facial shapes using these controls. Best of all, you have your control at your fingertips with the NURBS curve, as opposed to hunting for the BlendShape node when doing facial animation.

Corrective BlendShapes

BlendShapes aren't solely used for facial animation. Sometimes we use BlendShapes to correct deformations in the model when it is skinned and animated.

Open sam_Corrective.ma in this Hour's files. This file has our character with some simple animation on his arm. However, when his arm bends, you can see that the elbow gets thinner and overall does not look right in the crease. To fix this, we will make a corrective BlendShape that automatically activates when he bends his arm. Do as follows:

▶ Duplicate the base model in the BlendShape group and rename it to rElbow_Correct.

▶ Add it to the BlendShape node by **Shift**-selecting Sam's body geometry, clicking Edit Deformers, Blend Shape, Add, and then clicking the options box ▢. Choose the only BlendShape node in the scene when the options box opens.

▶ To access your BlendShape channels in your scene, you can also click on Window, Animation Editors, Blend Shape. Do that now.

▶ Turn the channel rElbow_Correct up to 1. We are doing this so that we can see the effect of our sculpting in real time.

▶ Scroll the timeline to frame 24. The elbow is bent on our skinned character on this frame, so we will sculpt the elbow on the corrective BlendShape to make it work correctly.

▶ Select the rElbow_Correct mesh, use the Sculpt Geometry tool and the Move tool on the vertices, and create a slight bulge near the inside of the elbow, as in Figure 15.12.

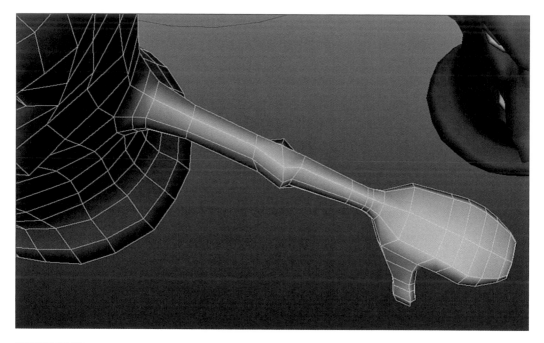

FIGURE 15.12
The elbow with a slight bulge added. This will correct the pinching that occurs when Sam bends his elbow.

Using the methods we discussed in Hour 9, we are going to add this shape as a Driven Key:

▶ Select lElbow_FK_CTRL in our skinned model.

▶ In the Animation menu set (**F2**), click on Animate, Set Driven Key, Set....

▶ Click on Load Driver.

▶ In the BlendShape window (reopen it if you've close it), click on Select at the bottom of the sam_BlendShape tab.

▶ Back in the Set Driven Key Window, click on Load Driven.

▶ Now in the top-right column of the Set Driven Key window, choose RotateY. In the bottom-right column (the driven channels), find the rElbow_Correct channel and select it.

▶ Make sure you are on frame 24 and click on Key. This shape is now keyed to be at a weight of 1 when the elbow is bent.

▶ Go to frame 1.

▶ In the BlendShape window, turn the weight of rElbow_Correct to 0.

▶ In the Set Driven Key window, click on Key. When the arm is straight, the elbow corrective BlendShape is not needed.

▶ Click on Play in the Timeline and watch as the BlendShape automatically dials in and out to correct bad deformations on a model.

▶ You can delete the animation on the elbow while on frame 1 because it is no longer needed.

You can use this method to correct any number of bad deformations on a model. You may also notice there is already a corrective BlendShape on Sam's mouth for when the jaw is opened. Select the jaw controller and rotate it down; you will see that the corners of the mouth smooth like they would in reality. You can make any number of corrective BlendShapes to finalize the deformations on a skinned model.

Other Uses for BlendShapes

As mentioned before, BlendShapes aren't necessarily only used to create facial animation. Sometimes a BlendShape is a good replacement for any number of deformations you have done to a model. One example would be if you wanted to make a model look like it is damaged. If you have a car model that needs to be animated in a crash, you could use a BlendShape of a dented bumper that you animate as the car hits a wall.

A BlendShape could be used to animate the page of a book turning, or to give a little bit of life to a falling leaf. You can even apply a BlendShape to a NURBS curve, so any resulting geometry or any animated effects using curves could get some added variety through the use of BlendShapes.

VIDEO

Mirroring BlendShapes

When you are creating BlendShapes and their controls, it is common to need to have individual control on either side of the face. Rather than create a specific left and right BlendShape for each facial pose, we can take advantage of the Paint BlendShape Weights tool. Look in the Bonus folder for a video showing you exactly how to accomplish this.

Summary

BlendShapes is a powerful animation tool in Maya, giving the user the ability to dynamically animate a model on the component level with relative ease. They serve as the foundation of facial animation in Maya. Remembering to start with clean geometry; creating BlendShapes is as easy as sculpting in Maya. When they are done, connect the weights of the shapes to controllers for ease of access. Corrective BlendShapes can make up for errant deformations in skinning, and beyond the obvious uses, BlendShapes can augment or replace all the other deformer types in Maya for some very interesting results.

Q&A

Q. My entire model is moving when I adjust the weight of a BlendShape. What is happening?

A. At some point, the pivot was changed in your model. Did you freeze transformations? BlendShapes work by moving vertices to a new position based on their relative position to the pivot. Make sure you do not freeze transformations.

Q. After I added a BlendShape node to Sam, none of the controls work. Why?

A. Deformation order is of the utmost importance here. What is happening is the deforms from the clusters and the skin are happening to the model, and then the BlendShape node is moving all of the vertices back to their original position. You must have skipped the step of accessing the All Inputs menu and reordering the inputs to put the BlendShape *first*.

Q. Can I split a shape so that it only affects the left or the right side of the face?

A. Yes, this is easy to do. Simply add the BlendShape to the BlendShape node twice, and then use the Paint BlendShape Weights tool in the Edit Deformers menu to paint the influence of a certain BlendShape. The tools and controls are the same as the Paint Skin Weights tool and the Paint Cluster Weights tool, so it should be straightforward to use.

Q. I added a BlendShape, and the name is something like Base1 and I want to change it. Where can I do that?

A. Go to Window, Animation Editors, Blend Shape. You can rename any channel by typing in a new name at the bottom of the channel's slider and pressing **Enter**.

Workshop

The workshop contains quiz questions and exercises to help you solidify your understanding of the material covered. Try to answer all questions before looking at the "Answers" section that follows.

Quiz

1. What tools are the most useful for creating BlendShapes?

2. How do you activate reflection on the Move tool in the quickest way?

3. What is the highest weight of a BlendShape by default?

4. What do we call a BlendShape that is used to fix deformation in the model?

5. Are BlendShapes additive, subtractive, multiplicative, divisive, or none of these?

Exercise

Create a library of BlendShapes for Sam. I have included the most common BlendShapes in his model as well as some good corrective shapes, but there are dozens that could be helpful to animators using this rig. Also, when you are adding the controls, add the connections to mouth_ CTRL, nose_CTRL, brow_CTRL, and so on, depending on what kind of BlendShape it is.

Answers

1. The Sculpt Geometry tool and Move tool (at the vertex component level) are the most useful tools for making BlendShapes, with reflection turned as well.

2. Reflection is accessible through the Tool Settings window, but the quickest way to activate it is to hold down **W** and LMB click and drag upward on the model.

3. A BlendShape's channel goes up to 1.0 by default, but you can type in any value you like into the channel and get overdriven results.

4. A corrective BlendShape fixes bad or undesired deformations on a skinned model.

5. BlendShapes are additive. Any BlendShape will add on top of another, which is why you must take care to not animate too many shapes at the same time.

HOUR 16

Animating Using Dynamics and Simulations

What You'll Learn in This Hour:

▶ Why dynamics and simulations are useful

▶ How to create active and passive rigid bodies

▶ How to simulate the scene

▶ How to cache a simulation to more easily scrub through the action

This chapter covers the clever stuff. Maya dynamics allow you to move, break, destroy, rebuild, bend, and twist objects based on real-world physics. But here is the good part: You don't have to have any in-depth knowledge of physics to use it. It would help, however, to take some time occasionally to observe how things around you react in the real world. Let's face it—nothing in the real world is keyframed or hand animated. It's all based on physics.

NOTE

Eek! Do I Have to Know Physics?

No, but it helps to observe how things react in the real world. For instance, when a bowling ball hits bowling pins, what usually happens? The bowling pins fly off, or fall over due to the impact. Why? Well, you can pretty much figure out that a very heavy bowling ball is going to knock anything that is lighter than itself out of its way. The reasons behind it are all due to physics, but just observing, plus a bit of common sense, will take you a long way toward getting started with the basics of physics-based dynamics.

In this Hour, you will be introduced to the basics of animating an object using dynamics based on real-world physics, and let Maya simulate the action for you. We will get started with an overview of what dynamics are and why you would want to use them. To get a solid grounding in the fundamentals, we will focus on active rigid bodies, which are objects that can actively react to fields, such as gravity, and passive rigid bodies, which play a role when creating your dynamic scene, but obviously not an active one. We will look at some of the fundamental settings to tailor the action to your own needs. We will also look at simulating, which lets Maya work out how to animate the scene according to the physical properties you have set up. Finally, you will learn to cache the scene (that is, store the calculations) to scrub through the action.

What Are Dynamics?

Dynamics describe how objects move based on real-world physics. You might be wondering why we would want to do that, when Hour 13, "Animation: Adding Movement to Your Scene," already covered the basics of keyframe animation. Well, imagine trying to animate explosions, curtains blowing in the wind, or a building crumbling to dust by keyframing. Wouldn't be too easy, would it? That's where dynamics come in. You can set up your objects—plus anything that needs to interact with or influence the objects—and then let Maya work out (simulate) all the complex physics calculations to animate your scenario.

What Are nDynamics?

Rigid body dynamics has been a part of Maya since its introduction back in version 1. It has been used in countless blockbuster productions and remains a solid foundation for dynamic simulations. nDynamics is a newer addition to Maya that is part of the Nucleus framework and creates a sort of family of dynamics, including nCloth, nParticles, and nHair. All nDynamic methods seamlessly interact with one another under the same Nucleus solver, which is more robust than the original Rigid Body Dynamics solver in that it calculates more iterations per frame. An example of this would be a bunch of marbles made from nParticles that sit within an nCloth bag and get poured onto a rug made from nHair. All will interact with one another without too much setup. The Nucleus solver will calculate all collisions across the family of dynamics. This Hour focuses on dynamics to get you started, but nDynamics is touched on in later Hours, including Hour 18, "Using Particles to Create Effects."

Physics in Action

The very simplest, fundamental, and well-known example of physics in action is an apple falling from a tree. It does so for a couple of reasons. First is its age and the fact that the stem that holds it on the branch is weaker than younger apples. The second reason is that our good friend gravity has been pulling that apple downward for a while now. Eventually, the apple can take it no longer and gravity wins, sucking the fruit to earth. The apple isn't solely governed by gravity, though. The apple has its own unique properties, and we refer to these in Maya as "attributes."

When describing to a friend an apple you are about to eat, you might tell them it's a big, shiny, red apple. Maya also keeps track of size (scale), color, and material attributes that might make the apple shiny or dull. However, it also can keep track of the apple's physical properties, which dynamics can use to work out (simulate) how it would be influenced by other objects or events in Maya. An apple has mass, it has a slippery or rough surface (friction), and it may also be soft or hard, which allows it to "bounce" or compress. When we create our objects, we tell Maya about their attributes. Even if you don't quite know the settings, you can start making a guess. A large rock would have more of a mass property than a feather, for instance, and a bowling ball would have a greater mass than a bowling pin.

NOTE

What Is Mass?

Mass is not quite the same thing as weight. Weight varies according to gravity, so a person would weigh less on the moon than they do on the earth. Mass relates rather to the quantity of matter in an object as well as its resistance to change in its own state of motion. You can think of it as how stubborn an object is about starting motion—or stopping motion once it has got going. So, if you flick a balloon that's at rest, it will merrily fly off on its way. If you put a finger out to stop it, it will easily stop. Want to try the same thing with a bowling ball? Best not to. A bowling ball won't fly off easily if you flick it, nor is it likely to stop at a gentle finger touch—you are more likely to hurt your finger. A bowling ball is far more reluctant to change its state of motion than a balloon; hence, the bowling ball has a greater mass.

What Does Simulating Mean?

Once we have told Maya about the physical attributes of a given object, we can set up a few other things in the scene (which we will get to in a moment) and then allow Maya to simulate (calculate), frame by frame, the scenario we have set up. So in our "apple falling from the tree" example, rather than having to work out ourselves where the apple should be in each frame as gravity pulls it to earth, as well as how it reacts to the ground, we can let Maya do the hard work and calculate all that for us. Once the simulation is complete, we can then view it in real time. This is called "simulating our scene."

Getting Started with Rigid Bodies

We have been talking about an apple falling from a tree, so let's build and simulate this in Maya. In recent and past versions of Maya are many different tools that allow the user to access dynamics and physics-based tools. Even just one look at the tools available on the Dynamics shelf (see Figure 16.1) can be overwhelming if you are new to dynamics. Fortunately, Maya has built-in help at hand. If you have a look at the Dynamics shelf, and rest your mouse over each button, an onscreen tooltip will appear, giving a brief description of each tool.

FIGURE 16.1
The Dynamics shelf contains commonly used tools for creating physics-based animations.

TIP

Missing Tooltips?

When you rest your mouse over a tool button in Maya, you should be given an onscreen tip to let you know what the button is. If the tooltip doesn't appear, you can check your settings in Maya. Go to Windows, Settings/Preferences, Preferences. In the "Interface, Help" category, look for the "Tooltips: Enable" check box in the Popup Help section. Click to enable or disable, as you wish.

We will be using some of the available tools in this Hour, which will focus on the basics of good-old Maya rigid body dynamics. However, you will also see settings for soft bodies on the menu. Maya soft and rigid body dynamics have been core components of Maya for many years, and they provide a nice foundation for you to move on to more complex dynamics when you are ready. Soft bodies are objects that are soft—and just like soft objects in the real world, they can squash, bend, and are generally flexible. Rigid bodies are the opposite. Rigid bodies are hard and inflexible objects.

Creating the Scene

To get started, you can either create your own scene or open up dynamic_apple_start.ma, which gives you a simple tree with a branch, a hanging apple, and a simple cube as the ground plane. Figure 16.2 shows your starting scene. It's always a good idea to start off by saving your scene with a different name so that if things go wrong, you can reopen the original and try again. Therefore, go to File, Save Scene As and then save your scene as myApple (either myApple.ma or myApple.mb will do). See Hour 3, "File Types and Managing Assets," for more detail on file types if you are interested in the differences between the two.

If you prefer to create your own scene, you can follow the modeling techniques covered earlier in this book to do so. Remember that you can start with some basic geometry shapes (primitives) and manipulate them into the scene's objects. To create your own apple tree scene, first create the ground using a squished polygon ("poly" for short) cube. Next, use a few manipulated poly cylinders to create a crude tree and a branch for your apple to fall from. The apple will be a simple sphere, again manipulated to take the general form of an apple. If you want it to look more realistic, you should grab an apple or look up an image of one online to take note of its different angles. It is not completely round, and has almost flat surfaces at the top and bottom, with a stem sticking out of the top. The stem can be created by selecting the faces at the very top of the apple (surrounding its center vertex) and then extruding these out a few times to take shape. Once the apple has been created, place it just under the branch, with its stem just touching the branch itself.

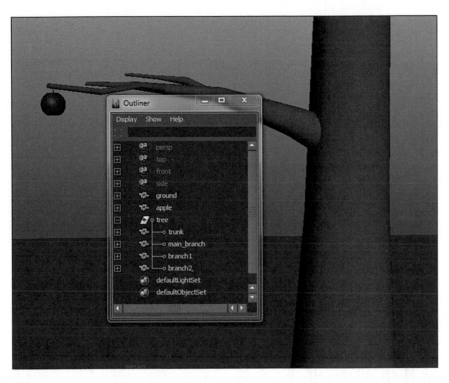

FIGURE 16.2
Get started by opening dynamic_apple_start.ma, or create your own simple apple tree scene.

TIP

Delete Construction History

Once you have completed modeling, it's often a good idea to delete the construction history to make things a bit more efficient. Select the object and use Edit, Delete by type, History (or press **Shift+Alt+D**). Be aware that this is not a hard-and-fast rule, however, because there may be times in rigging, for example, when it is necessary to keep some of the history. It's therefore a good idea to save your scene before deleting the history, so that you can return to it if you need to.

Whether you use the scene provided or make your own, it's always best to keep the geometry clean and of low polygon count. So, for example, there is no need here to have the cube for the ground with many subdivisions for the width, height, and depth—one of each will do. This keeps the polygon count low, and helps to speed up simulations times. It is also possible to take the simulated data and apply this to a more complex object later on.

Getting Dynamic

Now that the scene is ready, we need to tell Maya what is dynamic (that is, what should be used in the simulation and act as an object that has physical attributes). First of all, you need to understand that there are a few different types of dynamic attributes we can apply to each object. Earlier, we mentioned soft and rigid bodies. If we want some geometry in Maya to be dynamic and be able to be affected by gravity and so on, we need to make that object an active rigid body. If we wanted the object to be soft (more flexible), we would use the soft body option.

A passive rigid body creates an object that accepts collisions from an "active" rigid body, but it won't be affected by gravity. That is their relationship: active and passive. Our apple will be "active" because we need gravity to pull it to the ground. The ground itself and the tree will be "passive," though. After all, we don't want the ground to be affected by the falling apple and to float downward from our scene as it hits!

Once we create either type of rigid body, whether active or passive, Maya will create a "rigid body solver" that is basically the dynamics "brain" used to simulate (calculate) the dynamics.

Let the Apple Fall from the Tree

To let the apple fall from the tree, follow these steps:

▶ Open dynamic_apple_start.ma or use your own scene.

▶ Select the tree group in the Outliner.

▶ Use **F5** or the drop-down list in Maya's top-left corner to display the Dynamics menu set.

We are going to keep it easy to follow along by using the menu options, but feel free to find the equivalent button on the Dynamics shelf instead. For example, the active and passive rigid body buttons have icons of bowling pins, and are located right under the Dynamics label on the Shelf, as in Figure 16.3.

FIGURE 16.3
Rigid body buttons on the Dynamics shelf.

▶ With the tree group selected, choose Soft/Rigid Bodies, Create Passive Rigid Body, as shown in Figure 16.4.

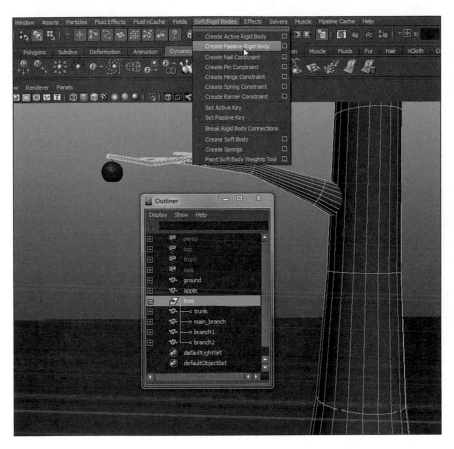

FIGURE 16.4
With the tree group selected, create a passive rigid body from the soft/rigid bodies menu in the Dynamics menu set.

You may notice that there is now a tiny little x in the scene. This is to show us that this object has dynamic attributes. A new node will also appear at the root of the tree group in the Outliner, with an icon that looks like a pin and bowling ball (see Figure 16.5).

▶ Select either the small x in the scene or the rigidBody1 node in the Outliner to open up the passive body attributes for the object in the Channel Box on the right side of your Maya scene, as shown in Figure 16.6. We aren't going to touch anything here right now; just have a look to get a feeling for what sort of things you can do.

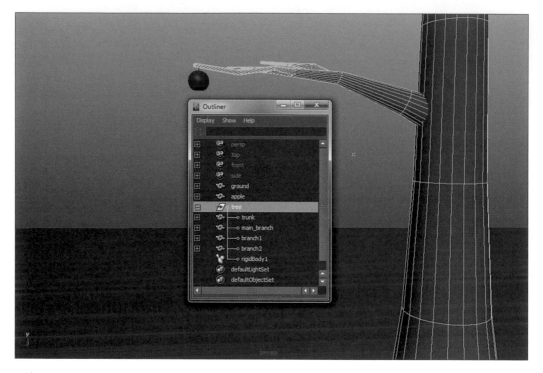

FIGURE 16.5
Once you have told Maya to treat the tree group as a rigid body, a small green cross will appear in the scene, and a new rigidBody1 node will appear in the outliner.

TIP

Toggle Between the Channel Box and Attribute Editor

You can use the Attribute Editor or the Channel Box to view and edit attributes. The Channel Box gives you access to a list of commonly used attributes, and the Attribute Editor provides access to all the attributes related to the selected object. Use **Ctrl+a** to toggle between the two.

▶ We need to make the ground a passive rigid body now, so select the ground and choose Soft/Rigid Bodies, Create Passive Rigid Body.

This time, you may wonder where the new rigid body node you just created has gone. When you created the rigid body for the tree, the tree was already a group and therefore Maya just added the node to the group. But because the ground is a single object, there was initially no need to create a group for it. However, now that the rigid body has been created, Maya has grouped it with the ground. If you expand the ground node in the Outliner, you will see the new rigid body underneath.

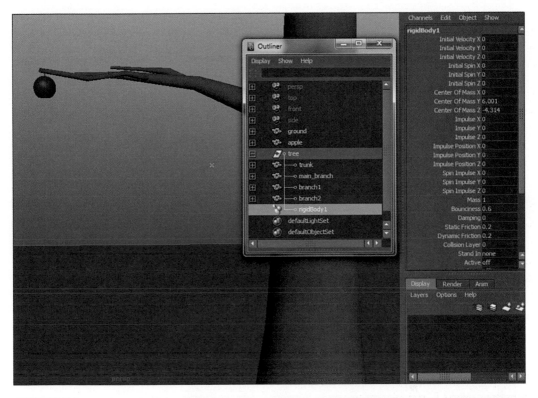

FIGURE 16.6
Select the green cross or the rigidBody node in the Outliner to display the rigid body attributes in the Channel Box.

▶ Now select the apple. This time, we want to create an active rigid body, but we also want to select some options along the way. Whenever you see a small square option box next to a menu item, it means extra options are available. So, go ahead and choose Soft/Rigid Bodies, Create Active Rigid Body, Options □, as in Figure 16.7.

The Rigid Options dialog box should now be displayed, as in Figure 16.8. If it isn't, retrace your steps and make sure you select the options box next to the Create Active Rigid Body menu item. These options display the initial dynamic attributes the apple will have.

▶ To give the rigid body a more descriptive name, use the Rigid Body Name field (see Figure 16.8) to type in **active apple**.

▶ Before clicking Create, have a look at the other attributes. There is no need to adjust anything else at this point, but you can see that the values such as mass, friction, and initial spin all could be changed if we wanted to. We can change these attributes later, so for now just click Create.

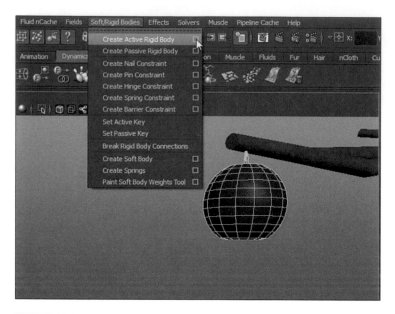

FIGURE 16.7
Choosing the square options box next to any menu item will let you select different options along the way.

FIGURE 16.8
The Rigid Options dialog box.

Once you have created the active rigid body, you will see in your Outliner that, once again, a rigid body node has appeared. Your outliner should now look like Figure 16.9. Go ahead and save your file.

FIGURE 16.9
Outliner showing all the rigid body nodes for our simulation.

Simulating the Apple Falling

We have created the scene and told Maya which objects we want to participate in the dynamics. Now we need to tell Maya to perform the simulation. To follow along, either continue to use your own scene or open up dynamic_apple_mid.ma. An apple doesn't fall from the tree to the ground instantly, so we need to make sure our scene has enough time to see our simulation. Check your Timeline duration and make sure its set to something like 500 frames by changing the value in the playback range end time field located toward the lower-right corner of your Maya screen, as shown in Figure 16.10. Next, click the play button next to the Timeline. Nothing happens. Why? Well, we haven't added any gravity to make the apple fall, so let's do that now.

FIGURE 16.10
The playback range fields let you change the duration of your animations by typing in the desired number of frames.

TIP

Stopping Playback

If you notice you forgot to set something up, or need to make adjustments, or have already seen all you want to see before playback has finished, you can press the **Esc** key on the keyboard to stop the playback.

To add gravity, do as follows:

▶ Continue using your scene from the previous stages, or open up dynamic_apple_mid.ma. The rigid bodies should be set up, and the next task is to add gravity.

▶ Select the apple group and choose Fields, Gravity from the Dynamics menu set. Remember, you can use **F5** to bring up the Dynamics menu set if you need to. Now let's try that play button again!

Our apple drops and hits the ground. (Great, Newton would be proud!) But did the apple bounce too much, or not at all? It's likely that Maya just used its default settings, which made the apple react more like a bouncing ball than an apple! In the real world, how the apple reacts to the ground would depend on the surface it landed on, plus the nature of the apple itself. An apple landing on grass or concrete would only bounce a small amount, and possibly roll. So, we need to adjust some attributes to make it more believable.

NOTE

Scrubbing the Timeline

You cannot scrub the Timeline while using active dynamics unless it has been cached. See the section on rigid body solvers about caching for more information.

▶ Save your scene and open up the apple group in the Outliner to select the rigid body node, which we named "active apple" earlier. This will display the attributes you can adjust to make the simulation more believable.

▶ With the active apple rigidBody node selected, we are going to have a look at adjusting some of the attributes, including Mass, Static Friction, and Bounciness. Figure 16.11 shows the default settings for each. It's not a good idea to change more than one thing at a time when you are experimenting; otherwise, you will not know which setting improved the simulation and which made it worse. So, we will look at each one in turn.

▶ First, we are going to have a look at Mass. The default value for Mass is 1. If we change this value to something like 500, press **Enter**, and then click the Play button, the apple falls at about the same rate as it did before, but its greater mass impacts the ground with more force and therefore it doesn't bounce quite the same. This is the effect of an object that weighs a lot more and is much more dense. The greater the mass, the greater the impact of the collision with passive or rigid body objects. Let's put this number back to 1 and press **Enter**.

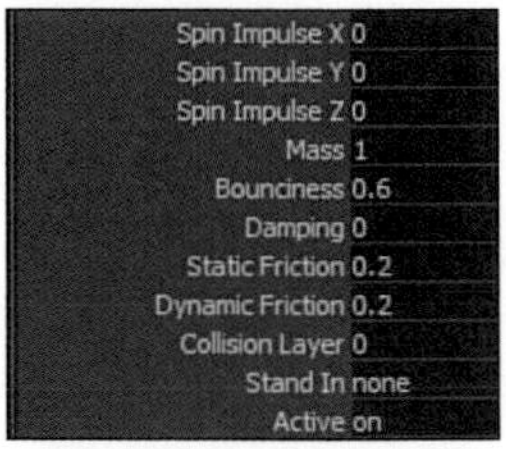

FIGURE 16.11
Default settings for some of the rigid body attributes.

TIP

Playback Speed

If your playback shows your apple dropping almost instantly, check your playback settings. In Windows, Settings/Preferences, Preferences, look for the Settings, Time Slider category and under Playback Speed, set Speed to Real-Time 24fps. Save your settings so the change takes effect.

▶ With the active apple rigid body still selected, let's look at Static Friction. Maya's default value is 0.2, but let's change this to 200. Now press **Enter** and click Play. It now takes a little bit longer for the apple to fall, and because we intersected the apple into the trunk a little, its high Static Friction attribute means it takes longer to finally be affected by the pull from gravity. We could use this value in another scenario, perhaps for a ball that we want to gently pick up speed while rolling down a hill. The ball would take a while to get rolling, and the higher this value the longer its friction will have with the surface. Let's put this value back to 1 and press **Enter**.

NOTE

Static Versus Dynamic Friction

Right underneath Static Friction you will notice Dynamic Friction. Dynamic Friction comes into play when we are using more than one active rigid body to modify resistance against each other. Because we are dealing with just one apple, there is no need to adjust Dynamic Friction.

▶ Bounciness will adjust how much the object bounces. The default value is 0.6, but for the sake of comedy and science, let's change this to a higher number first. Try **5** and press **Enter** and then click Play. Our apple has just taken its first steps into space!

▶ The default value for Bounciness was set to 0.600, which was too bouncy for an apple, and changing it to 5 didn't help, so let's lower this to 0.100. Press **Enter** and play the simulation. Now we see there is a lot less bounce, which is a more natural look, but maybe we could lower it a bit more, to 0.020 or even less. Play with these settings for different results and use your own judgment to determine what works best for you. The suggested final settings are shown in Figure 16.12, but use whatever settings you prefer. You can also open up dynamic_apple_final.ma to see our final scene in action.

FIGURE 16.12
Suggested final settings, but you should use whatever settings you like.

BONUS

Extra Dynamics Scene

Take a look in this Hour's source files and you will notice there is an extra dynamics scene. A ball has been set up to roll down a twirly slide, roll onto the ground, and knock over a pin. Have a look at the settings we used for the rigid and passive bodies to see how we have accomplished this. Then, why not try to make your own?

The Rigid Body Solver

To access the rigidSolver attributes, select any of the rigid body nodes. If necessary, use **Ctrl+A** to display the Attribute Editor. With any of the rigid body nodes selected, we can see in the Attribute Editor a tab for the rigidSolver. Click on that tab. At this point in time, it's probably a good idea to just understand that if we have a much more complicated scene, Maya will struggle to give perfectly accurate results based on the default settings of the solver. For instance, if our scene contained lots of complicated geometry, we may need to change the Step Size value and decrease it for greater accuracy over longer simulation times.

Creating a Cache

We would also create what is called a "cache" if we had a more complex scene. When we create a cache, Maya performs the necessary simulations and stores them into memory so that it doesn't have to recalculate the simulation. Once a cache is created, we are then able to scrub back and forth on the Timeline with ease, something that isn't possible without caching.

To cache a simulation:

▶ Select all geometry that has dynamic attributes (in our case, the tree, ground, and apple).

▶ Choose the Solvers menu and then select Memory Caching, Enable.

Now if we play our simulation through until the end, Maya will hold that information in memory. Once it's played through, you will see that you can scrub through the Timeline area.

NOTE

Delete and Cache Again to See Changes

If you need to make a change to anything in the scene, no matter how small, you will need to delete the old cache and create a new one. Select all the geometry that has dynamic attributes and choose Solvers, Memory Caching, Delete, to remove the existing cache. To re-cache, choose Solvers, Memory Caching, Enable. Remember to select all of the dynamic geometry to do this.

Summary

In this Hour, you had a look at dynamics so that you can let Maya simulate physics-based animations that would be challenging to create using keyframe techniques. Although the "apple falling from a tree" example could have been keyframed instead, this simple example introduced you to setting up your scenes for soft/rigid body dynamics. The apple needed to be an active rigid body, so that it could actively react to the gravity field you added. The tree and the ground were set up as passive rigid bodies so that Maya could calculate how the apple would react to the surfaces that it hit. If the ground had not been a passive rigid body, Maya would assume it didn't count in the simulation, and thus the apple would have fallen straight through.

Q&A

Q. Shouldn't everything be active if I'm using dynamics?

A. Not necessarily. Active rigid bodies actively react to other dynamic nodes and fields, such as gravity and other dynamic objects. If you made the ground an active rigid body, it too could react to the apple, and would merrily be pushed downward and out of your scene as the apple landed (bringing the apple along with it, because the apple would have nothing to stop it).

Q. Why don't my changes show up when I click Play?

A. If you have created a cache, Maya will replay according to the settings and simulation used at the time. To see updates, delete the current cache and create a new one.

Q. How can I add some spin on my apple?

A. Select the active apple rigidBody node that is in your apple group and try adjusting attributes. Try adjusting Spin Impulse X, Y, and/or Z. You can also adjust Initial Spin of X, Y, and Z. Remember to adjust attributes one by one to see what they do; otherwise, you won't know which is doing what.

Q. Why isn't my apple dropping?

A. Double-check that you have added a gravity field to the apple. Gravity works naturally in the real world, but you have to set it up specifically in Maya. If your apple partially goes through the ground, double-check that your ground is a passive rigid body.

Workshop

The workshop contains quiz questions and exercises to help you solidify your understanding of the material covered. Try to answer all questions before looking at the "Answers" section that follows.

Quiz

1. If you want an active rigid body to bounce off a floor, what would we have to make the floor?

2. When you create either an active or rigid body object, what does Maya create automatically to calculate the dynamic attributes?

3. Once you have an active rigid body and a passive rigid body, what is also required to make the objects fall or interact?

4. Newton, Gravity, and Turbulence are types of what within Maya dynamics?

5. If a heavy scene with lots of rigid and passive body objects isn't playing or calculating correctly, what attribute within the rigid body solver could you adjust to a lower value for a better calculation?

Exercise

Why not try creating a tree with different fruits using the new knowledge you have. Either create your own from scratch or use dynamic_apple_start.ma as a base. See how far you can push the simulation and your knowledge. Perhaps make some fruits bigger or more like coconuts and see if you can add different dynamic properties to each object. You can vary the size and shape of the trees, too, just to add variety. Perhaps make the tree a little taller to compensate for more fruits.

You could even create a separate tree close by with more fruits on its branches. You could create some large rocks or boulders on the ground and make these passive objects to see how they influence the objects as they land.

Now, of course, you don't want to have all the fruit dropping from the trees at the exact same time, but you can easily offset them by keying their Active state, as shown in Figure 16.13. For example, if you want one apple drop to be delayed, turn off its Active property at frame 1 by selecting the rigidBody for the apple and setting its Active state to off. Right-click the Active field and choose Key Selected. Then go to frame 100, set Active to on, and right-click to Key Selected. This way, gravity will not start affecting the apple until frame 100, when it then becomes an active object.

FIGURE 16.13
The Active property of a rigid body can be keyed on and off, to delay the influence of dynamic fields.

Answers

1. A passive rigid body. Even though we don't need the floor to respond to gravity or other fields, Maya still needs to know that it should be taken into account when dealing with dynamics.

2. A Rigid Body solver—the brains behind the simulation.

3. Gravity, or some sort of other field.

4. Fields. Check out the Field menu to see what other fields are available.

5. Step Size, which can be accessed by selecting any rigid body, going to the Attribute Editor, and clicking on the rigidSolver tab.

HOUR 17
Scripting and Automating Common Tasks

What You'll Learn in This Hour:

▶ How to use MEL commands to start to automate tasks

▶ How to use the Script Editor for creating scripts and watching MEL in action

▶ How to look up more commands using the MEL Command Reference

▶ How to save your script to a shelf so that it can run at the touch of a button

MEL is Maya's core scripting language. MEL stands for Maya Embedded Language, so it is hardly surprising to find it embedded right into Maya's core. As you work in Maya, MEL is busy behind the scenes executing the code to make pretty much everything you do in Maya happen. In fact, MEL isn't just behind the scenes at all, because Maya lets you see the MEL in action as you work! This means you learn the basics of MEL scripting by working as normal in Maya, but keeping an eye on what MEL is doing. Maya also lets you work with Python-style scripting if you prefer. You can make use of MEL or Python to automate repetitive tasks or complete complex tasks. Almost everything you can do using Maya's graphical interface can be automated and extended using MEL or Python.

NOTE

Saving Scripts to a Shelf

Maya lets you create a script and save it to a shelf so that all you need to do is click the icon on the shelf and run your script. You will learn how to save your scripts to a shelf in this Hour.

This Hour provides an overview of the basics you need to get started with MEL scripting. You will use the Script Editor within Maya to enter commands and also to watch commands being generated as you work manually in Maya. You will learn how to make use of those commands to help you use scripts to automate tasks by creating a few planets and lots of stars using MEL. This Hour also covers how to look up commands using the MEL Command Reference, and how to save commands to a shelf, so you can run them at the touch of a button.

MEL Scripting Basics

The quickest way to see MEL is action within Maya is through the command line at the bottom of your Maya screen. The left side of the command line has a label reading "MEL" (or "Python"), with a field next to it ready to accept MEL or Python commands. The right side of the command line is the feedback area that shows the results of commands as well as any error messages. As you work in Maya, keep an eye on the bottom right of the command line to see some MEL commands and responses appear.

It is traditional for a first scripting assignment to print out "Hello World" to the display because it's about the easiest thing to get started with. In a new empty scene in Maya, look for the Command Line at the bottom of your Maya screen. Check that the lower-left corner reads "MEL," as Figure 17.1 shows. You can swap between MEL and Python by clicking on the label, but for this Hour, we will stick to MEL.

FIGURE 17.1
Type a command into the command line on the left and then press Enter to execute the command and see the results on the right.

TIP
_____

Showing the Command Line

If the command line is missing, use Display, UI Elements and then turn on Command Line to show it again.
_____

> ▶ Now let's create a simple Hello World message using a MEL print statement. Type `print "hello world"` into the command line and press **Enter**.

> ▶ You should see that your "hello world" text has been printed out to the command response area. Figure 17.1 shows the left side of the command line, which is used to enter commands, and the right side, which shows any results.

> ▶ Now type `polySphere` into the command line and press **Enter** to create a polygon sphere. You should see that a new polygon sphere has been added to your scene, and the command response area shows the results. But better than that, you should now see the sphere in the viewport!

NOTE

MEL Is Case Sensitive

If you typed in **polysphere** with a lowercase s and pressed **Enter** to execute the code, Maya will have given you an error message. This is because MEL is case sensitive, which means you have to pay attention to whether you are using uppercase or lowercase letters, because MEL knows the difference. MEL only recognizes the command if the spelling is right, *including* the capitalization. That means MEL doesn't know what a polysphere is, but does know what a polySphere is. It might help you to know that commands in MEL start with a lowercase letter, and subsequent compound words are usually capitalized, as is the case with `polySphere`.

TIP

Repeat Commands Using Command History

If you want to repeat a command, click in the command line and use the up and down arrows to scroll through the command history. Once you have the command you want, press **Enter** to execute it.

Typing into the command line got us started, but it isn't going to get us very far if we don't discuss some more commands. It also isn't going to help us much when we want to perform more complex tasks that require quite a few lines of code. Fortunately, the Script Editor will help us out with both tasks.

Writing Scripts in the Script Editor

The Script Editor is far more sophisticated than the command line, and it lets you type in a single line of commands, or scripts containing numerous lines of code. It also lets you see a lot more of the MEL commands being executed in Maya as you work. You can also choose to venture into Python instead of MEL. For this Hour, we will stick to MEL:

▶ Open up the Script Editor in Maya by clicking on the Script Editor button on the lower right of your Maya screen, as Figure 17.2 shows. You can also use Window, General Editors, Script Editor if you prefer. The Script Editor will open, as shown in Figure 17.3.

FIGURE 17.2
Use the Script Editor button in the lower-right corner of your Maya screen to open up the Script Editor.

The Script Editor window lets you type in (or load up) single-line or multiline scripts in MEL or Python in the bottom input pane and see their output in the history pane in the top half of the window, as shown in Figure 17.3.

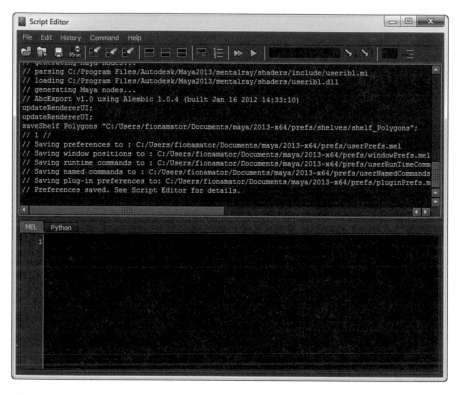

FIGURE 17.3
The Script Editor window shows MEL command history in the top pane and lets you type your own commands into the bottom pane.

The MEL tab in the bottom input pane is used to type in MEL commands, and the Python tab is used for Python commands. We are going to stick to MEL for this Hour, so let's get started:

▶ Type the command `sphere` into the MEL tab input area and press **Ctrl+Enter** to execute the command and create a NURBS sphere.

Pressing **Enter** (also known as **Return**) from your alphanumeric keyboard will simply take you to the next line to continue typing in your code. We use **Ctrl+Enter** to let Maya know we want to execute (that is, run) the command.

TIP

Change Font Size

If you want to change the size of the font in the top or bottom pane to make it easier to work with, just use **Ctrl** and MMB scroll in the pane you want to adjust.

As Maya executes the command, it is removed from the input pane, but will appear above in the history pane, along with any message to show the results. Sometimes this can be just what you want, but more often than not, you will probably still want to keep the command in the input pane, to add to it or use it again another time. If you want to keep the commands in the input pane after execution, select the commands first and press **Ctrl+Enter**. We will do this as we get slightly more ambitious and create a NURBS sphere and a polygon sphere at the same time.

▶ Type the following into the input pane:

```
sphere;
polySphere;
```

▶ To execute both commands, select both commands first and use **Ctrl+Enter**. The selected commands will remain in the bottom pane when you execute the code.

You might be wondering why we needed the semicolons when we didn't need them before. MEL is a scripting language, and just like any other language, it has grammatical rules you need to follow, called "syntax." When you use more than one command, Maya needs to know where the end of each command is. If you try leaving out the semicolon after `sphere`, Maya will think that the `polySphere` command is still part of the sphere command, and get very confused and will give you an error message in the history pane. In theory, the last semicolon after `polySphere` is optional because no other commands follow it and Maya will guess you are done. It is a bit lazy to let Maya guess things, and also a bit risky because Maya might guess wrong! It is therefore good practice to end your commands with semicolons, even if you think Maya will let you get away with leaving them out, so that is what we will be doing from now on.

NOTE

Keeping Commands in the Input Pane

MEL gives you plenty of choices to execute your code, including **Ctrl+Enter** (alphanumeric keyboard) and **Enter** (on the numeric keypad). You can also RMB click and drag in the input pane to choose Execute from the marking menu, or use the Command menu and then Execute. Whatever method you use, if you want to keep your commands in the input pane after executing the code, then *select* the text first.

TIP

Rescuing Commands from the History Pane

If you execute commands and forget to select the text first, the commands will disappear from the input pane, but you should be able to rescue them from the history pane. Locate and select the commands you need from the history pane and then MMB drag them back into the input pane.

Learning MEL from Maya in Action

We aren't going to get very far by only knowing the commands for a `sphere` and a `polySphere`. Plus, we didn't even make full use of those commands, because MEL provides options known as "flags" to help set values as we go. Fortunately, we can use Maya to help us find out more. One of the quickest ways to learn basic MEL commands is to work manually in Maya and observe the MEL in action in the Script Editor's history pane—and that is what we are about to do.

NOTE

Turn Interactive Creation Off for Now

Maya lets you interactively create objects by clicking and dragging on the grid to place them just where you want. Although this can be useful, it somewhat masks the MEL that displays in the history window. We are going to turn off interactive creation so we can more easily capture the MEL behind the creation of the objects. This also makes sure that objects start at the same place in the scene, which is (000) on the grid, so that any commands work the same here and in your own scenes.

- ▶ To make the MEL easier to see, and to make your own scenes consistent with the exercises here, turn off the interaction creation options. For NURBS, go to the Create menu and then to NURBS Primitives and make sure that Interactive Creation (toward the bottom of the menu) is turned off (unchecked). For polygons, use Create, Polygon Primitives. Make sure Interactive Creation is turned off here, too.

- ▶ Create a polygon sphere by using the Create, Polygon Primitives, Sphere. MEL will run the code to create a polySphere, so you should see the following command appear in the history pane:

  ```
  polySphere -r 1 -sx 20 -sy 20 -ax 0 1 0 -cuv 2 -ch 1;
  ```

You can see that MEL has added a few more things after the polySphere command that we didn't use when we created a polygon sphere earlier. These options, known as "flags," are used to set values as you go. The flags are denoted by a dash in front, and the values that flags accept are known as "arguments." The arguments all expect a certain type of data. For instance, the first flag -r is setting a radius and expecting an integer (whole) or float (decimal) number, which is 1 in this case. The -sx and -sy flags set the subdivisions for x and y both to 1, and they expect whole numbers (integers) as values. The -ax flag sets the primitive axis to Y, and expects three values for x, y, and z (that is, 0 1 0). The -cuv flag is used to create UVs and needs a number, too. The -ch flag is used to turn construction history on or off and needs a number, but in this case it just wants either 0 to turn the history off or 1 to turn it on. This is because MEL is expecting a simple Boolean value (a value that is just a choice between on and off, true or false, or 0 or 1).

NOTE

Basic Data Types

MEL (and just about any other scripting language) uses different types of data that you will need to be aware of. Flags and attributes all expect particular types of data, and if you provide the wrong kind you will get an error. The main types of data to be aware of in this Hour are integers, floats, strings, and Booleans, as described in Table 17.1.

TABLE 17.1 Basic MEL Data Types

Data Type	MEL	Example	Description
Integer	int	-3, 45, 8976, -578	Whole numbers.
Float	float	-0.01, 3.25, 786.00	Decimal numbers.
String	string	"hello world"	A string of characters used to work with text.
Boolean	boolean	0, 1, on, off, true, false	Used to indicate true or false. Either type in **true**, **1**, or **on** for true, or **false**, **0**, or **off** for false

Maya used default values to create the polygon sphere, but we can copy the command from the history pane by MMB dragging it into the input pane and then make some changes to get a bit more adventurous with creating our own objects in MEL. Let's create a new polygon sphere with a radius of 3, for example. Maya just assumes default values if we leave any of the flags out, so all we need is polySphere -r 3.

MMB drag the polySphere command from the history pane into the input pane. Delete flags and values you don't need, and change the radius value to 3. You should then end up with the following command to execute:

```
polySphere -r 3;
```

Remember to select the text first, and use **Ctrl+Enter** to execute it.

TIP

Echo All Commands

By default, the history pane doesn't show all the MEL that is running as you work in Maya. If you want to see more of the details, go to the History menu in the Script Editor and turn on Echo All Commands. You can always turn it back off if you find it to be overkill. Be sure to keep it turned off for this Hour, though.

You should be aware that flags have short names that are quicker to type, such as `-r`, or long names, such as `-radius`, which are more descriptive. We are going to stick to the short names for this Hour. The short names are quicker to type; plus, if you forget what any are, they are easy to look up, as you will see shortly. However, when creating your own scripts, feel free to add the more descriptive long names if you feel this will help you learn and remember what the scripts are for.

TIP

Clearing the History and Input Panes

When you are trying to capture a MEL command by carrying out a task and then copying the code from the history pane, starting with a clear pane can help distinguish the commands you need from any previous commands. To clear a pane, use the Edit menu in the Script Editor to choose Clear History, Clear Input, or Clear All.

Getting Help on Commands

If you already know the name of the command, but aren't sure what the flags are, or what type of information the flags are expecting, you can type `help` and then the name of the command into the input pane. For example, execute the following command:

```
help polySphere;
```

Maya will bring up a synopsis of the use of the command (`polySphere`, in this case) with its flags and the data types needed in the history pane, as shown in the top half of Figure 17.4. You can also get quick help by typing in the command, selecting it, RMB dragging, and then releasing over Quick Help from the marking menu that pops up. The Quick Help tab opens up on the right of the input pane, showing the command and a list of its short and long flags names, as shown by Figure 17.4.

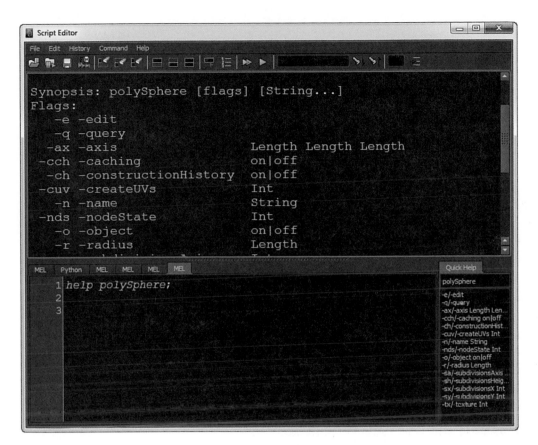

FIGURE 17.4
Type **help** followed by the command you want to look up to show a synopsis in the history pane (top), or RMB click and drag the command to bring up the Quick Help tab (right).

NOTE

Line Numbers

Figure 17.4 includes line numbers in the bottom pane. Line numbers are very useful when you're trying to debug your code (hunting down and fixing errors). Any error messages will include line numbers, so it's helpful to include the line numbers in your input pane, too. Use the Command menu within the Script Editor to choose Show Line Numbers to switch them on.

TIP

Extra Tabs

Extra tabs can be useful when writing or temporarily storing commands, as Figure 17.4 shows. You can add an extra tab for input by RMB clicking in the input pane and holding to bring up the marking menu. Drag and release over New Tab to create an additional tab. Maya will ask you whether you want a MEL or Python tab. Stick to MEL for this Hour.

For more comprehensive help, it is worth getting familiar with MEL's command reference. It is quite common place for even the most experienced programmers to look up commands in the command reference. Maya's main Help menu and the Script Editor's Help menu both have options to select MEL Command Reference. A browser window will open with commands grouped in alphabetical order and by category, as shown by Figure 17.5. Either scroll through all the commands on the main page or use the categories and alphabetical listings to search for the command you want. You can also type into the By Substring(s) field if you already have an idea of what you are looking for. You can also select the command in the input pane and use Help within the Script Editor to choose Help on Selected Command to go straight to the command you want.

Once you have found the command you are looking for, you should see that the command reference provides more information than the quick Help options within the Script Editor. The top of the page contains a synopsis of the command, including the flags it can use, expected data types for each flag, plus a description of what the command does. You might find it particularly helpful to scroll down to the very bottom of the page, where examples of code are provided. The examples can often help you understand how to use the command.

NOTE

MEL Syntax

You will come across the term "syntax" when using the MEL Command Reference, and also when MEL throws out any error messages that mention syntax. MEL is a scripting language, and just like any other language it has its own grammatical rules known as syntax. This pretty much means that you have to pay particular attention to things such as spelling, when to use uppercase and lowercase letters, when to use a semicolon or a period, when to use quotation marks (and when not to), and where to use brackets and even what kind of brackets to use. If you don't get things just right, MEL will let you know by giving you an error message.

TIP

Color-Coded Highlights

The Script Editor uses color-coded highlights when it recognizes MEL commands, which give you a quick way of checking that MEL is recognizing the commands as you type them. For example, sphere would be color-highlighted in the input pane, whereas Sphere would not be. Because MEL is case sensitive, Sphere is not recognized as a command due to the capital S at the beginning. Not seeing the highlights when expected is a good cue to double-check what you have typed.

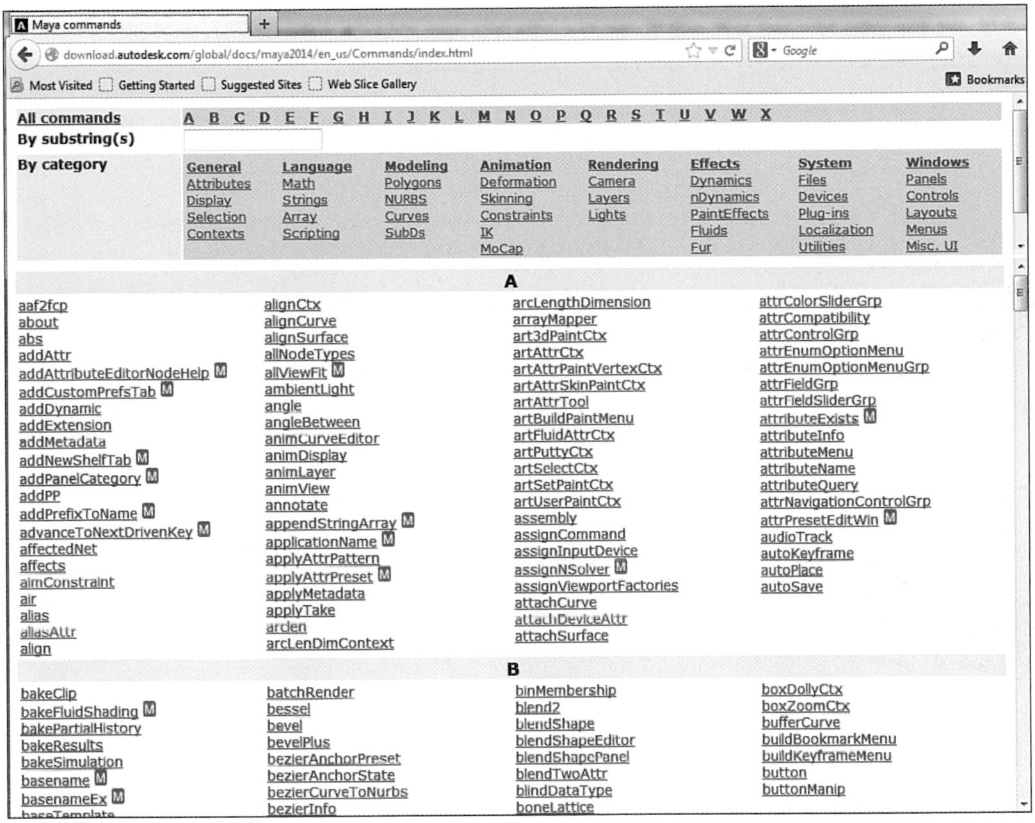

FIGURE 17.5
The MEL Command Reference lists commands alphabetically or in groups according to category.

Creating a Universe with MEL

Let's get busy. We are going to use MEL to create a few planets out of spheres, plus place some stars at random points in our universe:

▸ Start with a new empty scene, and open up the Script Editor by clicking the Script Editor button at the bottom right of your Maya screen.

▸ Make sure Interactive Creation is set to off, as described earlier in the "Learning MEL from Maya in Action" section. This just makes it easier to follow along and be consistent with this exercise. Use History, Clear All from the Script Editor to clear out any previous code in the history and input panes to start from scratch.

▶ We are going to use MEL to create a polygon sphere, but then move it as soon as it has been created, so type and execute the following commands:

```
polySphere;
move -r -1 2 4;
```

Remember to select the text before using **Ctrl+Enter** if you want to keep it in the input pane after you execute it.

You should see that a polygon sphere is created in the scene. The -r flag within the move command stands for "relative" and will move the selected object by taking into consideration its current position and then adding on the values that are specified for x, y, and z (-1, 2, and 4 in this case). If you prefer, you can use the -a (absolute) flag to disregard the current position of the object and move it straight to the coordinates specified. The move command worked because the sphere was still selected after we created it. This is often fine, but at times it is better to specify the object you want to move. Naming objects as you create them comes in very handy for all sorts of things, including making it easier to understand what is happening, problem solving if things are going wrong, and using the names to make sure we are moving the right object. So this is what we will do:

▶ Type in and execute the following:

```
polySphere -n "earth";
move -r 6 0 -5 "earth";
```

The -n flag lets us name the polySphere "earth" as we create it. The name needs quotation marks to let MEL understand that it is a string of characters we were using, rather than the name of an existing command. We then used the name "earth" at the end of the move command to specify the name of the object we want to move.

▶ Keep the earth in your scene, and now let's create the sun and scale it to make it bigger than the earth. Type in and execute the following:

```
polySphere -n "sun";
scale -r 3 3 3 "sun";
```

▶ Next, we will create Mars, but instead of scaling Mars, we will use its radius flag to set the size from the start. Type in and execute the following:

```
polySphere -r .5 -n "mars";
move -r 9 0 -7 "mars";
```

We are going to get a little more ambitious with Saturn, because Saturn needs a ring of course! We are going to use a NURBS sphere for Saturn, just to get more practice creating different types of geometry, and a polygon torus for its ring.

▶ Type in and execute:

```
sphere -r 1.1 -n "saturn";
move -r 13 0 -10 "saturn";
polyTorus -r 1.6 -sr 0.1 -n "ring";
rotate -r 15 0 0 "ring"; move -r 13 0 -10 "ring" ;
```

These commands create a NURBS sphere named "saturn," with a radius of 1.5, and move it into position. They then create a polygon torus named "ring," rotate it by 15 degrees, and move it to the same position as "saturn." The torus uses the -sr flag, which we haven't seen before. The -sr flag can be used to set the value of the section radius (that is, essentially how fat or thin your torus is).

Before moving on to learning some intermediate techniques for working with commands, let's print out the traditional "hello world" and learn about print statements and comments too. Comments are used to annotate scripts. To specify that a single line of text is a comment, use two forward slashes (//) at the beginning of the line. If you want the comments to span more than one line, start off with a forward slash followed by an asterisk (/*), type in your comment, and end the comment with an asterisk followed by a forward slash (*/), as Figure 17.6 shows. MEL will pass the comment onto the history pane, but will not execute anything within the comment. Print statements are also passed on to the history pane, but the difference between comments and print statements is that comments are purely for making notes. You can pass arguments on to print statements, however, to help get feedback from your commands, which you will see in the "Creating the Universe with MEL: Intermediate" section.

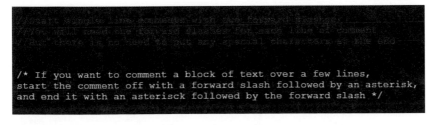

FIGURE 17.6
Two styles of commenting in MEL.

▶ Type in and execute the following code to print out a "hello world" message:

```
print ("hello worlds \n");
```

NOTE

Printing to a New Line

If you want to create a new line when using the print statement, use \n. The "n" stands for new line, but we can't just use the letter *n* by itself, or MEL will think we are trying to print it. The backslash is therefore used for an "escape character," to denote that the following character (the *n* in this case) needs to be used in the command.

Listing 17.1 shows all the commands for this section, including some comments to help you understand what the commands are doing.

Listing 17.1   Script for Creating the Universe Through MEL: Basic

```
//create the earth & move into position
polySphere -n "earth";
move -r 6 0 -5 "earth";
//create the sun & triple its size
polySphere -n "sun";
scale -r 3 3 3 "sun";
//create mars with a radius of .5 & move into position
polySphere -r .5 -n "mars";
move -r 9 0 -7 "mars";
// create saturn with radius of 1.1 & move into position
sphere -r 1.1 -n "saturn";
move -r 13 0 -10 "saturn";
//create the ring & rotate it & move into position
polyTorus -r 1.6 -sr 0.1 -n "ring";
rotate -r 15 0 0 "ring";
move -r 13 0 -10 "ring";
//print out "hello worlds" followed by a new line
print ("hello worlds \n");
```

TIP

Saving Scripts

Commands that you type into the input pane of the Script Editor will generally stay there until you (or Maya) do something to make them disappear. To store them more permanently, MMB drag them to a shelf, as shown in the section "Making Use of the Shelves," later in this Hour. You can also save a script using File, Save from the Script Editor menus.

BONUS

Scripts

Take a look in this Hour's folder and you will notice we have included the completed basic script for you, plus the intermediate one. We have also included a README file to provide you with instructions on how to load or copy and paste the scripts. As an added bonus, we have included a short but useful script that lets you hide and show NURBS curves and locators. This is very useful to show or hide animation rigs. There is also a great arc-tracking script that is really handy when you're trying to create polished animations.

Creating a Universe with MEL: Intermediate

We are going to introduce some intermediate scripting techniques here, but you can skip straight to the "Making Use of the Shelves" section if you have had enough of MEL for now. In this section, we are going to create a star, but we are also going to introduce some random numbers, plus variables, and explain what is happening in a moment.

▶ In the Script Editor, type in and execute the following:

```
//create a star of random radius
//& put it into a random position for x y & z
polyPrimitive -r (rand(0.01,0.11));
float $tX = rand(-18,18);
float $tY = rand(-18,18);
float $tZ = rand(-18,18);
move -r $tX $tY $tZ;
```

Remember to select the text and use **Ctrl+Enter** here, because you will want to use these commands again soon.

We have introduced a couple new things here: variables (starting with "$") and the rand function. Rand is a mathematical function that generates a number between the minimum and maximum numbers we set as arguments. Therefore, rand(0.01, 0.11) generates a random number anywhere between 0.01 and 0.11, whereas rand(-18, 18) generates a number between negative and positive 18. Also notice that when we set the radius using the rand function, we need some extra brackets around it to tell MEL to work out the random number first, then set the radius to that value.

We also introduced variables to help move the star to a random position. Variables are containers that store data for reuse when you need them. $tX, $tY, and $tZ are each variables, set up to store float (decimal) numbers that we can use to set the values of the x, y, and z translation.

You can use whatever name you want for variables, but MEL requires that you start the name off with a dollar sign, and it is helpful to name them to describe or at least hint at what they are for. We also assigned our `$tX`, `$tY`, and `$tZ` variables each a value between -18, and 18, as generated by the rand function again (for example, `float $tX = rand(-18, 18);`). The move `-r $tX $tY $tZ;` command used our variables with the random values to move the star into place.

This might seem a huge amount of work for just one star, but you can use what you just learned to help quickly generate as many stars as you want, all in random positions throughout your universe, as illustrated by Figure 17.7.

FIGURE 17.7
The universe with the sun, a few planets, and many stars, all generated almost instantly with MEL.

MEL and other scripting languages provide ways for you to automatically loop through commands that you want to repeat, and because we want more than one star, it is worth having a look. One of the most commonly used loops in MEL is the `for` loop, so let's look at that. If we want 100 stars, for example, we can use the same commands from earlier, but surround them with a `for` loop plus curly brackets, as follows:

```
int $i;
for ($i=0; $i < 100; $i++){
    float $radius = rand(0.01,0.11);
    float $tX = rand(-18, 18);
    float $tY = rand(-18,18);
    float $tZ = rand(-18,18);
    polyPrimitive -r $radius;
    move -r $tX $tY $tZ;
};
```

The `int $i;` line creates a variable called $i that can store integers (whole numbers) to act as our index (or counter). Next, within the first line of the `for` loop, `$i=0;` sets the value of our counter to 0, and if we jump to the end of that line, `$i++` is increasing the counter by 1 each time the `for` loop runs. Each time the `for` loop runs, it executes the block of commands in the curly brackets. Thus, we have our counter, and the counter is going to increase every time MEL executes the block of commands. However, we also need a way for MEL to know when to stop the loop, and this is where the condition in the middle of the first line of the `for` loop comes in. The condition `$i < 100;`, is essentially saying, "keep running the `for` loop while the counter $i is less than 100, but stop it as soon as it reaches 100 (or more)."

If you execute the `for` loop commands, you should see 100 stars almost instantly created in your scene. The $i counter was set to 0 to start with. The `for` loop then ran and created one star, and increased $i to 1. It then checked to see if $i was less than 100, and since it was, it continued and repeated the commands. It finally stopped when the counter $i had reached 100, and we had 100 stars.

You can use some MEL to select everything and delete it from your scene, so we can clear the scene, ready to create more. Use the `select -all; delete;` commands to delete everything in the scene, and let's create even more stars. In fact, let's create a random number of stars. We can use variables, plus the `rand` function to help out again. For example, we can use two integer variables to store the minimum and maximum numbers of stars we want to create ($min and $max). We can then use these variables within the `rand` function to make sure it generates a number of stars between the minimum and maximum values, and we can assign that number to the variable for the actual number of stars we are going to create ($noOfStars). The following commands give an example of requesting a minimum of 300 stars and a maximum of 600 stars:

```
//create variables for the min and max no of stars
int $min = 300;
int $max = 600;
```

```
//create variable to store the actual number of stars
//that will be a random number between $min and $max
int $noOfStars = rand ($min, $max);
```

Setting up and assigning values to the variables isn't going to generate the right number of stars unless we remember to replace the "100" within the condition in the `for` loop to `$noOfStars`. Therefore, the first line of the `for` loop should be this:

```
for ($i=0; $i < $noOfStars ; $i++){
```

You can do lots of other things with MEL, and we are going to have a look at just a couple more. At times, we might want to find out the value of a particular attribute of an object to use elsewhere. For example, suppose we want to set the value of the "ring" translation to the same as "Saturn," but we don't know what those translation values are. There are a couple of ways we can do this. One way is to use the `getAttr` command to get the translation values from "saturn," and use `setAttr` to set the translation values for the "ring" to the same thing. Once again, variables will help to store the information from "saturn" so we can reuse it for the "ring." Have a look at the commands in Listing 17.2, and then we will discuss them in more detail.

Listing 17.2   Using getAttr and setAttr to Set the Ring's Coordinates

```
//declare & initialize variables
//to store saturn's translation values for x, y and z
float $satTx = 0;
float $satTy = 0;
float $satTz = 0;
// create saturn with radius of 1.1 & move into position
sphere -r 1.1 -n "saturn";
move -r 13 0 -10 "saturn";
//get saturn's position
$satTx = `getAttr saturn.translateX`;
$satTy = `getAttr saturn.translateY`;
$satTz = `getAttr saturn.translateZ`;
print ("Saturn's coordinates are: " + $satTx + " " + $satTy + " " + $satTz +"\n");
//create the ring & rotate it
polyTorus -r 1.6 -sr 0.1 -n "ring";
rotate -r 15 0 0 "ring";
//set the rings x y z position to the same as saturn's;
setAttr ring.translateX $satTx;
setAttr ring.translateY $satTy;
setAttr ring.translateZ $satTz;
```

We did a few new things in these commands. First, we declared our variables for saturn's translation at the start, and because we didn't yet know saturn's translation coordinates, we initialized each value to 0 to begin. Creating variables at the start of your commands helps you keep track of them so you can easily find and update them when needed. Second, we used `getAttr`, as in `$satTx = ``getAttr saturn.translateX``;`. The `getAttr` command can be used to find out and get the value of a node's attribute. Because we had already named "saturn," all we had to do was use saturn's name, followed by a dot to tell MEL to look for the value of the attribute, and then specify the attribute we were looking for (`translateX`, in this case). You should also notice the backquotes around ``getAttr saturn.translateX``. These are used to tell MEL that you not only want to look at the value, but you want to capture the return value ("get" the value). In this case, we are getting the value of saturn's `translateX` attribute and assigning (storing) it to the `$satTx` variable.

Phew, that seems like a lot of work once again, so we need to put everything to good use by setting the value of the ring's translation to the same thing. This time, we just need to tell MEL to set the attribute for the ring's translation to the same as saturn's (and we already know saturn's). That is what we are doing with commands such as `setAttr ring.translateX $satTx;`. The `setAttr` command sets the attribute of `ring.translateX` to `$satTx`, which is saturn's translation value for x, which we got earlier. There's no need to use the backquote characters here because we are setting values, not getting them. We then need to make sure we set the values for y, and z, too.

Print statements can be used to access and print values of attributes to help us see what is happening as well as what is going wrong if there is a problem. For instance, look at the following command:

```
print ("Saturn's coordinates are: " + $satTx + " " + $satTy + " " + $satTz +"\n");
```

This will print out the text within the quotation marks, plus saturn's translation values for x, y, and z, which you have specified by using variables such as `$satTx`. The variables do not need quotations because you set them up so that Maya knows they are named variables. You need quotations around the text, though, so that Maya knows that they are strings of characters you want to use, rather than commands it should be looking for. The plus signs (+) are used to add more into your print statement, and you might recall from earlier that \n tells MEL to create a new line when you are done.

Finally, as one last touch before we leave our MEL script to create a universe, let's just finish off with a few lines to print out a hello to the worlds. We might also want to add a line to tell us how many stars we actually created. The following commands will do just that:

```
print "hello worlds \n";
print ("I just made " + $noOfStars + " stars!\n");
print "******************************** \n";
```

Notice that the "hello worlds" line doesn't need brackets because it is a simple string of characters. The line that prints out the $noOfStars needs the brackets because it is a bit more complex—it is printing a string, adding in a value from a variable, and then adding in another string again. The final line just adds a row of asterisks to the history pane as a finishing touch to let you know that this is the end of the commands you just executed. The complete code is provided in Listing 17.3.

Listing 17.3   Creating a Universe Through MEL: Intermediate

```
//Script to create a few planets, and lots of stars!
//variables for creation of the stars
int $max = 600;
int $min = 300;
int $noOfStars = rand ($min, $max);
//variables to store saturn's translation values
float $satTx = 0;
float $satTy = 0;
float $satTz = 0;
//create the earth & move into position
polySphere -r 1 -n "earth";
move -r 6 0 -5 "earth";
//create the sun & triple its size
polySphere -n "sun";
scale -r 3 3 3 "sun";
//create mars with a radius of .5 & move into position
polySphere -r .5 -n "mars";
move -r 9 0 -7 "mars";
// create saturn with radius of 1.1 & move into position
sphere -r 1.1 -n "saturn";
move -r 13 0 -10 "saturn";
//get saturn's position
float $satTx = `getAttr saturn.translateX`;
float $satTy = `getAttr saturn.translateY`;
float $satTz = `getAttr saturn.translateZ`;
//print out saturn's position just to check
print ("Saturn's coordinates are: " + $satTx + " " + $satTy + " " + $satTz +"\n");

//create the ring & rotate it
polyTorus -r 1.6 -sr 0.1 -n "ring";
rotate -r 15 0 0 "ring";

//set the rings x y z position to the same as saturn's;
setAttr ring.translateX $satTx;
setAttr ring.translateY $satTy;
setAttr ring.translateZ $satTz;

//create a star of random radius and put it into random position
//but do it for $noOfStars times...to create $noOfStars stars!
int $i;
for ($i=0; $i < $noOfStars ; $i++){
    float $radius = rand(0.01,0.11);
```

```
    float $tX = rand(-18,18);
    float $tY = rand(-18,18);
    float $tZ = rand(-18,18);
    polyPrimitive -r $radius;
    move -r $tX $tY $tZ;
};
print "hello worlds \n";
print ("I just made " + $noOfStars + " stars!\n");
print "******************************** \n";
```

CAUTION

Expression Editor in Maya

Maya also provides an Expression Editor to create scripted expressions within Maya. Although the expressions use syntax similar to MEL, there are some differences. The Expression Editor can be found using Windows, Animation Editors, Expression Editor. If you decide to use it, make sure to look up "Differences between expression and MEL syntax" in Maya's Help first.

Making Use of the Shelves

One quick way to take advantage of Maya's capabilities to automate tasks without having to delve deep into scripting is to create your own custom shelves with icons for tasks you perform. You can collect icons from other shelves, capture them from the menus as you complete tasks, or grab the code from the Script Editor to add it to the shelf.

To add a script, select the commands from the input panel of the Script Editor and then MMB drag it onto the shelf you want. Alternatively, use File, Save to Shelf from the Script Editor. A new icon will appear on the shelf that you can just click to execute the script. Let's get some scripts on the shelf:

▶ Click on your Custom Shelf tab to open it up to add your own shortcuts to.

▶ We will start off with a small script that is useful for clearing your scene. In your Script Editor input pane, type in select -all; delete;. These commands are the ones you learned would select everything in a scene and delete it. Select the commands in the input pane and MMB drag them all the way to the Custom Shelf tab.

Maya might hesitate for a short while, but then a new icon will appear on the shelf. Create a few objects in your scene and then click your new icon; they should disappear as Maya executes the commands from your shelf icon.

▶ If you created the universe script from earlier in this Hour, go ahead and, in the input pane, select all the text from that, too. MMB drag it onto the Custom Shelf tab. Now you can create a universe at the click of a button!

If you want to make an alteration to a script that has already been saved to a shelf, MMB drag the icon from the shelf back to the input pane of the Script Editor. Make the changes and then MMB drag back to the shelf. Another icon will appear, so just delete the original. If you prefer, you can RMB click the shelf icon and then click Edit to open up the Shelf Editor. Use the Command tab within the Self Editor to edit your code right there.

TIP

Adding to a Shelf

Add scripts to a shelf by MMB dragging the commands from the input pane of the Script Editor right onto the shelf you want. To copy an icon from one shelf to another, **Ctrl+MMB** drag the icon to the tab of the shelf you want to copy the icon to. If you want to add a tool, just MMB drag from the Toolbox onto the shelf. You can also add menu items. First, click the shelf you want to add the menu item to. Next, open the menu as usual but use **Ctrl+Shift** to click the menu item you want to add. There will be a short delay, but then your new icon should appear.

Instead of storing all your shortcuts on the Custom Shelf, you can create your own shelf instead, which comes in handy when you're working on particular tasks or projects. For instance, you might want to create a shelf for modeling with all your favorite tools, menu items, and even some scripted commands, too. You might have a different shelf for rendering, which includes some favorite lights as well as shortcuts to the Render View window and the Hypershade, for example. To create, delete, edit, or even load preexisting shelves, use the drop-down arrow to the left of the shelves to access menus to work with the shelves, as Figure 17.8 shows.

FIGURE 17.8
Use the drop-down arrow to the left of the shelves to access menus to modify the shelves.

This Hour was mainly about scripting, but using custom shelves with added favorite shortcuts and scripts can really help you automate your tasks, too.

Summary

This Hour introduced you to some basic MEL scripting to help you automate tasks. You were also introduced to some intermediate scripting techniques that provide even more scope to automate your own tasks. We focused on MEL because MEL is Maya's embedded scripting language, but Python is useful, too. This Hour should have got you started, but if you really want to learn to make your own scripts, make sure you use the MEL Command Reference to look up new commands you might find useful. Also, remember that you can use the history pane within the Script Editor to carry out tasks in Maya and learn from the MEL that comes up there.

Q&A

Q. **Where can I look up new commands?**

A. Use the Help menu within Maya's main window or use the Script Editor to look up any new commands or to get more detail on ones you already know in the MEL Command Reference.

Q. **Why am I getting an error for a command that I know is right?**

A. Double-check everything in the command itself, such as whether you have used lowercase instead of uppercase (or vice versa) or forget the hyphen on a flag. If you are sure the command is right, start looking at the commands that precede it. If you miss a semicolon from the line before, for example, MEL will get confused and think your new command is part of the old one, and is very likely to generate errors.

Q. **Why isn't my `move` command moving the object where it should?**

A. Double-check the flags you use in the `move` command. Remember that `-r` will move the object relative to its current position, whereas `-a` will move it straight to the position you specify.

Q. **Why do my commands change color sometimes and not others?**

A. The Script Editor color-codes your commands as you input them, as long as you have typed them correctly, including paying attention to when to use uppercase and lowercase letters. If something is not highlighting when you think it should, double-check to see if you have entered it correctly.

Workshop

The workshop contains quiz questions and exercises to help you solidify your understanding of the material covered. Try to answer all questions before looking at the "Answers" section that follows.

Quiz

1. How can you execute your commands but keep the text in the input pane?

2. If your commands disappear from the input pane when you execute them, how can you get them back?

3. How can you quickly find out what flag to use for setting the height of a `polyCube`?

4. How can you save your script to a shelf?

5. What is a variable?

Exercise

If you haven't already tried the "creating the universe" script, now is a good time to do so. If you already have, then try to add a few more objects to it. Maybe a `polyCube` and a `polyTorus` as space debris, for example, or some kind of spaceship. Try to look up at least three commands · you haven't used before and try them out. Finally, because this Hour was all about scripting and automating common tasks, think about what common tasks you do. Use the Custom Shelf tab, or create a custom shelf of your own, and then add some icons from other shelves and from the menus too. Finally, remember to use the Script Editor to watch the MEL commands that appear as you work, and try to create a few commands to add to your shelf to help you along the way. Remember that even the best programmers use command references to learn more, so get used to looking up anything you don't know in the MEL Command Reference.

Answers

1. Select the text first and then use **Ctrl+Enter** to execute.

2. Select the commands from the history pane and MMB drag them back into the input pane.

3. To get quick help, type in and execute `help polyCube` to get a synopsis in the history pane, or select `polyCube` and RMB drag to access Quick Help in the input pane.

4. Select the commands in the input pane and MMB drag them to the shelf you want to save them to.

5. A variable is like a container that can store data. Variable names in Maya start with a dollar sign ($).

HOUR 18
Using Particles to Create Effects

What You'll Learn in This Hour:

▶ How to create and emit particles
▶ How to modify the look and speed of your particles
▶ How to copy attributes by using presets
▶ How to cache your scene to enable real-time playback

Particles are used in lots of different ways for many different effects and media. If you need to create dust and debris from explosions, fireworks, smoke, rain, tornados, and more, particles are for you. Imagine creating and animating numerous tiny specks of dirt and elements by hand. Fortunately, you don't have to. Maya's particle systems let you emit customized particles to suit your needs.

NOTE

Particles Are for More Than Just Dust

Particles are not just for small specks of dust, dirt, and other tiny elements. You can also use the particle systems in Maya to emit other objects that you need en masse, such as wasps swarming from a nest.

In this Hour, you will get an overview of Maya's particle systems, focusing on nParticles, and can follow along by creating a vapor trail for an animated character flying around with a jet pack. You will learn how to create and emit particles, how to make adjustments to their look and speed, and how to cache your scene to view it in real time. You will also learn how to use presets to copy attributes from one node to another to save time when setting up extras.

What Are Particles?

Maya particles are largely physics-based points in 3D space that can be displayed in a variety of ways, including as dots, blobby surfaces, and streaks. Particles are used in lots of different ways for many different effects and media. We have already mentioned dust and debris from explosions, but particles aren't just limited to small points. We can tell each particle to use an object (geometry) instead. This is called "geometry instancing" and can usually be seen in blockbuster movies such as *The Matrix*, where the sentinels and other robots appear en masse. The animators can animate certain parts of objects such as the sentinels and then attach them to a particle system to have many of them (sometimes hundreds) all follow a similar path or pattern rather than animate each and every one individually.

Particles can be seen on TV, in games, and in the movies as natural background extras. Imagine requiring bubbles of air rising up underwater. Who wants to animate a million of those by hand? No, we'll leave all this to Maya's powerful particle system to create the smoke, fire, water, dust, tornados, plasma, explosions, and so on. The list is long!

What Is an Emitter?

Particles have to come from somewhere, however, and they are nothing without an emitter. An emitter is where particles are born and shoot out from. To create the particles, we must create an emitter to give birth to the particles and emit them into the scene. Emitters can release particles from a point in 3D space or from geometric objects. An example of this would be to have grains of sand emitting from a hand or an entire body, much like the effect in the movies *Spiderman* and *The Mummy*. Once the emitter has been created, we can tweak many attributes to control our particles, all based on physics. We can add forces such as gravity fields, Newton fields, turbulence, and many more. These attributes give us an almost completely unlimited amount of options to play with.

Particles or nParticles?

Maya's nParticles are similar to Maya's "standard" particles but are powered by Maya's nucleus dynamic simulation framework. nParticles have a few different attributes and options and can integrate and collide with other nDynamic systems in Maya, such as nMeshes and nCloth right out of the box. By this, we mean that if you use Maya standard particles and you want a particle to bounce off of a cube, you need to tell the particle to collide with the cube. This would be similar to what we did in Hour 16, "Animating Using Dynamics and Simulations." Using Maya's standard dynamic system in Hour 16, we specified the apple as an active rigid body and the ground as a passive rigid body so that the simulation knew that the apple could react to the ground. However, if you do the same thing with an nParticle and a cube that has been converted to an nCube, they will automatically interact with each other. nParticles also have the ability to simulate other natural elements such as water. Standard particles and nParticles have many features in common, however. Therefore, when we refer to the term "particles" without specifying which kind, the topic applies to either type of particle system.

It would be good to start with the basics of Maya nParticles, so let's get started!

Getting Started with nParticles

We are going to get started with Maya's nParticle system, using the Sam character introduced in Hour 8, "Character Modeling." Sam has been given some basic animation, plus a jet pack for you to create a vapor trail for using nParticles:

▶ Open particles_v1.ma from this Hour's source files to see Sam and his jet pack, as shown in Figure 18.1.

FIGURE 18.1
The particles_v1.ma file is all ready to go with a character and his jet pack.

NOTE

Camera for Composition

The particles scenes provided on the DVD for use in this Hour have a camera, called Camera_MAIN, provided to give you a composed view of the scene. We have replaced the top viewport panel with Camera_MAIN, although you can use the Panels menu within the viewport to switch back to the top view if you prefer. Camera_MAIN has been locked to avoid accidental changes. For more information on working with cameras, see Hour 14, "Creating and Adjusting Cameras."

If you click on the Camera_MAIN viewport and click Play (from the lower-right corner of your screen), you will see that Sam has some basic animation applied which has him take off, become slightly unstable before deciding to call it a day and land. The animation doesn't make a whole lot of sense yet, until we create the vapor trail. What we need here are some jet pack effects, and for this, we will use nParticles. Follow the steps below to add the vapor trail:

TIP

Animating Sam

We have only provided some basic animation on Sam. Therefore, if you would like to have a go at improving or changing it, you can show Sam's animation controllers by using the Show menu in one of the viewing panels to reveal NURBS curves. Character animation is beyond the scope of this book, but feel free to have a try if you're interested.

▶ Use the drop-down menu set list located at the top-left corner of your Maya screen to select the nDynamics menu set, as shown in Figure 18.2.

FIGURE 18.2
You can swap to the nDynamics menu set by using the drop-down menu set list in the top-left corner of your Maya screen.

▶ Once you have the nDynamics menu set selected, you should see some available menus that include nParticles.

▶ From the nDyamics menu set, select the nParticles menu and then Create nParticles. You can see from Figure 18.3 that a few options are available. The top half of the menu options are essentially asking how we want to emit the particles, and the bottom half of the menu options are asking what type of particle we would like to emit.

▶ Figure 18.3 shows that we have the choice of Points, Balls, Cloud, Thick Cloud, or Water. All of these have different attributes. We are going to use Cloud nParticles created from a point emitter (rather than being emitted from an object).

▶ Double-check that Cloud is selected and then choose Create Emitter.

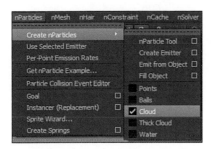

FIGURE 18.3
Create nParticles lets you choose the particle type in the lower half of the menu options as well as how you want to emit the particles from the top.

Maya has now created an emitter, along with the all-important nucleus dynamic systems, which enable everything to work. The emitter has been placed right on the ground in the middle of Sam's base. You can switch to wireframe mode by pressing 4 on your keyboard to see it, as shown in Figure 18.4. You can also see from the Outliner that an emitter node, nParticle node, and nucleus node have been created. Switch back to shaded view by pressing 6 on the keyboard when you are ready to continue.

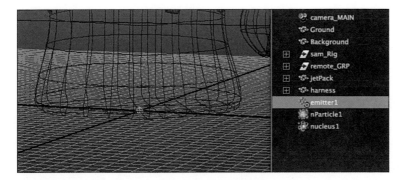

FIGURE 18.4
An emitter should appear at the base of Sam, and the Outliner should now have nodes for an emitter, nParticle, and nucleus.

▶ Click the Play button (lower right of your Maya screen) to see the particles being discharged from the emitter on the floor. You will see that as Sam moves, the particles keep emitting from the ground rather than from the jet pack. We need to position the emitter inside one of its jets, and make sure that it moves along with Sam.

▶ To position the emitter inside one of the jets, select the emitter from the Outliner and translate it until it is just up inside the hole of the first jet. If we were to click Play now, we would see Sam fly off but the emitter stay put. To fix this, we need to parent constrain the emitter to the jet pack. This will enable the emitter to always follow the jet pack, even if we change the animation of Sam later on.

▶ To find the Constrain menu, change to the Animation menu set by pressing **F2** or by using the drop-down list in the top-left corner of your Maya screen and then choose Animation. The Animation menu set should appear, along with the Constrain menu.

▶ In the scene, select the jet pack geometry and then hold **Shift** down to select the emitter.

▶ With the jet pack and emitter selected, choose Constrain and then Parent to constrain the emitter to the jet pack. Now if we click Play, we can see the particles emitting from the parented emitter, moving along with the jet pack.

TIP

Jet Pack Still Misbehaving?

If for some reason the jet pack remains on the ground, it is possible that you constrained the jet pack to the emitter, rather than the other way around. Use the **z** key to undo, and try again. Make sure that you select the jet pack first, then **Shift**-select the emitter before trying again.

▶ Once you are satisfied that the emitter is moving along with the jet pack, save your file.

The jet pack particles don't quite have the look we are after, however, so let's begin tweaking them in the next section.

NOTE

Parent Constraint Versus Parenting

Rather than parent constraining the emitter to the jet pack, we could have first selected the emitter, **Shift**-selected the jet pack, and pressed **p** on the keyboard. This would create a permanent parent/child relationship, rather than a constraint, which can be animated on and off. A constraint was used instead so that the emitter remains easy to find in the Outliner, rather than being moved in the hierarchy under its parent.

Editing the Attributes of an Emitter

In the previous section, we created a point emitter that releases particles directly, and then we parent constrained the emitter to a jet pack to make it appear that the jet pack was emitting the particles. We are going to continue modifying our nParticles apparently emitted from the jet pack, but it is worth noting that Maya also provides different options for emitting nParticles. Both nParticles and standard particles can be emitted from points on a surface, points on a curve, all CVs and vertices of a selected object, as well as selected vertices, CVs, and edit points. Additionally, nParticles and standard particles can be emitted from volume shapes such as cones, spheres, and cylinders.

We can control the direction, quantity, speed, and initial direction of emitted particles by setting attributes while we are creating the emitter, or by adjusting attributes on the emitter once it has been created. Select the square options box next to the menu label to set options as you create, as shown in Figure 18.5.

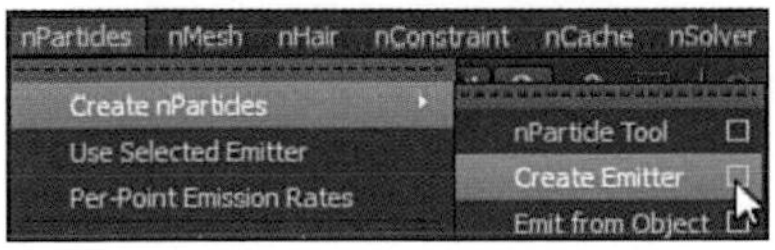

FIGURE 18.5
Select the square options box on any menu item, such as Create Emitter, to set options as you go.

TIP

Emitting nParticles from an Object

To emit nParticles from an object, select the object. Then use the nDynamic menu set to choose nParticles, Create nParticles, Emit from Object.

Emitter attributes can also be modified once created, which is a good thing because we need to change some attributes on our emitter. Follow the steps outlined here to adjust some attributes to improve your vapor trail—and learn more about emitters and particles as you go:

▶ Continue with the file you created earlier, or open particles_v2.ma to start with Sam with a default emitter parent constrained to his jet pack. If you click Play to see the particles that are being emitted, you should see that the particles are not really coming out as a nice vapor trail, but rather are coming out from all directions. This is because our emitter is set up as an "omni" emitter. This will be adjusted in the next steps.

NOTE

Emitter Types

An emitter can come in the form of an omni, directional, surface, curve, or volume emitter. An omni emitter discharges particles in all directions (omnidirectional), whereas a directional emitter emits in the direction specified by its Direction X, Y, and Z attributes. Surface emitters release particles from positions on or near polygonal or NURBS surfaces. Similarly, particles from curve emitters are released from positions on or near a curve. Finally, particles from volume emitters are discharged from a closed volume such as a cube or sphere shape.

▶ In your scene, select the emitter in the Outliner, and let's look in the Attribute Editor at the different types of emission available. If necessary, use **Ctrl+a** to bring up the Attribute Editor, as shown in Figure 18.6.

FIGURE 18.6
The attributes for the emitter can be modified through the Attribute Editor.

TIP

Display the Attribute Editor

Use **Ctrl+a** to toggle between the Channel Editor and the Attribute Editor. Alternatively, you can use the Editor buttons in the top-right corner of your Maya screen, as Figure 18.7 shows. Be aware that versions of Maya previous to 2014 will only have three buttons rather than the four shown in Figure 18.7.

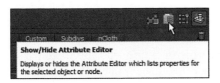

FIGURE 18.7
You will find the button for the Attribute Editor in the top-right corner of your Maya screen.

▶ We want to change the type of our emitter from Omni to Directional. With the emitter selected, expand the Basic Emitter Attributes section, if necessary, by clicking on the drop-down arrow to the left of the label. Figure 18.8 shows the Basic Emitter Attributes section expanded to reveal the Emitter Type options.

▶ Click the drop-down list next to the Emitter Type menu to select Directional instead of Omni, as Figure 18.8 shows.

FIGURE 18.8
Click the drop-down list next to Emitter Type to change the type to Directional.

▶ If we click Play now, we can see the particles coming out in a more uniform way, but they are going in the wrong direction, so we need to make further adjustments. Therefore, with the emitter still selected, return to the emitter attributes in the Attribute Editor and scroll down to the Distance/Direction Attributes, as shown in Figure 18.9. The default value of Direction X is 1.000, which is why our particles are going in the wrong direction.

▶ Set the value of Direction X to 0, and set the value of Direction Y to -1.000. This should enable the particles to travel downward.

▶ Click Play to check the flow of the particles and you should see them emitting downward from the jet pack, which is the correct direction for this example. If you scroll through the available attributes for our emitter, you will see there are many attributes we can still modify. For instance, within the Distance/Direction Attributes section, we can add a bit more spread to the particles. The Spread attribute controls the emission spread angle for Directional and Curve emitters. Think of a cone and the particles emitting from the point of the cone and spreading out into the outer area. Smaller values will give a more concentrated stream of particles (a more narrow cone), and larger values (up to 1) a wider cone. Setting the value to 1 produces an emission angle of 180 degrees, and a value of 0.5 produces an angle of 90 degrees.

▶ With the emitter selected, adjust the Spread value to between 0 and 1. Click Play to see how changing these values affects the stream of particles.

▶ With the emitter still selected, when you have finished experimenting with the Spread attribute, set the value to 0.15 and click Play. Figure 18.9 shows our final values for the Distance/Direction Attributes, but you can set them to your own preferences.

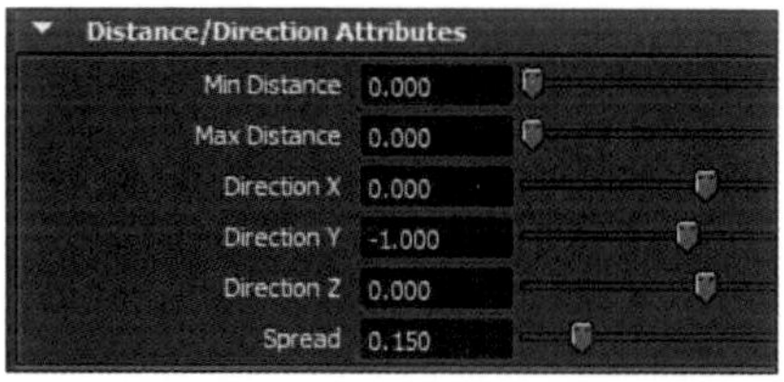

FIGURE 18.9
In the Distance/Direction Attributes section, set Direction Y to -1.000, Spread to 0.150, and the other distance attributes to 0.000.

Your jet pack should now have a nice stream of particles flowing from it. We can still adjust some more attributes to further improve it, however. In addition to modifying attributes for the emitter, we can modify the attributes for the particles themselves:

▶ Select nParticle1 in the Outliner to open the attributes for this node.

▶ In the Attribute Editor, click on the tab for nParticleShape1 so that we can make a small adjustment to the size of the particles.

▶ To find the radius of the particles, expand the Particle Size section by clicking on the arrow next to the label. Increase the value of the radius until you get the look you want. We have chosen 0.500 for this example. Figure 18.10 shows the Radius attribute located in the Attribute Editor.

▶ Save your file.

TIP

Adjusting the Radius of Particles
To get instant visual feedback about the size of your particles, play the animation until the particles just start to come out of the jet pack and then stop. Adjusting the value for the particle radius will now be reflected in your viewing panel.

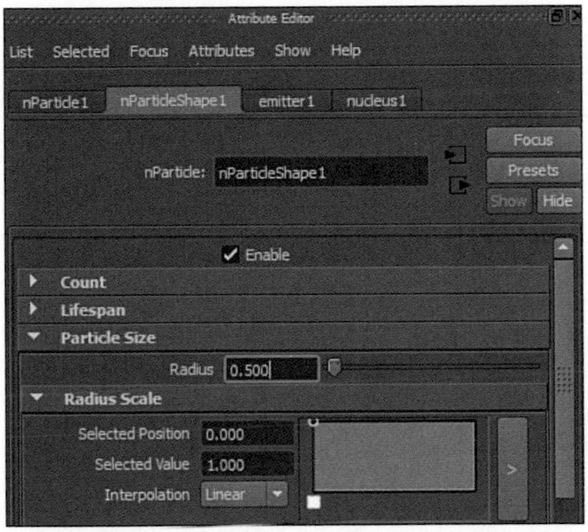

FIGURE 18.10
Select the nParticle node and then the nParticleShape tab in the Attribute Editor to find the particle radius attribute.

Making More Adjustments

Next we want to animate and change the speed of the particles. Currently, the particles just slowly emit from the jet pack without the force one would expect. Follow these steps to animate the speed of the particles:

- ▶ Continue with your own file, or open particles_v3.ma to start from this point.

- ▶ Select the emitter to make further adjustments.

TIP

Tabs in the Attribute Editor

If you look at Figure 18.10, you will see that the nParticleShape1 node attributes are showing, but there are also tabs available in the Attribute Editor for the emitter and nucleus nodes. To swap between the particles, emitter, and nucleus attributes, simply select the relevant tab.

- ▶ Scroll down to Basic Emission Speed Attributes and increase Speed to 5.000 and also enable Scale Rate by Speed. Speed acts as a multiplier for the original emission speed when Scale Rate by Speed is enabled. A value of 1 leaves the speed as it is, a value less than 1 reduces the speed, and a value greater than 1 increases the speed. Our value of 5 will multiply the original emission speed by 5.

NOTE

Counting Particles

If you want to see how many particles are being emitted, select the nParticle1 node and make sure to also select the nParticleShape1 tab in the Attribute Editor. Expand the Count section and then click Play. When you stop playback, the Count figure will update to reflect the number of particles that have been emitted up to that point in time (frame).

▶ With the emitter selected, scroll up to Basic Emitter Attributes to adjust the rate at which the particles are being emitted per second. Set the value for Rate (Particles/Sec) to 500 to give us a lot more particles.

▶ Click Play, and you should notice that more particles are now emitted. However, although the particles are now looking more like a vapor trail, they are still being emitted before we need them. If you look at the animation, Sam presses the buttons to start the jet pack around frame 25. We don't want our particles to start emitting until then, so we can animate the Rate attribute to emit zero particles until we need them.

▶ Make sure you are on frame 1 on your Timeline, and with the emitter selected, in the Attribute Editor turn the Rate down to 0.

▶ Right-click inside the Rate value field and select Set Key, as shown in Figure 18.11. Because the rate is now zero particles per second, our particles won't be emitted at all now. The value field will turn red to indicate you have successfully set a key.

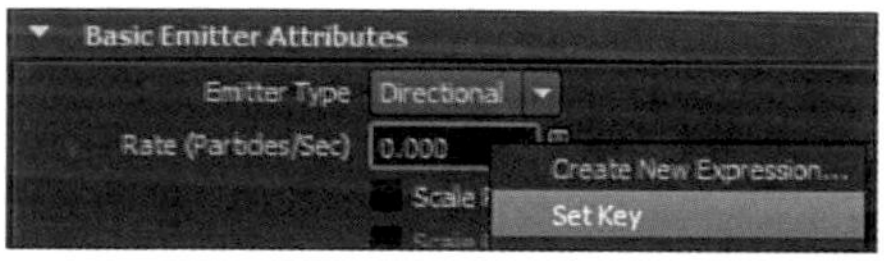

FIGURE 18.11
Right-click inside a value box to set a key for animation.

▶ Play the animation to around frame 25, until just before Sam hits the buttons.

▶ At frame 25, with the emitter still selected, right-click inside the Rate value field again and once more select Set Key. Setting a key on the Rate value as 0 on frame 1 and frame 25 keeps the rate constant at 0 between those frames. This means we won't emit particles between frame 0 and frame 25.

▶ As soon as Sam hits the buttons, we want to start emitting particles. However, because they are unlikely to come out all at once, we need to give them the time to build up to full speed. We are therefore going to set a key for the full rate at frame 35. So, scroll to frame 35 on the Timeline, change the Rate value to 500, and right-click to set a key. This means that at frame 25, no particles will be emitted, but then will begin to emit on frame 26, and build up until they are emitting at 500 particles per second by frame 35.

▶ Play the animation to see the effect. The beginning has been improved, but how about the end? When we reach the landing part of the animation, Sam releases the buttons, and it is here where we want to animate the value of the particle rate back to zero.

You may think that going to frame 420 and then setting a key to 0 in the Rate value is the way to go, but this will only animate the rate from 500 down to 0 over a long period of time. To be more precise, because we set the rate to 500 at frame 35, the rate would be decreasing from 500 at frame 35 through to 0 at frame 420, which is not what we want. Instead, we need to anchor the value of 500 at the point we want the particles to start to switch off. Let's set the Rate value at 500 on frame 400, and then trail it down to 0:

▶ Scroll through the Timeline to frame 400. With the Rate value at 500, right-click the value field to set a key.

▶ Scroll through the Timeline to frame 420 and change the Rate value to 0. Right-click the value to set a key. The particles should now start to decrease from 500 particles per second at frame 400, and trail off to 0 at frame 420. Save your file before continuing.

Now play the scene. The particles only start emitting at the point where Sam hits the buttons. They also finish at about the right time when he lets go of the buttons! Great! Now we have a more focused vapor stream.

TIP

Adjusting the Rate Animation

To adjust the keyframes for the particle rate values, select the emitter to show the keyframes on the Timeline. With the emitter selected, you can also use the Graph Editor to modify your animation by selecting Window, Animation Editors, Graph Editor. Also note that other attributes can be animated by right-clicking their values in the Attribute Editor to set a key.

Changing the Color of Particles

The particles we created are blue, which gives a nice slightly cartoony feel to our vapor trail, but this might not be what we want. The next step is to fine-tune the shading:

▶ Continue to use your own file, or open particles_v4.ma from this Hour's source files to start from here.

▶ Select the nParticle1 node in the Outliner, and click on the nParticleShape1 tab in the Attribute Editor.

▶ Scroll down to the Shading section in the Attribute Editor. You may have to expand it by clicking on its arrow to the left of its label. Here, we can tweak opacity, color, and incandescence, and even change the particle render type.

▶ To achieve a smoky look, first expand the Color section within the Shading section. You will see a white circle and a blue circle above a rectangular color ramp, as shown in Figure 18.12.

FIGURE 18.12
The Color settings found in the Shading section of the nParticlesShape attributes allow you to modify the colors of your particles.

▶ The smoky look can be achieved by changing the white circle to a dark gray and changing the blue circle to a light gray. To do this, first click to select the white circle above the color ramp, and then click on the color swatch next to Selected Color. Choose a dark gray.

▶ Next, click on the blue circle above the ramp to select it. Using the Selected Color swatch, change the color to a light gray.

▶ Once you have finished adjusting the settings to your liking, save the file.

Copying Attributes by Using Presets

Now that we have our particle system working just the way we want it to, we need to create another one for the other jet on the other side. We do not have to repeat all the preceding steps, however. Have no fear: We can save a preset of the first particle system and use this on the second one. Presets let you save attributes on one node and then apply them to another. Do as follows:

▶ Continue with your own file, or open particles_v5 to start from here.

▶ Select the emitter node in the Outliner.

▶ Click on the Presets button toward the top of the Attribute Editor, as shown in Figure 18.13. Select the option Save pointEmitter Preset and give the preset a name, such as emitterSAM, and then save it.

FIGURE 18.13
Use Presets to save attributes from one node and load them onto another.

▶ Select the nParticle1 node in the Outliner and click on the nParticleShape1 tab. Use the Presets button to save this as a preset by repeating the preceding steps. Give the preset a name, such as nParticleShapeSAM, and save.

▶ We now need to create a new emitter and place it up inside the second jet. Follow the steps toward the beginning of the "Getting Started with nParticles" section to create a new emitter, place it inside the second jet, and parent constrain it to the jet. There is no need to adjust the attributes, however, because that is the purpose of using the preset. Once you have constrained the emitter to the jet pack, return to these steps to use the preset.

▶ Once the new emitter is in place, select it and in the Attribute Editor, click on the Presets button again. This time select the name of the saved preset from the list that appears and choose Replace, as shown in Figure 18.14.

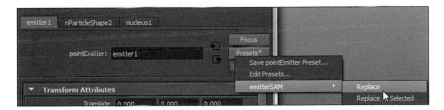

FIGURE 18.14
With the new emitter selected, click the Preset button in the Attribute Editor to select the saved emitter (emitterSAM) and then choose Replace.

▶ Select the new nParticle2 node created when you created the new emitter. Click on the nParticleShape2 tab to use the Presets button to replace this node with the saved nParticleShapeSAM preset.

▶ You may find that the emitter jumps to the position of the other emitter. Don't worry; simply move it back into place.

VIDEO

Setting Presets

Watch the bonus video included in this Hour's files for a quick run-through of setting presets to help your workflow. Presets save time by letting you save attributes on one node and apply to another when needed.

▶ Now we have to reassign the keyframes from the first emitter to the second emitter. Select the first emitter and make a selection over the keyframes in the Timeline by **Shift** dragging from frame 0 to the end of the Timeline. Alternatively, you can double-click the Timeline to select all the keyframes.

▶ Once the frames on the Timeline have been selected, all the frames will be highlighted and the Timeline will turn red. With the Timeline still red, right-click the Timeline to select Copy.

▶ Now go to frame 1 and select the second emitter. Right-click on the Timeline (still on frame 1) and select Paste to paste the keys from emitter1 onto emitter2. Click on Play. When you are happy with your scene, save the file.

Creating a Cache

It is likely that there will come a time when Maya starts to moan about the amount of particles in the scene. In fact, it may already be doing it with the current scene by displaying error messages. For example, you may get an error saying that nucleus evaluation has skipped due to a large frame rate. There are a couple ways around this. To keep previewing our animation, we can use Playblast to see it in real time. To do this, select the panel you want to playblast and then go to the Window menu and select Playblast. Alternately, you can right-click the Timeline to select Playblast. This lets you view the scene in real time, but you do have to wait until Maya creates the Playblast in order to see it.

Next up is caching, which is a process where Maya performs the calculations necessary and then stores the sequences for you to recall them at the time of playback. This means that if you cache your scene, you can also then scrub back and forth on the Timeline. Cache files can be quite large, however, depending on your scene, so keep an eye on your cache folder within your project. To create a cache, follow these steps:

▶ Continue with your own file, or open particles_v6.ma to start from here.

▶ To cache a scene, select the particles that need caching; in the Outliner, select nParticle1 and use **Ctrl** on the keyboard to also select nParticle2.

▶ If necessary, swap to the nDynamics menu set, but using the drop-down menu set list in the top-left corner of your Maya screen.

▶ With nParticle1 and nParticle2 selected, choose the nCache menu and then click Create New Cache. Maya will now automatically play through your Timeline and cache the scene for you.

TIP

Deleting the Cache

Remember that if you need to tweak something in your scene, you will have to delete the cache and re-create it again. Otherwise, Maya will continue to play the cached sequence and you will not see your changes. To delete the cache, on the nDynamics menu set, choose the nCache menu and then Delete Cache.

As a final note about particles, remember there are many attributes you can tweak on the emitter node, particles node, and even on the nucleus node. It's always a good idea to just tweak one thing at a time while you are learning, though, so that you can pinpoint what attribute is responsible for the changes.

Summary

In this Hour, you had a look at particles to create effects. You specifically looked at Maya's nParticle system, which you used to create a vapor trail for a jet pack. An emitter was used to discharge the nParticles from a point in your scene. The emitter was parent constrained to the character's jet pack so that it could move along with the jet pack, and provide the appearance of particles being emitted from the jet pack itself. This Hour also covered editing attributes to customize the look and speed of your particles, plus copying the attributes across to other nodes using presets. In order to view the scene in real time, we also covered creating a cache.

Q&A

Q. Why isn't my jet pack moving with Sam?

A. You may have accidentally parent constrained the jet pack to the emitter rather than the emitter to the jet pack. Either retrace your steps or find the parent constraint in the Outliner and delete it. Select the jet pack and then **Shift**-select the emitter to re-create the parent constraint.

Q. Can I kill off some of my particles as new ones still are emitting?

A. Yes, you can specify a lifespan for particles and nParticles so that they fade away after reaching a specified age. To do this, select the shape node for the particle or nParticle and then modify the lifespan attributes.

Q. How can I change the particle type from a cloud to a streak?

A. To change the render type of the particles from a cloud to a streak (or blobby surfaces and so on), select the nParticle, and in the Attribute Editor, use the nParticleShape tab to find the Shading attributes. Within this section, you can select from a variety of render types.

Q. I'm getting an error message about nucleus evaluations skipping frames when I try to play my scene. What can I do?

A. Cache your scene to store the sequence of events and enable Maya to play it back in real time.

Workshop

The workshop contains quiz questions and exercises to help you solidify your understanding of the material covered. Try to answer all questions before looking at the "Answers" section that follows.

Quiz

1. What attribute do we need to keyframe to limit or initiate an amount of particles coming from our emitter?

2. When we create an emitter, what does Maya automatically create for us?

3. What can we use to copy attributes from one particle emitter node to another?

4. Do we have to add gravity to our particle once we create an emitter?

5. What can we use to play our scene in real time?

Exercise

Why not try creating a fun effect with instances? Rather than settle for particle types that Maya provides for you, you can create your own objects and have them emitted as particles instead. Using your existing scene, create a polygon cube. In the Outliner, select the cube and then **Ctrl**-select nParticle1. Use the nDynamics menu set to choose the nParticles menu and then Instancer (Replacement). Your particles have now been replaced with instances of the cube. You can scale and change the color or texture of the cube, and the changes will be reflected in your instanced cube particles. You can then hide the original cube by selecting it and setting its Visibility attribute to 0 in the Channel Box.

If you have animation on your cube or other object, it will also be carried over all instances. The particles can be replaced with any object you can think of. The jet pack could be emitting thousands of animated monkeys if you wanted!

Answers

1. The emitter's Rate (Particles/Sec) attribute, which is found in the Basic Emitter Attributes section. Rate refers to the particles per second that are being emitted.

2. An nParticle node and a nucleus node, assuming we are using nParticles. If we were using standard particles instead from the Dynamics menu set (rather than nDynamics menu set), Maya would create a particles node along with the emitter.

3. We can save a preset and use that on another node to copy across the attributes.

4. No, there is no need because gravity is built into the nucleus node. If you select the nucleus node and look in the Attribute Editor, you will see a section for Gravity and Wind.

5. We can create a cache. However, we need to remember to delete the cache and create a new one if we make changes to the scene.

Lighting Your Scene Correctly

What You'll Learn in This Hour:

▶ How to add lights to your scene

▶ The fundamentals of three-point lighting

▶ How to deal with shadows

▶ How to link lights to specific objects

Maya has many different ways to help an artist light a scene. Lighting a scene correctly depends on the look you wish to achieve or replicate. Lights can be set up to replicate the type of lighting you would find outside on a sunny day, or set a mood for interior lighting. Lighting can match the realism found in the real world, or can be designed to add drama or subtlety. Studio lighting of cars, food, or models as seen in the glossy magazines can also be replicated. What is nice about lighting in Maya is the fact that it provides you with the tools to be artistic and experiment with different moods. Whether aiming for realism, dramatic effect, cartoon world stylization, or artistic effects, the choice is up to you. However, in order to get the correct look that you are aiming for, it's a good idea to first learn the basics of lighting, as discussed in this Hour.

NOTE

Lighting, Materials, and Rendering

To get the correct look you are aiming for, you should be aware that lighting, rendering, and working with materials that you apply to surfaces all go hand in hand. For example, you cannot create a shiny apple in Maya without applying a material to the apple object, which has been set up to let the surface shine. Plus, you need a light to shine on the surface and you need to render the final image! Hour 7, "Creating Node Networks in the Hypershade," covers materials. This Hour touches on rendering the final image to get you started with lighting, but also see Hour 21, "Rendering Final Imagery," if you're interested to know more about rendering.

In this Hour, you will get an overview of lighting in Maya, including fundamental principles of three-point lighting, which is a classic technique used in the real-world for studio, photography, and theatrical lighting, and is also commonly used in 3D worlds, too. You will learn how to create and place lights, how to cast shadows, and how to tweak the attributes of the lights and shadows to aim for the look you want. You will also learn how to use light linking to specifically target which objects you want to illuminate.

Lighting Basics

When lighting a scene in Maya, you can start by thinking of choosing lights for a room in your own home. In the real world, you would decide what kind of lights you want and how many. You would also choose how bright they should be, what kind of shades they would have, and where you want to place the lights. For example, you might decide upon a bright ceiling light, plus a couple more subdued table lamps. Similarly, in Maya, you can select from a few different light types, place them where you want, and modify their intensity, color, shadows, and other attributes to simulate the looks you would get from your ceiling light, your shaded bulbs, or any other light source. There are many similarities between lighting a 3D scene and lighting in the real world. However, there are also some fundamental differences you can take advantage of. For example, once you have created and positioned your light, it is up to you to decide whether or not you want the light to cast shadows, and it's up to you to decide how sharp or how soft the shadows are. You can even decide to cast shadows on particular objects and leave other objects out. There are many choices to get the look you are aiming for, but whether you are aiming for realistic lighting or dramatic artistic lighting, a good place to start is by observing light in the real world.

Observing Light and Shadows

Observing how light works in the real world will help provide you with the skills to light scenes as you wish in Maya. As you observe light, make particular note of how shadows are softer or harder, longer or shorter, depending on the different strengths, direction, and position of the light source. Also notice how light can bounce from one surface to illuminate another, and how light can cause color to bleed from one material to another. Light also reflects, gets absorbed, or refracts depending on the type of material it hits. *Reflection* refers to light waves bouncing back off the surfaces, *absorption* soaks in light, and *refraction* refers to light that bends as it passes through a surface. For example, a glass will disperse, refract, reflect, illuminate, and cast a shadow from direct light. A dull rubber eraser is more likely to absorb the light, although depending on its color (for example, a bright red eraser), it may bleed its color onto a nearby surfaces such as a piece of white paper. The eraser will cast a shadow in direct light, and it will have a soft close proximity shadow known as occlusion, which doesn't need strong light to be seen.

Try playing with different materials in the real world, and moving them in front of light and close to one another. Use different types of light, such as a flashlight, table lamp, and outdoor light, at different times of the day and in different weathers, for example. It will also be helpful to look at real-world photography techniques to consider applying them to your 3D scene. Useful techniques include those used to bounce light into an otherwise dim area, or to highlight that perfect specularity across a contour of a shiny new sports car or to light a shot of some tasty mouthwatering food. Observation is the key to understanding lighting.

Creating Lights and Shadows

Lighting is a key aspect of your scene, interacting with the materials that you apply, and setting the mood for the piece. A typical lighting workflow includes planning the look that you are going for, such as where the light and shadows are coming from, and how strong you want the light and shadows to be. The next step is to create the lights and move them into place. Lights that you create in general do not automatically cast shadows, so you will need to decide which is the main source of light (or lights) that you want to cast shadows from and turn on the shadows. Although you may initially find it strange that Maya lights do not instantly cast shadows, as you work more with Maya lighting you will see the benefits. Choosing which lights do or do not cast shadows lets you light with fine precision. The attributes of the lights and shadows can be tweaked to get just the look you are going for. For example, you can adjust the intensity and color of each light individually, and you can also decide whether to have soft or hard shadowed edges, and even what color the shadows should be. Once your lighting and shadows are in place, you can then add some supplementary lighting effects such as glows, fog, or even lens flares. This section will discuss how to create lights and shadows as well as how to make adjustments. Once the basics are covered, we will move on to a three-point light setup, which is a commonly used lighting technique in visual media. To follow along as you go, open up a file to experiment as you read:

▶ Create your own simple scene containing a few polygon primitive shapes such as spheres and cubes, or open lighting_v1.ma from this Hour's source files on the bonus DVD. This scene contains a few colorful spheres for you to light.

BONUS

Scene Files

Take a look in this Hour's source files and you will find a few scene files for you to experiment with. We have included a scene with some colored spheres for you to light. We have also included some scenes at various stages of a three-point lighting setup that is covered in the "Getting Started with Three-Point Lighting," later in this Hour.

▶ To create a light, use the Create menu from any of the menu sets and then select Light to choose from the available light types, as shown in Figure 19.1. Choose the Spot Light option for now. Light types are discussed next.

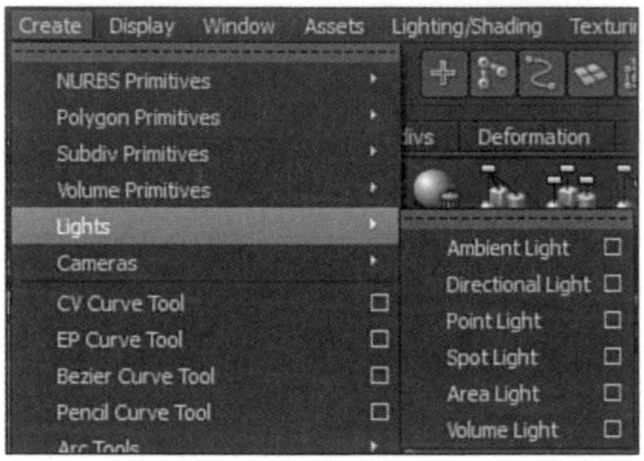

FIGURE 19.1
Create direct lights in Maya by using any menu set to choose Create, Lights and then choose from the available light types.

TIP

Creating Lights from the Rendering Shelf

You can also use the buttons on the Rendering shelf to create the desired light type, as shown in Figure 19.2.

FIGURE 19.2
The Rendering shelf has buttons to create ambient, directional, point, spot, area, and volume lights.

Maya Light Types

Looking at the Create, Lights options in Figure 19.1, you can see that Maya provides six different light types: ambient, directional, point, spot, area, and volume lights. All the lights have common attributes, such as color, intensity, and shadow options. However, each type of light also has its own set of unique attributes that make it useful in particular lighting scenarios, just as different types of light are useful for different purposes in the real world. For example, real-world spotlights are great for studio, stage, sports, and security, but you are more likely to choose domestic bulbs to light the interior of your own home. Maya provides lights to simulate real-world lights, including Maya spot lights for real-world spotlights and Maya point lights for bulbs.

A Maya spot light shines a beam of cone shaped light out from a small point in space. It is a very versatile light, similar to a flashlight, car headlight, or, of course, a spotlight in the real world. Spot lights are also useful to simulate table lamps with shades, overhead lighting, and to target very specific areas or even wide-reaching areas. The bottom row of Figure 19.3 shows some spheres lit with spotlights in Maya. Notice that the light comes from the direction that the spot light is aimed toward, and that the shadows are cast out from that single angle. Because spot lights emit a beam of light from one point in space to another, it is important to position the spot light where you want the light to come from, and to point the spot in the direction of the surface you want to illuminate. You will also need to make sure the cone angle of the beam is wide enough to encompass the target.

FIGURE 19.3
Spheres illuminated in Maya to show the direction of the light source and shadows cast. Top left uses a single point light, top right a directional light. The bottom left and bottom right each use a single spot light.

TIP

Following Along

If you would like to experiment as you follow along, open lighting_v1.ma from this Hour's source files or use your own scene to create any of the lights discussed. Later in the Hour, we provide a more structured exercise in the "Getting Started with Three-Point Lighting" section.

Point lights emit light in all directions from a point in space. They are commonly used to simulate the illumination from an incandescent light bulb or spherical-shaped lights. Notice that because the light rays come from different directions, the shadows are also cast out in many directions, as Figure 19.3 top left shows. Where you place the point light in the scene is important, but the angle is not. Because the light is emanating from all directions, unlike a spot light with a focused beam, there is no need to angle it to aim it in a particular direction.

▶ To add a shadow, select the light and find the Shadows section in the Attribute Editor. You can choose between Use Depth Map Shadows and Use Ray Trace Shadows, which are discussed in more detail shortly. For now, check Use Depth Map Shadows to turn them on.

Directional lights emit parallel rays of light from an infinitely far away distance. A common use for directional lights is to simulate rays from the sun or moon. In some ways, directional lights are the opposite of point lights. Because the parallel rays of directional lights are coming from a great distance, the actual position you place the directional light does not make a difference. To explain this further, think of the beam of the spotlight. The rays are emitting out from one point in space as a cone shaped beam in the distance. Elements outside the beam will miss out on receiving the illumination from the spotlight. The parallel beams coming from the directional light, on the other hand, simulate rays from a light source such as the sun that will encompass the whole scene. However, although the position isn't critical, the direction is. Because the directional light is emitted in a single direction, it is important to set the angle to the direction you want. The top-right image of Figure 19.3 shows spheres lit by a directional light.

TIP

Previewing Lights in the Scene

On any of your viewport panels, use Lighting, Use All Lights to see the effects of your lights in a pre-view mode as you work, or press **7** on your keyboard. Use Lighting, Use Default Lighting, or press **6**, to return to your normal view when done. You can also render the image to see the more complete look by using the Rendering menu set to choose Render, then Render Current Frame. Rendering is covered in more detail in Hour 21.

Figure 19.4 shows the different icons used to represent lights in Maya for each light type. When the type of light you select emits light from a single direction, as is the case for directional, spot, and area lights, the icons all have an indicator to let you know what direction the light is being emitted from. Directional and spot light icons use directional arrows, and the area light icon uses a center pointer as the indicator. Because ambient, point, and volume lights do not emit light in one single direction, there is no need for the icon to indicate directionality.

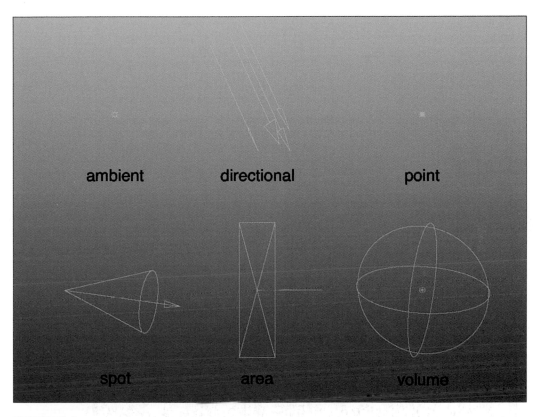

FIGURE 19.4
Icons for different light types in Maya. Where direction is important, the icon will have an indicator, as the directional, spot, and area light icons show.

Ambient lights provide general soft diffuse illumination emitting from all directions, but in contrast to the point light, have no visible point of emission. Ambient lights can be used to fill in shadowed areas that need a bit of lifting, but should be used with care. Ambient lights do not add any specularity (reflections of bright areas) to the scene. Additionally, ambient lights do not contribute toward bump map calculations, intended to simulate elevations and depressions in surfaces. Thus, although potentially useful, ambient lights can flatten out your scene, robbing it of depth and richness if used unwisely.

Area lights are physically based two-dimensional rectangular lights useful for simulating light coming through large areas, such as windows, recesses, and overhead lighting. They can also be used to simulate reflections of windows on surfaces. Area lights should be positioned where you need them, and rotated into place to angle them in the desired direction. Scaling the icons for directional, spot, point, and ambient lights will not make a difference to how the light source is emitted for those lights. However, scaling does impact area lights. You can scale the area light icon to match the size of the area you want to have the light emitted from (matching the size of a window, for example).

Volume lights emit light from a volumetric shape. By default, creating a volume light will provide a spherical volume that you can resize to simulate light from a small candle, for example, or enlarge to encompass a room. Altering the size influences how far the light reaches. It is also possible to change the volumetric shape to a box, sphere, cylinder, or cone by adjusting the Volume Light Attributes, Light Shape attributes of the volume light in the Attribute Editor.

TIP

Direct (Local) Versus Indirect (Global) Illumination

This Hour focuses on direct illumination, which provides local illumination through direct beams of light emitting from a light source. However, in the real world, light also bounces across surfaces, further contributing to illumination in the scene as it goes. Think of the example of the red eraser on a white background, with the color of the eraser bleeding onto background. Maya lets you simulate such real-world inter-reflected light through global illumination options in the mental ray renderer. Global illumination is beyond the scope of this book, but if you are interested to know more, have a look at Hour 21 to learn about rendering in general, and then have a look at the global illumination options that mental ray provides.

Casting Shadows

Shadows are vital to add realism to your scenes. Without shadows, objects will appear to hover off ground, making it more difficult to distinguish foreground objects from background ones. Shadows can be used to add contrast to elements in your scene as well as to add dramatic effect. By default, lights created in Maya previous to version 2014 will have all shadows turned off. Maya 2014 lights, on the other hand, have a shadow type known as "raytraced" turned on by default, although not necessary ready to appear because additional render settings have to be set. The additional settings and shadow types are discussed shortly. Meanwhile, to see the available shadow types, or to turn shadows on or off, select the light and use the Shadows section of the Attribute Editor, as detailed here:

▶ Using your own file, or lighting_v1.ma with a spot light created, select the spot light.

▶ In the Attribute Editor, scroll down to the Shadows section to see that Maya provides a choice between Use Depth Map Shadows and Use Ray Trace Shadows. In Maya 2014, Use Ray Trace Shadows will be on by default, but previous versions of Maya will have no shadows turned on. Check the box next to Use Depth Map Shadows to turn on depth map shadows for this Hour.

Depth map shadows are easy to use and quicker to calculate than raytraced shadows, and they can produce similar results, so we will use them during this Hour. Depth maps are essentially a form of texture that Maya layers over your scene to produce your final image when rendered. The default resolution of the depth map is 512, although you can increase this resolution to improve the quality of your shadows. For example, if the edge of the shadows appear jagged, increase this resolution to try to smooth out the edges. You can also increase the Filter size, which controls the softness of the edges.

NOTE

Shadow Quality

The quality of shadow edges is also linked to rendering quality. See Hour 21 for more detail on improving shadow renders.

Raytraced shadows can produce soft and transparent shadows, which are physically more accurate than depth map shadows but can also be very time consuming to produce. Raytracing involves Maya calculating rays of light emitted from the light source to their destination—the camera. We will stick to depth map shadows in this Hour, but if you are interested in trying out raytraced shadows, you will also need to make sure that Raytracing options are turned on within the Render Settings in order for the shadows to appear. Maya 2014 does this by default for renders that use mental ray, but otherwise you will need to make sure to switch on the settings yourself. You can use the Render Settings button at the top of your Maya screen to access render settings, but see Hour 21 for further detail.

TIP

Casting Shadows per Object

If you want some objects to cast shadows, but others not to, first select the objects (rather than the light). Next, find the Render Stats attributes for the objects in the Attribute Editor. You can then choose whether or not to have the objects cast shadows, receive shadows, and more. You can even choose to hide the objects by turning off Primary Visibility, but still have them cast a shadow.

Positioning Lights

Maya lets you choose from a few different methods to accurately place your light in the scene. Complete the following steps to practice placing your lights. Where you actually position them is not important at this stage, although you may want to try to light an object nicely as you practice. In the three-point lighting example later in the Hour, we will position lights more accurately:

▶ Use your own file, with a spot light created, or continue to use lighting_v1.ma with the spot light you created earlier.

▶ Select the spot light in the Outliner, or its icon in the scene view, to move (**w** on your keyboard), rotate (**e**), and scale (**r**) like you would any other object in Maya. Note that scaling will not affect the intensity of most lights. It will instead only make the icon larger in most cases.

▶ You can also use the Channel Box to input numerical values to place lights precisely where you want. This is particularly handy when trying to match the height or angle of a light. For example, you could copy over the Translate Y value from one light to another to copy the height and rotational values to match an angle.

TIP

Switching Panel Layouts to Help You Work

Changing your panel layouts by switching between single- and four-scene views can help you position your lights or any other object. Viewing four panels at once provides more viewing angles, whereas a single view provides a larger viewing area. Therefore, a common workflow is to switch back and forth between the two. If already in single viewport layout, you can switch to the four-scene view by simply tapping the spacebar. To return to a single view, click on the panel you want (for example, perspective) and then tap the spacebar. Alternatively, you can switch using the Single Perspective View button in the Toolbox on the left side of your Maya screen, as shown in Figure 19.5 (top), or the Four View button, as shown in Figure 19.5 (bottom).

FIGURE 19.5
The Single Perspective View button (top) and the Four View button (bottom), located on the left side of your Maya screen, let you swap between different layouts.

Look Through Selected

Maya also provides an interactive placement mode to let you look through a spot, area, or directional light. With this method, you look through the light as if you were looking through the lens of a camera. Use your **Alt** and LMB, RMB, and MMB drags to angle and position the light, as if adjusting a camera view:

▶ With your spot light selected, use your scene view menus to choose Panels, Look Through Selected. You should now notice a green circle that represents the boundary spot light's cone, with you looking through it onto the scene. Objects outside this boundary will not be illuminated by the spot.

▶ Figure 19.6 gives an example of looking through the spotlight in lighting_v2.ma. The inner circle represents the boundary of the cone of light. The outer edge represents the penumbra area, which blurs the edge of the light to give it the appearance of losing intensity around the edge to give a softer look. Spotlights are covered in more detail later in this Hour.

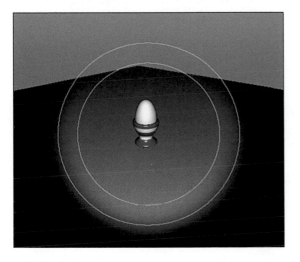

FIGURE 19.6
Selecting the spot light and choosing Panels, Look Through Selected lets you view your scene directly through the cone of the spot light.

▶ In the view that lets you look through your spotlight, use your **Alt** key and mouse buttons to position and angle the light.

▶ Once you are done experimenting, to exit out of Interactive Placement mode, switch back to perspective view by selecting Panels, Perspective, Persp or use the Single Perspective View button shown in Figure 19.5.

Light Manipulators

Certain light sources in Maya can be adjusted interactively in the scene view by selecting the light and then pressing t on your keyboard or clicking on the Show Manipulator Tool button from the Toolbox, as shown in Figure 19.7. In Maya 2014, if you do not see the Show Manipulator Tool button in the Toolbox, press t on your keyboard to activate the tool, and the button should appear for future use in your current Maya session.

FIGURE 19.7
The Show Manipulator tool lets you interactively place and adjust your light.

▶ With your spotlight selected, press **t** on your keyboard, or click on the Show Manipulate Tool button shown in Figure 19.7. Manipulators will appear around your light, as shown in Figure 19.8.

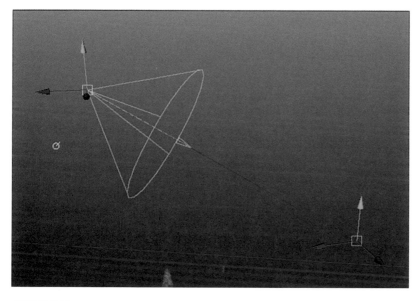

FIGURE 19.8
You can show the light's manipulator tools to interactively place and adjust the light.

▶ Position your light using the manipulator at the top of the spot light. To aim the spot light, use the manipulator at the opposite end.

You can also interactively modify additional attributes of the light by clicking on the small blue index icon that appears near the light, as shown in Figure 19.8. Clicking repeatedly cycles through various options according to the light source. Although this is useful, if you are new to Maya, you may find adjusting attributes in the Attribute Editor easier to begin with.

Common Light Attributes

Although the different light types in Maya all have unique attributes to make them suitable for specific purposes, they also have some key attributes in common with each other. Figure 19.9

shows some of the attributes for the point light that are commonly found on other Maya light types.

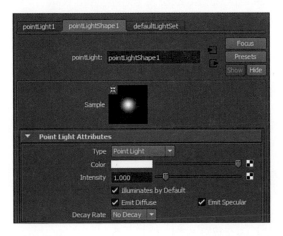

FIGURE 19.9
Maya lights have some attributes in common, such as Color and Intensity.

Each light has a Type attribute that defines the Maya light type, as shown in Figure 19.9. Clicking on the drop-down list for Type lets you change the type of light you have created. This is useful when you have already positioned your light and then realize that a different light source would be better. Rather than delete the light, you can change from one type to another. Be aware that it is often better to just delete the light and create a new one to avoid any possibilities of confusion in the lighting calculations potentially caused by the swap.

Changing the color of lights can have a significant impact on the final look for your scene. Color can be adjusted by clicking on the color swatch next the label for the Color attribute shown in Figure 19.9, or by using the adjacent slider.

Intensity for each light can also be adjusted through use of the slider adjacent to the Intensity attribute shown in Figure 19.9. Higher values make the lights brighter, and lower values decrease the brightness. If the slider does not provide a high enough value, just type the value you want into the value field.

The Decay Rate shown in Figure 19.9 can be used to simulate real-world lighting falloffs. In the real world, light intensity decreases (decays) the further the beam is away from its source. Think of shining a flashlight into darkness. The light will only travel so far before fading away into the distance. By default, Maya lights do not decay, so to turn on decay, select from one of the options on the drop-down list. A quadratic decay is often used to simulate realistic lighting decay. Be aware that you may have to increase the intensity of the light significantly to make it reach your object if you do apply decay. In fact, instead of increasing intensity by single digits, you may have to think in terms of increasing intensity by 10 or even 100 or more.

Other significant common attributes shown in Figure 19.9 include the Illuminates by Default option, which generally acts as the on/off switch for your light. The Emit Diffuse and Emit Specular options control whether or not you want to emit diffuse light or the specular light (bright reflections). Figure 19.10 shows a sphere with a shiny (specular) Blinn material applied and lit normally with both options on by default on the left. You can see that the sphere has color and a specular highlight. The middle image shows the same sphere lit by specular light only. If you look closely, you will see only the specular highlight has been lit, but because there is no diffuse light, the object has no color and cannot be seen. This can be useful to add to additional lights to really make the specular highlights pop without affecting the general color. The final image on the right shows the sphere lit by diffuse light only. Its specular highlight is gone, but the diffuse color remains.

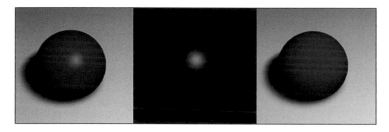

FIGURE 19.10
A Blinn material sphere lit with a spotlight emitting diffuse and specular light (left), the same sphere lit with specular only (middle), and the sphere lit with diffuse light only (right)

NOTE

Material Settings Are Important

Properties of materials that you apply to your surfaces interact with the lights to help get the look you want. The shiny sphere in Figure 19.10 (left) is shiny because the light is emitting both diffuse and specular rays *plus* the Blinn material is set up to have specular attributes. A lambert material would have appeared like the sphere in Figure 19.10 (right) because it does not have specular properties. This shows the importance of knowing your materials. See Hour 7 for more information on materials.

Spot Light Attributes

In addition to the common attributes just listed, each light has its own unique attributes. Creating lights and adjusting the attributes one by one to get a feel for what they do will help you explore the possibilities. Discussing all the attributes is beyond the scope of this Hour; however, spot lights are a special case due to their versatility and are therefore worth a mention here.

Just like any other light, you can adjust a spot light's color, intensity, decay, and whether it illuminates at all or uses just specular or just diffuse light. Additionally, you can adjust its cone angle and other attributes to create a hard or soft edge to the light that lands on the surface. See Figure 19.11 for commonly used spot light attributes.

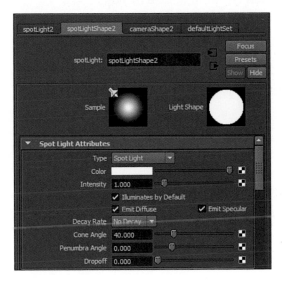

FIGURE 19.11
Commonly used spot light attributes.

The Cone Angle in the Spot Light Attributes section lets you set values for the cone boundary. Smaller values decrease the size of the cone, thus narrowing the beam. Larger values increase its size and correspondingly widen the beam. The Penumbra Angle can be adjusted to blur the outer edge to give the light a softer appearance, as the light from the cone decreases in intensity in this area. Use the adjacent slider or type in the value you want to use. The Dropoff values let you control the intensity and light falloff from the center to the edge.

TIP

Light Shape Sample

As you adjust attributes such as the intensity, cone, penumbra angle, and dropoff, the Light Shape sample shown in Figure 19.11 provides a preview of the intensity and shape that the spot light will cast.

Getting Started with Three-Point Lighting

Three-point lighting is a commonly used technique for lighting almost any subject within visual media, including stage, screen, and photography. A three-point lighting setup requires at least three different light sources, each with a different purpose: a key light, a fill light, and a back light.

The key light is the main source of illumination that sets the direction of the light. Setting the angle, intensity, and color of the key light also sets the mood for your shot. As the main light source, it also sets the tone for casting shadows. The key light is normally placed to the side of the camera, aimed toward the subject, with the fill light on the opposite side. Placing the key light so that it illuminates the subject from one far side will provide strong contrast and can set a dramatic mood. Aiming the key light from a more central position will create less contrast in general.

The main purpose of the fill light is to control the darkness of the shadowed areas and fill in some subtle lighting to the areas that the key light doesn't quite reach. For example, when lighting a person or a computer-generated character, you might want to lighten up strong shadows under the nose and chin. The fill light is normally placed still facing the subject, but on the opposite side of the camera to the key light. The fill light is normally softer and less intense than the key light because its purpose is to fill in some of the darker areas rather than act as the primary (or key) light source.

The back light is placed behind the subject, aimed toward the subject's back. At times it is angled more to one side to target that particular side more than the other. If you look in almost any glossy magazine, for example, you are likely to quickly spot people who have a strong highlight over one shoulder coming from a back light largely targeting that side of the body. Illuminating the subject from behind provides a rim of light that enhances dimensionality and helps the subject to pop out from the background. It is also, therefore, often referred to as the "rim light."

TIP

Four-Point Lighting

Four-point lighting is similar to three-point lighting but adds a fourth light behind the subject aimed at the background. Four-point lighting setups are used when the background needs some extra illumination, or to help eliminate or lessen the effect of shadows cast by objects in the foreground.

Creating the Key Light

Now that you have an idea of what the purpose of a three-point lighting setup is, let's get started lighting a scene. We want to create a good strong light from a 45-degree angle in front of the subject to be our key light. Placing the key light at a 45-degree angle can provide contrast without being overdramatic, so this is what we will do in our exercise. Once we have created the key light, we will go on to add our fill light to help lift the ambience of the whole subject. We will then add our back (or rim) light to help the subject pop out by highlighting the outline rim of the object from behind. Follow these steps to light a scene with three-point lighting, and learn some tips along the way:

▶ Open the scene lighting_v2.ma, which contains a simple egg in an egg cup to light, from this Hour's source files.

NOTE

Render Camera

We have created a camera called Camera_MAIN with a composed view of the scene for you to work with for scenes in lighting_v2.ma through lighting.v6.ma. We swapped the top view panel to show the Camera_MAIN view by using the Panels menu in that viewport to select Perspective, Camera_MAIN. If you select the camera and look in the Channel Box, you will note that the attributes in the Channel Box have been grayed out. This is because we have locked the camera so you cannot accidentally change it. If you want to switch back to top view, use the Panels menu within the viewport to select Orthographic, Top. To switch back again to the Camera_MAIN view, use the Panels and then Perspective, Camera_Main. See Hour 14, "Creating and Adjusting Cameras," if you are interested to learn more about working with cameras.

To get an idea of how the lights will affect the scene, you can render along the way, because Maya does not fully calculate the lighting until you do. Rendering final imagery is covered in more detail in Hour 21, but it will be helpful to introduce the basics now, to see how our scene starts off and to see how it progresses as the lighting is changed:

▶ To view the current render, select the view that you want to render (Camera_MAIN in this case). From the Rendering menu set, choose Render, then Render Current Frame. The shot renders with Maya's default lighting. Although this gets the job done initially, it certainly can be improved by adding our own lighting.

▶ We are going to use a spot light for our key light, so from any of the menu sets, choose the Create menu and then select Lights, Spot Light. A spot light will appear in your scene partially hidden by the egg cup. We will move the light into position shortly, but first let's see how the render appears now.

NOTE

Key, Fill, and Back Lights in Maya

When looking at the types of light you can create in Maya, you probably noticed that there were no options for key, fill, and back lights. This is because it is up to you to choose what type of light you would like to create to act as a key, back, or fill light. It is then up to you define its purpose by its position and other settings.

▶ Once you have created your spot, choose the Render menu to then select Render Current Frame.

▶ Continuing with your own scene or lighting_v2.ma, select the newly created spot light to get ready to move it into place.

Because the purpose of the spot light is to act as a key light, our goal is to move it so that it is in front of the egg and off to the side at about 45 degrees and pointing down at the egg. Figure 19.12 provides an indicator of where the lights should be placed, but if you would like a more specific idea, save your current file and open up lighting_v6 to make note of the placement of each light. Once you understand what you are aiming for, return to your lighting_v2.ma file to create and position each light yourself using the following steps.

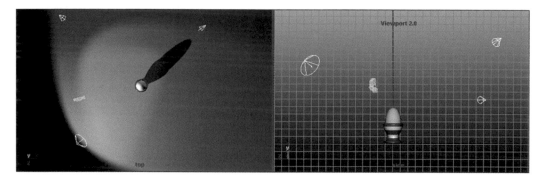

FIGURE 19.12
A three-point lighting setup in top view (left) and side view (right). The camera is in green, the key light is the wide-angled spot, the fill is the spot on the opposite side of the camera from the key, and the back light is the spot behind the egg.

To quickly preview how your lights are affecting the scene in real time, you can use the Viewport 2.0 or High Quality Renderer option on your viewport to preview the effects. The next step tells you how:

▶ In your perspective viewing panel, use the Renderer menu to select Viewport 2.0. This enables Maya's hardware rendering through the use of your graphics card to preview real-time effects such as lighting and shadows.

▶ You can toggle between textured view with the default viewport lighting and textured view plus lighting by pressing 6 and 7, respectively. For now, we want to press 7 to active lighting in our viewports.

TIP

Viewport 2.0

If your graphics card does not support Viewport 2.0, use the Renderer menu on the perspective viewport to select High Quality Renderer instead. If your machine does not support that either, you will have to resort to occasionally rendering your scene as described at the beginning of the "Creating the Key Light" section. You can find more detail in Hour 21.

▶ Select the spot light. Then, using your preferred method of positioning the spot light, translate it in front of the egg cup.

▶ Pull it back just behind the camera in top view, but still in front of the egg cup. Translate it up in Y until its about parallel to the camera and then rotate it downward at about 45 degrees or so to aim it at the egg.

▶ Figure 19.12 shows the suggested placement of the key spot light in the top and side views. The camera is the green icon and the key light is the wide-angled spot. With the spot light selected, use the Attribute Editor to locate the Spot Light Attribute section and use the Intensity attribute to increase the intensity in the light's attributes to 1.500.

▶ With the light sill selected, use the Attribute Editor to scroll to the Shadows section. If you're using Maya 2014, the Use Ray Traced Shadows option will be on by default, although no shadow types will be on if you're using previous versions. Either way, we want to instead use depth map shadows, so check Use Depth Map shadows. Shadows should now appear.

▶ Now we can see that our key light is casting a strong shadow and we don't even have to render. However, you can also use the Rendering menu set to choose Render, Render Current Frame if desired.

▶ Now we can see that the edge of the light (the cone) is very harsh. To soften this, raise the Penumbra Angle setting to 10. If the slider does not move up to 10, you can just type it in. Now the light falls off nicely.

▶ Before we create our next light, change this light's name to "Key" by double-clicking the light in the Outliner and renaming it. Save your file.

Creating the Fill Light

To create the fill light, to help control the darkness of the shadowed areas and provide overall subtle illumination, complete the following steps:

▶ Continue with your previous file, or open lighting_v3.ma to start with a key light already created.

▶ Use Create, Lighting, Spot Light to create another spot light.

▶ Move the spot light into a similar position as the key light, but on the opposite side of the camera and a little bit higher up in Translation Y. The fill light position is shown in Figure 19.12. The fill light is the light on the opposite side of the camera to the wide-angled key light (top view), and the one that is positioned uppermost in the scene in side view in Figure 19.12.

▶ With the light still selected, in the Spot Light Attributes section of the Attribute Editor, turn down the Intensity on the new spot light to 0.500 and adjust the Penumbra Angle to 10. Widen the cone angle to about 50.000.

▶ If you're using Maya 2014, use the Shadows section of the Attribute Editor to switch off Use Ray Trace Shadows. This is not necessary in previous versions of Maya because no shadows are cast by default anyway, which is what we want here.

▶ Name this light "Fill" and save your file.

NOTE

Pick and Choose Lights to Cast Shadows

We did not turn shadows on for the fill light because its purpose is to fill in a bit more light, and not to cast shadows. If all our lights had shadows, the scene would most likely look unrealistic, with shadows would be coming from everywhere. Turn on shadows only when you need them.

Creating the Back Light

Once the key and fill lights have been created, we have more control of the overall lighting of our subject and can adjust accordingly for different effects. Next, we want to add our back light as follows:

▶ Continue with your previous scene, or open lighting_v4.ma to use a scene with the key and fill lights already created.

▶ Use Create, Lighting, Spot Light to create another spot light and name the new light "Backlight."

▶ If you're using Maya 2014, use the Shadows attributes in the Attribute Editor to turn off Use Ray Traced Shadows. Lights in previous versions of Maya should not cast shadows by default anyway.

▶ Position the light approximately opposite the camera behind the egg, and aimed at the egg. Adjust to place and angle the spot light to the back and left of the egg to try to pick up a highlight on the side of the egg shell. This is where our viewport lighting feedback comes in handy.

▶ Render to see the result by using the Rendering menu set to select Render, Render Current Frame.

You should notice a few things. First, we wanted no shadows to come from the back light or the fill light. Shadows are unnecessary for some lights you create and can actually cause confusion when used incorrectly. The key light is the main shadow-casting light here, so there is no need to add shadows to the other lights. The other thing to note is that the back light is affecting the ground, which is not what we want. We only want the subject to be backlit. Fortunately, this can easily be resolved by breaking the connection between the backlight and the ground, as the next section shows.

Breaking Links

Maya lets you pick and choose which lights illuminate which objects. By default, the lights and shadows affect all objects in the scene, but it is possible to break the links between the lights and the objects. The following steps will show you how:

▶ Continue with your own file, or open lighting_v5.ma with a key, fill, and back light already created.

▶ Switch to the Rendering menu set by pressing **F6** on your keyboard, or by using the drop-down menu set list in the top-left corner of your Maya screen.

▶ Use the Outliner to select the floor and use **Ctrl** to also select the backlight.

▶ With floor1 and backlight selected, use the Rendering menu set to choose the Lighting/ Shading menu and then select Break Light Links.

▶ Use Render, Render Current Frame to see the results; you should notice that the backlight is now only affecting the eggcup.

TIP

Linking Lights

You can link lights to particular objects (excluding other objects) or objects to particular lights. Using the Rendering menu set, choose Lighting/Shading, Light Linking Editor. To link a light to objects, based on selecting the light first, choose Light-Centric. To link based on selecting the object first, choose Object-Centric. Use the dialog box that opens to link lights to objects by selecting them simultaneously in the left and right panels, or unlink them by deselecting.

▶ We can do the exact same thing with the fill light. Select floor1 and **Ctrl**-select the fill light. Use Lighting/Shading, Break Light Links to break the links between the light and the selected object.

- ▸ If you now render your image, you should notice the fill light no longer affects the floor. We want to leave the key light illuminating the floor and casting its shadow, but the cone angle could be widened to spread the light out more and provide a softer shadow.

- ▸ With the key light selected, use the Attribute Editor to change Cone Angle to 100.

- ▸ If you render the image, you will see that this has given the egg a much softer shadow, but because we have a larger cone angle, it would be a good idea to also turn up the depth map shadow resolution to improve the results.

- ▸ With the key light selected, use the Shadows section of the Attribute Editor to turn Resolution (underneath Use Depth Map Shadows) up to 2048.

As a few last tweaks, you can try experimenting by changing the color of the lights. A nice touch would be to mimic the blue of the sky bouncing off of the egg shell, so try changing the color of the backlight to blue. Render to see the results. Once you have tried that, you can also change the color of the key light to resemble the color of the sun. An off-white or yellow would do the trick here.

You may also want to change the color of the shadow to a midnight blue, by adjusting Shadow Color in the Shadows section of the spot light's attributes. Experiment with different intensities of light to create greater highlights. Perhaps try turning different light completely down to see exactly how the individual lights work. The lighting_v6.ma scene from this Hour's source files on the bonus DVD provides a suggested finalized lighting setup.

VIDEO

Setting Good Light Presets

Watch the bonus video included in this Hour's files for a quick run-through of setting good light presets. Using light presets will help you light your scenes more efficiently by letting you save and reusing favorite settings for your lights.

Summary

In this Hour, you learned about the different light types in Maya, how to create them, how to modify their key attributes, such as intensity and color, and how to create and modify shadows. Using the three-point lighting techniques discussed in this Hour will help you light subjects in the real world as well as your 3D worlds. Remember that no matter what look you are aiming for, your observations of lighting will help you to re-create what you want in Maya. Also, remember to make use of Maya's facilities to pick and choose what scene elements you want to light, what lights you want to cast shadows, and what objects you want to have shadows. As a final tip, if you are aiming for realism, make sure your shadows make sense according to the direction of the primary light source. For example, if bright light is coming in from one direction, it makes sense to cast shadows from that light rather than from others.

Q&A

Q. Why don't I have any shadows?

A. Lights in Maya do not in general automatically cast shadows. To turn on shadows, select the light and turn on Use Depth Map Shadows in the Attribute Editor, or Use Ray Trace Shadows. If using raytraced shadows, you will also have to check that Raytracing options are turned on in the render settings.

Q. How can I turn off a shadow on a particular object?

A. Select the object and in the attributes for the object (rather than for the light), find the Render Stats attributes. Here, you can choose whether an object casts shadows and/or receives shadows.

Q. What can I do about jagged depth map shadow edges?

A. Increase the resolution for the depth map shadows in the Attribute Editor. You can also increase the filter size. See Hour 21 to learn about improving the quality of the render.

Q. I keep turning up the intensity of my light but nothing seems to happen. What's going on?

A. If you have set a decay rate, you will also have to increase the intensity of the light significantly. Rather than bumping up the values by single units, try increasing by units of tens, hundreds, or even thousands. If you have not used decay rates, make sure that the light is turned on and that it is positioned so that you can see its effects.

Workshop

The workshop contains quiz questions and exercises to help you solidify your understanding of the material covered. Try to answer all questions before looking at the "Answers" section that follows.

Quiz

1. What are the main light sources needed for three-point lighting?

2. How can we adjust a light's position in a more dynamic way?

3. How can we stop a light hitting a surface but allow it to hit another?

4. What can we adjust to make the edges of a spot light softer?

5. Apart from spot lights, what are the other types of light can we create in Maya?

Exercise

Try to find some good photographic reference online or in a magazine and see if you can mimic that particular lighting by using the lights covered in this Hour. Additionally, familiarize yourself with how the properties of lights and materials interact with each other in Maya by using your own scene, or lighting_v1.ma, with a spot light or light of your choice. Change the material properties of the spheres to see how the light affects the changes to the properties of the surfaces. You may have noticed that the blue sphere in lighting_v1.ma (and in some of the figures used in this Hour) does not have a shiny specular highlight. This is because it uses a lambert material that has no specular properties.

As a final suggestion, now that you know how to light a scene, you may want to go back through exercises you have completed in previous Hours to light up your work.

Answers

1. Three-point lighting uses a key light source for main illumination, a fill light to essentially provide control for the more shaded areas, and a back (or rim) light to make the subject pop from its background.

2. Use the panels menu to look through the selected light to adjust it as if looking through a camera lens.

3. We can use light linking to set up specific links between lights and objects, and break links between objects if necessary.

4. Adjusting the spot light's penumbra angle can add softness to the edge. Use dropoff to control the intensity from its center to its outer ring.

5. In addition to spots, Maya provides directional, area, ambient, volume, and point lights.

HOUR 20
Applying Hair and Cloth for Realism

What You'll Learn in This Hour:

▶ How to apply hair and fur to your models
▶ How to make hair and fur dynamic
▶ How to create nCloth objects and change their properties
▶ Animating with hair and nCloth

To add an extra layer of realism and visual quality, you can apply hair and cloth effects to your Maya scenes. Characters seem more lifelike with dynamic hair and fur, and there is no limit to the number of effects you can achieve with Maya's nCloth. From a simple fur to a complex hairdo, and from a tattered waving flag to a fully simulated toga, hair, and cloth pack a lot of visual punch.

NOTE

Dynamics and nDynamics

This book covers Maya's legacy dynamics system in Hour 16, "Animating Using Dynamics and Simulations," and saves nDynamics for this Hour. We wanted to cover both systems, but with so much overlap, it made sense to save nDynamics for our discussion of nCloth. Suffice it to say that all of the principles are the same between the two systems—it's just that in Maya 2014, all of the nDynamics are integrated together, so that nMeshes, nCloths, and nParticles can all be working in the same system.

In this Hour, you will see how to apply hair and fur to your models, and then how to turn on dynamics to affect these systems. Then we will create a simple nCloth and apply some dynamics to it. Finally, we will look at our Sam model with hair and cloth applied to demonstrate the correct workflow for animating a scene with hair and cloth in it.

Applying Fur and Hair

Applying fur and hair is simplest on polygonal meshes. Create a new Maya scene and then create a polygonal sphere by clicking Create, Polygonal Primitives, Sphere.

Loading Fur

By default, the Fur plugin is not loaded. Click on Window, Settings/Preferences, Plugin Manager. In the Plugin Manager, scroll down until you find Fur.mll and check both Loaded and Auto-Load.

Applying Fur

Follow these steps to apply fur to an object:

▶ Select the pSphere you created.

▶ Switch to the Rendering menu set by pressing **F6**.

▶ Click on Fur, Attach Description, New.

▶ A default fur will appear on the sphere you created, like in Figure 20.1.

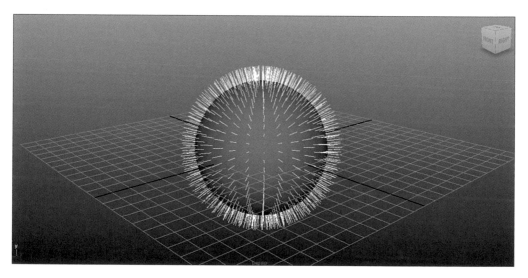

FIGURE 20.1
The default fur applied to the sphere. We will need to apply attributes to this fur to get it to look anything like real fur.

▶ Select the fur by clicking it.

▶ In the Attribute Editor (**Ctrl+A**), select the FurDescription1 tab.

▶ Click on Presets, Duckling, Replace.

▶ The fur now has taken on the attributes of the Duckling preset, which makes the fur pressed down against the surface of the sphere and is finer and yellow colored.

▶ Click on Render, Render Current Frame. It should resemble Figure 20.2.

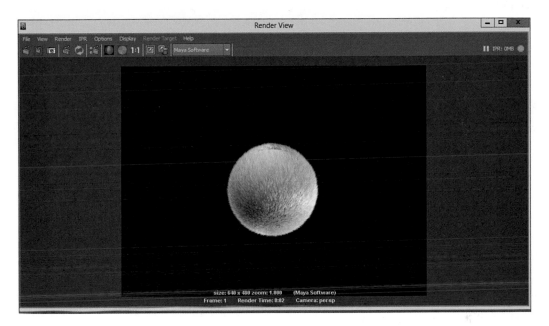

FIGURE 20.2
In just a few clicks, we were able to create a fairly attractive fur on this sphere. The attributes are all customizable, so we have little limit to our imagination with fur.

Modifying Fur Attributes

Select the fur once again and take a look in the Attribute Editor at FurDescription1. Many of the attributes are self-explanatory, such as Length and Curl. A few attributes are a little tricky, such as Scraggle and Clumping, but with a little experimentation and use of the Help menu, you can wrangle these attributes to your will. Perhaps the easiest way to modify attributes is to type in values in the Attribute Editor and press **Enter**. However, if you would like to assign textures to the values (to have a different color on a different section of fur, for instance), you can do one of two things. First, you can drop a texture file onto almost any of the Map slots in the Details tab in the Attribute Editor. (Scroll down in FurDescription1 to the Details tab. Opening this will show all of the attributes. Opening each of these attributes will expose the Maps slots that can then be applied a texture.) Alternatively, you can use the Paint Fur Attributes tool. Click on Fur, Paint Fur Attributes Tool. In the pop-up box, choose Length as the fur attribute and then click the brush on the fur. Open the Tool Settings window by clicking Window, Settings/Preferences, Tool Settings. What will appear is the familiar painting tool settings you've encountered when painting Skin Weight maps or Cluster Weight maps or 3D textures. Change the settings of the brush and practice painting the fur attributes in panel. Figure 20.3 shows the result of using the scale operation and painting on the top of the sphere, effectively making a bald spot there.

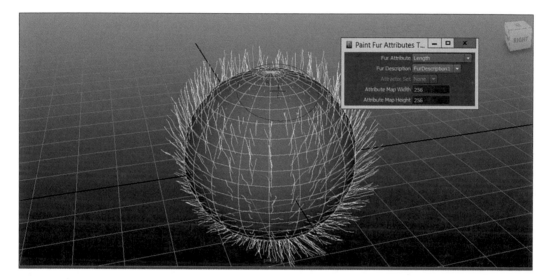

FIGURE 20.3
The familiar paint tools work the same with the Paint Fur Attributes tool. Here, I've painted the Length attribute to a small value on the top of the sphere, making a bald spot.

▼ TRY IT YOURSELF

Experiment with Fur

Apply all of the different fur presets to different objects and practice changing the attributes.

1. Go through the different attributes and adjust them to see the result in panel. Some attributes, such as inclination, are easier to visualize when painting fur attributes rather than adjusting in the Attribute Editor.

2. Do some test renders, and when you have created your own settings that look cool, save them as your own presets!

Applying Hair

Applying hair is very similar to applying fur; however, Maya's nHair is a much more powerful system than the fur system, albeit more cumbersome to set up. Follow these steps:

- Create a new Maya scene, and a polygon sphere in that scene.

- Select the sphere and then switch to nDynamics by clicking on the nDynamics menu set in the top-left corner of the Maya UI (nDynamics does not have a hotkey).

- Click on nHair, Create nHair.

- A default hair system is created and applied to your sphere, as shown in Figure 20.4.

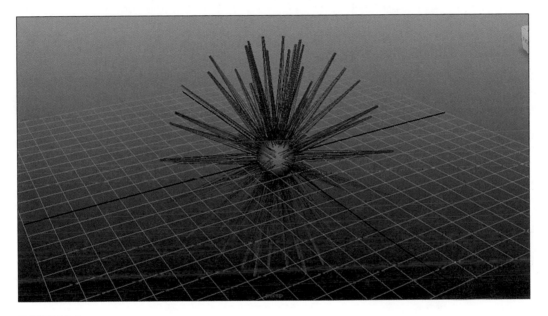

FIGURE 20.4
Although it is as easy to create as a fur system, a hair system has many more parts and offers much more control.

- Select the hair system by clicking on it.

- Open the Attribute Editor (**Ctrl+A**).

Notice that not only is there a greater number of nodes created for a hair system, but none of them have presets. This is because Maya assumes (and rightly so) that all hair systems you will ever create will need detailed and specific control curves to describe the position and shape of the hair. Whereas hair needs to be styled explicitly, fur can normally be controlled with parametric controls and maps.

Hair Attributes

Your nHair system comes with a few nodes. The transform node pfxHair1 should be ignored. The pfxHairShape1 node contains mesh output as well as information on control curves. And the hairSystemShape1 node contains global attributes for the hair system. As with the fur attributes, you should be able to experiment with these attributes and get a feel for what they do in conjunction with checking the Maya Help menu. There are more attributes, but they were created sort of "behind the scenes." These attributes are contained by the follicles.

Follicles and Curves

A *follicle* is essentially a point that "emits" a hair in a hair system. It has its own attributes, many of which are identical to the hairSystemShape's attributes, that can override the values if you so choose. In the Outliner (Window, Outliner), expand the group hairSystem1Follicles. There are dozens. Maya created these automatically for you, but the way hair actually works in Maya is a little tricky: A hairSystem contains all of the follicles that are styled and rendered according to the hairShape.

Select the follicles on the top of the sphere in the Persp pane and press **Delete**. Notice that the follicles and the hairs they were generating are missing now, as shown in Figure 20.5.

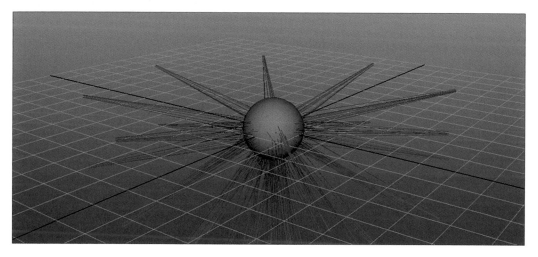

FIGURE 20.5
Hair grows out of follicles, which once deleted no longer generate hair.

The hairSystem is still displaying the rest of the follicles, though. This is another major distinction between a hair system and a fur system—individual follicle control.

Let's control the remaining follicles with curves. Follow these instructions:

▶ Click on Create, EP Curve Tool.

▶ In the side or front panel, click and create a wavy curve out of the top of the sphere, like in Figure 20.6.

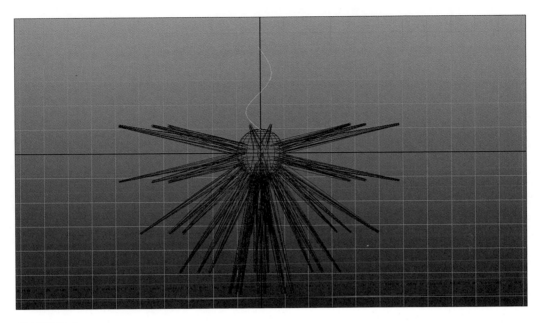

FIGURE 20.6
The wavy NURBS curve from the top of the sphere will serve as a new hair guide.

▶ **Shift**-select the sphere and click on nHair, Make Select Curve Dynamic.

▶ Select the curve again and click on nHair, Assign Hair System, hairSystemShape1.

As you can see, Maya creates a follicle and "grows" the hair along this curve. The interesting thing about using curves is you can now edit the CVs of a curve and "groom" the resultant hair. Most hair workflows start with building the general hair shape with curves and generating follicles from those curves.

TIP

Guide Curves

You can have Maya generate curves for your hairs after the hair system is created by clicking on nHair, Add Output Curves to Hair.

Creating Dynamic Hair and Fur

On their own, the Hair and Fur tools add a nice level of realism and detail to your scenes. However, to add the most sophistication possible from these tools, the hair and fur should move with the character. Next, you will learn how to turn on dynamics for hair and fur.

nHair and Dynamics

By default, all nHair is dynamic. Click Play on your hair scene and watch the hairs fall to the side of the sphere. To adjust the dynamics of a hair curve, you can adjust the Dynamic Properties tab in the Attribute Editor. Additionally, you can create Dynamics Overrides by enabling that tab in the Attribute Editor with a follicle selected. Let's edit these dynamic properties and watch the effects:

- ▶ Select the hair and open the Attribute Editor.

- ▶ Expand the Dynamic Properties tab.

- ▶ Change Bend Resistance to 200.

- ▶ Rewind the scene to frame 1 and press Play.

Instead of drooping down to the sides like before, the hair now remains fairly stiff. Experiment with the other dynamic properties and see what each attribute does to the movement of the hair. I've saved my scene with these settings as hair_Demo.ma.

Fur and Dynamics

Fur is *not* dynamic by default. In fact, you have to "borrow" a hair system's dynamics for use with a fur system. This is still very quick to achieve, however:

- ▶ Open fur_Dynamics.ma in this Hour's files.

- ▶ This scene is a basic fur attached to a sphere. Select the sphere.

- ▶ Change to the nDynamics menu set by choosing it from the menu set drop-down list in the top-left corner of the Maya UI.

- ▶ Click on nHair, Create Hair and then click the options box ☐.

- ▶ Change the Output setting to NURBS Curves and click Create Hairs.

- ▶ Select the sphere and click on nMesh, Create Passive Collider.

- ▶ Switch to the Rendering menu set by pressing **F6**.

- ▶ Select any one of the output curves from the hairSystemShape1 in panel.

- ▶ Click on Fur, Attach Hair System to Fur, hairSystemShape1.

- ▶ Play back the animation.

The fur is "borrowing" the dynamics from the hair curves you created. Each hair has influence on the furs around it and moves them as the animation plays back. You also made sure the hair would not intersect the sphere by making it a passive collider as well.

nCloth and nDynamics

In Maya 2014, Autodesk has consolidated all of the dynamics of cloth, hair, and particles into the nDynamics system. This is great because artists can now create a variety of systems using all of these dynamics types that affect each other. For instance, particles can bounce off hair and land on a cloth, and tear the cloth when enough of them accumulate. Because of this consolidation, making nCloths and making objects interact with nCloths is faster than ever.

Let's first make an object an nCloth. Open nCloth_Start.ma in this Hour's files and follow these directions:

▶ You will see a tablecloth in the air over a ball object. Change to the nDynamics menu set by choosing it from the menu set drop-down list in the top-left corner of the Maya UI.

▶ Select the table cloth object.

▶ Click on nMesh, Create nCloth.

▶ Click Play on the scene.

The tablecloth object falls straight downward, and goes right through the ball. This is because the ball has not been changed into an nMesh yet. All objects that are going to interact in an nDynamics simulation must be nMeshes, nParticles, nHair, and so on.

▶ Select the ball.

▶ Click on nMesh, Create Passive Collider.

▶ Click on Window, Settings/Preferences, Preferences. Click on the Time Slider menu on the left of the Preferences window, and in the settings box that opens on the right, make sure under Playback that Playback Speed is set to "Play every frame."

▶ Also change Max Playback Speed to 24fps.

▶ Save and close this menu. Click on Play on the Timeline and watch the dynamics.

As you can see, the tablecloth is now colliding with the ball. It falls and wraps around the ball realistically, after only a few clicks in Maya. There are many different dynamic property of nCloth, all accessible in the Attribute Editor when selecting an nCloth. The properties control things such as stretching, bending, and even how much a cloth can be pulled before tearing. You can go through the attributes and play with them, or you can load some presets and see how the attributes are set, to create your own effects in the future.

▶ Select the tablecloth, and open the Attribute Editor.

▶ Go to the nClothShape1 tab and in the top-right corner, click on Presets, Silk, Replace.

▶ Play back the animation.

Notice now how the cloth floats down very slowly, and only bends gently around the ball. Try to load other presets and see if you can modify their attributes to get your desired cloth type.

Attaching nCloth to Other Objects

Cloth is rarely independent in a scene; it is almost always attached to another object in some way. You'll see now how to attach an nCloth to another object using nConstraints:

▶ Open nCloth_Flag.ma in this Hour's files.

▶ Play back the animation. You will notice the flag blows away instead of being attached to the flagpole like it should be.

▶ Switch to component mode by pressing **F8**.

▶ Select the two vertices that are on the top and bottom of the flag and closest to the flag-pole, as in Figure 20.7.

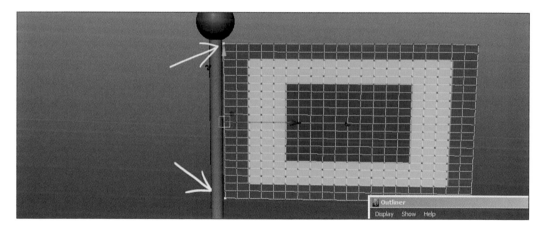

FIGURE 20.7
Select these two vertices for making our nConstraint.

▶ Click on nConstraint, Transform.

▶ Play back the animation.

Notice how the flag is now behaving as if it is connected to the flagpole. You have created an nConstraint, which is a dynamic constraint using an nMesh. Simply put, the dynamicCon-straint1 node that was created is almost like a controller for the vertices we chose. You can par-ent that object, animate, and so on, and the vertices will follow along. There are many kinds of nConstraints: attaching components to components, slide on surface, and more. You should experiment with each one to see which type works the best for your purposes.

Characters and Clothes

A huge amount of the cloth workflow that is done in CG deals with characters and clothing. You can use the exact same nConstraints as you would for any other nCloth to make sure the character's clothing stays attached. The most common workflow for creating clothes is to duplicate the body geometry and sculpt it into shape. I've done that for Sam, and you can begin this section with the file sam_Cloth_Start.ma:

▶ Open sam_Cloth_Start.ma in this Hour's files. In this file, Sam is in his default pose with a t-shirt model on, like in Figure 20.8.

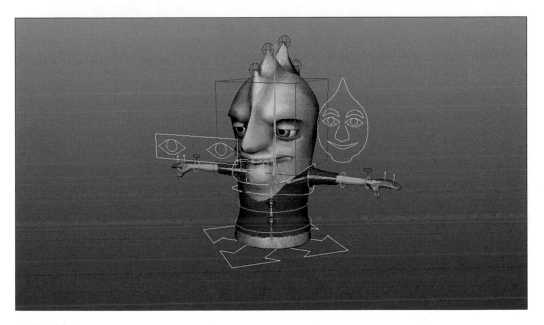

FIGURE 20.8
Sam and his red t-shirt.

▶ Select the t-shirt model and change to the nDynamics menu set by choosing it from the menu set drop-down list in the top-left corner of the Maya UI.

▶ Click on nMesh, Create nCloth.

▶ Click on Sam's body geometry and click on nMesh, Create Passive Collider.

▶ Play back the animation.

Because Sam's t-shirt is so close in shape to Sam's geometry, no constraints need to be set up for it to not fall off his body in a default pose. However, we want to make sure that certain areas stay in place, so we will create an nConstraint to ensure this:

▶ Select the t-shirt model.

▶ Switch to component mode by pressing **F8**.

▶ Select the vertices of the collar and the outermost ring of vertices that make up the sleeves, as in Figure 20.9.

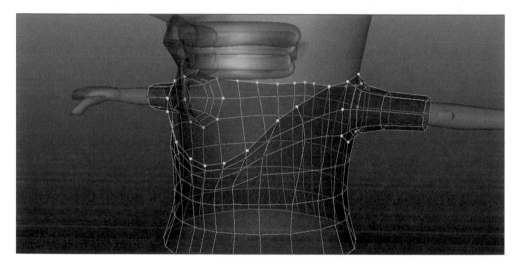

FIGURE 20.9
By selecting these vertices, we will be able to make a constraint that keeps the collar and sleeves in place.

▶ Press **Shift** and LMB click on Sam's body geometry.

▶ Click on nConstraint, Point to Surface.

▶ Play back the animation.

Now the t-shirt is really looking like it will stay in place as you animate Sam. The t-shirt body and the ends of the sleeves are free, but the collar and the base of the sleeves near the shoulder are going to move along with the surface that we constrained them to. You will need to constrain either a small part or a large part of your nCloth to your characters, depending on how the cloth is behaving and what the garment looks like. For instance, a toga should be able to mostly hang free, but a long sleeve shirt might need to be constrained in many places to avoid intersections and tears.

Animating with Hair and nCloth

For the most part, you can animate your characters like normal when they have hair and cloth applied, except for one major difference: You have to give extra time for the hair and cloth to precalculate into position before the character begins moving—meaning if your character starts a scene hanging from a ledge, you have to give Maya some "run-up" frames to calculate what the hair and cloth should look like in a start position that you choose. For this reason, many productions make sure their shots start on frame 101 instead of 1, giving FX artists 100 frames to calculate the start position of the character. Follow along to see how to do this:

- ▶ Open sam_Cloth_Hair_Start.ma. You will notice that Sam has his red t-shirt as well as a braided goatee. Classy.

- ▶ To make sure that the hair and cloth calculate correctly, we need to make sure the pose is saved at frame 1. Change your selection mask to just curves by deselecting all of the other object types in the selection mask menu at the top of the Maya UI, like in Figure 20.10.

FIGURE 20.10
Changing the selection masks to only allow curves to be selected speeds up this step.

- ▶ Now LMB drag a selection box around the entire character, selecting all of his controls.

- ▶ On frame 1, press **S** to set a key. You have just now made sure that the character's pose is set to default on frame 1.

- ▶ On frame 101, set an interesting start pose on Sam. Move him off of his origin, change the spine and arm poses, and do something with the head as well. It can be anything you want; mine is shown in Figure 20.11.

- ▶ Remember to set a key on your controls if you do not have AutoKey on.

- ▶ Rewind the scene to frame 1 and then play back the animation. (Your scene should still be playing back every frame from when we set it in the last section.)

- ▶ Notice that the t-shirt and goatee calculate into place and are ready for the scene to begin on frame 101 now.

As you can see in Figure 20.12, the nCloth and nHair calculate nicely if you give them enough time to. Because we will never be creating animation that starts from a default pose, beginning an animation scene on frame 101 is a good practice in order to allow the FX artists to have the frames they need to perform the calculations on the scene to add a lot of realism.

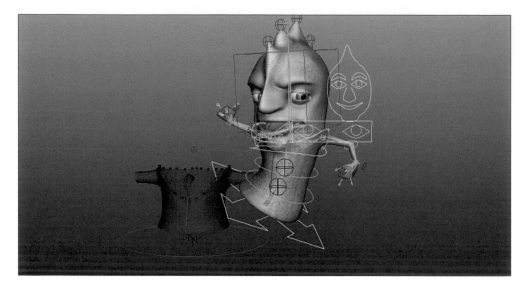

FIGURE 20.11
The pose I chose for Sam on frame 101. Notice how the clothes and hair do not move along with Sam. This is normal, because the clothes and hair need to calculate into place, which requires us to play back the animation (displaying every frame) so it has a chance to do so.

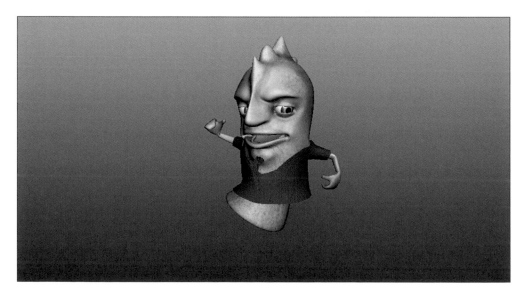

FIGURE 20.12
This pose looks cool! The shirt and goatee simulated nicely into place, and now the animation can start from this frame without breaking the dynamics.

VIDEO

Common Hair and Fur Settings

In this bonus video, I walk through applying fur and hair and the common presets. I also show off how to use curves to create hair follicles as well as loading hair examples into your scenes to examine them.

Summary

Adding nHair and nCloth to your scenes can be a great way to add extra realism. Indeed, characters frequently require clothing and hair or fur. To know these skills is to take another step closer to being a very well-rounded artist in Maya. We first took a look at how to apply fur and fur presets. We then created nHair and took a look at the different nodes that combine to create this amazing dynamic effect. We next investigated the dynamics that come built into nHair, and then borrowed those dynamics to make a fur system dynamic as well. Next, we explored nCloth and how to create collider objects and nConstraints. We then saw a common method for creating clothing for a character, with the t-shirt made from duplicating Sam's geometry. Next, we applied what we discussed in the entire Hour to create dynamic hair and cloth on our Sam rig, but not before making sure that we give enough "run-up" frames for Maya to calculate the correct position of the dynamics at animation start. Cloth and Hair offer an amazing amount of cool effects with very few mouse clicks in Maya. Experiment with these effects to add interesting dynamics and realism to your scenes.

Q&A

Q. I apply a fur to an object, but it does not show up. Why?

A. Make sure you are viewing all object types in your panel. In your panel, click Show, All.

Q. I have no presets for my fur. How can I make them available?

A. Presets are available in the Attribute Editor on the furDescription tab. You are most likely looking at the FurFeedbackShape instead. Switch tabs in the Attribute Editor.

Q. When I apply hair and play back the scene, the hair flies all over the place. What's wrong?

A. More than likely, your scene is playing back at 24fps, but Maya cannot calculate the hair that fast on your machine. Set your playback to "play every frame" by clicking on Window, Settings/Preferences, Preferences. Click on the Time Slider menu on the left of the Preferences window, and in the settings box that opens on the right, make sure under Playback that Playback Speed is set to "Play every frame."

Q. **When I apply cloth, it still intersects my character, even though I have added it as a passive collider. Why?**

A. Adjust the attributes in the Collisions tab in the Attribute Editor. You may have to adjust the scale of the collisions to make sure the vertices don't intersect.

Workshop

The workshop contains quiz questions and exercises to help you solidify your understanding of the material covered. Try to answer all questions before looking at the "Answers" section that follows.

Quiz

1. What menu set contains fur?

2. Why have hair, particles, and cloth been consolidated into a single system?

3. An object that collides with nCloth objects is called what?

4. Is Maya's fur dynamic?

5. Why is it not a good idea to create animation on frame 1 when using a character with hair or cloth attached?

Exercise

Try to create your own wardrobe and hair for Sam. I made a simple t-shirt and a goatee, whereas you might make a hula skirt and a long ponytail. Be creative! The more you experiment and practice with hair and cloth, the more easily you'll be able to add this extra realism to your scenes in the future.

Answers

1. The Rendering menu set contains the Fur menu.

2. Hair, cloth, and particles have been consolidated in nDynamics so they can all interact with each other.

3. A "passive collider" can collide with any nMesh.

4. Not by default. You must create an nHair and then attach the dynamic curves to the Fur to drive the fur dynamics.

5. All dynamics need to be calculated, so if you create a start pose for your animation on frame 1, you are not giving Maya any time to simulate the cloth or hair. Start from the default pose on frame 1 and then animate the character into your start pose on frame 101.

HOUR 21
Rendering Final Imagery

What You'll Learn in This Hour:

▶ How to generate final images through rendering

▶ How to render single images in Render View

▶ How to create batch renders to render animated sequences

▶ What main settings you will need to use to set up your renders

Rendering is the step you use to generate the final images for your scene. You can render frames out to a variety of commonly used image formats, such as TIFF (tiff), TARGA (tga), JPEG (jpg), or select different options including Maya's own IFF (iff) format. Maya lets you define the size and resolution you want and which frames you want to render, either as single images or using Batch Rendering to render out animated sequences. But rendering is more than choosing your image format and resolution. Rendering is about making choices related to quality and speed as well as what rendering engine you want to use, which will impact the final outcome. The rendering engine (or renderer) is the brains behind all the calculations to generate the final look of the light and shadows, the motion, and the effects and all the elements in your scene. Maya provides different renderers for your use, including Maya Software and Mental Ray, to name two very popular ones. Each renderer has its own unique set of features to help you achieve the look you want. Depending on what you have set up in your scene, rendering a single frame can take anywhere from a fraction of a second, to minutes, or longer to perform all the calculations required to generate the final look. This means there are often tradeoffs to be made between the speed and the quality of the renders, but fortunately Maya provides tools and settings to help with those decisions along the way.

NOTE

Rendering, Lighting, Materials

Rendering is the step that generates your final images, and there are many important settings to help you get the quality and look you are aiming for. However, the final look also depends on what lighting and shadows you use, plus what materials you apply to the surfaces. Therefore, at some point make sure you have a look at Hour 7, "Creating Node Networks in the Hypershade," and Hour 19, "Lighting Your Scene Correctly."

In this Hour, you will learn how to use rendering to generate single images using Render View, and also animated sequences using Batch Rendering. You will also learn how to make comparisons between renders as you make adjustments by keeping images in Render View. Interactive Photorealistic Rendering (IPR) lets you tweak your scenes and see the results in close to real time, so we will take a look at that too. We will also, most importantly, look at some of the settings you will need to successfully render out your images.

Render Basics

As you create your scenes in Maya, the viewports render objects so that you can work with them efficiently, but this is not the final quality render. Figure 21.1 shows the viewport view of a scene on the left, and on the right the final image that has been rendered using Mental Ray, which is one of the rendering engines Maya provides. When we talk about rendering, we usually mean generating the final image, similar to that shown in Figure 21.1 (right). You should notice that the render on the right shows that the lights, shadows, colors, and particles have all been calculated, generating quite a different look from the viewport scene on the left.

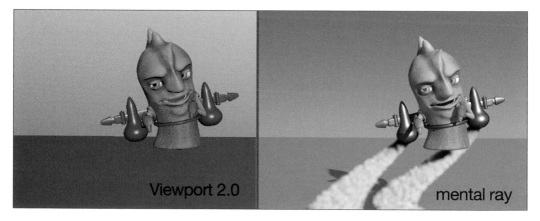

FIGURE 21.1
Viewport scene view (left) versus a rendered image (right).

A few render engines are bundled inside Maya, including Maya Software, Maya Hardware, Maya Vector, and Mental Ray. Maya Software is Maya's own renderer that works efficiently with Maya, and produces good results without too much fuss. The Mental Ray renderer has a wider feature set, including sophisticated options to simulate real-world lighting. The most popular features of Mental Ray over Maya Software are global illumination, physical sun and sky, final gather and caustic light, and much more. A combination of these features with some setup and understanding can allow the artist to create more realistic-looking images than using of Maya Software. You can also create render passes to separate elements such as shadows, occlusion, specularity, and reflections, to name a few. The tradeoff is more complexity over using Maya Software; plus, Maya Software has its own advantages, such as letting you render things such as Maya's paint effects whereas Mental Ray doesn't.

Maya Vector renderer lets you render in a stylized format (such as cartoon-like) or in 2D vector formats such as Adobe Flash. Maya Hardware rendering, which puts your computer graphics card to work, is faster than software rendering, but not always as high quality. However, it can be very useful for rendering dust particles and fairy dust.

Maya Software is the easiest to get started with, so we will focus on that, but we will mention Mental Ray along the way, too. Both are very popular and commonly used renderers, so it's worth having a look at both.

Render Buttons

The Render buttons (shown in Figure 21.2) at the top of your Maya user interface are very useful for your rendering workflow in Maya. The buttons provide easy access to render your images and adjust settings. This Hour will cover how to do all that, but first let's have an overview of the buttons that will be used throughout.

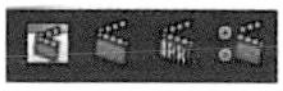

FIGURE 21.2
The buttons in the Rendering buttons group provide easy access to create and adjust renders.

Let's look from left to right at the buttons shown in Figure 21.2. The first opens the Render View window, which has many useful features to deal with rendering images. The second renders the current frame. The third button opens Render View with the IPR (Interactive Photorealistic Rendering) feature active, which lets you tweak your scene and see how it affects the render in real time. The final button on the far right gives you access to Maya's rendering settings. The settings enable you to select the image size and resolution you want to render, to pick the renderer you would like to use, and to adjust features to change the quality versus speed of your renders.

Rendering Single Images

You can render a single image with the click of a button. To learn about rendering a single image, and experiment as you are following along, complete these steps:

▶ Open up rendering_v1.ma from this Hour's source files, or use any of your own scenes. Rendering.v1.ma is a modified version of the scene used in Hour 19. We have lit the scene a bit differently and have animated the diffuse color and glow intensity on the eggMAT material of the egg to give you a short and manageable animated scene to work with.

▶ Click on the viewport that contains the scene composition that you want to render. In this case, just to get started, click on Perspective View and compose the scene to your liking.

▶ Click on the Render Current Frame button toward the top-right corner of your Maya screen to render. The Render View window opens, and renders your image according to the Render Settings, which we will have a look at shortly.

TIP

Rendering the Current Frame

To select a specific frame for rendering, scrub along the Timeline or click Play and then stop when you reach the frame that you want to render. You can then render the frame by using the Render Current Frame button, shown in Figure 21.2 (second to the left).

Render View

The Render View window in Maya has many features to view renders of single frames. It can be used both as a previewing tool and to render out a finalized single image. Just select the viewport that has the scene composed as you want it, scrub along the Timeline to the frame you want, and click the Render Current Frame button.

▶ If you haven't already done so, with rendering_v1.ma open, click on Perspective View and click the Render Current Frame button, which will open the Render View window, and render the image. Use this scene, or a scene of your choice, to experiment with any of the features discussed in this section.

Render View renders the frame that has been selected from the viewpoint or camera view that you have selected, as shown in Figure 21.3. If you change your scene composition in Perspective View and click the Render Current Frame button again, you should see that the new render shows the updated composition. You can also scrub along the Timeline to select a different frame for rendering and then render that, too.

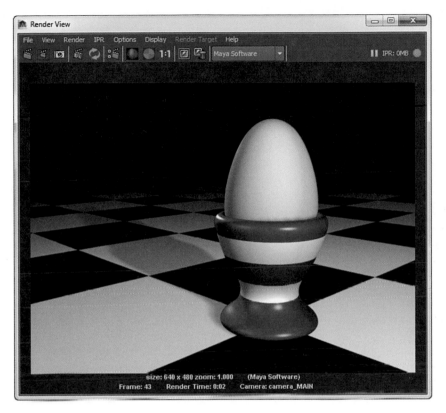

FIGURE 21.3
Render View lets you render single images.

Looking along the top of the Render View window, you will see menus and buttons are provided to access further features. One thing to note right away is that the button located below the File menu looks like the Render Current Frame button you used earlier, but is actually slightly different. It is the Redo Previous Render button, which will render from the same camera/viewport previously used. To render a different camera:

▶ Click on the viewport that contains the camera view you want to render and then use the Render Current Frame button at the top of your Maya screen. If necessary, you can use the Panels menu within the viewports to change to any existing camera first. Alternatively, use the Render menu within the Render View window and then select Render to choose from a list of available cameras.

NOTE

A Rendering Camera

We have provided a camera called camera_MAIN with a composed view of the scene for you to render from if you would like to. We have replaced your top view with the camera_MAIN view. You should also note that camera_MAIN has also been locked to prevent accidental changes. See Hour 14, "Creating and Adjusting Cameras," for more information on working with cameras.

▶ You can also swap between renderers by using the Select Renderer list at the top of the Render View window. If Mental Ray is not listed, you will have to load it. See the tip on loading Mental Ray and Maya Vector to do so.

TIP

Loading Mental Ray and Maya Vector

If Mental Ray is missing from your renderers list, use Windows, Settings/Preferences, Plugin Manager to find and load Mayatomr.mll. Also, check Auto Load, if you want it to be automatically loaded in the future. If the Maya Vector renderer is missing and you would like to use it, too, then use the Plugin Manager to load the VectorRender.bundle also.

▶ To zoom in and out of the image in Render View, or pan around to view any sections of particular interest (use the normal **Alt** and mouse buttons as you would use on any viewport). To return back to the original size, use the 1:1 Display Real Size button.

Render View provides useful information about your render at the bottom of its window. This includes the image size, zoom ratio, and renderer used along the top row, and frame number, render time, and camera along the bottom, as Figure 21.4 shows. Monitoring render times here is a good habit to get into. Keeping an eye on how changes affect render times helps you decide whether or not the changes are worth keeping. Remember that a few more seconds on a single image might not make much difference, but they can add up when dealing with multiple images in animations.

FIGURE 21.4
Render View provides details about the render at the bottom of the window.

TIP

Render Settings

Render View renders using the current settings in Render Settings. You can either use the Render Settings button on the top of your Maya screen or use Options, Render Settings within Render View to open up the Render Settings window.

Rendering Regions

Waiting for an entire new image to be rendered each time you make a change and want to see what is happening can be very time consuming. Fortunately, Maya gives you the option to render regions of the image instead. Rendering just a region saves time, and also helps you problem solve quickly by re-rendering just the area you need. For example, if you want to soften shadows or the falloff area from a spot light cone, selecting a region to render along the targeted edge provides quick feedback. To render a region, follow these steps:

▶ In Render View, marquee select a region by clicking and dragging over part of the image. A red marquee line should appear, indicating the boundary of your selection, as shown in Figure 21.5. To modify the region, simply click and drag to marquee select again.

▶ Once you have a red boundary, indicating that a region has been selected for render, click the Render Region button in the Render View window, as shown in Figure 21.5.

▶ You can zoom closer to a region by using **Alt** RMB, or you can use View, Frame Region from the Render View menus. Use the 1:1 Return to Real Size button to return to the original size.

TIP

Automatically Render Regions

You can automatically render the region as you drag by using the Options menu within Render View to turn on Auto Render Region. Just be aware that the time-saving tradeoffs are balanced by the risk of accidentally setting off a render when you click and drag!

TIP

Auto Resize and Rendering Regions

When you zoom in to a render region, or any other area of the image, by default the next render will zoom you back out. If you prefer to keep your zoom ratio intact, use the Options menu on the Render View to disable Auto Resize.

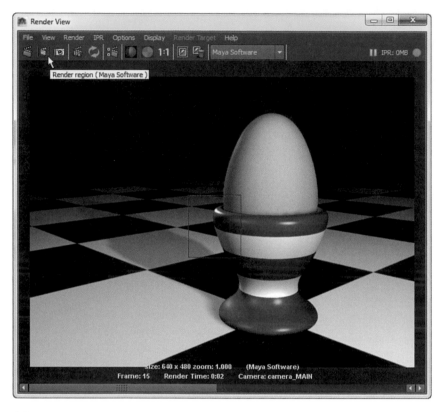

FIGURE 21.5
Render regions let you marquee select an area to quickly preview changes without waiting to render the entire image.

Comparing Saved Images

You will probably want to make adjustments to the scene and will also want to see whether your adjustments are making things better, worse, just different—or if the changes are even noticeable! Render View lets you keep renders in the window to compare between different versions, as shown in Figure 21.6.

Follow these steps to keep and compare images within Render View:

▶ Render an image and then click the Keep Image button within Render View to store it for viewing later, as shown in Figure 21.6 (left).

▶ Scrub along the Timeline to a different frame, or make a change to your scene, such as changing a light color or intensity, a material color, or any other change of your own choice. Render the image again. Click the Keep Image button to keep the new render in Render View as well.

▶ If you want to remove an image, click on the Remove Image button, as shown in Figure 21.6 (right).

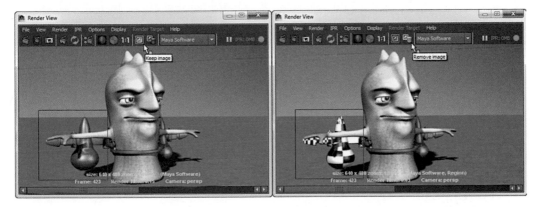

FIGURE 21.6
Use the Keep Image button to keep images within Render View, and use the Remove Image button to delete. Drag the bottom scroll bar to view stored images.

You should notice that once you keep an image in Render View, a scroll bar appears at the bottom to let you easily scroll between images, as shown in Figure 21.6. You can save multiple images, from any camera or any frame. You can also keep images from other scenes, too. Even if you accidentally close the Render View window, the images are still safely stored in Render View, although they are not saved if you close and reopen Maya.

TIP

Commenting

Render View lets you annotate saved images in the window by right-clicking the Keep Image button and selecting Keep Image With Comment. Commenting can help keep a record of changes, to let you retrace your steps if you need to.

To save images permanently, use the File menu within Render View to choose Save Image in the format you specify. By default, Maya will place saved images into the images folder of the project directory that you are working with. You can also load an existing image by using File, Open Image.

Fine-Tuning with IPR

For instant feedback on changes, Interactive Photographic Rendering (IPR) can be used for Maya Software or Mental Ray. IPR lets you make a change and have it almost instantly update in

Render View as you go. To tune your scene with Interactive Photographic Rendering, follow these steps:

▶ Click on the IPR rendering button on your Maya user interface, or use the Redo the previous IPR render button within Render View. If you are rendering using Maya Software, the image will render as normal; however, if you are using Mental Ray, the image will appear in wireframe, as shown in Figure 21.7.

▶ Marquee select a region to fine-tune in IPR by dragging over the image. You can select the whole image, or just a region, although the larger the region size, the slower IPR will update the render. As you drag, you should see the region rendering, as shown in Figure 21.7. Now you can make changes in your scene and have them almost instantly show up in the region you have selected.

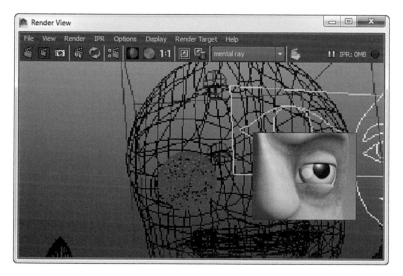

FIGURE 21.7
A Mental Ray IPR render. IPR lets you select one or more regions and have the render update interactively in close to real time as you make changes in your scene.

TIP
Add to the Region
If you want to add regions to the IPR, just click and drag while IPR is on. Newly selected regions will automatically be added to the IPR render.

Render Settings

Use Render Settings to choose the renderer you want to use as well as to control the quality versus speed of the render and the image size, resolution, format, and other settings that will impact the final look. Render Settings apply to single images as well as to any animated sequences. To access render settings, follow these steps:

▶ Open Render Settings by clicking the Render Settings button on the top of your Maya scene, or use Options, Render Settings within Render View.

The Render Settings window opens up with a Common tab for basic settings you will want to make no matter what renderer you choose, plus render-specific tabs to give you access to the unique feature sets that the selected renderer offers. Figure 21.8 shows the Render Settings window open with Mental Ray selected as the renderer.

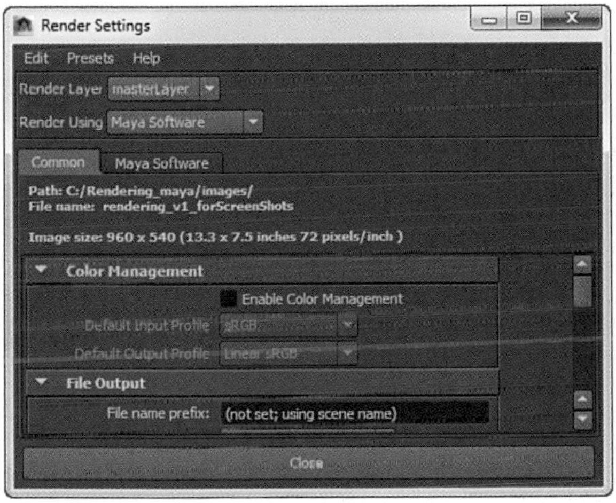

FIGURE 21.8
The Render Settings window with available tabs specific to the renderer selected, such as the Mental Ray options shown here.

▶ To select the type of renderer, use the Render Using drop-down list to choose from the available list, as shown in Figure 21.9. If you want to use Mental Ray and it is in not on the list, you will need to load it first. To load it, use Windows, Settings/Preferences, Plugin Manager to find Mayatomr.mll. Turn on Loaded to load and Auto Load if you want it to automatically load in the future.

FIGURE 21.9
Select from the Render Using list to choose from the available renderers.

Common Settings

Regardless of your choice of renderer, you will need to set up some basics, such as filename, path, image size, format, camera that you want to render, and the frames you want. The settings on the Common tab let you do all this, as shown in Figure 21.10. If you have a version of Maya that is previous to Maya 2014, do not be concerned if you do not see the Scene Assembly and Render Options sections shown in Figure 21.10. They are new additions for Maya 2014, and we will not need them in this Hour. Let's have a look at some important settings that you should be aware of.

FIGURE 21.10
The Common tab in Render Settings lets you set fundamental options such as filename and image size and format, plus the frame range you want to render.

The File Output section is for entering the filenaming conventions, including filename, image format, and numbering system. By default, Maya uses your scene name as the filename, as shown in Figure 21.11, but you can type into the File Name Prefix field to enter your own if you prefer. The path that the images will be rendered to is, by default, the image directory for the project that you have set. If you want to change the path to another, at the top of the Render Settings window, use Edit, Change Project Image Directory.

The Image format by default is Maya's own Maya IFF image format, which is the best quality and most efficient format for Maya to work with. However, other standard formats that are commonly used alternatives, such as TIFF (tiff) and JPEG (jpg), can be selected from the drop-down list shown in Figure 21.11.

FIGURE 21.11
The File Output section lets you enter a filename, image format, and frame/animation extension to set up where Maya puts the numbers in the filename.

To render out a range of frames, you first need to set up a filenaming convention that includes how to use numbering for the images. Use the Frame/Animation Ext: list (as in Figure 21.11) to select anything other than the Single Frame extension options. The format of "name.#.ext" is one of the most commonly used, however, because many applications will understand this format. This means that the name of the file will be first, followed by the number of the image, then the extension (the format of the image). For example, renders from a file named myScene with an image format of tiff would become myScene.1.tiff, myScene.2.tiff, and so on.

Once you have chosen something *other* than the Single Frame options from Frame/Animation Ext:, Maya knows you want to render more than one frame, so the Frame Padding section (grayed out in Figure 21.11) will become active, and so will Frame Range. Use Frame Padding if you want to give the image number the same number of digits by adding in preceding 0's. For example, a Frame Padding setting of 3 would create the series as 001, 002, and so on.

Any time you want to render more than one frame, you will want to make sure to enter a Start and End frame in the Frame Range section. By default, Maya renders starting from frame 1, and ending at frame 10, as shown in Figure 21.12. Therefore, unless you just want 10 frames, make sure to enter your own settings! New to Maya 2014 is the Skip Existing Frames option, shown in Figure 21.12. Enable this when you have already rendered some images, but have deleted some and want to keep others. This will save time by letting the renderer detect existing frames and only render out the missing ones.

FIGURE 21.12
Frame Range lets you enter the starting and ending frame you want to render.

NOTE

Frame Range

To access the Frame Range or Frame Padding, set up Frame/Animation Ext: to anything other than Single Frame options; otherwise, Maya assumes you only have one frame to render! Once you have selected something like "name.#.ext," Frame Range and Frame Padding will then become active.

The Renderable Cameras section is used to tell Maya which camera or cameras you want to render your scene from. By default, the perspective camera is your renderable camera, but you can switch cameras or add more to the list by using the drop-down list next to any camera. To swap one renderable camera for another, use the drop-down list next to the existing renderable camera that you don't need and then select from the cameras available. To add an additional one, use the drop-down list next to any camera to select Add Renderable Camera. Figure 21.13 shows an example. An additional camera will appear. If it is not the one you want, use the drop-down list next to the newly added renderable camera to switch.

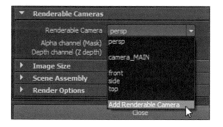

FIGURE 21.13
Use the drop-down list next to any existing camera to make it renderable by selecting Add Renderable Camera.

TIP

Make Unwanted Cameras Unrenderable

Rendering from cameras that you don't need to can waste time and resources, especially when you're rendering animated sequences with many frames. To make a camera unrenderable, click the trash can icon next to it in the Renderable Cameras section of the Common tab.

The Image Size section is used to set image size and resolution, as shown in Figure 21.14. Maya lets you choose from a variety of industry-standard resolutions by using the drop-down Presets list, or you can just type a custom size directly into the Width and Height boxes if you prefer. Make sure you select Maintain Width/Height Ratio if you want to keep the same width to height ratio as you currently have. This allows you to type in either the width or height, and Maya will work out the other for you. You can also change Resolution and Resolution Units settings to adjust the resolution and size from the display-ready resolution of 72.00 pixels per inch (ppi), to something more suitable for print, such as 300 ppi, if needed.

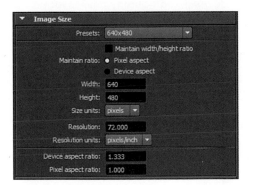

FIGURE 21.14
Use Image Size to set up the size and resolution of your images.

TIP

Resolution Gate

Use the Resolution Gate button (blue sphere) along the top of the camera's viewport to see how any changes in resolution affect the composition. Anything in your scene appearing outside the gate will not show up in the render for that camera, so you will need to adjust the resolution or the camera composition if you want them included.

Quality Presets

When dealing with improving quality of renders, you are likely to come across the terms *aliasing* and *anti-aliasing*. Aliasing artifacts are the jagged or stair-stepped edges that sometimes appear around edges in your scene, such as shadowed edges or areas of high contrast. Anti-aliasing is the process of smoothing out these areas to improve the appearance. Improving the anti-aliasing will improve the quality of the render, but also usually means longer render times. Decreasing the quality can speed up your workflow while you are making adjustments, but can make the jagged lines more obvious. The choice between quality and speed is really up to you. It is beyond the scope of this Hour to cover all the options you can choose to improve the quality of your renders, but you can make a start by looking at the existing presets that Maya provides.

BONUS

Rendering Presets

Presets save time and energy by letting you reuse custom settings. You will find a few useful additional presets for rendering from this Hour's section on the DVD. Make sure to also have a look at the video tutorials on setting presets from Hour 18, "Using Particles to Create Effects," and Hour 19. These tutorials will help you gain a better understanding of using presets.

Maya lets you control the quality of your renders to provide quick draft-quality renders for pre-viewing, or full production quality renders, which take longer but are much better quality for final renders. You also have a number of other presets in between these two options. For Maya Software rendering, use the Maya Software tab to select between Quality presets listed in the Anti-aliasing section, as shown in Figure 21.15 (left). In versions of Maya previous to 2014, with Mental Ray rendering, use the Quality Presets list at the top of the Quality tab. For Maya 2014 Mental Ray rendering, use the Presets menu, as in Figure 21.15 (right), at the top of the Render Settings Window, combined with options for quality in the Sampling section of the Quality tab.

FIGURE 21.15
Use presets Maya Software's Anti-aliasing Quality (left) or the Quality tab (right) in Mental Ray to choose what quality of render you want.

If you want to see what a difference rendering quality makes, open up rendering_v1.ma from this Hour's source files. Use the Render View window to render a frame, and use the Keep Image button at the top of the Render View window to save the renders. Next, change some of the quality settings and repeat. For example, try rendering in Maya Software at Preview quality and compare it to Production quality by scrubbing between the saved images in the Render View window. Rendering_v1 was created for Maya Software rendering, but it doesn't hurt to see what happens when you render it in Mental Ray too.

TIP

Turning on Raytraced Shadows

If you have created lights with raytraced shadows, you will need to turn on raytracing in Render Settings to see them. Raytracing settings can be found in the Raytracing Quality section on the Maya Software tab if you're using Maya Software to render. If using Mental Ray, look for Raytracing options on the Quality tab. Maya 2014 made a few updates to the raytracing settings, so you might find that Mental Ray has already turned on raytracing by default, but it is always a good idea to check. Also note that you can use the Raytracing options both in Render Settings and in attributes for the shadow on the lights that use them to improve the look of raytraced shadows.

Rendering Animations with Batch Render

Batch rendering is used to render a range of frames or an entire animated sequence. In theory, rendering using batch render is as simple as setting up a few things and then launching a batch render, but that is rarely a good idea without careful checks first. Rendering out sequenced images can be time consuming, and it can be frustrating if you don't form good habits early on. Otherwise, you might find yourself waiting for a batch render of your beautiful animation, only to find you rendered from the wrong camera, at the wrong resolution, and only got 10 frames out, because you forgot to set the frame range to the end! Even worse is when you forget to set your filename and path, and so your bad render just overwrote files that you wanted to keep! It is therefore important to have a good workflow practice of checking and rechecking before you render. So let's first have a look at the settings we want to use.

Check Render Settings for Batch Rendering

Before setting off the render, you should make sure your project directory is set. Plus, you should set up the basics in common settings, and any quality settings or other features that you want to use. These common settings were discussed in the previous section, but Table 21.1 shows a reminder list. The first two columns list the main settings to watch out for. The third column provides suggested settings if you want to render the sample file render_v1.ma.

▶ Open rendering_v1.ma or a scene of your own choice.

▶ Click the Render Settings button to open up Render Settings. Use the suggested settings within Table 21.1 to set up the scene for a batch render. If you're using your own scene instead, make sure to enter settings that make sense for your scene.

▶ Once you have finished setting up your render, save the file to get ready to batch render.

TABLE 21.1   Suggested Batch Rendering Settings to Check

Section	Setting	Exercise Setting
Render Settings Window		
	Render Using	Maya Software
	Common Tab	
File Output	Filename	eggRender
	Image Format	JPEG (jgp)
	Frame/Animation Ext	name.#.ext
	Frame Padding	3
Frame Range	Start Frame	1.000
	End Frame	48.000
Renderable Cameras	Renderable Camera	camera_MAIN
Image Size	Presets	640x480
	For Maya Software Rendering: Maya Software Tab	
Anti-aliasing Quality	Quality	Production quality
Raytracing Quality	Raytracing (on or off)	Raytracing on
	For Mental Ray Rendering: Quality Tab	
	Quality Presets	N/A
Raytracing	Raytracing (on or off)	N/A

TIP

File Information

By default, Maya will render images to the image directory of the current project. The path is shown at the top of the Common tab, as you can see in the example in Figure 21.16. Filename, frame range, and image size are also shown.

FIGURE 21.16
Use the top of the Common tab to double-check your path, filename, and numbering, plus frame range, image size, and resolution.

To Batch Render

Once you have checked your settings, it is a good idea to preview some frames first, just to make sure everything is in order. Scrub along the Timeline and then use the Render Current Frame button to check a few frames. Once you think you are all set to go, you might also want to save your file before you launch the render. Batch renders sometimes go wrong, and you don't want any crashes to lose your settings:

▶ Continue with your previous file, or open up render_v2.ma from this Hour's source files, to start with a file already set up for batch rendering in Maya Software.

▶ To launch the batch render, use the Render menu set to select Render, Batch Render.

▶ Once the batch render is running, you can keep an eye on how it is getting along in a couple different ways. If you look at the lower-right corner of your Maya screen, you should see progress messages in the Command feedback bar. You can also open up the Script Editor using the button in the very bottom right of your Maya screen. You should see progress indicators whiz by, letting you know which frame is being rendered.

▶ To preview the most recently rendered image while the batch render is in progress, use Render, Show Batch Render from the Render menu set. Maya's image viewer FCheck should open up with the most recently rendered frame.

▶ To cancel the render if there is a problem or you have changed your mind, from the Render menu set, just go to Render, Cancel Batch Render. You will then be asked to confirm whether or not you want to cancel.

You can continue to work with Maya while batch rendering, but you might notice that it is sluggish compared to normal. This is because the batch rendering is taking up some of the resources.

TIP

Batch Rendering with Maya Closed

Batch rendering will continue to run even with Maya closed. If you close Maya and then decide you want to cancel the batch render, you will need to use **Ctrl+Alt+Del** to select the Task Manager. In the Process tab, select the Render.exe process and click the End Process button.

NOTE

Video Formats

By rendering to an image sequence, if the render goes wrong at some point, you can still most likely salvage some of the images and only have to render out the missing ones. This wouldn't be possible if rendering straight to a video format such as AVI or MOV. Once you render as a sequence, you can then use an application such as Adobe After Effects or Adobe Premiere Pro, or one of the freely available applications to convert your sequences to the video format that you want.

Viewing in FCheck

Maya comes bundled with its own image viewer called FCheck. You can use this to view your renders. To launch FCheck through Maya, use Maya's File, View Image to view a single image, or File, View Sequence to play a sequence of images. To launch FCheck through Windows, use Start, All Programs, Autodesk, Autodesk Maya 2014, FCheck. For earlier versions of Maya, look in the Autodesk Maya folder for the Maya version that you have.

Figure 21.17 shows FCheck open with a rendered image. If necessary, use the File menu and select Open Image to open a single image, or select Open Animation to open a sequence. To play a sequence, use the Play button located toward the top-left corner of the scene. To scrub through, drag with your mouse.

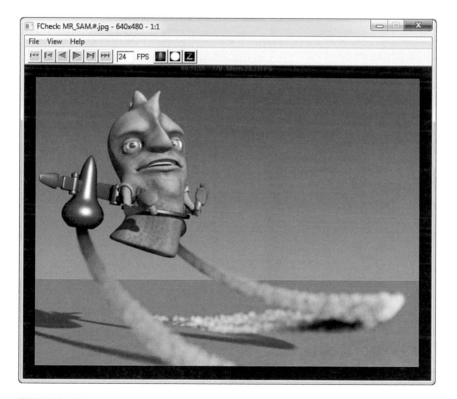

FIGURE 21.17
Maya's FCheck image viewer lets you view single images or animated sequences

Summary

In this Hour, you learned about rendering. You can render out single frames, or multiple frames from animated sequences using batch render. Speed versus quality of renders is always a factor, but you can use Maya's Render View to keep images to compare, and you can use IPR to help make those decisions. Rendering the look you want depends on making the right lighting, shadows, and materials choices, too. For example, when shadow edges aren't quite how you want them, if improving render quality isn't getting what you want, you might have to go back to the shadows on the lights to make adjustments there. The great thing about rendering in Maya is that Maya provides many features to help you along the way.

Q&A

Q. Why can't I enter a frame range?

A. You need to make sure you select a Frame/Animation extension such as "name.#.ext." Otherwise, Maya will think you only want to render a single frame and not let you access the frame range options.

Q. Why doesn't my render match the composition I set up?

A. You may have selected the wrong camera or viewport. In Render View, use the Render menu to then choose Render again and select the correct camera. If you're batch rendering, double-check that the camera you want is renderable.

Q. How can I see my images once they are rendered?

A. You can use FCheck, which is bundled with Maya, or can use most other image viewers. You can open FCheck from Maya by using File, Open Image or File, Open Animation.

Q. How can I speed up my renders for previewing?

A. You can use the quality settings to reduce the quality of your renders to something like draft or intermediate quality. Check out the Maya Software tab if you're using Maya Software, or Mental Ray's Quality tab if you're using Mental Ray in versions of Maya earlier than 2014. Use the Presets menu from the top of the Render Settings window if you're using Mental Ray in Maya 2014, and also reduce the quality options in the Sampling section of the Quality tab. You can also reduce the image size using the Common tab for Maya Software or Mental Ray.

Workshop

The workshop contains quiz questions and exercises to help you solidify your understanding of the material covered. Try to answer all questions before looking at the "Answers" section that follows.

Quiz

1. How do we render lots of images together in sequence?

2. If Mental Ray isn't loaded, where can you load it?

3. What is the common frame/animation extension used when rendering sequences?

4. What can be used in the Render window for real-time feedback?

5. How can a render be stopped while it is still in progress?

Exercise

Maya allows the artist to render in layers, too, so that you can tweak individual elements for greater control when compositing in postproduction. Render layers can be added by selecting the geometry you want to add to a layer and creating a new render layer under the Render tab in the Channel Box or Layer Editor. You can name these layers, and Maya will create extra folders in the images folder for the specific objects in any one layer. For example, we could render the particles separately and control their color when post-processing the image. Create a simple scene with just a few objects, and add each one to its own render layer. Don't panic if some of your objects seem to disappear! Just click back on the masterLayer to reveal them all again.

As a final suggestion, now that you know how to render a scene, you may want to go back through exercises that you have completed in previous hours to render your work.

Answers

1. Maya provides batch rendering to render out any of your image sequences.

2. You can use Windows, Settings/Preferences, Plugin Manager to find and load Mayatomr.mll to load Mental Ray.

3. A commonly used frame/animation extension format is "name.#.ext." This puts the file-name first, then the image number, and then the image extension.

4. IPR (Interactive Photorealistic Rendering) can be used to select regions to render, and see changes made to the scene update in near to real time. IPR is available for Maya Software and Mental Ray.

5. Use the Render menu set to choose Render, Cancel Batch Render to cancel a batch render in Maya. If you have closed Maya, you will need to use **Ctrl+Alt+Del** to select the Task Manager and then, in the Process tab, select the Render.exe process and click the End Process button.

HOUR 22
Working with Film

What You'll Learn in This Hour:

▶ How to import a piece of footage in your scene

▶ How to conform your animation to a tracked camera

▶ What camera and render settings are needed for working with film

▶ How to avoid lighting issues and other problems with film

Maya is the de-facto standard 3D application for the film industry. As such, the tools for working with film are top notch. We have cameras with ample customization options to match real-world film, as well as render settings to make your shots seem real.

NOTE

Stocking Up

If you cannot create your own plates for practice, you may want to download some professionally created plates from sites such as www.istockphoto.com and www.shutterstock.com. These sites contain lens info and have good support for using their footage as plates for 3D scenes.

In this Hour, you find out how to import and adjust a filmed background, lay out your scene to work with a tracked camera, and use common settings that will get you on your way to working with film in an everyday setting.

Importing a Film Plate

To import a film plate, we import an image or image sequence as an image plane to a camera. As such, we need to create our camera that will serve as our shot camera. Follow these steps to import a moving plate to our scene:

▶ Create a new Maya scene.

▶ Click on Create, Cameras, Camera.

- ▶ Rename this camera "shot_Cam."

- ▶ Change a panel to view through this camera by clicking within a panel on Panel, Perspective, shot_Cam.

- ▶ In the shot_Cam panel, click on View, Image Plane, Import Image.

- ▶ Navigate to this Hour's files and choose still_Plate.png.

- ▶ It will load into the camera and your scene should look like mine (see Figure 22.1).

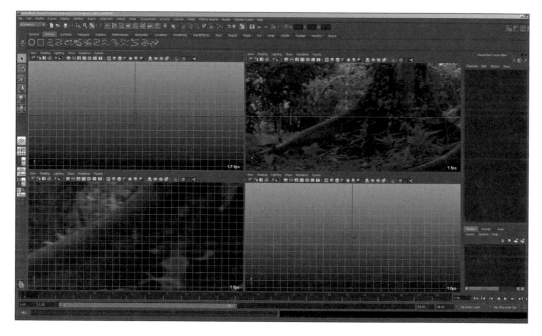

FIGURE 22.1
The shot_Cam with the image plane loaded.

As you can see, the shot_Cam has an image plane loaded now. This is similar to how we added an image plane for modeling reference; however, we're interested in setting up the camera to match this angle. First, let's change a few settings on the image plane to make things easier for us to work:

- ▶ In the shot_Cam panel, click on View, Image Plane, Image Plane Attributes, shot_Cam, imagePlaneShape1.

- ▶ This loads the Attribute Editor and the image plane's tab.

▶ In the Attributes, change the display to Looking Through Camera. Seeing the image plane in all panels is distracting.

▶ Change the Display mode to RGB. Even though PNGs have an alpha channel, we do not need to see through the plate, so leaving Maya to calculate the alpha wastes system resources.

▶ Scroll down to the Placement tab and change the Depth setting to 1000. This pushes the image plane far backward so that objects do not intersect it.

▶ In the shot_Cam panel, dolly and orbit the camera so that the grid looks like it is positioned on the forest floor, like mine does in Figure 22.2.

FIGURE 22.2
The grid is our guide as to the floor of the forest.

It is also a good idea to create a *very* large ground plane to give yourself an idea of the horizon to further gauge the proper camera position. Follow these steps:

▶ Click Create, Polygon Primitives, Plane.

▶ In the Channel Box, scale the plane to 1000 in ScaleX and ScaleZ.

▶ Switch to wireframe mode by pressing the **4** key.

▶ Adjust the camera one more time with an eye on the new horizon line. It should look like mine in Figure 22.3.

FIGURE 22.3
The plane gives us a good feeling of where the horizon is our scene.

The last attribute to try to match is the focal length. Ideally, a supervisor working on set will be recording the lens information for each shot. This shot has a focal length of 50mm. I have saved this scene as still_Frame.ma.

Using a 3D Tracked Camera

Nearly every single camera used in film is dollying, panning, zooming, and so on. This movement needs to be translated into 3D movement that Maya understands before you can animate within the scene. I have included a tracked camera that we are going to use to get a little bit of practice setting up the scene as well as a moving background plate.

Setting Up the Scene

First, we need to open the tracked camera and see what kind of information is contained within the shot. Follow these instructions to get a sense of the workflow of using a tracked camera:

► Open tracked_Start.ma. Notice that a camera and tracking markers are placed in the scene. If your camera does not display the image plane, you will need to go into the Attribute Editor for the shot_Cam. In the image_PlaneShape1 tab, browse to the /plates/ plate directory in this Hour's files to relink the file.

► While in the Attribute Editor, change the settings to make the image plane display only "looking through camera," like we did in the last section. Also, change the display to RGB, just like we did in the last section.

▶ In the Attribute Editor, in the shot_CamPlane1 tab, notice how Use Image Sequence is checked. This is the attribute that tells Maya to read a sequence of images for the plate.

NOTE

Sequence Numbering

Maya prefers the images in a sequence to be numbered with a period delineating the image name and then image number (for example, imageName.001.png).

▶ In the Attribute Editor, in the Image Plane Attributes section, is an attribute called Frame Cache. This is the number of frames Maya will save to memory for fast playback. The problem is, if your cache is too small, Maya will constantly change the cached frames and you will not have smooth playback. If you have at least 8GB of RAM, change this value to be 240, the number of frames in our sequence.

▶ Now we are ready to place the camera. You cannot do this by just moving the camera itself; it has keyframes on it.

▶ Create a locator by clicking on Create, Locator.

▶ Scale it up to be very large in the Persp panel, like mine in Figure 22.4.

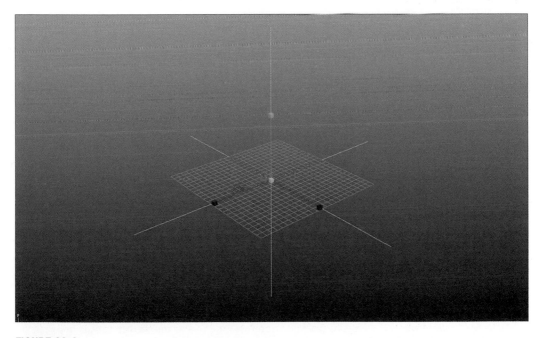

FIGURE 22.4
The locator will help us position and align the camera.

▶ Select the shot_Cam and then **Shift**-select the locator. Switch to the Animation menu set by pressing **F2**. Click on Constraint, Point. Then click on Constraint, Orient.

▶ In the Outliner, click the plus sign next to the locator's node, expanding its hierarchy.

▶ Select both the point and orient constraints in the Outliner and then press **Delete**. You just quickly aligned the locator to the camera object.

▶ In the Outliner, select the cam_Group. **Ctrl**-select the locator in the Outliner and press **P** to parent it.

▶ Select the locator and look at the Channel Box. There are minute rotations in all of the channels. We want the camera to generally be parallel to the ground because we know it was shot that way on set. Therefore, select all of the rotate channels and type in **0** to zero them.

▶ Move the locator off the ground and back far enough that you can see the grid, as in Figure 22.5.

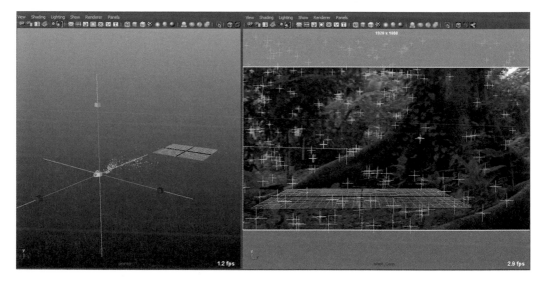

FIGURE 22.5
The camera placed with grid in view. We will import an object to work with scale now.

Scene Scale

Scale is a tricky issue when it comes to tracked cameras. One of the major differences between a moving camera and a static camera is that scale does not matter with a static camera. You can simply scale your scene to make the character appear to be any size you like. Conversely, you can scale your character to fit the scale of the camera if the character rig supports it. Regardless of what method you use, the movements in the camera have a scale to them that needs to match the size of the world and hence your characters. You cannot begin to adjust this scale until you get an object into the scene:

▶ Import sam_Scale.ma into this scene by clicking File, Import.

▶ As you can see in Figure 22.6, he is much too large.

FIGURE 22.6
Yikes, Sam is too large for this scene.

▶ We can either scale the character up, or scale the camera down. Let's do the latter because even though Sam scales well, it is best to leave the character alone if you can.

▶ Select the locator. Move the pivot of the locator to the world origin by pressing **W** to switch to the Move tool, holding down the **D** key and the **X** key simultaneously, and MMB clicking on the world origin.

▶ Now scale the locator up until Sam is about half the size he looks now. My scale is shown in Figure 22.7.

▶ When you are done, it's a good idea to lock all of the channels to avoid accidental movement. Select the camera and **Shift**-select the locator, go into the Channel Box, LMB drag on all of the transform channels, right-click on the selected channels, and choose Lock Selected.

FIGURE 22.7
This looks about right. Sam is appearing to be a normal scale now.

▶ Because the tracking locators are a little annoying, you can select one of them, press the **Up Arrow** key on your keyboard to select the parent group, and then press **Ctrl+H** to hide the tracking locators.

▼ TRY IT YOURSELF

Learning Scale Through Practice

One of the major issues in working with film is scale. Practicing working with scale will help very much if you are thinking about entering the feature film business.

1. Import objects of different sizes into your scene and try to come up with the best scale and camera position/orientation to match it.

2. Keep practicing with every model you can get your hands on, but remember: The camera's movement scales with the group node you are scaling. In other words, if there are little bumps or jostles in the camera, they will be amplified if you scale the camera up or down. Ask yourself if the object should be bigger in camera because it is actually bigger in world space, or if it should just be closer to the camera?

Masks

If you want a character move behind an object in the plate, you need to learn to load masks. A *mask* is a piece of footage that has an alpha channel determining where the image is see-through, so you can choose what objects to place in front of the character. Follow these steps to create a mask for the tree that is in the foreground:

▶ In the shot_Cam panel, click on View, Image Plane, Import Image.

▶ Navigate to this Hour's source files and find the plates/mask directory. Choose any of the .png files in that directory.

▶ Check the Use Image Sequence check box in the Attribute Editor.

▶ Make sure the mask is displaying properly by changing the Color Offset attribute to white, and it should look like my scene in Figure 22.8.

FIGURE 22.8
The mask is blocking the tree in the foreground.

▶ Change the display settings to Looking Through Camera, but do not change the display from RGBA—we need the alpha channel to display in order to see objects that are not masked.

▶ In the Placement section of the Attribute Editor, change Depth to 1. This is so that nothing will get in between the object and the mask.

▶ Return the Color Offset setting to black.

This mask was created in a separate program and then exported for our use in this scene. There is no automatic way within Maya to mask objects, so you will need to do some prep work on your scenes if complex masking is essential to getting your animation done. Truthfully, though, in production there is frequently not enough time to get masks perfect in time for the animation stage (compositors typically start work on a shot midway through animation).

▶ Select the group sam_Geo and move him to the right of the screen until he is partially covered by the mask.

▶ If it is working correctly, it will look like Figure 22.9.

FIGURE 22.9
Sam is behind the mask and therefore looks like he is peeking out from behind a tree.

More Camera Settings

The following settings will further help you customize your camera to give you more render-friendly settings, and to help you match real-world cameras.

Clip Planes

Two of the settings that deal with scale are Near and Far Clip Planes. These settings adjust how close an object has to be to the camera to be rendered, and how far the object has to be to be rendered. However, the near clip setting also controls how close polygons can be to each other before they will seem to visually intersect. This is occurring right now in Figure 22.9 in Sam's eyelids. Select the shot_Cam and go into the Attribute Editor. In the Camera Attributes, set Near Clip Plane to .1. His eyelids should fix.

Film Back and Film Gate

These settings are finally applicable to our scene. You need to know the camera's make and model to get accurate settings to put into these attributes. These settings control how much of a lens's viewable area actually gets captured by the image sensor or the film inside the camera. Imagine a projector showing a huge image onto a small projector screen, and the image spilling over the sides onto the wall behind. Having the wrong film back settings is similar to this. We do not need to worry about these settings as the tracking software recognized the HD video aspect ratio and estimated the film back. You can see there are many presets for Film Back, and on feature projects that use film, these can come in handy.

Common Render Settings

It is highly uncommon to render the image planes when you are working with film. It is much more likely that you will be compositing the characters and objects back into the shot using compositing software later on. Set the Display Mode to "none" in the image plane's attributes in the Attribute Editor before rendering.

If you are using any useBackground materials to catch shadows from objects, these materials "pick up" the image planes also, so hiding them is important.

If you are using Final Gather to have bounced light in your scene, you should know that image planes do not cast and receive Final Gather points. It can be a nice trick to get your character looking more like it is actually in the scene by setting the Environment color to a "darkened average" of the colors in the plate. Our forest plate is very dark and green, so that kind of color would do. Be careful not to make it too bright or saturated.

Aspect Ratios and Resolution

The image plane will always render to fill the film gate—meaning that if you render an aspect ratio different from your image plane (and film gate), you will be missing the image plane on the top and bottom, or left and right, of your render. For instance, if your plane is 1920×1080 (1.77 aspect ratio), and you render at 500×1080, then you will have a render with the film gate compressed into the width of the available resolution. In Figure 22.10, this is exactly what happened; notice how there is blank area on the top and bottom of the image. You can gain this area back by setting a different "Fit Resolution Gate" in the Film Back settings of your camera; however, this is cumbersome and not very widely used. In all but a few cases, you will want to render at the same aspect ratio and resolution as your film.

FIGURE 22.10
The aspect ratio of your render will affect how the plate is rendered. In addition, the Fit Resolution Gate settings in the camera shape will change how the image plane renders.

Color

One extra render issue that needs to be addressed is color. Depending on the format of the plate, you will need to render in 8-bit, 16-bit, or 32-bit color. If you are working with a plate that is an 8-bit-per-channel format, such as .png or .jpg, it is overkill to render at a higher bit depth. Alternatively, if you are compositing the final image into film, you need to set your render bit depth to at least 16 bits per channel to match the color quality of film. To do that, follow these instructions:

▶ Click on Window, Rendering Editors, Render Settings.

▶ If you are using Maya Software, in the Common tab there is a section called File Output. In the Image Format drop-down box, choose Maya 16 IFF or Tiff 16 TIF. These two formats will automatically switch the software renderer to render at that bit depth.

▶ If you are using Mental Ray, switch to the Quality tab. At the bottom of this tab, there is a Frame Buffer section. Changing the Data Type setting to RGBA Half 4×16 or RGBA Float 4×32 will choose either 16-bit or 32-bit color, respectively. You must remember to choose a compatible output file format in the Common tab, though, or the color quality will be lost.

BONUS

Bonus Plates and Scenes

You will find this Hour's Bonus folder has some extra plates and Maya scenes. Open these reference objects and characters into them, and practice working with scale.

Summary

Whether it is a reference image or an image sequence, applying a filmed image to your scenes is a common practice for digital artists. We begin with importing a simple still image and setting up our camera to create some animation within this scene. Some of the common camera and image plane parameters were discussed. We then looked at working with image sequences and tracked cameras. Orienting the camera and setting scene scale were demonstrated; then we imported a mask into our scene. Finally, a few of the common camera, render, and image output settings pertaining to film were discussed.

Q&A

Q. My scene has a black background when I open it. What's wrong?

A. The file path is probably incorrect for the image plane. Set your project to this Hour's folder, or wherever you have saved the source files that go with this chapter. The image plane may need to be reloaded after doing so.

Q. I cannot see my image plane, even though I know that importing worked. What is wrong?

A. Make sure your panel is set to display cameras. To be sure you can see image planes, in your camera's panel, click Show, All.

Q. There are little bumps in the camera movement in the tracked camera scene. Is this normal?

A. No tracked camera is 100% perfect. Although sometimes we get very close, there might be little bumps and hitches. These are easy to stabilize when you're compositing the scene later, so at a certain point, the artist tracking a shot will hand off the scene to animation.

Q. **When I import a mask, it is behind my character. Why?**

A. Sounds like you forgot to move it close to the camera so that no objects can pass between the mask and the camera. Change the Depth settings in the image plane's attributes.

Workshop

The workshop contains quiz questions and exercises to help you solidify your understanding of the material covered. Try to answer all questions before looking at the "Answers" section that follows.

Quiz

1. How many image planes can be imported onto a camera?

2. How do you ensure you will have smooth playback when dealing with an image sequence?

3. Which is better, scaling a character to match a camera, or scaling a camera to match a character?

4. What setting must you check to make sure your mask's alpha channel will be used?

5. Which file formats support greater than 8-bit color when rendering with Maya Software?

Exercise

Take a few photos from your personal library and load them as image planes in Maya; then set up cameras and scenes to match the footage. Next, import some characters and try to compose the shot by matching the perspective (focal length) and scene scale. Practice creating realistic compositions that you might see in a film!

Answers

1. Infinite, or as many as your machine can handle!

2. You want to set the Frame Cache attribute to a number greater than the number of images in the sequence so that Maya will store them in memory.

3. Always scale the scene to match the character, even if the character's rig is fully scalable.

4. In the image plane's attributes, check to make sure Display Mode is set to RGBA.

5. Maya 16IFF and Tiff16 are both 16-bit file formats, suitable for rendering images that are going to be composited into film.

HOUR 23
Correct Project Management and Scene Workflow

What You'll Learn in This Hour:

▶ How to take advantage of Maya's project directory structure

▶ What are good project settings and workflows

▶ What are some common issues in project management

▶ How to set up an animated project from start to finish

We covered the Maya default project structure briefly in Hour 3, "File Types and Managing Assets." Although we touched on the normal project directories that Maya creates for you, we did not talk specifically about taking advantage of this structure. Using Maya's organizational tools to your advantage can mean the difference between a smooth project and rough sailing.

NOTE

About the Scene File Locations

So far, we have been operating with this book in a way that has allowed you to open each scene file smoothly and without issue. That is because all of the files you need to open a scene are located within a single directory. By default, Maya will look in the same directory as the scene file for linked assets, such as textures, caches, and reference files. We will break away from the default and set up a project the right way now.

In this Hour, you find out how to make the most of the organizational tools that Maya has built into it. We will then discuss the best settings for your projects and how to come up with an efficient workflow for organizing your scenes and assets. We will point out common pitfalls so you can avoid them when you are working. Finally, we'll follow a scene through an entire simple production pipeline to see it start to finish. Although the methods described in this Hour are not revolutionary or even unique to Maya, they are pivotal to the success of a project.

The Maya Project Structure

The Maya project was covered briefly in Hour 3. Let's take another look at the Set Project window in Figure 23.1, accessed through File, Project Window.

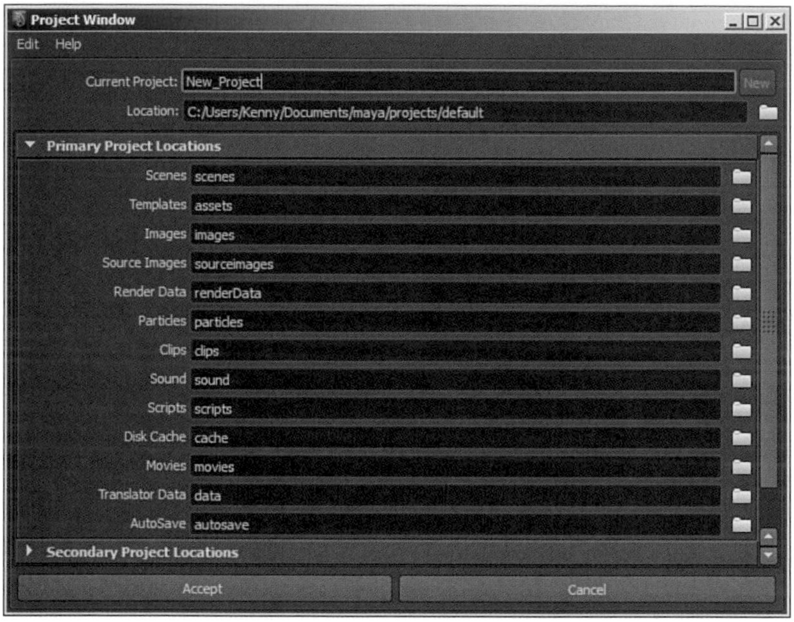

FIGURE 23.1
The Project Window in Maya shows you the directory in which your project exists, and the directories that Maya will save the file to by default.

Setting your project (File, Set Project) and creating a new project through the Project Window tells Maya to create or read the workspace.mel script file, which contains details about the locations of the directories and files in your project. With this kind of automation, the best practice is to always save your files in the same directories. However, Maya's defaults can make it so that the files start to fill directories very quickly. For instance, if you save the in-progress scenes for your character models, the in-progress rig files for your character rigs, and every single revision of a dozen animated shots in the same "scenes" directory, you will have to wade through hundreds of files in order to find the right one. Instead, we separate "assets" from "scenes." The distinction will be that a scene is any Maya file that contains manipulation done to final assets. Assets go into scenes, not the other way around.

Take a look at Figure 23.2, where the folder structure of a default Maya project is laid out.

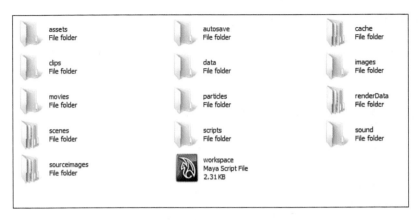

FIGURE 23.2
The default Maya project structure as seen in Windows.

The very first folder is named "assets." This is where your assets will live, including character models and rigs, props and environments, textures and plates, and anything else that is combined together to make a moving, finished image. (Why we will not be putting textures into source images is explained a little later.)

Naming Conventions

With everything going into folders of their own, we need to make sure that a proper naming convention is adopted so that files almost "sort themselves." You should be able to tell at a glance what the status or revision is of an asset, what type of file the asset is, and what the file contains. Here is my favorite naming convention, applicable to almost every single asset type that you can use in a Maya scene:

```
assetName_assetType_versionNumber_Notes.extension
```

Let's come up with a few examples of this naming convention for assets. For instance, if you are saving the fifth revision of a color map for Sam's skin, and the note you want to leave for yourself is that it is a work in progress (WIP) and still needs speckles, then you might save the file like this:

```
Sam_skinColor_v05_WIPNeedsSpeckles.tga
```

Why are the notes after the version number? If you save multiple versions of the same asset, you want them to sort alphabetically by the version number, and not by the notes.

If you are saving the tenth revision of a rig file for Sam and it just needs the controllers to be put into correct display layers, then the file would look like this:

```
Sam_rig_v10_WIPDisplayLayersForCTRLS.ma
```

At a glance, you can tell everything that is happening in that scene, what needs to be done, and where the file should go. As long as you follow this naming convention, and choose and repeat your name for every task, you should be fine. You don't have to call the file in which you are creating a control rig the "rig" file; instead, you can call it the "ctrl" file or the "puppet" file—as long as you call it the same thing every time.

For scenes, the naming convention is similar:

```
projectName_sequenceLabel_shotLabel_task_versionNumber_notes.extension
```

So, the third version of an animation file in the project "Sam Runs Away," in the "Boat Chase" sequence, and the second shot in the sequence in which you have added overlap to the spine, would look like this:

```
SRA_BOAT_020_anim_v03_overlapInSpine.ma
```

You can abbreviate your project names and your sequence names however you like—again, as long as you are *consistent*. The same goes for the task names. "Anim" is a fine abbreviation for animation, but you might like something even shorter. Also, numbering your shots by tens means that you can add up to nine shots between two present shots without having to mess up your naming convention. So, the first shot is 010, the second 020, and so on.

Adopting and sticking to a set-naming convention is absolutely essential in a production environment. There is no leeway for your own structure; you are expected to adhere strictly to the established naming convention if you want to be a hire-able artist. So learn to be organized!

Directory Structure Issues

A little while ago, we established that every single asset, no matter what, goes into the Assets directory. That includes texture files. Maya creates the sourceImages directory for you, though, so why not use that folder?

The reason is simple. You are going to be creating a directory for every single asset that you have in your project. Each character, prop, and environment needs its own folder. The issue comes down to choosing to create one directory for each asset, and then multiple subdirectories that have the same name, or one directory for each asset *type*, and then multiple subdirectories for each asset. Allow me to demonstrate further.

Under the first system, you have an assets directory, and let's say a character (Sam) and a prop (Hammer), and all of the associated assets to go with these assets. The directories would look like this:

```
Project\Assets\Characters\Sam\models
Project\Assets\Characters\Sam\rigs
Project\Assets\Characters\Sam\sourceimages
```

and

```
Project\Assets\Props\Hammer\models
Project\Assets\Props\Hammer\rigs
Project\Assets\Props\Hammer\sourceimages
Etc.
```

See how in the preceding structure, there is only one directory named Sam, and one named Hammer. Here's the other way to organize this:

```
Project\sourceImages\Sam\
Project\Assets\models\Sam
Project\Assets\rigs\Sam
Etc.
```

This is a huge problem. If you want to know where all of the files associated with a single asset are, you will have to hunt around or (even worse) search for the directories that share the same name. Having up to a dozen directories all called "Sam" is not organization, it's madness. And although the poor sourceImages directory will be mostly deserted in a project set up by these specifications, there will be many other sourceImages directories within the assets' folders to make up for it!

Referencing Pipeline

We've been using scene files that have all of the connected assets present in the same directory as the scene itself. However, in production, a "referencing pipeline" is much more common. This practice makes use of "references," which is Maya's way of bringing an asset into a scene by reading the asset file but not importing the asset fully. Rather, it is almost like a link that is updated any time the scene is reloaded. The benefits of this kind of workflow are immense; the most major positive effect is that you can update an asset file, and then all of the scene files that reference that asset will "pick up" the revised asset the next time the scene is read. You can change a texture file, fix a rig problem, or replace an asset entirely, and the changes will propagate to scenes with the click of a button. The other major benefit is scene overhead and drive space. Because a referenced file is not actually imported into the scene, the scene files stay very small. A few hundred kilobytes is normal for an animation file—even one that references a 200MB rig file and a 50MB environment. Rather than import or start from the asset file itself, use references. To see how referencing works, follow these steps:

▶ Create a new scene in Maya.

▶ Click on File, Create Reference.

▶ The normal File dialog box will open.

▶ Select sam_rig_v02_final.ma and click on OK.

▶ Sam will appear in your scene exactly as if he was imported.

▶ Save this scene by going to File, Save As.

▶ Name it reference_Test.ma.

▶ Navigate to the folder where you saved the file and see how large the file is. It is very small.

▶ Now let's take a look at the Reference Editor to see some more of the functions that referencing allows us to do.

▶ Click on File, Reference Editor. It should look like Figure 23.3.

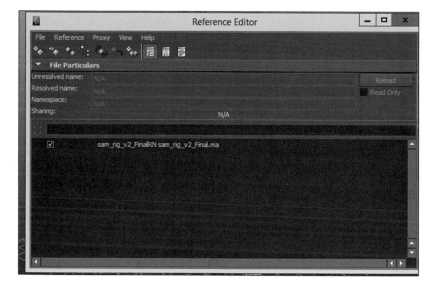

FIGURE 23.3
The Reference Editor with the Sam rig loaded.

Checking or unchecking a reference simply loads it or unloads it from a scene. This is not the same as importing or deleting the reference. It just means that temporarily the reference will be removed from view and you can continue to work on the scene until you are ready to bring the reference back. It is very useful if you have a scene with multiple characters to reduce scene overhead and work efficiently. In the Reference menu, you can Reload and Replace Reference, the two most common commands after loading and unloading. Reloading a reference simply tells Maya to re-read the asset file and make any updates to the reference contained within. Replacing the reference allows you to choose a new asset that should take the current asset's place. Be warned that if you replace a reference and the new reference has a different hierarchy or naming convention, Maya may not be able to reconnect all of the information in the scene.

You may lose information such as render layers, animation, and so on. Careful riggers know not to make too many changes to the hierarchy or controls, and usually a new character rig can replace an old one with minimal damage. Even on high-end productions, though, a rig update can spell trouble for the animators. Save multiple versions of your scenes (and assets) to prevent data loss.

Relative and Absolute Paths

Take a look at the top of the Reference Editor window again. Select the Sam reference and see the path that loads into the very top bar of the Reference Editor. Mine says:

```
D:/SamsTeachYourselfMaya/Chapters/23/sam_rig_v2_Final.ma
```

This is what is called an absolute path. It is the path to the directory with no context or relation to the Project directory. For maximum compatibility between machines and within a studio, relative paths are recommended. Relative paths simply means that the Project directory is considered the "base directory" and that all paths should be written relative to the Project directory. So if my Project directory is in D:\SamsTeachYourselfMaya, then the relative path for this rig is now:

```
/Chapters/23/sam_rig_v2_Final.ma
```

TRY IT YOURSELF ▼

Replace Absolute Paths with Relative

Replace all of the paths in your scene with relative paths. First, make sure your project is set to this Hour's directory:

1. Starting in the Reference Editor, delete the parts of the path up to the point where the Project directory is removed. Pressing Enter should reestablish the path and set it for the loaded reference. If you made a mistake, Maya will ask you to correct it.

2. Go into the Hypershade and select Sam's textures. Double-click on them to open the Attribute Editor, and find the File tabs to see the paths for Sam's textures. Chances are, the textures haven't loaded yet anyway.

3. Replace the texture's paths with relative paths as well.

Good Project Workflows

When you are creating a project from scratch, practicing good workflow will save you headaches down the road. Following a strict naming convention is a great start. Also, creating a template project directory that can be copied and renamed for each one of your new projects saves you the time of having to create the directories each time. This template contains other support-ive directories within it, and also distinguishes which directory is going to be used as the actual Maya "Project." Take a look at Figure 23.4 and you will see what is meant by this.

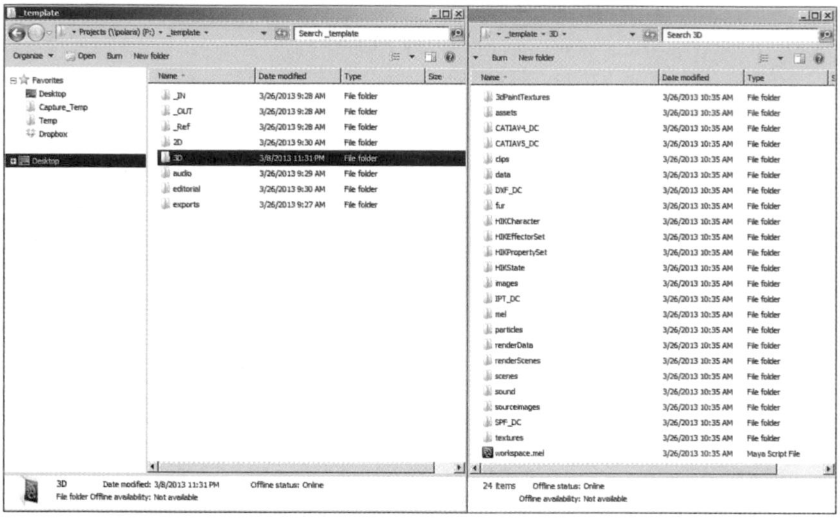

FIGURE 23.4
The template directory contains some supportive directories for our project.

As you can see, the template directory has subdirectories for other parts of an animated project like audio and editorial. The "3D" directory contains the normal Maya Project directories. You will "Set Project" to the "3D" directory.

Other good workflow is to create your scene directories in advance as well. Within the scenes directory, you create an animation, lighting, and fx directory within each shot and within each sequence. So, a template shot directory might look like this:

```
3D\scenes\sequence\shot\anim
3D\scenes\sequence\shot\light
3D\scenes\sequence\shot\fx
```

In a large project, the simple task of creating directories can take hours and hours. Organizing ahead of time will pay off greatly in the long run.

Pull or Push Workflows

The one major decision that needs to be made in terms of file management and workflow is whether you want to using a "Pull" workflow or a "Push" workflow. With a Pull workflow, you are always making sure that you are updating your scene files with the latest assets. When an asset is updated, it is up to you or another artist to load the new asset into their scenes. For example, if you just saved Sam_rig_v03.ma, then all of the animators that are currently using Sam_rig_v02.ma will need to replace their references in their Maya scenes to "pull" the update. The advantage of this workflow is that you are sure an asset update will not break working scenes. The disadvantage is that you will have to manually update all of the scenes that use an asset. On a long project, this could mean hundreds of scenes.

With a Push workflow, there is a single file that is overwritten to "push" updates into scenes using an asset. This file is normally labeled "Published" or "Final" or some other label reserved for the single pushed file. You would still be working on Sam_rig_v03.ma, but when you save it, you would save it as Sam_rig_v04.ma and then save it again and overwrite Sam_rig_PUB.ma. All animation scenes are using the PUB file already, so when they reopen their scenes, the new asset will load in. No manual updating is necessary. The pros and cons are the opposite of a Pull workflow. While you are doing a lot less work to update your scenes when an asset is published, there is the potential that a scene could break and you would then have to manually downgrade the asset to the previous version.

Most major studios employ a combination of Push and Pull, depending on the asset and the stage of production. For personal projects and small projects, a Push workflow works nicely.

Project X Workflow Case Study

Let's follow a project called Project X through the pipeline. This project is a commercial that has three shots starring one character named Sam who is playing with a beach ball in a beach environment.

First, we will copy the template folder and rename it to "ProjectX".

We will start by creating our character. His models will be saved in:

```
ProjectX\3D\assets\characters\Sam\models
```

As we continue to revise the model and get closer to final, the naming convention will follow our strict pattern:

```
Sam_model_v10.ma, Sam_model_v11.ma, etc.
```

When it is finished, save the model as:

```
Sam_model_PUB.ma
```

As you rig the character, save the files in the following directory:

```
ProjectX\3D\assets\characters\Sam\rigs
```

Textures can be placed in:

`ProjectX\3D\assets\characters\Sam\sourceimages`

At the same time you are working on the character rig, you may be modeling the beach ball and the beach environments as well; save them in their respective directories:

`ProjectX\3D\assets\props\ball\models`
`ProjectX\3D\assets\sets\beach\models`

When all of the assets are complete, you save PUB versions of them. As you start the three shots, you copy the shot template directory (which contains anim, fx, and light subdirectories) three times into the seq1 directory and name them as follows:

`ProjectX\3D\scenes\seq1\010`
`ProjectX\3D\scenes\seq1\020`
`ProjectX\3D\scenes\seq1\030`

When you create your shots, you will start by referencing in the three assets needed:

`ProjectX\3D\assets\characters\Sam\rigs\Sam_rig_PUB.ma`
`ProjectX\3D\assets\sets\beach\rigs\beach_rig_PUB.ma`
`ProjectX\3D\assets\props\ball\rigs\ball_rig_PUB.ma`

Then you save the resulting file as follows:

`ProjectX\3D\scenes\seq1\010\anim\seq1_010_anim_v01_sceneSetup.ma`

As you work, you save new versions and notes until your animation is complete. Then you create a new scene and *reference* your animation file into the scene. Save this new scene as follows:

`ProjectX\3D\scenes\seq1\010\light\seq1_010_light_v01_animComplete.ma`

Remember, the note can be whatever you want it to be, just keep it after the version number.

When the scene is finally complete, you will render the images to:

`ProjectX\3D\images\renders\seq1\010\v01\`

If you have followed proper naming convention, been tidy with your directories, and did not deviate from good workflow, the only difficulties you have with the project should be artistic ones.

BONUS

Good Project Example

This Hour's Bonus file is a Project directory structure within the Bonus folder. Open the Project folder labeled "Project X" and notice how each folder has a template folder already inside. To create new subdirectories, copy and rename the "_template" folders to whatever you choose. For instance, within the 3D\assets\chars\ directory, copy the "_template" directory and rename it "Sam." This new directory will contain all of the subdirectories you need for this character. Explore the project and feel free to use this structure for all of your projects.

Summary

Proper project workflow is essential to completing your work on time and on budget. Starting with Maya's project directory structure, we can take advantage of where Maya saves files by default. When we save files, we must keep absolute adherence to a naming convention; otherwise, files will quickly become disorganized and cluttered. We must decide on a Push or Pull workflow, depending on the needs of the project and the size of the team. We can even save ourselves a lot of time by setting up some templates to be used on projects in the future rather than reinventing a pipeline every time.

Q&A

Q. When I set my project, it asks me if I want to create a default workspace. Why?

A. This is because the folder you have chosen does not have a workspace.mel file within it. This file is used by Maya to determine the paths of your project. If you are sure the project you want to set exists, make sure you selected the correct directory, because all existent projects contain a workspace.mel file.

Q. Can I have multiple Maya projects within the same directory?

A. Not within the same directory, but two subdirectories can both be Maya projects. This used to be the way that things were done; set your project to the asset or the scene that you were working on. Up until Maya 2008 or so, it made sense, but modern Maya depends so much on scattered files that this is not advisable.

Q. I want to name my published files "Final" or something else. Is that okay?

A. That is totally fine, as long as you keep a consistent naming convention.

Q. What do I do if there are no sequences in my project, because it is just one shot?

A. You can remove directories that are not necessary, but I would still have a shot directory in your 3D/scenes directory. Call it 010 for consistency. Overall, you will be working on projects with many shots and sequences, so do not get lazy and put all of your scenes in the 3D/scenes directory.

Workshop

The workshop contains quiz questions and exercises to help you solidify your understanding of the material covered. Try to answer all questions before looking at the "Answers" section that follows.

Quiz

1. How do you set your project in Maya?

2. Which workflow depends on artists to update their own scenes with new assets?

3. When you are saving a file, where do the notes go in the filename?

4. What goes in the 3D/sourceimages folder?

5. Why are scenes that make use of referenced assets small in file size?

Exercise

Create your template directories for your projects. Create a template for the assets folders (sets, props, characters) as well as a shot template to go into your sequences (anim, light, FX). Decide and stick to a naming convention, and test your new project template on one of the Hours in this book by moving the files into their appropriate directories, referencing assets if necessary, and saving files with version numbers and comments.

Answers

1. Click on File, Set Project.

2. A "Pull" workflow means that each scene needs to be manually updated to the latest assets.

3. Notes always go after the version name, so that when you sort alphabetically, your revisions will always stay in order.

4. Nothing goes into this folder. You should create a new sourceimages folder in each one of the asset's folders in the 3D/assets directory.

5. Referenced files are read by Maya but not imported into the scene. Only the edits done to references are saved into a file, such as animation information, adjustment of attributes, and layers.

Ideal Settings, Preferences, and Hotkeys

What You'll Learn in This Hour:

▶ How to check or change settings and preferences

▶ What different settings and preferences to check or change when needed

▶ How to use hotkey shortcuts to quickly work with many of Maya features

▶ How to delete user preferences files to restore Maya back to the defaults

One look at Maya's user interface will tell you that there are a lot of features available in Maya. Behind the scenes of those features are numerous settings, too. Fortunately, Maya's default settings come in handy for most of your needs, at least to get started. But sometimes you will prefer other settings because of a certain task or project you are working on, or just because you like a different setup better. Maya lets you specify your own user preferences and settings for the user interface, tools that you work with, how objects are displayed, and how you prefer to work with many of its features. Maya also provides you with a large range of keyboard shortcuts known as "hotkeys" to help your workflow, too. You will need to know some right away, and will most likely want to pick up others depending on what you are working on. Ideal settings, preferences, and hotkeys are really what you want or need for your task or project. But whether you're just starting out or are an experienced user, it's a good idea to have a look at what is available. And just in case you make some changes, and wish you hadn't, Maya also provides options to reset everything back to Maya's defaults.

NOTE

Default Settings and Preferences

Maya lets you change all sorts of settings and preferences to help you work the way you want to, but every now and then, you might regret a change you make and not know how to fix it. Fortunately, as you will find out in this Hour, Maya has options to let you restore things back to the default settings.

In this Hour, you will learn about some of the settings and preferences that are already provided as defaults for you in Maya, and how to change them to meet your needs. You will also learn how to restore to default settings just in case you make a change and then regret it. Plus, you will learn about using some of the most commonly used keyboard shortcuts, known as "hotkeys," to speed up your workflow.

Settings and Preferences Basics

The default settings that Maya provides right out of the box will get you a long way to completing any task you want to do, but it is good to be aware of what settings you are taking for granted so that you can change them when you need to. Specifying your own preferences throughout Maya not only aids your workflow by saving time, but it also helps prevent errors through incorrect settings. Animators have to be careful to animate at the correct number of frames per second, for example, so they should check settings before they begin work.

You can access the main settings and preferences for Maya through the Window menu, and then select Settings/Preferences to choose from the listed options, as shown in Figure 24.1.

FIGURE 24.1
Use Windows, Settings/Preferences to access settings and preferences for the features you use in Maya.

TIP

Shortcut to Preferences

You can use the Preferences button located toward the lower right of your Maya screen to go straight to the Preferences window ▣.

Figure 24.1 shows that there are also settings for tools and hotkeys, plus editors for shelves and panels, and even color, too. Hour 17, "Scripting and Automating Common Tasks," touches upon the Shelf Editor and customizing shelves, so have a look if you are interested to know more. This Hour focuses on the Preferences window, which gives you access to your main user preferences and also points out some particular things to pay attention to.

NOTE

Tool Settings and Menu Options

The tools you use and many of the menu items you select also have options you can set. Instead of using Window, Settings/Preferences to change tool settings for the tools in the Toolbox, simple double-click the tool button for the tool you need. Menus items also often have options to set. To access options from menus, click on the option box next to a menu item's name. Maya will remember the settings and options you choose for tools or menu items, so if you don't want to be surprised by anything unexpected next time, use the Reset Tool button on the Tool Settings window or look for Edit, Reset Settings on the windows you use to put everything back to their defaults when you are done.

User Preferences

You can set preferences for Maya's features through the Preferences window. To access Preferences, select the Window menu, then Settings/Preferences, and then Preferences. The Preferences window will open, as Figure 24.2 shows.

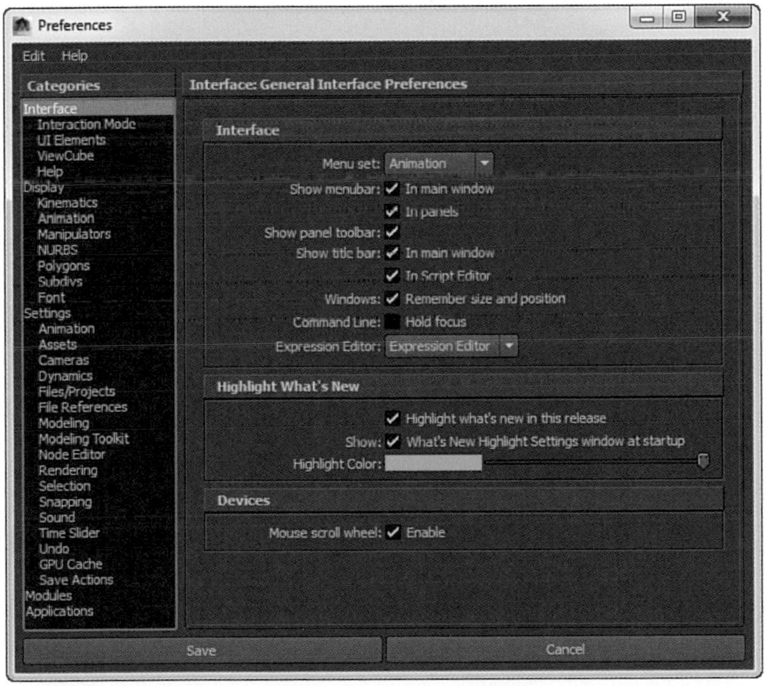

FIGURE 24.2
The Preference window lets you access preferences for many of Maya's features.

The preferences are divided into categories, which are listed in main groups on the left side of the Preference window. To check or change preferences, click on the category you want on the left panel and make the changes using the right. Table 24.1 gives a brief description of each main group.

TABLE 24.1   Preference Window Main Categories

Category Group	Use the Categories Listed To:
Interface	Customize the general look of the user interface by showing or hiding menus and other user interface elements.
Display	Change how objects and related features you work with are displayed.
Settings	Set default values for tools, features, and related operations used for particular tasks or projects.
Modules	Improve system response by disabling any unneeded software modules that Maya loads by default.
Applications	Specify which application Maya should use for opening and viewing specific image or movie file types.

Let's have a closer look at some of the options for working with the user interface, display, and main settings from the Preferences window next.

Customizing the User Interface

The Interface category group within the Preferences window is where you will find preferences for the look of Maya's interface. The general Interface category, shown in Figure 24.2, lets you choose which menu set for Maya to load up when you start, plus provides options to show or hide menu bars in the main window or within the panels. Maya 2014 also lets you decide whether to highlight new features and what color to highlight them. Use the UI Elements category to hide or display additional UI (user interface) elements such as the shelves, Time Slider, Command Line.

TIP

Show/Hide UI Elements with Maya's Display Menu

The Display menu from the main Maya menus also lets you pick and choose UI elements to show and hide. Maya provides hotkeys to let you hide unwanted elements, so it's a good idea to know where to go to find them again if you hide anything by accident!

Still within the Interface grouping, the ViewCube category lets you show or hide the ViewCube, as shown in Figure 24.3 (left). The ViewCube can be useful to navigate between scene views. You can click to change views to perspective, front, side, top, or right, or tumble in perspective view by dragging. You can also use the ViewCube category to show or hide the Compass. The Compass can sit underneath the ViewCube to give you a north/south/east/west perspective orientation, as Figure 24.3 (right) shows.

FIGURE 24.3
Use the ViewCube category (left) to show or hide the ViewCube and Compass (right).

The Help category within the Preference window lets you show, hide, or change the display of the in-view help messages that appear for certain tools, operations, and features. The font size for the messages can be changed, too, plus how long the messages are displayed for. ToolClips, which were introduced in Maya 2014, can be enabled or disabled here, or modified to have the popup only display the tool name and shortcut without the ToolClip contents.

TIP

Color Settings

You can change the colors of your user interface, wireframes, manipulators, viewport background, and any of the other default color settings for pretty much anything you work with in Maya. Go back to Window, Settings/Preferences and then select Color Settings. If you decide to have a play, rest assured you can set everything back to normal by using Edit, Reset to Defaults right within the Color Editor window.

TIP

Panel Layouts

You can also change the layout and contents of the panels of your viewports to help you work on specific tasks. For instance, if focusing on fixing final renders, you could use a three-panel layout. The top-left panel might host the Render View window, and the top right your perspective view. The panel underneath might show the Hypershade so that you can tweak materials while checking the render as you go. To change layouts and panels, either use the options from the Panel menu within a viewport panel, or go back to Window, Settings/Preferences and then select the Panel Editor. Within the Panel Editor, you will find a Layout tab where you can choose from or create your own panel layout.

Display Preferences

The Interface category group we just discussed is all about changing the general look of Maya's graphical user interface. The Display categories, on the other hand, enable you to check or change preferences related to the display of objects and the features related to the objects that you work with. Animators and riggers would want to check out the Kinematic preferences to adjust the display size of joints, for example. Modelers, on the other hand, might want to have a look at the preferences for how NURBS, polygons, and subdivisions are displayed. Texture displays are also dealt with in the general Display category. You can increase the resolution of textures displayed to improve their appearance within Maya, or decrease this for a bit more working speed. Furthermore, if you notice that your texture swatches within materials attributes or the Hypershade show up as empty squares instead of previews of the textures, you can also bump up the maximum resolution for the texture swatches here, if needed. Generally, whatever task you are working on, you can look through the Display category group to find something of use.

NOTE

Display Menu Options

The Display menu from Maya's main menus lets you access preferences for displaying objects and features. An important one for modelers to know is turning on or off backface culling, by using Display, Polygons, Backface Culling. This lets you hide or show the object's backface to speed the display or manipulation. Showing or hiding normals and softening and hardening edges are found here, too. Plus, you'll find Heads Up Display to display your polygon counts and such. However, the Display menu isn't just for the modelers. For instance, animators and riggers can alter the size of joints by going to Display, Animation, Joint Size.

TIP

Manipulator Size

The size of the manipulators can be changed by going to the general Display category, but you should note that a much quicker way is to use the hotkey shortcuts of + to increase the manipulator size and - to decrease. Hotkeys are Maya's keyboard shortcuts, which we will discuss later in this hour.

Settings Preferences

The Settings category group within the Preference window is one you should check out to define preferences and default values for tools, plus related operations when working on specific projects or tasks. You should be aware of some of the main settings whatever the task, but animators definitely need to check these out!

The main Settings category lets you choose your world coordinate system and working units, as shown in Figure 24.4. Notice that you can change the world coordinate system from Maya's default settings of using Y as the up coordinate to Z if you are used to working with Z as up in other packages, or if you have a project that requires it. You can also set measurement units and working angles. Animators will need to set the time units here to the frames per second their project requires.

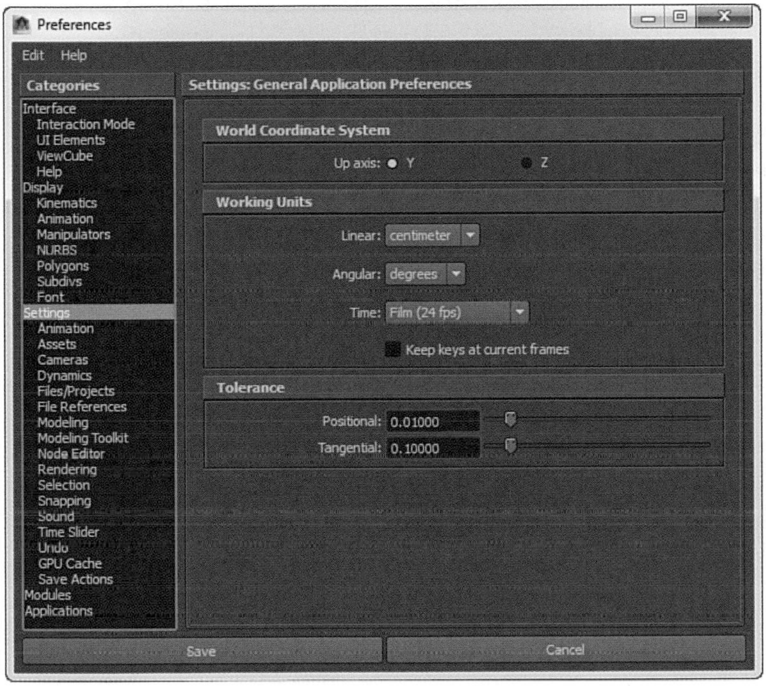

FIGURE 24.4
The Settings category within the Preferences window lets you set default values for features and operations that you will use for carrying out tasks and projects.

NOTE

Undo

If you check out the Undo category, you will see that Maya lets you specify the number of actions it will store in the undo queue. By default, Undo is set to 50, which means Maya will let you reverse up to 50 actions. You can increase this by typing into the Queue size field, or you can even switch on Queue infinity to have an unlimited number of Undos. Although an infinite number of available Undos sounds great, be aware that it can also use up a lot of memory and make Maya more sluggish when the queue gets too big.

TIP

AutoSave

If you want to have Maya automatically save your work periodically, you can use the Files/Projects settings to turn on AutoSave and then specify how often you want to save.

Whether you're modeling, rendering, working with dynamics, or just generally working with Maya, it is a good idea to have a look through the categories that might apply to your tasks. Animators need to double-check settings using a few different categories from the Settings group. Table 24.2 lists some useful settings animators should be aware of.

TABLE 24.2   Settings Category Group for Animators

Category	Section	Description
Settings (General)	Working Units, Time	Set the frames per second.
Animation	AutoKey	Indicate whether you want to use AutoKey to automatically set keys as you make changes to a previously keyed object. Also used to specify whether you want AutoKey to key all the attributes or just the ones that have been changed.
	Tangents	Set default in and out tangents, and whether or not to use weighted tangents by default.
Sound	Waveform display	Display the top, bottom, or all of the sound waveform.
	Repeat on hold	Use to have the sound repeat at the current time as you hold down LMB on the Time Slider. The sound continues when you scrub to the next time. This is useful when lip syncing to locate a particular sound.
	Repeat size	How much sound is repeated when using Repeat on Hold as described. Sets the number of frames of sound you want to repeat.
Time Slider	Playback start/end	Use to set the playback range for the Time Slider.
	Animation start/end	Use to set the animation range.
	Height	Can be used to increase the height of the Time Slider, which is useful when you are working with sound to see more of the sound waveform details.

Category	Section	Description
	Playback speed	Specify the speed at which your scene plays. Note that playing every frame depends on how powerful your machine is, and therefore can vary from machine to machine. If you want to play back using the frame rate you are working with, choose from the fps options instead. If you don't see the fps you want, you need to go to Settings to set up the time units first.

The Grease Pencil tool is new to Maya 2014. It lets you draw right on the screen with a virtual marker. Although of particular interest to animators, it can be used to mark up your screen to help in whatever task you are doing. Double-click the tool to adjust settings for the tool itself. You can also set preferences for how the frames that use Grease Pencil are displayed in the Time Slider. Use the Time Slider category within the Preferences window, and then the Time Slider section to find options for Grease Pencil. You can choose to have Grease Pencil frames displayed on the time slider for the active camera only, to display frames for all sequences regardless of camera, or to hide the Grease Pencil frame indicators altogether.

Saving and Deleting Preferences

Maya stores your customized settings in user preference files. This way, Maya is all ready to go according to your own preferences each time you use it. To save preferences, use File, Save Preferences. Make sure you have enough space on your disk to save, though, because Maya won't let you know if you don't! The preference files are stored in the paths shown in Table 24.3, depending on the operating system you use.

TABLE 24.3 Paths for Preference Files

Operating System	Path
Windows XP	\Documents and Settings\<username>\My Documents\maya\<version>\en_US\prefs.
Windows Vista and Windows 7	\Users\<username>\Documents\maya\<version>\en_US\prefs.

Operating System	Path
Mac OS X	/Users/<username>/Library/Preferences/Autodesk/ maya/<version>/prefs. Note: To open the Preferences directory using Mac OS X Lion, select Finder, Go, Go to Folder and type the path directory (/Users/<username>/ Library/Preferences).
Linux (64-bit)	~<username>/maya/<version>/prefs.

If you need to restore the preferences to the defaults for any reason, close Maya and locate the user preference files on your system, as shown by Table 24.3, and delete the preference files you want to restore. Maya will next open with the default preferences back in place.

TIP

Restoring to Defaults

Don't forget that the tools and features of Maya also have options to reset to default. Within the tool settings or the windows that you use, look for the Reset Tool button, or Edit, Reset Tool, Edit Revert to Saved (preferences window), or Edit, Reset Setting.

NOTE

Saving Preferences on Exit

The Save Actions category lets you set whether or not to save preferences upon exiting Maya.

Hotkeys

Hotkeys are Maya's keyboard shortcuts that help your workflow by providing quick access to navigate your scene, work with tools and objects, display and hide features, and just about anything else you can think of. Before we talk about specific hotkeys, the hotbox and marking menus that Maya provides are worth a mention because some of the hotkeys we are about to discuss bring up the hotbox and marking menus.

Hotbox and Marking Menus

Maya's hotbox and marking menus provide access to Maya's entire feature set right on the active viewport. In any viewport, hold the **spacebar** down to bring up the hotbox, and you will see what seems like a screen full of menus, as shown in Figure 24.5 left. Although this can seem overwhelming at first, as you become more familiar with Maya, using the hotbox can help your workflow. To access any menu from the hotbox, hold the **spacebar** to show the hotbox and then click the menu you want, but keep your LMB pressed down. The menu options will appear, and you can then drag down to the item you want and release the LMB to select it.

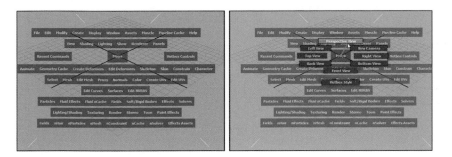

FIGURE 24.5
Holding down the spacebar will show the hotbox to let you choose from Maya's menus from the viewport (left). Click and hold the LMB over the central Maya label to bring up a marking menu for changing views (right).

Maya also provides marking menus that let you quickly select actions to perform. Marking menus appear in the viewports when you use particular key and mouse combinations. For example, if you hold the **spacebar** down to reveal the hotbox, and then click and hold your LMB on the word Maya in the center, a marking menu will appear to let you change to perspective, side, front, or top view, as shown in Figure 24.5 (right). Maya 2014 will also let you choose from a few other views, too, as shown in Figure 24.5. To select an item from a marking menu, LMB drag in the direction of the item you want to select. As soon as you see the item highlighted, release the mouse. There is no need to be precise. Maya lets you quickly sweep near, on, or beyond the item to select, as shown by Figure 24.6.

NOTE

Using Hotkeys to Access Marking Menus

Some marking menus are assigned to hotkeys; for example, you can hold down the **h** key plus hold down your LMB to bring up the marking menu that lets you switch between menu sets, as shown in Figure 24.6.

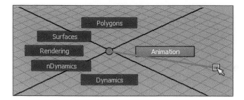

FIGURE 24.6
Use h+LMB in any viewport to bring up the Menu Set marking menu.

TIP

Context-Sensitive Marking Menus

RMB on a selected object to bring up context-sensitive marking menus for the object you are working with. For example, RMB on a polygon to switch between component and sub-object modes using a marking menu.

Common Hotkeys

As you have learned, hotkeys are keyboard shortcuts that let you quickly access many of the features in Maya. The list of hotkeys that Maya provides can be overwhelming, but some commonly used ones are good to know. Have a look through the hotkeys listed here and try them out as you go, using a scene of your choice. We point out some hotkeys to pay particular attention to in the paragraphs that follow, but look through the tables to find more. Try to familiarize with a basic set first, and as you become more familiar with Maya, try adding some others to your repertoire.

Probably the most important hotkeys to learn are the ones that let you move around your viewports as you work. Use the **Alt** key and hold down your left, middle, or right mouse button to tumble (orbit), track (move left to right, or up and down), and dolly (move forward and back), as Table 24.4 shows.

TABLE 24.4 Tumble, Track, Dolly

Hold + Drag	Function
Alt+LMB	Tumble (orbit)
Alt+MMB	Track (left-right, up-down)
Alt+RMB	Dolly (forward-back)
or	
ALt+LMB+MMB	

TIP

Tumble, Track, and Dolly in Other Maya Windows

Try using your **Alt** key and mouse buttons in other Maya windows, such as Render View and the Graph Editor, and you will see that some of the windows let you move around them just as you would in your viewports.

Have a look through Table 24.5 to try out some of the hotkeys that you will find useful for your general workflow. Two important hotkeys to learn from this table are **Ctrl+a** and the **spacebar**. **Ctrl+a** switches between the Attribute Editor and the Channel Box. Because almost everything you do in Maya requires working with attributes, this is a good one to learn! You will also often want to toggle between different panel layouts as you work. *Tap* the **spacebar** to toggle between single-perspective view and a four-panel view layout. Just be aware that *holding* the **spacebar** down brings up the hotbox instead.

TABLE 24.5 Window and Views

Press	Function
Ctrl+a	Bring up or switch between the Attribute Editor and Channel Box
Spacebar (tap)	Toggle Panel Layout
f	Frame selection in the active panel
Shift+F	Frame selected in all views
a	Frame all in the active panel
Shift+A	Frame all in all views
[	Undo view (camera) move
]	Redo view (camera) move
Ctrl+spacebar	Switch between standard and full-screen view
Alt+b	Switch between a gradient, black, dark gray, or light gray background color

TIP

The Spacebar

Tapping the **spacebar** toggles between panel views (single-perspective and four-panel view by default). Holding the down **spacebar**, however, brings up the hotbox to let you access all of Maya's features from your viewport.

CAUTION

Maya Is Case Sensitive

Maya is case sensitive, so using an uppercase character instead of a lowercase one will give you a different hotkey. Lowercase **z** is used for Undo, but uppercase **Z** is Redo, for example.

Use the QWERTY keys on your keyboard to access commonly used tools. The **q** key lets you select, **w** move, **e** rotate, and **r** scale. The **t** key shows the manipulator tool. And if your manipulator handles are too big or too small, use + to increase or - to decrease their size, as Table 24.6 shows.

TABLE 24.6 Tool Operations

Press	Function
Caution	Complete current tool
Insert	Enter tool Edit mode (or hold down **d** for Mac users)
q	Select
w	Move
e	Rotate
r	Scale
t	Show Manipulator (tailored for selected object, such as lights)
Ctrl+t	Universal Manipulator (combines move, rotate, and scale tools)
y	Last tool used (that is *not* select, move, rotate, or scale)
+ or =	Increase manipulator size
- (minus)	Decrease manipulator size

TIP

Tool Marking Menus

Hold your LMB with either **q**, **w**, **e**, or **r** pressed down to access the marking menu options for the tool you selected.

Maya lets you view your scene in different ways to help you with the task at hand, as Table 24.7 shows. Much of the time you might prefer to work in shaded mode with textures on by pressing **6**, although if you want to see the geometry without the textures, you can turn them off by pressing **5**. If you are modeling and trying to tweak a few vertices, you might want to press **4** to view in wireframe mode. When working with lights and shadows, pressing **7** will come in handy.

TABLE 24.7   Viewport Display

Press	Function
4	Wireframe
5	Shaded
6	Shaded + Textured
7	Shaded + Textured + Use All Lights

Maya's menus are grouped into menu sets, and you can choose the set you want to work with according to the task you are doing. Use **F2** through **F6** to switch between commonly used menu sets, as shown in Table 24.8. If you prefer, you can press **h+spacebar** to bring up a marking menu that lets you switch between the menu sets. You can also hide menus in your panels to get more working space, and show them once again when you need them, as listed in Table 24.8.

TABLE 24.8   Menus

Press	Function
F2	Animation menu set
F3	Polygons menu set
F4	Surfaces menu set
F5	Dynamics menu set
F6	Rendering menu set
h+LMB (hold)	Menu set marking menu
Shift+m	Show/hide Viewport panel menu
Ctrl+Shift+M	Show/hide Viewport panel toolbar
Ctrl+m	Show/hide main menu bar
h+LMB	Switch between menu sets using a marking menu

TIP

The Paint Effects Panel

Pressing **8** will bring up the Paint Effects panel, with the Paint Effects tool all ready to go. That's great if you meant to do that, but it can be a nuisance if you didn't. A quick way to exit is to press **8** again to close the panel, and then press **q** to switch away from the Paint Effects tool.

Table 24.9 lists some useful commands. Where would we be without good old Undo to reverse unwanted actions? To use undo in Maya, all you need to do is press the z key although if you are used to using **Ctrl+z** in other packages, this will work too. **Shift+Z** lets you redo. Another particularly useful key is g to repeat your last action. Just created a NURBS sphere and need another one? Press g. Just extruded a face on a polygon and need to extrude another face? Select the face, and press g. Have a look through Table 24.9 to see what else you might find useful.

TABLE 24.9   Commands

Press (or Hold)	Function
F1	Help.
z (or Ctrl+z)	Undo.
Shift+Z	Redo.
Ctrl+a	Show, or switch between Attribute Editor and Channel Box
(Hold) Space	Hotbox.
(Hold) RMB	Marking menu.
Insert	With Move tool, switches between move pivot and move object.
(hold) d	With Move tool, hold d and LMB to move pivot. This is also useful for Mac keyboards with no Insert key.
g	Repeat last action.
Ctrl+g	Group.
Ctrl+d	Duplicate.
p	Parent.
Shift+P	Unparent.
Alt+Shift+D	Delete history.
Ctrl+x, Ctrl+c, Ctrl+v	Cut, Copy, Paste. (Mac users can use Cmd or Ctrl for these.)
Ctrl+n, Ctrl+o, Ctrl+s	Create a new scene, open a scene, or save a scene. (Mac users can use Cmd or Ctrl for these.)
Shift+S	File, Save Scene As (new to Maya 2014).
Ctr+r	Create file reference.

There are many useful hotkeys for modeling in Maya. Most of the hotkeys listed in this section will help, but Table 24.10 through Table 24.13 show quite a few more. Modelers should make sure to know to right-click objects to choose between object and component mode, and be sure to learn how to access pivot points by using the Insert or Home key. You can also hold down the **d** key to access pivot mode.

TIP

Pivot Mode for Mac Users

Mac users can hold down the **d** key to access pivot mode because Mac keyboards have no Insert key!

Modelers will also find it helpful to display different degrees of object smoothness by selecting the object and then pressing **1**, **2**, or **3** on the keyboard, as shown in Table 24.10. Using **1** can help you model by keeping complexity down to a minimum, showing the geometry in rough format. Pressing **3** can help you preview how it will look when smoothed.

TABLE 24.10   Object Smoothness

Press with Object Selected	Function
1	Default polygon mesh display (no smoothing)
2	Cage plus smooth polygon mesh display
3	Smooth polygon mesh display
1	NURBS rough
2	NURBS medium
3	NURBS fine

Right-clicking an object will let you access the marking menus to let you switch between objects and components, but you can also use the hotkeys listed in Table 24.11. Notice, too, that you can grow your selection regions by using > and shrink them by using <.

TABLE 24.11   Component Editing and Selection

Press	Function
F8	Object/Component mode
F9	Polygon vertex
F10	Polygon edge
F11	Polygon face
F12	Select, UV
Shift+>	Grow polygon selection region
Shift+<	Shrink polygon selection region
Ctrl+F9, Ctrl+F10, Ctrl+F11, Ctrl +F12	Convert polygon selection to vertices, edges, faces, or UVs

NOTE

Mac OS X Keyboard

If you're using a Mac, the Exposé hotkeys (**F9**, **F10**, **F11**) may conflict with Maya's hotkeys. As a workaround, either edit the Maya hotkeys by using the Hotkey Editor in Window, Settings/Preferences or change the Exposé hotkeys in the System Preferences panel of the Mac OS X machine.

When moving objects or components, you can use **x**, **c**, or **v** to snap to a grid, curve, or point, as shown in Table 24.12. For example, select an object and then press **w** to activate the Move tool. Next, hold down the **x** key as you LMB drag the Move tool's manipulator in the direction you want to go. You should see your object snapping to the grid as you pull it along. If you use MMB drag instead, you can click on the area you want and the object will jump straight to it. The **j** key is also useful when you want to rotate something by 45 degrees, for example. Holding down **j** will snap the rotations to discrete intervals so that you can snap to 15, 30, then 45 degrees as you rotate.

TABLE 24.12   Snapping

Hold	Function
x	Snap to grid
c	Snap to curve
v	Snap to point
j	Move, rotate, scale
Shift+J	Move, rotate, scale relative

Maya scenes can quickly fill up with many different objects. Sometimes it is useful to hide selections with **Ctrl+h**, so that you can focus on what you need. If you want to isolate the object you want to work with, use **Shift+I** to temporarily hide the other objects. When you want your other objects back, make sure you have no objects selected and then use **Shift+I** again. See Table 24.13 for more hotkeys related to displaying and hiding objects.

TABLE 24.13   Showing and Hiding Objects

Press	Function
Ctrl+h	Hide selection
Shift+H	Show selection
Ctrl+Shift+h	Show last hidden

Press	Function
Alt+h	Hide unselected objects
Shift+I	Isolate the selection for viewing

DID YOU KNOW?

Finding Hidden Objects

You can use the Outliner to find hidden objects and display them again. Use Window, Outliner and then find your missing object on the list. Objects that are hidden have their Visibility attribute set to 0 and are grayed out on the list. Once you have found the one you want, turn its Visibility attribute back on in the Channel Box by typing **1**. Alternatively, you can find the object in the Outliner and use **Shift+H** to show it again. Note that Isolate works a bit differently. If you have isolated something and want everything back, make sure to have nothing selected and then use **Shift+I** again to exit isolation view.

Animation hotkeys let you set a key by pressing **s**, and play and pause your animations using **Alt+v**. Another useful hotkey involves holding the **k** key down and using your LMB to use a virtual slider to drag in the viewport or Time Slider to scrub through your animation. Have a look through Table 24.14 for some more hotkeys to try.

TABLE 24.14   Animation and Playback

Press	Function
s	Set key.
i (press and release)	Insert keys tool for Graph Editor.
Shift+W	Set translation key.
Shift+E	Set rotation key.
Shift+R	Set scale key.
k (hold)+LMB	Virtual Time Slider mode. Press and hold and then scrub the Timeline.
Shift+S+LMB	Keyframe and tangent marking menus.

If you are working with an animated sequence, you are going to want to play it within Maya, and to pause play or step through the animation. See Table 24.15 for playback hotkeys.

TABLE 24.15   Playback

Press	Function
Alt+v	Toggle between play and stop
Alt+,	Move back one frame
Alt+.	Move forward one frame
,	Go to previous key
.	Go to next key
Esc	Stop playback (if animation is playing)

Table 24.16 gives you a few extra hotkeys to try out.

TABLE 24.16   Extras

Hold + Drag	Function
\+ with MMB	2D Pan tool
\+ with RMB	2D Zoom tool
\ (press)	Enable/disable 2D Pan/Zoom (click with camera selected)
Shift+Q+LMB	Component marking menu
Alt+q	Polygon marking menu
q, w, e, or r with LMB	Selection, move, rotate, or scale marking menu
Up, down, left, or right arrow	Walk up, down, left, or right in current hierarchy (selected object or components)
Alt + up, down, left or right arrow	Move selected object up, down, left, or right by one pixel

BONUS

Hotkeys

This Hour covered many of the hotkeys available in Maya, but there are plenty more (for working with paint effects and for modeling, for example). You will find a comprehensive listing in this Hour's folder on the DVD. We have provided a list by category and an alphabetical listing by hotkey. Alternatively, you can search for All Maya Hotkeys using Maya's Help menu, or you can use Window, Settings/Preferences, Hotkey Editor, List All.

Summary

This Hour covered hotkeys, marking menus, and the hotbox to help you speed up your workflow. It also covered useful settings and preferences you can use to set up Maya and its features for working on particular tasks—or just because that's the way you prefer things! The key point to remember from this Hour is that if you make changes and regret it, you can close Maya and then delete your own user preference files to have Maya reopen the next time with everything set back to the defaults.

Q&A

Q. Where have all my menus and toolbars gone?

A. It is possible that you accidentally hid them. Try using **Ctrl+spacebar** to see if you are in full-screen view. If that didn't work, use **Ctrl+spacebar** to get back to where you were. Next, try using Display, UI Elements to locate your missing user interface elements. You can also look in Window, Settings/Preferences, Preferences and then the Interface category group.

Q. Why isn't my hotkey doing what it should?

A. Maya is case sensitive, so double-check that you are using the proper case for the character used for the hotkey. Also, double-check that you haven't accidentally left Caps Lock on.

Q. How can I change the background color in the viewports?

A. **Alt+b** will toggle through a few options for the background color, but otherwise use Window, Setting/Preferences, Preferences, Color Editor to customize.

Q. Where have my manipulator handles disappeared to?

A. If the handles on your manipulators have disappeared, it is possible you accidentally used a hotkey to make them either so small that you cannot see them or so big that the Maya viewport can't contain them. Either use the hotkeys **+** (to increase) and **-** (to decrease) to resize, or use your Preference window to find the Manipulators category and adjust the size there.

Workshop

The workshop contains quiz questions and exercises to help you solidify your understanding of the material covered. Try to answer all questions before looking at the "Answers" section that follows.

Quiz

1. Where can you set up your frame rate if you are animating?

2. Where can you turn on AutoSave if you want to use it?

3. How can you reset things back to their defaults?

4. Where is the button that opens up the Preferences window without going to the Window menu?

5. Where can you increase the number of actions Maya will let you undo?

Exercise

Have a look through the list of hotkeys and start to learn and use some of the ones you feel most comfortable with. Also, experiment with some of the settings and preferences discussed— and even ones we didn't discuss—to become more comfortable setting up and using Maya to meet your own needs.

Answers

1. Use the Preferences window, General Settings category to set up the time value for the number of frames per second (fps) you want to use.

2. AutoSave options are found in the Preference window, within the Files/Project category.

3. Within the tools or windows that you might have changed, look for the Reset Tool button, or Edit, Reset, or even Edit, Restore. If that doesn't do the trick, you will have to close Maya, delete your user preference files, and reopen Maya to restore everything back to the defaults.

4. The button located second to the bottom on the lower right of your Maya screen should open up the Preferences window and bypass the Window menu.

5. Undo has its own category in the Preference window. You can increase the value up to infinity if you want, but be aware that the Undo queue can start hogging resources and even slow down Maya if it has numerous actions stored up.

Index

How can we make this index more useful? Email us at indexes@samspublishing.com

X-Y-Z

Sams **Teach Yourself**

When you only have time
for the answers™

Whatever your need and whatever your time frame, there's a Sams **Teach Yourself** book for you. With a Sams **Teach Yourself** book as your guide, you can quickly get up to speed on just about any new product or technology—in the absolute shortest period of time possible. Guaranteed.

Learning how to do new things with your computer shouldn't be tedious or time-consuming. Sams **Teach Yourself** makes learning anything quick, easy, and even a little bit fun.

Sams Teach Yourself Android Game Programming in 24 Hours

Jonathan S. Harbour
ISBN-13: 9780672336041

HTML, CSS and JavaScript All in One

Julie C. Meloni
ISBN-13: 9780672333323

Sams Teach Yourself JavaScript in 24 Hours

Phil Ballard/Michael Moncur
ISBN-13: 9780672336089

Sams Teach Yourself Node.js in 24 Hours

George Ornbo
ISBN-13: 9780672335952

Sams Teach Yourself jQuery Mobile in 24 Hours

Phillip Dutson
ISBN-13: 9780672335945

Sams Teach Yourself books are available at most retail and online bookstores. For more information or to order direct, visit our online bookstore at **informit.com/sams**.

Online editions of all Sams Teach Yourself titles are available by subscription from Safari Books Online at **safari.informit.com**.

SAMS

REGISTER

THIS PRODUCT

informit.com/register

Register the Addison-Wesley, Exam Cram, Prentice Hall, Que, and Sams products you own to unlock great benefits.

To begin the registration process, simply go to **informit.com/register** to sign in or create an account. You will then be prompted to enter the 10- or 13-digit ISBN that appears on the back cover of your product.

Registering your products can unlock the following benefits:

- Access to supplemental content, including bonus chapters, source code, or project files.
- A coupon to be used on your next purchase.

Registration benefits vary by product. Benefits will be listed on your Account page under Registered Products.

About InformIT — THE TRUSTED TECHNOLOGY LEARNING SOURCE

INFORMIT IS HOME TO THE LEADING TECHNOLOGY PUBLISHING IMPRINTS Addison-Wesley Professional, Cisco Press, Exam Cram, IBM Press, Prentice Hall Professional, Que, and Sams. Here you will gain access to quality and trusted content and resources from the authors, creators, innovators, and leaders of technology. Whether you're looking for a book on a new technology, a helpful article, timely newsletters, or access to the Safari Books Online digital library, InformIT has a solution for you.

informIT.com

THE TRUSTED TECHNOLOGY LEARNING SOURCE

Addison-Wesley | Cisco Press | Exam Cram
IBM Press | Que | Prentice Hall | Sams

SAFARI BOOKS ONLINE

informIT.com THE TRUSTED TECHNOLOGY LEARNING SOURCE

PEARSON

InformIT is a brand of Pearson and the online presence for the world's leading technology publishers. It's your source for reliable and qualified content and knowledge, providing access to the top brands, authors, and contributors from the tech community.

Addison-Wesley **Cisco Press** EXAM/**CRAM** **IBM Press.** QUE° ‡ PRENTICE HALL **SAMS** | Safari²

LearnIT at InformIT

Looking for a book, eBook, or training video on a new technology? Seeking timely and relevant information and tutorials? Looking for expert opinions, advice, and tips? **InformIT has the solution.**

- Learn about new releases and special promotions by subscribing to a wide variety of newsletters. Visit **informit.com/newsletters**.

- Access FREE podcasts from experts at **informit.com/podcasts**.

- Read the latest author articles and sample chapters at **informit.com/articles**.

- Access thousands of books and videos in the Safari Books Online digital library at **safari.informit.com**.

- Get tips from expert blogs at **informit.com/blogs**.

Visit **informit.com/learn** to discover all the ways you can access the hottest technology content.

Are You Part of the IT Crowd?

Connect with Pearson authors and editors via RSS feeds, Facebook, Twitter, YouTube, and more! Visit **informit.com/socialconnect**.

Try Safari Books Online FREE for 15 days

Get online access to Thousands of Books and Videos

FREE 15-DAY TRIAL + 15% OFF
informit.com/safariebooktrial

 Feed your brain

Gain unlimited access to thousands of books and videos about technology, digital media and professional development from O'Reilly Media, Addison-Wesley, Microsoft Press, Cisco Press, McGraw Hill, Wiley, WROX, Prentice Hall, Que, Sams, Apress, Adobe Press and other top publishers.

 See it, believe it

Watch hundreds of expert-led instructional videos on today's hottest topics.

WAIT, THERE'S MORE!

Gain a competitive edge

Be first to learn about the newest technologies and subjects with Rough Cuts pre-published manuscripts and new technology overviews in Short Cuts.

Accelerate your project

Copy and paste code, create smart searches that let you know when new books about your favorite topics are available, and customize your library with favorites, highlights, tags, notes, mash-ups and more.

* Available to new subscribers only. Discount applies to the Safari Library and is valid for first 12 consecutive monthly billing cycles. Safari Library is not available in all countries.

Addison Wesley · AdobePress · Cisco Press · FT Press · IBM Press · Microsoft Press · New Riders · O'REILLY

Peachpit Press · PEARSON IT Certification · PRENTICE HALL · que · SAMS · vmware PRESS · WILEY · wro

Your purchase of **Sams Teach Yourself Maya® in 24 Hours** includes access to a free online edition for 45 days through the **Safari Books Online** subscription service. Nearly every Sams book is available online through **Safari Books Online**, along with thousands of books and videos from publishers such as Addison-Wesley Professional, Cisco Press, Exam Cram, IBM Press, O'Reilly Media, Prentice Hall, Que, and VMware Press.

Safari Books Online is a digital library providing searchable, on-demand access to thousands of technology, digital media, and professional development books and videos from leading publishers. With one monthly or yearly subscription price, you get unlimited access to learning tools and information on topics including mobile app and software development, tips and tricks on using your favorite gadgets, networking, project management, graphic design, and much more.

Activate your FREE Online Edition at
informit.com/safarifree

STEP 1:   Enter the coupon code: SIHJQZG.

STEP 2:   New Safari users, complete the brief registration form.
            Safari subscribers, just log in.

If you have difficulty registering on Safari or accessing the online edition,
please e-mail customer-service@safaribooksonline.com

Addison Wesley   Adobe Press   ALPHA   Cisco Press   FT Press   IBM Press   Microsoft   New Riders   O'REILLY

Peachpit Press   PRENTICE HALL   QUE   Redbooks   SAMS   SAS Publishing   vmware PRESS   WILEY   WROX